PowerShell Troubleshooting Guide

Minimize debugging time and maximize troubleshooting efficiency by leveraging the unique features of the PowerShell language

Michael Shepard

[PACKT] enterprise 🞬
PUBLISHING   professional expertise distilled

BIRMINGHAM - MUMBAI

PowerShell Troubleshooting Guide

First published: November 2014

Production reference: 1211114

Published by Packt Publishing Ltd.
Livery Place
35 Livery Street
Birmingham B3 2PB, UK.

ISBN 978-1-78217-357-1

www.packtpub.com

Cover image by Michal Jasej (milak6@wp.pl)

Credits

Author
Michael Shepard

Reviewers
Christian Droulers
Rob Huelga
Steve Shilling

Acquisition Editor
Meeta Rajani

Content Development Editor
Adrian Raposo

Technical Editors
Tanvi Bhatt
Pragnesh Billimoria

Copy Editors
Simran Bhogal
Maria Gould
Ameesha Green

Project Coordinator
Kinjal Bari

Proofreaders
Simran Bhogal
Joel T. Johnson

Indexer
Monica Ajmera Mehta

Production Coordinator
Alwin Roy

Cover Work
Alwin Roy

About the Author

Michael Shepard has been working with computers since the early '80s, starting with an Apple II in school and a Commodore 64 at home. He started working in the IT industry in 1989 and has been working full-time since 1997. He has been working at Jack Henry & Associates, Inc. since 2000. His focus has changed over the years from being a database application developer to a DBA, an application admin, and is now a solutions architect. In his years as a DBA, he found PowerShell to be a critical component in creating the automation required to keep up with a growing set of servers and applications. He is active in the PowerShell community at Stack Overflow and projects at CodePlex. He has been blogging about PowerShell since 2009 at http://powershellstation.com.

I'd like to thank my employer, Jack Henry & Associates, Inc., for allowing me the freedom over the last few years to both learn and teach PowerShell. My wonderful wife, Stephanie, and my children, Simeon and Gwen, also deserve thanks for humoring me when I can't stop talking about PowerShell, and for giving me some breathing room to write.

About the Reviewers

Christian Droulers is a late-blooming software developer. He only started programming in college and has not stopped since. He's interested in beautiful, clean, and efficient code.

Steve Shilling has worked in the IT industry commercially since 1987, but started with computers in 1982 writing BASIC programs and debugging game programs written by others. He has broad knowledge about Unix, Windows, and Mainframe systems. He primarily lives in the Unix/Linux world automating systems for deployments and businesses, and has spent many years working in system administration, software development, training, and managing technical people. He remains in the technical field of expertise providing knowledge and experience to companies around the world to make their systems stable, reliable, and delivered on time. His experience has taken him through many different industries covering banking and finance, insurance services, betting exchanges, TV and media, retail, and others, allowing him to have a unique perspective of IT in business where most have only worked in one industry.

Steve works for TPS Services Ltd., which specializes in IT training and consultancy, life coaching, management training, and counselling. The IT part of TPS Services Ltd. specializes in Linux/Unix systems for small, medium, and large organizations, and the integration of Linux and Windows systems.

www.PacktPub.com

Support files, eBooks, discount offers, and more

For support files and downloads related to your book, please visit www.PacktPub.com.

Did you know that Packt offers eBook versions of every book published, with PDF and ePub files available? You can upgrade to the eBook version at www.PacktPub.com and as a print book customer, you are entitled to a discount on the eBook copy. Get in touch with us at service@packtpub.com for more details.

At www.PacktPub.com, you can also read a collection of free technical articles, sign up for a range of free newsletters and receive exclusive discounts and offers on Packt books and eBooks.

https://www2.packtpub.com/books/subscription/packtlib

Do you need instant solutions to your IT questions? PacktLib is Packt's online digital book library. Here, you can search, access, and read Packt's entire library of books.

Why subscribe?

- Fully searchable across every book published by Packt
- Copy and paste, print, and bookmark content
- On demand and accessible via a web browser

Free access for Packt account holders

If you have an account with Packt at www.PacktPub.com, you can use this to access PacktLib today and view 9 entirely free books. Simply use your login credentials for immediate access.

Instant updates on new Packt books

Get notified! Find out when new books are published by following @PacktEnterprise on Twitter or the *Packt Enterprise* Facebook page.

Table of Contents

Preface

PowerShell Troubleshooting Guide uses easy-to-understand examples to explain the PowerShell language, enabling you to spend more of your time writing code to solve the problems you face and less time agonizing over syntax and cryptic error messages. Beginning with the foundations of PowerShell, including functions, modules, and the pipeline, you will learn how to leverage the power built into the language to solve problems and avoid reinventing the wheel. Writing code in PowerShell can be fun, and once you've learned the techniques in this book, you will enjoy PowerShell more and more.

What this book covers

Chapter 1, *PowerShell Primer*, provides a brief introduction to some of the most important entities in the PowerShell language including cmdlets, functions, scripts, and modules. A special emphasis is placed on the importance of the pipeline in PowerShell operations.

Chapter 2, *PowerShell Peculiarities*, includes a number of features of the PowerShell language, which are unusual when compared with other mainstream programming languages. Examples of these topics are output from functions and non-terminating errors.

Chapter 3, *PowerShell Practices*, shows a few ways that the scripting experience in PowerShell can be improved, either in performance or in maintainability. A lengthy discussion of the various output cmdlets is included.

Chapter 4, *PowerShell Professionalism*, gives examples of practices that might not be as familiar to traditional system administrators but are common among professional developers. These practices will help scripters create more reliable products and be more confident when making changes to existing codebases.

Chapter 5, Proactive PowerShell, presents a number of practices that, when applied to code, will result in more flexible code with fewer bugs. In a sense, this is pre-emptive troubleshooting, where we create our code thoughtfully in order to reduce the need for troubleshooting later.

Chapter 6, Preparing the Scripting Environment, covers the idea of knowing the characteristics of the environment in which your scripts are running. We also spend some effort trying to weed out network connectivity issues.

Chapter 7, Reactive Practices – Traditional Debugging, shows how to perform traditional troubleshooting in PowerShell using the debugging features of the console and the ISE, along with other techniques. It wraps up with an example of how using the wrong PowerShell feature to perform an operation can lead to poor performance.

Chapter 8, PowerShell Code Smells, explains the concept of code smells (signs of poorly implemented code) and compares it with antipatterns, best practices, and technical debt. It then shows some ways that PowerShell code might begin to smell.

What you need for this book

Most of the examples in the book will work with PowerShell Version 2.0 and above. In places where a higher version of the engine is required, it will be indicated in the text. You should have no problems running the provided code on either a client installation (Windows 7 or greater) or a server installation (Windows Server 2008 R2 or greater).

Who this book is for

This book is intended for anyone who has some experience with PowerShell and would like to expand their understanding of the language design and features in order to spend less time troubleshooting their code. The examples are designed to be understood without needing any specific application knowledge (for example, Exchange, Active Directory, and IIS) in order to keep the intent clear. A few sections are aimed at system administrators specifically. This is due to the different skill set that most administrators bring to the table compared with developers. However, the points made are applicable to anyone using PowerShell.

Conventions

In this book, you will find a number of styles of text that distinguish between different kinds of information. Here are some examples of these styles and an explanation of their meaning.

Code words in text, database table names, folder names, filenames, file extensions, pathnames, dummy URLs, user input, and Twitter handles are shown as follows: "The Get-Help cmdlet has a number of switches that control precisely what help information is displayed."

A block of code is set as follows:

```
param($name)
    $PowerShellVersion=$PSVersionTable.PSVersion
    return "We're using $PowerShellVersion, $name!"
```

When we wish to draw your attention to a particular part of a code block, the relevant lines or items are set in bold:

```
#find largest 5 items in the directory tree
dir -recurse |
    tee-object -Variable Files |
    sort-object Length |
    tee-object -Variable SortedFiles |
    select-object -last 5
```

Any command-line input or output is written as follows:

```
Get-ChildItem "c:\program files" -include *.dll -recurse
```

New terms and **important** words are shown in bold. Words that you see on the screen, in menus or dialog boxes for example, appear in the text like this: "It features a button labeled **Scan Script**, a gear button for options, and a grid for results."

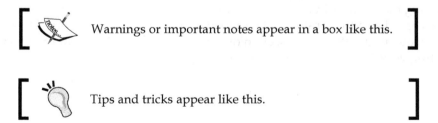

Warnings or important notes appear in a box like this.

Tips and tricks appear like this.

Reader feedback

Feedback from our readers is always welcome. Let us know what you think about this book—what you liked or may have disliked. Reader feedback is important for us to develop titles that you really get the most out of.

To send us general feedback, simply send an e-mail to feedback@packtpub.com, and mention the book title via the subject of your message. If there is a topic that you have expertise in and you are interested in either writing or contributing to a book, see our author guide on www.packtpub.com/authors.

Customer support

Now that you are the proud owner of a Packt book, we have a number of things to help you to get the most from your purchase.

Downloading the example code

You can download the example code files for all Packt books you have purchased from your account at http://www.packtpub.com. If you purchased this book elsewhere, you can visit http://www.packtpub.com/support and register to have the files e-mailed directly to you.

Errata

Although we have taken every care to ensure the accuracy of our content, mistakes do happen. If you find a mistake in one of our books—maybe a mistake in the text or the code—we would be grateful if you would report this to us. By doing so, you can save other readers from frustration and help us improve subsequent versions of this book. If you find any errata, please report them by visiting http://www.packtpub.com/submit-errata, selecting your book, clicking on the **errata submission form** link, and entering the details of your errata. Once your errata are verified, your submission will be accepted and the errata will be uploaded on our website, or added to any list of existing errata, under the Errata section of that title. Any existing errata can be viewed by selecting your title from http://www.packtpub.com/support.

Piracy

Piracy of copyright material on the Internet is an ongoing problem across all media. At Packt, we take the protection of our copyright and licenses very seriously. If you come across any illegal copies of our works, in any form, on the Internet, please provide us with the location address or website name immediately so that we can pursue a remedy.

Please contact us at `copyright@packtpub.com` with a link to the suspected pirated material.

We appreciate your help in protecting our authors, and our ability to bring you valuable content.

Questions

You can contact us at `questions@packtpub.com` if you are having a problem with any aspect of the book, and we will do our best to address it.

1
PowerShell Primer

This chapter will give you a very brief overview of the main features of the PowerShell language. By the end of the chapter, you will be familiar with the following topics:

- Cmdlets
- Functions
- Scripts
- Pipelines
- Variables
- Modules

Introduction

Windows PowerShell (or just PowerShell, for short) was introduced by Microsoft in late 2006 accompanied by little fanfare. In the last seven years, PowerShell has gone from being what might have seemed like a research project to what is now the mainstay of Windows automation and is included in every Windows operating system and most of the major Microsoft products including Exchange, System Center, SQL Server, SharePoint, and Azure.

PowerShell is often thought of as a command-line language, and that is an accurate (but incomplete) view. Working on the command line in PowerShell is a joy compared to MS-DOS batch files and most of the command-line tools that IT professionals are used to having at their fingertips work with no changes in the PowerShell environment. PowerShell is also a first-class scripting language where the knowledge you gain from the command line pays off big time. Unlike MS-DOS, PowerShell was designed from the beginning to be a powerful tool for scripting. Unlike VBScript, there is an interactive PowerShell console that allows you to iteratively develop solutions a bit at a time as you work your way through a sequence of objects, methods, and properties.

PowerShell includes several different elements that work together to create a very powerful and flexible ecosystem. While this chapter will give you an overview of several of these pieces, be aware that the PowerShell language is the subject of many books. For in-depth coverage of these topics, refer to *PowerShell In Practice* by Don Jones, Jeffery Hicks, and Richard Siddaway, *Manning Publications*.

Cmdlets

In PowerShell, a **cmdlet** (pronounced "command-let") describes a unit of functionality specific to PowerShell. In version 1.0 of PowerShell, the only way to create a cmdlet was by using managed (compiled) code, but 2.0 introduced **advanced functions**, which have the same capabilities as cmdlets. Built-in cmdlets exist to interact with the filesystem, services, processes, event logs, WMI, and other system objects. Some examples of cmdlets, which also show the flexibility in parameter passing, are shown as follows:

- `Get-ChildItem "c:\program files" -include *.dll -recurse`: This cmdlet outputs all `.dll` files under `c:\program files`

- `Get-EventLog Application -newest 5`: This cmdlet outputs the five most recent entries in the `Application` event log

- `Set-Content -path c:\temp\files.txt -value (dir c:\)`: This cmdlet writes a directory listing to a text file

Cmdlets are named with a two-part construction: verb-noun. Verbs in PowerShell describe the actions to be performed and come from a common list provided by Microsoft. These include `Get`, `Set`, `Start`, `Stop`, and other easy-to-remember terms. The `Get-Verb` cmdlet provides the list of approved verbs with some information on how the verbs can be grouped. The following screenshot shows the beginning of the list of verbs and their corresponding groups:

PowerShell nouns specify on which kind of objects the cmdlet operates. Examples of nouns are `Service`, `Process`, `File`, or `WMIObject` Unlike the list of verbs, there is no managed list of approved nouns. The reason for this is simple. With every new version of Windows, more and more cmdlets are being delivered which cover more and more of the operating system's features. An up-to-date reference for verbs along with guidance between similar or easily confused verbs can be found at `http://msdn.microsoft.com/en-us/library/ms714428.aspx`.

Putting nouns and verbs together, you get full cmdlet names such as `Get-Process` and `Start-Service`. By providing a list of verbs to choose from, the PowerShell team has gone a long way toward simplifying the experience for users. Without the guidance of a list such as this, cmdlet authors would often be forced to choose between several candidates for a cmdlet name. For instance, `Stop-Service` is the actual cmdlet name, but names such as `Kill-Service` and `Terminate-Service` would both convey the same effect. Knowing that `Stop` is the approved verb not only makes the decision simple, it also makes it simple to guess how one would terminate a process (as opposed to a service). The obvious answer would be `Stop-Process`.

Cmdlets each have their own set of parameters that allow values to be supplied on the command line or through a pipeline. Switch parameters also allow for on/off options without needing to pass a value. There is a large set of common parameters that can be used with all cmdlets. Cmdlets that modify the state of the system also generally allow the use of the `-Whatif` and `-Confirm` risk mitigation parameters. Common parameters and risk mitigation parameters are covered in detail in *Chapter 5, Proactive PowerShell*.

The big three cmdlets

When learning PowerShell, it's customary to emphasize three important cmdlets that are used to get PowerShell to give information about the environment and objects that are returned by the cmdlets. The first cmdlet is Get-Command. This cmdlet is used to get a list of matching cmdlets, scripts, functions, or executables in the current path. For instance, to get a list of commands related to services, the Get-Command *service* command would be a good place to start. The list displayed might look like this:

```
PS C:\Users\mike> get-command *service*

CommandType     Name                             ModuleName
-----------     ----                             ----------
Function        Get-NetFirewallServiceFilter     NetSecurity
Function        Set-NetFirewallServiceFilter     NetSecurity
Cmdlet          Get-Service                      Microsoft.PowerShell.Management
Cmdlet          New-Service                      Microsoft.PowerShell.Management
Cmdlet          New-WebServiceProxy              Microsoft.PowerShell.Management
Cmdlet          Restart-Service                  Microsoft.PowerShell.Management
Cmdlet          Resume-Service                   Microsoft.PowerShell.Management
Cmdlet          Set-Service                      Microsoft.PowerShell.Management
Cmdlet          Start-Service                    Microsoft.PowerShell.Management
Cmdlet          Stop-Service                     Microsoft.PowerShell.Management
Cmdlet          Suspend-Service                  Microsoft.PowerShell.Management
Application     services.exe
Application     services.msc
```

The thought behind listing Get-Command as the first cmdlet you would use is that it is used to discover the name of cmdlets. This is true, but in my experience you won't be using Get-Command for very long. The verb-noun naming convention combined with PowerShell's very convenient tab-completion feature will mean that as you get familiar with the language you will be able to guess cmdlet names quickly and won't be relying on Get-Command. It is useful though, and might show you commands that you didn't know existed. Another use for Get-Command is to figure out what command is executed. For instance, if you encountered the Compare $a $b command line and didn't know what the Compare command was, you could try the Get-Command command to find that Compare is an alias for Compare-Object.

PowerShell provides aliases for two reasons. First, to provide aliases that are commands in other shells (such as dir or ls), which lead us to PowerShell cmdlets that perform similar functions. Secondly, to give abbreviations that are shorter and quicker to type for commonly used cmdlets (for example, ? for Where-Object and gsv for Get-Service). In the PowerShell community, a best practice is to use aliases only in the command line and never in scripts. For that reason, I will generally not be using aliases in example scripts.

A similar trick can be used to find out where an executable is found: `Get-Command nslookup | Select-Object Path` returns the path `C:\Windows\system32\nslookup.exe`.

The second and probably most important cmdlet is `Get-Help`. `Get-Help` is used to display information in PowerShell's help system. The help system contains information about individual cmdlets and also contains general information about PowerShell-related topics. The cmdlet help includes syntax information about parameters used with each cmdlet, detailed information about cmdlet functionality, and it also often contains helpful examples illustrating common ways to use the cmdlet.

> Pay attention to the help files. Sometimes, the problem you are having is because you are using a cmdlet or parameter differently than the designer intended. The examples in the help system might point you in the right direction.

The following screenshot shows the beginning of the help information for the `Get-Help` cmdlet:

```
Administrator: Windows PowerShell

PS C:\Users\Mike> get-help get-help

NAME
    Get-Help

SYNOPSIS
    Displays information about Windows PowerShell commands and concepts.

SYNTAX
    Get-Help [[-Name] <String>] [-Category <String[]>] [-Component <String[]>] [-Path <String>] [-Role <String[]>] [<CommonParameters>]

    Get-Help [[-Name] <String>] [-Category <String[]>] [-Component <String[]>] [-<String>] [-Role <String[]>] -Detailed [<CommonParameters>]

    Get-Help [[-Name] <String>] [-Category <String[]>] [-Component <String[]>] [-<String>] [-Role <String[]>] -Examples [<CommonParameters>]

    Get-Help [[-Name] <String>] [-Category <String[]>] [-Component <String[]>] [-<String>] [-Role <String[]>] -Online [<CommonParameters>]

    Get-Help [[-Name] <String>] [-Category <String[]>] [-Component <String[]>] [-<String>] [-Role <String[]>] -Parameter <String> [<CommonParameters>]

    Get-Help [[-Name] <String>] [-Category <String[]>] [-Component <String[]>] [-<String>] [-Role <String[]>] -ShowWindow [<CommonParameters>]

DESCRIPTION
    The Get-Help cmdlet displays information about Windows PowerShell concepts an
    functions, CIM commands, workflows, providers, aliases and scripts.

    To get help for a Windows PowerShell command, type "Get-Help" followed by the
    Get-Process. To get a list of all help topics on your system, type: Get-Help
    topic or use the parameters of the Get-Help cmdlet to get selected parts of t
    parameters, or examples.

    Conceptual help topics in Windows PowerShell begin with "about_", such as "ab
```

Another source of information in the help files are topics about the PowerShell language. The names of these help topics start with `about_`, and range from a few paragraphs to several pages of detailed information. In a few cases, the `about_` topics are more detailed than most books' coverage of them. The following screenshot shows the beginning of the `about_Language_Keywords` topic (the entire topic is approximately 13 pages long):

```
PS C:\Users\mike> get-help about_Language_Keywords
TOPIC
    about_Language_Keywords

SHORT DESCRIPTION
    Describes the keywords in the Windows PowerShell scripting language.

LONG DESCRIPTION
    Windows PowerShell has the following language keywords. For more
    information, see the about topic for the keyword and the information that
    follows the table.


        Keyword             Reference
        -------             ---------
        Begin               about_Functions, about_Functions_Advanced
        Break               about_Break, about_Trap
        Catch               about_Try_Catch_Finally
        Continue            about_Continue, about_Trap
        Data                about_Data_Sections
        Do                  about_Do, about_While
        DynamicParam        about_Functions_Advanced_Parameters
        Else                about_If
        Elseif              about_If
        End                 about_Functions, about_Functions_Advanced_Methods
        Exit                Described in this topic.
        Filter              about_Functions
        Finally             about_Try_Catch_Finally
        For                 about_For
        ForEach             about_ForEach
        From                Reserved for future use.
        Function            about_Functions, about_Functions_Advanced
        If                  about_If
        In                  about_ForEach
        InlineScript        about_InlineScript
```

The `Get-Help` cmdlet has a number of switches that control precisely what help information is displayed. The default display is somewhat brief and can be expanded by using the `-Full` or `-Detailed` switches. The `-Examples` switch displays the list of examples associated with the topic. The full help output can also be viewed in a pop-up window in PowerShell 3.0 or higher using the `-ShowWindow` switch.

> PowerShell 3.0 and above do not ship with any help content. To view help in these systems you will need to use the `Update-Help` cmdlet in an elevated session.

The final member of the big three is `Get-Member`. In PowerShell, all output from commands comes in the form of objects. The `Get-Member` cmdlet is used to display the members (for example, properties, methods, and events) associated with a set of objects as well as the types of those objects. In general, you will pipe objects into `Get-Member` to see what you can do with those objects. An example involving services is shown as follows:

Functions

Functions are similar to cmdlets and should follow the same naming conventions. Whereas cmdlets are compiled units of PowerShell functionality written in managed code like C#, functions are written using the PowerShell language. Starting with PowerShell 2.0, it has been possible to write advanced functions, which are very similar to cmdlets. It is possible to use common parameters and risk mitigation parameters with advanced functions. An example of a function is shown as follows:

```
function get-PowerShellVersionMessage{
param($name)
    $PowerShellVersion=$PSVersionTable.PSVersion
    return "We're using $PowerShellVersion, $name!"
}
```

Calling the function at the command line is straightforward, as shown in the following screenshot:

```
PS C:\Users\Mike> get-PowerShellVersionMessage Mike
We're using 4.0, Mike!
```

Scripts

Scripts are simply files with a .ps1 file extension, which contain PowerShell code. It is possible to parameterize a script file in the same way that you would a function using a Param() statement at the beginning of the file. If we were to store the following code in a file called Get-PowerShellVersionMessage.ps1, it would be roughly equivalent to the Get-PowerShellVersionMessage function in the previous section:

```
param($name)
    $PowerShellVersion=$PSVersionTable.PSVersion
    return "We're using $PowerShellVersion, $name!"
```

A security feature of PowerShell is that it won't run a script in the current directory without specifically referring to the directory, so calling this script would look like this:

```
.\get-powershellversionmessage –name Mike
```

The following screenshot shows the aforementioned code being stored in a file:

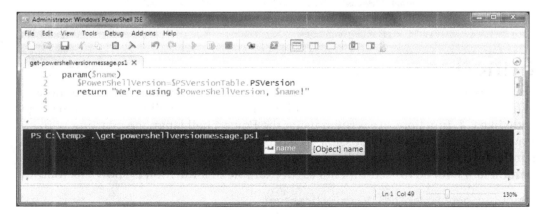

And the output would be (on the computer I'm using): **We're using PowerShell 4.0, Mike**.

> Depending on your environment, you might not be able to run scripts until you change the execution policy. The execution policy dictates whether scripts are allowed to be executed, where those scripts can be located, and whether they need to be digitally signed. Typically, I use `set-executionpolicy RemoteSigned` to allow local scripts without requiring signatures. For more information about execution policies, refer to `about_execution_policies`.

It is also possible to define multiple functions in a script. However, when doing so, it is important to understand the concept of scope. When a script or function is executed, PowerShell creates a new memory area for definitions (for example, variables and functions) that are created during the execution. When the script or function exits, that memory is destroyed, thereby removing the new definitions. Executing a script with multiple functions will not export those functions into the current scope. Instead, the script executes in its own scope and defines the functions in that scope. When the script execution is finished, the newly created scope is exited, removing the function definitions. To overcome this situation, the dot-source operator was created. To dot-source a file means to run the file, without creating a new scope in which to run. If there was a script file with function definitions called `myFuncs.ps1`, dot-sourcing the file would use the following syntax:

```
. .\myFuncs.ps1
```

Note that there is a space after the first dot, and that since the script is in the current directory explicit use of the directory is required.

Pipelines

PowerShell expressions involving cmdlets and functions can be connected together using pipelines. Pipelines are not a new concept, and have been in DOS for a long time (and in Unix/Linux forever). The idea of a pipeline is similar to a conveyor belt in a factory. Materials on a conveyor belt move from one station to the next as workers or machinery work on the materials to connect, construct, or somehow modify the work in progress. In the same way, pipelines allow data to move from one command to the next, as the output of one command is treated as the input for the next. There is no practical limit to the number of commands that can be connected this way, but readability does keep command lines from continuing forever. It can be tempting to string more and more expressions together to create a single-line solution, but troubleshooting a pipeline evaluation can be tricky.

When working with long pipeline constructions, consider breaking the line into several expressions to make the execution clearer.

Prior to PowerShell, pipelines dealt with output and input in terms of text, passing strings from one program to the next regardless of what kind of information was being processed. PowerShell makes a major change to this paradigm by treating all input and output as objects. By doing this, PowerShell cmdlets are able to work with the properties, methods, and events that are exposed by the data rather than simply dealing with the string representation. The PowerShell community often refers to the methods used by string-based pipelines as parse-and-pray, which is named after the twin operations of string parsing based on an understanding of the text format and hoping that the format of the output doesn't ever change. An example, shown in the following screenshot, illustrates this quite well:

```
Administrator: C:\Windows\system32\cmd.exe

C:\Users\Mike\Documents\PowerShellTroubleshooting\Images>dir
 Volume in drive C is C_Drive
 Volume Serial Number is 58BC-BCB6

 Directory of C:\Users\Mike\Documents\PowerShellTroubleshooting\Images

02/28/2014  09:37 PM    <DIR>          .
02/28/2014  09:37 PM    <DIR>          ..
02/28/2014  08:34 PM            25,303 3571EN_01_001.png
02/27/2014  09:44 PM            29,845 Image001.png
02/27/2014  09:45 PM            25,303 Image002.png
               3 File(s)         80,451 bytes
               2 Dir(s)  14,646,292,480 bytes free

C:\Users\Mike\Documents\PowerShellTroubleshooting\Images>
```

It's easy to think of the output of the MS-DOS `dir` command as a sequence of files and folders, but if the output is carefully studied, something different becomes clear. There is a tremendous amount of other information provided:

- Volume information
- Volume serial number
- A directory-level caption
- A list of files and folders
- A count of files

- The total size of those files
- The number of directories
- The space free on the drive

To work with this output and deal with, for instance, the file names, there's a tremendous amount of work that would need to be done to analyze the formatting of all of these elements. Also, there are several different formatting parameters that can be used with the MS-DOS `dir` command that would affect the output. By passing data between cmdlets as objects, all of this work is eliminated. The PowerShell `Get-ChildItem` cmdlet, which is similar to the MS-DOS `dir` command, outputs a sequence of file and directory objects if the current location is a filesystem location.

How pipelines change the game

To see how the choice of an object-oriented pipeline changes the way work is done, it is sufficient to look at the MS-DOS `dir` command. I am picking on the `dir` command because it has a simple function and everyone in IT has some level of experience with it. If you wanted to sort the output of a `dir` command, you would need to know what the parameters built into the command are. To do that, you'd do something like this:

```
C:\Users\mike>dir /?
Displays a list of files and subdirectories in a directory.

DIR [drive:][path][filename] [/A[[:]attributes]] [/B] [/C] [/D] [/L] [/N]
  [/O[[:]sortorder]] [/P] [/Q] [/R] [/S] [/T[[:]timefield]] [/W] [/X] [/4]

  [drive:][path][filename]
              Specifies drive, directory, and/or files to list.

  /A          Displays files with specified attributes.
  attributes   D  Directories                R  Read-only files
               H  Hidden files               A  Files ready for archiving
               S  System files               I  Not content indexed files
               L  Reparse Points             -  Prefix meaning not
  /B          Uses bare format (no heading information or summary).
  /C          Display the thousand separator in file sizes.  This is the
              default.  Use /-C to disable display of separator.
  /D          Same as wide but files are list sorted by column.
  /L          Uses lowercase.
  /N          New long list format where filenames are on the far right.
  /O          List by files in sorted order.
  sortorder    N  By name (alphabetic)       S  By size (smallest first)
               E  By extension (alphabetic)  D  By date/time (oldest first)
               G  Group directories first    -  Prefix to reverse order
```

It's clear that the designer of the command had sorting in mind, because there is a /O option with five different ways to sort (ten if you include reverse). That is helpful, but files have a lot more than five properties. What if you wanted to sort by more than one property? Ignoring those questions for a moment, does the collection of sorting options for this command help you at all if you were trying to sort the output of a different command (say an ATTRIB or SET command)? You might hope that the same developer wrote the code for the second command, or that they used the same specifications, but you would be disappointed. Even the simple operation of sorting output is either not implemented or implemented differently by MS-DOS commands.

PowerShell takes an entirely different approach. If you were to look at the help for Get-ChildItem, you would find no provision for sorting at all. In fact, PowerShell cmdlets do not use parameters to supply sorting information. Instead, they use the object-oriented pipeline. MS-DOS developers needed to encode the sort parameters for the dir command inside the dir command itself is because that is the only place that the properties exist (including sorting criteria). Once the command has been executed, all that is left is text, and sorting text based on properties is a complex parse-and-pray operation (which we have already discussed). In PowerShell, however, the output of Get-ChildItem is a sequence of objects, so cmdlets downstream can still access the properties of the objects directly. Sorting in PowerShell is accomplished with the Sort-Object cmdlet, which is able to take a list of properties (among other things) on which to sort the sequence of objects that it receives as input. The following are some examples of sorting a directory listing in MS-DOS and also in PowerShell:

Sorting method	DOS command	PowerShell equivalent
Sort by filename	DIR /O:N	Get-childitem | sort-object Name
Sort by extension	DIR /O:E	Get-ChildItem | Sort-object Extension
Sort by size	DIR /O:S	Get-ChildItem | Sort-object Size
Sort by write date	DIR /O:D	Get-ChildItem | Sort-object LastWriteTime
Sort by creation date	Out of luck	Get-ChildItem | Sort-object CreationTime
Sort by name and size	Out of luck	Get-ChildItem | Sort-object Name,Size

It can be clearly seen by these examples that:

- PowerShell examples are longer
- PowerShell examples are easier to read (at least the sorting options)
- PowerShell techniques are more flexible

The most important thing about learning how to sort directory entries using `Sort-Object` is that sorting any kind of objects is done the exact same way. For instance, if you retrieved a list of applied hotfixes on the current computer using `Get-hotfix`, in order to sort it by HotFixID, you would issue the `Get-Hotfix | Sort-Object -Property HotFixID` command:

```
PS C:\Users\mike> get-hotfix | sort-object HotFixID

Source     Description       HotFixID     InstalledBy            InstalledOn
------     -----------       --------     -----------            -----------
ASGARD     Security Update   KB2862152    NT AUTHORITY\SYSTEM    11/13/2013 12:00:00 AM
ASGARD     Security Update   KB2868626    NT AUTHORITY\SYSTEM    11/13/2013 12:00:00 AM
ASGARD     Security Update   KB2876331    NT AUTHORITY\SYSTEM    11/13/2013 12:00:00 AM
ASGARD     Update            KB2883200    asgard\Administrator   8/22/2013 12:00:00 AM
ASGARD     Update            KB2884101    NT AUTHORITY\SYSTEM    11/3/2013 12:00:00 AM
ASGARD     Update            KB2884846    NT AUTHORITY\SYSTEM    11/3/2013 12:00:00 AM
ASGARD     Update            KB2887595    NT AUTHORITY\SYSTEM    11/18/2013 12:00:00 AM
ASGARD     Update            KB2889543    NT AUTHORITY\SYSTEM    9/30/2013 12:00:00 AM
ASGARD     Update            KB2891214    NT AUTHORITY\SYSTEM    11/3/2013 12:00:00 AM
ASGARD     Security Update   KB2892074    NT AUTHORITY\SYSTEM    12/12/2013 12:00:00 AM
ASGARD     Security Update   KB2893294    NT AUTHORITY\SYSTEM    12/12/2013 12:00:00 AM
ASGARD     Security Update   KB2893984    NT AUTHORITY\SYSTEM    12/12/2013 12:00:00 AM
```

Another point to note about sorting objects by referring to properties is that the sorting is done according to the type of the property. For instance, sorting objects by a numeric property would order the objects by the magnitude of the property values, not by the string representation of those values. That is, a value of 10 would sort after 9, not between 1 and 2. This is just one more thing that you don't have to worry about.

What's the fuss about sorting?

You might be asking, why is sorting such a big deal? You'd be correct; sorting is not necessarily a tremendously important concept. The point is, the method that the designers of PowerShell took with the pipeline (that is, using objects rather than strings) that allows this sorting method also allows other powerful operations such as filtering, aggregating, summarizing, and narrowing.

Filtering is the operation of selecting which (entire) objects in the pipeline will continue in the pipeline. Think of filtering like a worker who is inspecting objects on the conveyor belt, picking up objects that are bad and throwing them away (in the bit bucket). In the same way, objects that do not match the filter criteria are discarded and do not continue as output. Filtering in PowerShell is done via the `Where-Object` cmdlet and takes two forms. The first form is somewhat complicated to look at, and requires some explaining. We will start with an example such as the following:

```
Get-ChildItem | Where-object {$_.Size -lt 100}
```

Hopefully, even without an explanation, it is clear that the output would be a list of files that have a size less than 100. This form of the `Where-Object` cmdlet takes a piece of code as a parameter (called a scriptblock), which is evaluated for each object in the pipeline. If the script evaluates to true when the object in the pipeline is assigned to the special variable `$_`, the object will continue on the pipeline. If it evaluates to false, the object is discarded.

PowerShell 3.0 made a couple of changes to the `Where-Object` cmdlet. First, it added an easier-to-read option for the `$_` variable, called `$PSItem`. Using that, the previous command can be rewritten as follows:

```
Get-ChildItem | Where-object {$PSItem.Size -lt 100}
```

This is slightly more readable, but Version 3.0 also added a second form that simplifies it even more. If the script block is referring to a single property, a single operator, and a constant value, the simplified syntax can be used, shown as follows:

```
Where-Object Property Operator Value
```

Note that there are no braces indicating a scriptblock, and no `$_` or `$PSItem`. The simplified syntax for our sample filter command is this:

```
Get-ChildItem | Where-Object Size -lt 100
```

Variables

PowerShell variables, similar to variables in other programming languages, are names for data stored in memory. PowerShell variable references begin with a dollar sign and are created by assigning a value with the assignment operator (the equals sign). Unlike many programming languages, you do not need to define variables before using them or even specify what type of information the variable is going to point to. For instance, the following statements are all valid:

```
$var = 5
$anothervar = "Hello"
$files = dir c:\
```

Note that while the first two assignments were simple (integer and string constants), the third involved executing a pipeline (with a single statement) and storing the results of that pipeline in a variable. The command in the third line returns a collection of more than one kind of object (it has files and folders). Note that there is no special notation required to store a collection of objects.

Several common parameters in PowerShell take the name of a variable in order to store results of some kind in that variable. The -ErrorVariable, -WarningVariable, -OutVariable parameters, and (new in Version 4.0) -PipelineVariable parameter all follow this pattern. Also, all of the *-Variable cmdlets have a -Name parameter. These parameters are expecting the name of the variable rather than the contents of the variable. The name of the variable does not include the dollar sign. In the following screenshot, you can see that the -outvariable parameter was passed the file value, which caused a copy of the output to be stored in the variable called file:

```
PS C:\temp> dir test.txt -outvariable file


    Directory: C:\temp


Mode                LastWriteTime     Length Name
----                -------------     ------ ----
-a---         3/11/2014     7:26 PM          0 test.txt

PS C:\temp> $file.LastWriteTime

Tuesday, March 11, 2014 7:26:08 PM
```

In short, referencing the content of the variable involves the dollar sign, but referencing the variable name does not.

Modules

In Version 1.0 of PowerShell, the only ways to group lists of functions were to either put script files for each function in a directory or to include several functions in a script file and use dot-sourcing to load the functions. Neither solution provided much in the way of functionality, though. Version 2.0 introduced the concept of modules. A PowerShell module usually consists of a folder residing in one of the directories listed in the PSModulePath environment variable and contains one of the following:

- A module file (.psm1) with the same name as the folder
- A module manifest (.psd1) with the same name as the folder
- A compiled assembly (.dll) with the same name as the folder

One tremendous advantage that modules have over scripts is that while every function in a script is visible when the script is run, visibility of functions (as well as variables and aliases) defined within a module can be controlled by using the `Export-ModuleMember` cmdlet.

The following module file, named `TroubleShooting.psm1`, re-implements the `Get-PowerShellMessage` function from earlier in the chapter using a helper function (`Get-Message`). Since only `Get-PowerShellVersionMessage` was exported, the helper function is not available after the module is imported but it is available to be called by the exported function.

```
function Get-Message{
param($ver,$name)
   return "We're using $ver, $name!"
}

function Get-PowerShellVersionMessage{
param($name)
   $version=$PSVersionTable.PSVersion
   $message=Get-Message $version $name
   return $message
}

Export-ModuleMember Get-PowerShellVersionMessage
```

Importing a module is accomplished by using the `Import-Module` cmdlet. Version 3.0 of PowerShell introduced the concept of automatic importing. With this feature enabled, if you refer to a cmdlet or function that does not exist, the shell looks in all of the modules that exist on the system for a matching name. If it finds one, it imports the module automatically. This even works with tab-completion. If you hit the *Tab* key, PowerShell will look for a cmdlet or function in memory that matches, but If it doesn't find one it will attempt to load the first module that has a function whose name matches the string you're trying to complete. Listing the cmdlets that have been loaded by a particular module is as simple as the `Get-Command -Module` module name.

Further reading

For more information, check out the following references:

- The Monad Manifesto at `http://blogs.msdn.com/b/powershell/archive/2007/03/19/monad-manifesto-the-origin-of-windows-powershell.aspx`

- Microsoft's approved cmdlet verb list at `http://msdn.microsoft.com/en-us/library/ms714428.aspx`
- `get-help get-command`
- `get-help get-verb`
- `get-help about_aliases`
- `get-help get-member`
- `get-help about_functions`
- `get-help about_functions_advanced`
- `get-help about_scripts`
- `get-help about_execution_policies`
- `get-help about_scopes`
- `get-help about_pipelines`
- `get-help where-object`
- `get-help about_variables`
- `get-help about_commonparameters`
- `get-help about_modules`

Summary

In this chapter, we have seen the main building blocks of PowerShell as a language. We have demonstrated how similar functionality can be implemented using a function, a script, and a module. An emphasis was placed on how PowerShell's use of an object-oriented pipeline gives tremendous advantages in terms of flexibility without re-implementing common features such as sorting and filtering in each function.

PowerShell provides an innovative programming and scripting experience. The next chapter will highlight various ways that the PowerShell language functions differently from other programming languages.

2
PowerShell Peculiarities

In many ways, PowerShell is different (as a language) than other traditional programming languages. Some of PowerShell's peculiarities will be presented in this chapter, as well as some guidance on how to avoid common pitfalls. Here are the topics we'll cover in this chapter:

- Strings (quoting, substitution, and escaping)
- Function return values
- Pipeline processing
- Error handling and non-terminating errors

PowerShell strings

In PowerShell, either double quotes or single quotes can be used to express string literals. For instance, the following values are the same:

```
"HELLO WORLD"
'HELLO WORLD'
```

Using both kinds of quotes can be useful when quoting strings which themselves contain quotes, such as the following:

```
"I can't stop using PowerShell"
'He said, "I like using PowerShell" all day long'
```

If a single quote is needed in a single-quoted string, you can double the quote (for example, 'can't is a contraction'). The same technique allows the use of double-quotes in a double-quoted string. Strings written this way can be somewhat confusing to look at and it is easy to lose track of the number of quotes. A simpler method of including a double quote character in a string is to escape it with the backtick (`` ` ``), also called a grave accent. The following string is an example: "the `` ` ``" character is a double quote".

A peculiar kind of string in PowerShell is called a here-string. Here-strings allow strings to cross several lines and also to contain quotes of either kind without any doubling. Here-strings begin with either @" or @' at the end of a line and end with "@ or '@ respectively at the beginning of a line. A common error is to indent the closing punctuation (so that it is not at the beginning of a line) which causes the here-string to not be terminated. The syntax highlighting in the **integrated scripting environment** (**ISE**) will provide a good visual cue that something isn't quite right in this situation. The following illustration shows a couple of correctly formatted here-strings and one that isn't correctly terminated. Note that the text after the final here-string shows an error and the code hint explains the problem:

```
$var=@"
this is a here-string
"@

$var2=@'
this is also a here-sring
    it spans more than one line.
        The indenting is preserved.
'@

$var3=@'
    This here-string is not properly terminated.
    '@

get-childitem
        White space is not allowed before the string terminator.
```

String substitution

The main difference between single- and double-quoted strings (both normal strings and here-strings) is that single-quoted strings are static while double-quoted strings perform string substitution. Variable references contained in double-quoted strings are replaced with string representations of the contents of the variable. For example, if the variable `$name` contains the value `"Mike"`, the double-quoted string `"My name is $name!"` would become `"My name is Mike!"`.

String substitution is a great timesaver. In many languages, embedding values in string output involves string concatenation, and code ends up with lots of expressions such as `"My name is "+$name+"!"`. If the desired output involves several variables, the expression will need to be broken down into more and more segments. However, embedding several variables in PowerShell is often as simple as including the variable names in the string.

For simple objects (such as strings, integers, and floating point numbers), the representation of the variable that is used in the string substitution is the same value that you would see if you used `Write-Host` (for example) to display the value. For complex objects, however, the value is the result of the object's `ToString()` method. This means, generally, the way `$var` is output is different from how `"$var"` is output, as shown in the following screenshot:

```
PS C:\temp> $var=get-service | select -first 1
PS C:\temp> $var

Status     Name                 DisplayName
------     ----                 -----------
Stopped    AeLookupSvc          Application Experience


PS C:\temp> "$var"
System.ServiceProcess.ServiceController
PS C:\temp> _
```

If a variable is an array, the value that is placed in a string is the value of each of the items in the array separated by the value of the built-in `$ofs` variable (which stands for output field separator). The default value of `$ofs` is a space, but it can be changed to create strings delimited by whatever is desired, as shown in the following screenshot:

```
$values='larry', 'moe', 'curly'

write-host "$values"

$ofs=","

write-host "$values"
larry,moe,curly
larry,moe,curly

PS C:\Users\Mike>
```

How string substitution goes wrong

String substitution is a simple concept, but there are a few common issues that people encounter with it. First, it is critical to realize that string substitution is only performed on double-quoted strings. For example, the string `'My name is $name!'` will not be changed in any way. A second common error is trying to embed something more complicated than a variable value in a string. For instance, if `$file` is a reference to a file, you might be tempted to use `"the file is $file.length bytes long"` and expect to have the length of the file replace `$file.length` in the string. The rule of string substitutions that the engine looks for a variable name and replaces it with a value. In this case, `$file` is the name of a variable and it will be replaced with the name of the file. The remainder of the string will be unchanged, as shown in the following code snippet:

```
$file=dir *.* | select -first 1

"the file is $file.length bytes long"
the file is C:\Users\Mike\.gradle.length bytes long
```

In order to include complicated expressions in a string, one approach is to use the subexpression operator `$()`; for example, `"the file is $($file.length) bytes long"`. Subexpressions in strings are not limited to property references, though. Any expression (including cmdlets) is allowed. The string `"the process started at $(Get-Date)"` is an example of using code in a string.

A second method to include complicated expressions in a string is to use the format operator, `-f`. Using the format operator involves preparing a string with placeholders numbered starting with zero and providing a list of values to be substituted. The previous example involving file lengths could be rewritten using the format operator as follows:

```
"the file is {0} bytes long" -f $file.length
```

Including more than one value is just as easy:

```
"the file {0} is {1} bytes long" -f $file.FullName,$file.length
```

There are several advantages to using the format operator over using string substitution. First, since the placeholders are short, the final string is much shorter in the code listing and will be easier to read on the screen and in a printout. Second, with the format operator, special formatting codes can be applied to the placeholders to format the values in specific ways. For example, formatting a date value in a long date format would use a placeholder such as `{0:D}`, and formatting a floating point value with two decimals would use `{0:N2}`. A reference for formatting codes can be found at `http://msdn.microsoft.com/en-us/library/26etazsy.aspx`.

Escaping in PowerShell strings

A common practice in programming languages is to use the backslash (\) as an escape character to allow special characters to be written in strings. PowerShell's integration as a scripting and command-line language necessitates that the backslash not be given any special meaning other than the traditional meaning as a path separator. Therefore, the backtick is used as the escape character. To include a dollar sign in a string without triggering substitution, you can escape the dollar sign with a backtick like so: `"the value of the variable `$var is $var"`. Notice that the first dollar sign is escaped with a backtick but the second one isn't, so the second `$var` will be replaced. This technique was mentioned earlier to include a literal double quote in a double-quoted string. An important point to remember is that substitution is not performed on single-quoted strings, so including an escaped single quote in a single-quoted string doesn't work.

The following is a table of allowed special characters in double-quoted strings:

Value	Meaning
`0	Null
`a	Alert (bell)
`b	Backspace
`f	Form feed
`n	New line
`r	Carriage return
`t	Horizontal tab
`v	Vertical tab

Function output

The example function included in *Chapter 1, PowerShell Primer*, used string substitution and returned the single result of that operation. As a reminder, here it is again:

```
function Get-PowerShellVersionMessage{
param($name)
    $PowerShellVersion=$PSVersionTable.PSVersion
    return "We're using $PowerShellVersion, $name!"
}
```

This pattern (that is, performing a calculation and returning the result) is common to procedural programming languages such as C#, Java, and Visual Basic. In PowerShell, however, functions are more complicated than the usage in this scenario in several ways.

In statically-typed languages, the type of a function (that is, the type of a value returned by the function) is either declared as part of the function definition or inferred by the compiler. In PowerShell, the only consideration of a type associated with the output of a function is in the help provided for the function. This output type can be used by a PowerShell host to guide IntelliSense in the environment, but does not place any restrictions on the function in any way. That is, there is no constraint on what types of objects a function outputs. For example, the help for `Get-Service` indicates that it outputs `System.Service.ServiceController` objects, as shown in the following screenshot:

```
Outputs
    System.ServiceProcess.ServiceController
    Get-Service returns objects that represent the services on the computer.
```

Because of this, when you use `Get-Service` in a pipeline, the environment can tell what properties are relevant, as shown in the following screenshot:

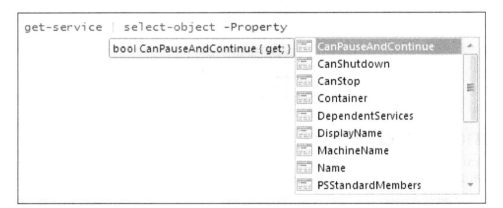

Downloading the example code

You can download the example code files for all Packt books you have purchased from your account at http://www.packtpub.com. If you purchased this book elsewhere, you can visit http://www.packtpub.com/support and register to have the files e-mailed directly to you.

As a specific example of the varying output types of a function in PowerShell, consider the `Get-ChildItem` cmdlet. A similar command in the .NET framework would be the `GetFiles` static method of the `System.IO.Directory` class, which returns an array of strings corresponding to the files in a directory. `Get-ChildItem`, on the other hand, generally outputs a list of `FileInfo` objects, but depending on the particular parameters used it might output nothing, a list of `FileInfo` objects, or a single `FileInfo` object. Consider the following code to see an example of this in action:

```
$files = Get-ChildItem -path *.exe

foreach ($file in $files){
    # do something interesting
}
```

The code follows a common pattern (that is, get a list of objects and use `foreach` to iterate through the list) and the intent of the code is plain. A problem arises in trying to interpret the `foreach` loop over a value that is not a list. If there are no `.exe` files in the current directory, `$files` will be empty. By this I mean that `$files` won't be an empty list; it will simply be `$null`. What about the situation where there is exactly one `.exe` file? Does it make sense to loop through a single file? Again, this is not a list with one file in it, it is a single `FileInfo` object.

In PowerShell Versions 1.0 and 2.0, the answer was to be more careful when storing lists in variables. By adding a type of `[array]` to `$files`, we have instructed the engine to make sure that what is stored in the variable is indeed an array. In this case, the zero and single object cases result in an empty list and a list containing one object. The loop now makes sense:

```
[array]$files = Get-ChildItem -path *.exe

foreach ($file in $files){
    # do something interesting
}
```

PowerShell Version 3.0 has a different approach to solving this problem. In this version, each non-null, non-collection object is given a Count property with a value of 1 and indexer that shows that the first item in the collection (at index 0) is the object itself. The built-in $null value has a Count property of 0. However, in the case of a null object, the indexer isn't really usable because the index needs to be less than the count (which is zero). These extra properties are added invisibly, that is, they do not show up in the output of Get-Member, but they can still be evaluated, as the following illustrates:

```
PS C:\Users\Mike> $files=dir | select -first 1
PS C:\Users\Mike> $files.Count
1
PS C:\Users\Mike> $files[0]


    Directory: C:\Users\Mike


Mode                LastWriteTime     Length Name
----                -------------     ------ ----
d----         9/8/2014   10:38 PM            .gradle


PS C:\Users\Mike> $files[1]
PS C:\Users\Mike> $null.Count
0
```

Pipeline processing

Another way that functions in PowerShell are different from other languages is how they interact with the pipeline. Functions in PowerShell output objects that can be picked up as input to subsequent functions or cmdlets. This in and of itself is not unique, but the timing of the output is different from other languages.

Consider the process of obtaining a listing of all of the files on a drive. For some drives this operation will be very lengthy, possibly taking several minutes to complete. In PowerShell though, the list of files begin to appear almost instantly. The process can take a while to be complete, but the function (Get-ChildItem) will output file and folder objects as each directory is scanned rather than waiting to have all of them collected in a list and returning the list all at once. This feature of built-in cmdlets is something that might easily be taken for granted, but when writing functions, the concept of a return value needs to be carefully considered.

Although PowerShell includes a return keyword, the use of return is optional and omitting it is even considered by some to be a best practice. PowerShell functions will return a value that is included after a return statement, but that is not the only kind of output in a function.

The rule for function output is simple. Any value produced in a function that is not consumed is added to the output stream at the time the value is produced.

Consuming a value can be accomplished in many ways:

- You can assign the value to a variable
- You can use the value in an expression, as an argument to a cmdlet, function, or script
- You can pipe the value to Out-Null
- You can cast the value as [void]

With that understanding, consider the following PowerShell functions, which all return a single value:

```
function get-value1{
    return 1
}

function get-value2{
    1
    return
}

function get-value3{
    1
}

function get-value4{
    Write-Output 1
}
```

The first function uses the traditional method to output the single value and end the execution of the function. The second includes the value as an expression that is not used and is thus added to the output stream. The return statement in the second function ends the execution of the function, but does not add anything to the output stream. The third function outputs the value just as the second did, but does not include the superfluous return statement. The final version uses the Write-Output cmdlet to explicitly write the value to the output stream. The important point to understand is that values can be output from a function in more places than just the return statement. In fact, the return statement is not even needed to output values from a function.

When writing a function, it is extremely important to ensure that the values that are produced in the process of executing are consumed. In most cases, values will be consumed by the natural activities in your function. However, sometimes values are produced as a side effect of activities and make it into the output stream inadvertently. As an example, consider the following code:

```
function Write-Logentry{
param($filename,$entry)
    if(-not (test-path $filename)){
      New-Item -path $filename -itemtype File
    }
    Add-Content -path $filename -value $entry
    Write-Output "successful"
}
```

The intent of the code is to create a file if it doesn't exist, and then add text to that file. The problem comes in when the file is created. The New-Item cmdlet writes a FileInfo object to the output stream as well as creating the file. Since the code doesn't do anything with that value, the FileInfo object from the New-Item cmdlet is part of the output of the function. It is very common on Stack Overflow to see PowerShell questions that involve this kind of error. Using New-Item (or the mkdir proxy function for New-Item) is often the source of the extraneous object or objects. Other sources include the Add() methods in several .NET classes, which in addition to adding items to a collection, also returns the index of the newly added item.

Pinpointing this kind of error in a function is often confusing because the error message will almost never indicate that the function is the problem. The error message will be downstream from the function where the output is used. In the Write-Logentry example function, instead of a value of "successful", the output could be an array of objects containing a FileInfo object and the value "successful". Trying to compare the result for a good value might look as follows:

```
$val=write-logentry c:\temp\newfile.txt "I have a bad feeling"

if ($val.StartsWith("s")){
   write-host "the function worked"
}
Method invocation failed because [System.IO.FileInfo] does not contain a method
named 'StartsWith'.
At line:13 char:5
+ if ($val.StartsWith("s")){
+    ~~~~~~~~~~~~~~~~~~~~~~~~
    + CategoryInfo          : InvalidOperation: (:) [], RuntimeException
    + FullyQualifiedErrorId : MethodNotFound
```

At first look, errors will seem like nonsense. What does PowerShell mean that it can't find a method called `StartsWith()`? Looking at the type of the variable shows that instead of the string that is expected, it contains an array, as shown in the following screenshot:

```
PS SQLSERVER:\> $val.GetType()

IsPublic IsSerial Name                                    BaseType
-------- -------- ----                                    --------
True     True     Object[]                                System.Array
```

Similar errors will occur when expecting a numeric result and trying to do calculations on the value. Doing calculations with arrays is probably not going to work, and if it does, it will not work as intended.

It is possible to collect all of the values that are to be output in a variable and wait to output the values until the end of the function, but this is not recommended. One simple reason is that this requires the function writer to keep track of all of the objects and to have memory allocated for the entire collection. Using the output stream naturally, that is, writing to the output stream as objects become available, allows downstream PowerShell cmdlets to work with them while the rest of the objects are being discovered.

The following is a practical example:

```
function find-topProcess{
   param([string[]]$computername)

   $computername |
      foreach{ Get-WmiObject Win32_Process |
               sort-object WorkingSetSize -Descending |
               Select-Object -first 5 PSComputerName,
                                      Name,
                                      ProcessID,
                                      WorkingSetSize

         }
}
```

This function takes a list of computer names and outputs the five processes on each computer that use the highest amount of memory. It could have been written as the following:

```
function find-topProcessBad{
  param([string[]]$computername)

    $processes=$()
    $computername |
        foreach{ $processes+=Get-WMIObject Win32_Process |
                 Sort-Object WorkingSetSize -Descending |
                 Select-Object -first 5 PSComputerName,
                                        Name,
                                        ProcessID,
                                        WorkingSetSize

        }
    return $processes
}
```

The final output would be the same, in that the same values would be returned in the same order. On the other hand, the way the output is seen by downstream pipeline elements is very different. In the first case, as each computer is scanned, the list of processes is sent to the output stream and then the next computer is considered. There is no local storage in the function at all. In the second case, the processes from each computer are appended to a list. The downstream pipeline elements won't see any output from this function until all of the computers have been scanned. If only a few computer names are being passed in, there is little difference. But if the list is hundreds or thousands of names long, or if the network latency is high enough that it takes a long time to get each set of results, it may be several minutes until any output is delivered. If the function is being called at the command line, it may not be obvious that anything is happening.

Another implication of the second example is that all of the objects need to be stored in a list in memory. This example used a small list of small objects (five) so the effect might not be seen. If the function returned all processes with all of the properties associated with those objects, the memory usage would be quite high. Memory allocation times will also factor into execution time as well.

 To help keep memory usage and execution time lower, try to write objects to the output stream immediately rather than storing them in a collection to be returned all at once.

PowerShell error handling

Discussions about error handling in PowerShell revolve around two things: the statements used in error handling, and what constitutes an error that needs to be handled.

The trap statement

PowerShell error handling had a rocky start. The Version 1.0 error handling statement was the trap statement. This statement is similar to the ON ERROR GOTO statement in Visual Basic 6. This was a functional way to do error handling, but it was not what most programming languages had been using for the last decade. If a trap statement is included in a scope, when an exception (called a **terminating error** in PowerShell terminology) occurs in that scope, the execution is stopped and the trap statement is executed. By default, trap statements handle any terminating error and can be written to only handle certain types of errors. In the scope of the trap statement, the $_ special variable contains the error or exception that was caught.

The default execution for a trap statement writes the error to the error stream (separate from the output stream) and continues the function after the statement that had the error. The break and continue keywords are used in a trap statement to either exit the function or to continue the execution without writing the error to the error stream.

The following screenshot shows an example of a trap statement without using break or continue. Notice that the error is written to the error stream and the execution of the function is resumed:

```
function test-trap1{
    trap {
        "an error occurred: $_"
    }
    $var = 1 / 0
    write-host "end of function"
}
test-trap1
an error occurred: Attempted to divide by zero.
Attempted to divide by zero.
At line:7 char:4
+     $var = 1 / 0
+     ~~~~~~~~~~~
    + CategoryInfo          : NotSpecified: (:) [], RuntimeException
    + FullyQualifiedErrorId : RuntimeException

end of function
```

The following screenshot shows an example of a trap statement using continue. Notice that the error is not written to the error stream and the execution of the function is resumed:

```
PS C:\Users\Mike>
function test-trap2{
    trap {
        "an error occurred: $_"
        continue
    }
    $var = 1 / 0
    write-host "end of function"
}
test-trap2
an error occurred: Attempted to divide by zero.
end of function

PS C:\Users\Mike>
```

Finally, an example of a trap statement using break. You will notice in the following screenshot that the error is written to the error stream and the execution of the function is not resumed:

```
function test-trap3{
    trap {
        "an error occurred: $_"
        break
    }
    $var = 1 / 0
    "end of function"
}
test-trap3
an error occurred: Attempted to divide by zero.
Attempted to divide by zero.
At line:7 char:4
+     $var = 1 / 0
+     ~~~~~~~~~~~~
    + CategoryInfo          : NotSpecified: (:) [], Parent
    + FullyQualifiedErrorId : RuntimeException
```

The reality of the trap statement is that it is rarely used except when only PowerShell Version 1.0 is available. The additional error handling features added in Version 2.0 are much more easily understood and less complicated.

If you find yourself having trouble following the execution path of a trap statement, try to rewrite the function using try, catch, and finally.

try, catch, and finally statements

Version 2.0 of PowerShell introduced traditional try, catch, and finally statements to the language, which work in a similar fashion to structured error handling in languages such as C#, Java, and VB.NET. In a try, catch, and finally construct, code that might throw a terminating error is enclosed in a try block. One or more catch blocks will be present to handle specific classes of errors. An optional finally block can contain code that is always executed whether an exception is thrown in the try block or not. In this model, there is no concern about the code in the try block being resumed or not. Once a terminating error occurs, the execution immediately jumps to the catch blocks to be handled. The remaining code in the try block is not executed. As is the case in the trap statement, in the catch block, the special variable $_ contains the error that occurred.

The next screenshot shows a simple example using try, catch, and finally. Note that there is a catch block for a specific type of error, but in this case the more general catch-all catch block was selected because the exception that is thrown does not match the specific exception type named in the first catch block.

```
PS C:\Users\Mike> function test-try{
    try {
        $var = 1/0
        "the function completed normally"
    }
    catch [System.Management.Automation.CommandNotFoundException] {
        "Couldn't find the command: $_"
    }
    catch {
        "Something else happened: $_"
    }
    finally {
        "this always executes"
    }
}

test-try
Something else happened: Attempted to divide by zero.
this always executes
```

Non-terminating errors

While the `trap` statement might be considered peculiar because languages generally include some sort of structured error handling like `try`, `catch`, and `finally`, PowerShell error handling is peculiar for a completely different reason. In the previous sections, we were careful to use the terminology **terminating error** to describe situations that triggered the error handling capabilities. The reason for this is that PowerShell includes another type of error, not surprisingly called a **non-terminating error**, which is not found in other languages.

To understand non-terminating errors, it is helpful to consider a typical PowerShell script operating in a datacenter that retrieves performance counters from several thousand servers using CIM. With CIM, an administrator can issue a request to all of these servers using a single cmdlet. Anyone who has worked in a datacenter knows that with a large number of servers, there will always be some that are not working quite right for some reason. The reason might be storage-related, network-related, an OS issue, or maybe the servers are simply offline for maintenance. In a typical programming model, attempting to access these servers will result in an error. If the error stops the execution flow, the remainder of the servers will not be able to provide information. What is worse is that the information that has already been retrieved will be lost as well since the statement that is doing the retrieval encountered an error so no assignment can be made to a variable (or anything else, for that matter).

This situation is not ideal. What an administrator would want is to retrieve what information is available and accessible, but also be able to see what errors occurred in order to log them or respond to them in some way. To address this concern, PowerShell introduced non-terminating errors. By default, a non-terminating error is written to the error stream, but does not trigger error handling (`try`, `catch`, `finally`, or `trap`).

An example of a non-terminating error uses the `Get-WMIObject` to access localhost and a non-existent computer, as shown in the following screenshot:

```
try {
  Get-wmiobject -computername NOBODY,Localhost -ClassName Win32_OperatingSystem
} catch {
  "something bad happened"
}
Get-wmiobject : The RPC server is unavailable. (Exception from HRESULT: 0x800706BA)
At line:5 char:3
+   Get-wmiobject -computername NOBODY,Localhost -ClassName Win32_OperatingSystem
+   ~~~~~~~~~~~~~~~~~~~~~~~~~~~~~~~~~~~~~~~~~~~~~~~~~~~~~~~~~~~~~~~~~~~~~~~~~~~~~~~~~~~
    + CategoryInfo          : InvalidOperation: (:) [Get-WmiObject], COMException
    + FullyQualifiedErrorId : GetWMICOMException,Microsoft.PowerShell.Commands.GetW
   miObjectCommand


SystemDirectory : C:\Windows\system32
Organization    :
BuildNumber     : 7601
RegisteredUser  : Mike
SerialNumber    : ███  █ ████  ██████   █████
Version         : 6.1.7601
```

Note that an error occurred (stating that RPC wasn't available on the NOBODY computer), but that the execution of `Get-WMIObject` continued accessing the localhost computer. The error handling code did not execute because the error in question is a non-terminating error.

This is often the desired outcome as explained previously. On the other hand, what if it is appropriate to execute the error handling code if a non-terminating error occurs? Cmdlets provide a parameter called `-ErrorAction`, which can be used to override the default behavior. The default value for `-ErrorAction` is `Continue`, which means to write the error to the error stream, add it to the `$Error` collection, and continue executing the current statement. To force the cmdlet to treat non-terminating errors as exceptions (terminating errors), use the value `Stop`. The possible values for the `-ErrorAction` parameter are listed in the following table:

Value	Meaning
Stop	Treats any errors as terminating errors (that is, throws an exception).
Continue	Writes the error to the error stream, adds it to the `$Error` collection, and continues the execution.
SilentlyContinue	Adds the error to the $Error collection and continues execution. Does not write the error to the error stream.
Inquire	Asks the user whether to continue or not.
Ignore	Continues execution without writing to the error stream or recording the error.
Suspend	Opens a nested prompt for interactive debugging (refer to *Chapter 7, Reactive Practices – Traditional Debugging*).

The following screenshot illustrates the use of a non-terminating error as an exception:

```
try {
  Get-wmiobject -computername NOBODY,Localhost `
                -ClassName Win32_OperatingSystem `
                -ErrorAction Stop
} catch {
  "something bad happened"
}
something bad happened
```

In this case, since the -ErrorAction was set to Stop, the execution of the cmdlet was terminated as soon as an error (in this case, a non-terminating error) occurred. The catch statement was triggered, the error was not written to the output stream, but it was written to the $Error collection.

Further reading

You can go through the following references for more information on this topic:

- get-help about_quoting_rules
- get-help about_PowerShell_Ise.exe
- get-help about_preference_variables
- get-help about_operators
- get-help about_escape_characters
- get-help about_return
- get-help about_trap
- get-help about_try_catch_finally
- get-help about_throw
- Learn about formatting codes at http://msdn.microsoft.com/en-us/library/26etazsy.aspx

Summary

In this chapter, we looked at several aspects of the PowerShell language that are implemented in ways different from other popular programming languages such as C#, Java, and VB.NET. On the topic of strings, types of quotes, string substitution, and escaping special characters were covered. The discussion of PowerShell functions focused on the types and number of objects returned and how functions in PowerShell write objects to an output stream throughout the execution of the function rather than returning all of the values at the end of execution. The final topic focused on error handling methods in PowerShell, including the trap statement from PowerShell Version 1.0, the more advanced `try`, `catch`, and `finally` statements included from Version 2.0, and the difference between terminating errors and non-terminating errors.

The focus of the next chapter will be on practices that will help keep PowerShell code performing well and easy to debug.

3
PowerShell Practices

In this chapter, we will discuss a few practices that will help PowerShell scripts run faster and produce the results that are expected. We will also cover optional output to the user and documentation in terms of built-in help along with the following topics:

- Filter left
- Format right
- Comment-based help
- Output using `Write-*` cmdlets

Filter left

As discussed in *Chapter 1, PowerShell Primer*, pipelines are a central feature of PowerShell. Cmdlets can sometimes create a tremendous amount of data though, and pushing that data through a pipeline does have performance implications in terms of memory and processor usage. Filter left is the principle that objects should be filtered as early as possible in the pipeline. Since pipelines flow from left to right, the filter should be as far to the left as it can be.

For example, the following pipelines have the same results and to show the SQL Server datafiles (`*.mdf`) in order of size:

```
dir c:\ -recurse | sort-object -Property Size -descending | where-object Extension -eq '.mdf'

dir c:\ -recurse | where-object Extension -eq '.mdf' | sort-object -Property Size -descending

dir c:\ -recurse -include *.mdf | sort-object -Property Size -descending
```

Even though the results are the same, the execution is about as different as possible. The first pipeline collects all of the files on the disk into a collection, sorts that list, and then selects the .mdf files. The second passes all of the files on the disk again, but filters them before sorting. The third example only creates objects for the .mdf files and only sorts those objects.

Using the Measure-Command cmdlet to get the time each of these takes to execute reveals the very different performance. Note that I have formatted the statements to make them easier to fit on the page. The measurement code is as follows:

```
Measure-Command {dir d:\ -recurse |
              Sort-Object -Property Size -descending |
              Where-Object Extension -eq '.mdf'} |
              Select TotalMilliseconds

Measure-Command {dir d:\ -recurse |
              Where-Object Extension -eq '.mdf' |
              Sort-Object -Property Size -descending } |
              Select TotalMilliseconds

measure-command {dir d:\ -recurse -filter *.mdf |
              Sort-Object -Property Size -descending } |
              Select TotalMilliseconds
```

And the following screenshot shows the results:

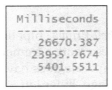

```
Milliseconds
------------
   26670.387
  23955.2674
   5401.5511
```

Putting the filter on the extreme left caused the code to take about 80 percent less time in this instance. Filtering before sorting provided a slight benefit, but not nearly this striking.

This seems like a simple example, but the principle is important. In production environments, there may be dozens or even hundreds of scripts running at the same time on a server, so the performance of each script is something that needs to be considered. When remoting is added into the mix the performance is magnified as the objects not only require memory but also network bandwidth. The difference between retrieving a list of all files on a server and pulling the single file that is needed is tremendous.

Filter left!
Make sure you keep the filtering parameters and cmdlets as far to the left in the pipeline as possible.

Format right

The next important practice in PowerShell is to format right. This means that any format cmdlets included in the pipeline should be at the far right of the pipeline. While filter left is primarily about efficiency, format right concerns the kinds of objects produced. To see this, have a look at the following output:

```
PS C:\Users\mike> get-service | get-member


    TypeName: System.ServiceProcess.ServiceController

Name                        MemberType    Definition
----                        ----------    ----------
Name                        AliasProperty Name = ServiceName
RequiredServices            AliasProperty RequiredServices = ServicesDependedOn
Disposed                    Event         System.EventHandler Disposed(System.Object, System.Eve
Close                       Method        void Close()
Continue                    Method        void Continue()
CreateObjRef                Method        System.Runtime.Remoting.ObjRef CreateObjRef(type reque
Dispose                     Method        void Dispose(), void IDisposable.Dispose()
Equals                      Method        bool Equals(System.Object obj)
ExecuteCommand              Method        void ExecuteCommand(int command)
GetHashCode                 Method        int GetHashCode()
GetLifetimeService          Method        System.Object GetLifetimeService()
GetType                     Method        type GetType()
InitializeLifetimeService   Method        System.Object InitializeLifetimeService()
Pause                       Method        void Pause()
Refresh                     Method        void Refresh()
Start                       Method        void Start(), void Start(string[] args)
```

First, you can see that the Get-Service cmdlet outputs the ServiceController objects. Piping those ServiceController objects to Format-List, though, produces a series of objects with indecipherable properties, as shown in the following screenshot:

```
PS C:\Users\mike> get-service | format-list | get-member


    TypeName: Microsoft.PowerShell.Commands.Internal.Format.FormatStartData

Name                                     MemberType Definition
----                                     ---------- ----------
Equals                                   Method     bool Equals(System.Object obj)
GetHashCode                              Method     int GetHashCode()
GetType                                  Method     type GetType()
ToString                                 Method     string ToString()
autosizeInfo                             Property   Microsoft.PowerShell.Commands.I
ClassId2e4f51ef21dd47e99d3c952918aff9cd  Property   string ClassId2e4f51ef21dd47e99
groupingEntry                            Property   Microsoft.PowerShell.Commands.I
pageFooterEntry                          Property   Microsoft.PowerShell.Commands.I
pageHeaderEntry                          Property   Microsoft.PowerShell.Commands.I
shapeInfo                                Property   Microsoft.PowerShell.Commands.I


    TypeName: Microsoft.PowerShell.Commands.Internal.Format.GroupStartData

Name                                     MemberType Definition
----                                     ---------- ----------
Equals                                   Method     bool Equals(System.Object obj)
GetHashCode                              Method     int GetHashCode()
GetType                                  Method     type GetType()
ToString                                 Method     string ToString()
ClassId2e4f51ef21dd47e99d3c952918aff9cd  Property   string ClassId2e4f51ef21dd47e99
groupingEntry                            Property   Microsoft.PowerShell.Commands.I
shapeInfo                                Property   Microsoft.PowerShell.Commands.I


    TypeName: Microsoft.PowerShell.Commands.Internal.Format.FormatEntryData

Name                                     MemberType Definition
----                                     ---------- ----------
Equals                                   Method     bool Equals(System.Object obj)
GetHashCode                              Method     int GetHashCode()
GetType                                  Method     type GetType()
ToString                                 Method     string ToString()
ClassId2e4f51ef21dd47e99d3c952918aff9cd  Property   string ClassId2e4f51ef21dd47e99
formatEntryInfo                          Property   Microsoft.PowerShell.Commands.I
outOfBand                                Property   bool outOfBand {get;set;}
writeStream                              Property   Microsoft.PowerShell.Commands.I
```

Once a formatting cmdlet has been executed, the only objects on the pipeline are PowerShell formatting objects which are only useful by the PowerShell host. As a general rule, the only cmdlets that can follow a formatting cmdlet in the pipeline are the output cmdlets that start with Out-. These output cmdlets are designed to interpret these formatting objects and render formatted output accordingly. Since pipelines always end in Out-Default, there's little danger of ever encountering one of these formatting objects unless something is included between the formatting cmdlet and the end of the pipeline, which is shown in the following screenshot:

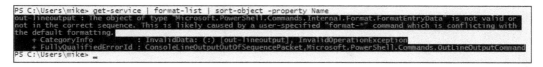

Trying to sort the objects after formatting them is a common mistake. It is clear from this example that the ServiceController is no longer present, and that attempting to use the properties of the original objects are going to fail.

Because of the destructive nature of formatting cmdlets, the best practice is to not use them in functions or scripts unless the output of the script or function in question never needs to be manipulated programmatically. In other words, use formatting only if the output is intended for people to use rather than as input to other scripts or functions.

> Avoid using formatting cmdlets in functions or scripts that may provide input for other functions or scripts. To show that the code uses formatting, consider naming the function or script with the verb Show (for example, Show-ServiceInfo).

Comment-based help

As mentioned in *Chapter 1*, *PowerShell Primer*, the help system in PowerShell is very useful. When writing functions and scripts in PowerShell, it is important to provide the same kind of documentation so users are able to use the code correctly.

In order to get the minimal amount of help available, the only requirement is to create a function. Take a look at the following screenshot, for example, shows the help content generated automatically for a simple function:

```
PS C:\Users\mike> function get-stuff{
>> param($stuffID, [switch]$inreverse)
>> #do something here
>> }
>>
PS C:\Users\mike> get-help get-stuff

NAME
    get-stuff

SYNTAX
    get-stuff [[-stuffID] <Object>] [-inreverse]


ALIASES
    None


REMARKS
    None


PS C:\Users\mike> _
```

There is even help for specific parameters, as shown in the following screenshot:

```
PS C:\Users\mike> get-help get-stuff -parameter inreverse

-inreverse

    Required?                    false
    Position?                    Named
    Accept pipeline input?       false
    Parameter set name           (All)
    Aliases                      None
    Dynamic?                     false
```

It should be clear that PowerShell is using the definition of the function to generate the help content. This is extremely helpful for several reasons, some of which are listed as follows:

- The syntax section is never out of sync with the definition. There is no need to worry about missing or misspelled parameters or whether the brackets are in the right places.

- It is not necessary to create a separate file (or any file at all) in order to have help for a function.

- Help for a function will be consistently displayed.

The help seen in the earlier examples is not nearly as complete as the help seen for cmdlets, such as Get-ChildItem or Get-WMIObject, so how does one provide the missing pieces of information? The answer is comment-based help.

Using comment-based help is a very simple process. The content for the help system is usually embedded in a function or immediately before the function in a comment or series of comments. The following screenshot illustrates this well:

```
function get-stuff{
param($stuffID,[switch]$inreverse)
<#
    .SYNOPSIS
        The get-stuff function uses the provided parameters to get some stuff
    .DESCRIPTION
        Get-stuff can get all of the stuff (by omitting the stuffID parameter),
        it can get a specific kind of stuff (by supplying the stuffID),
        and it can optionally provide the results in reverse (with the inreverse switch)
    .PARAMETER stuffID
        The ID of the stuff to retrieve
    .PARAMETER inreverse
        Indicated whether the results are to be output in reverse
    .EXAMPLE
        get-stuff -stuffID 1
    .EXAMPLE
        get-stuff -inreverse
#>
#do something useful
}
```

Given this function definition with embedded comment-based help, `get-help` now returns a much more complete topic:

```
PS C:\Users\mike> get-help get-stuff

NAME
    get-stuff

SYNOPSIS
    The get-stuff function uses the provided parameters to get some stuff

SYNTAX
    get-stuff [[-stuffID] <Object>] [-inreverse] [<CommonParameters>]


DESCRIPTION
    Get-stuff can get all of the stuff (by omitting the stuffID parameter),
           it can get a specific kind of stuff (by supplying the stuffID),
           and it can optionally provide the results in reverse (with the inreverse switch)


RELATED LINKS

REMARKS
    To see the examples, type: "get-help get-stuff -examples".
    For more information, type: "get-help get-stuff -detailed".
    For technical information, type: "get-help get-stuff -full".
```

As stated in the comments at the end of this topic, the examples are visible by using `get-help` with the `-Examples` switch. The following screenshot illustrates this:

```
PS C:\Users\mike> get-help get-stuff -Examples

NAME
    get-stuff

SYNOPSIS
    The get-stuff function uses the provided parameters to get some stuff

    -------------------------- EXAMPLE 1 --------------------------

    C:\PS>get-stuff -stuffID 1




    -------------------------- EXAMPLE 2 --------------------------

    C:\PS>get-stuff -inreverse

    do something useful
```

There is some flexibility in the precise placement of the comment as well as a tremendous variety of information that can be included. For complete details, refer to the `about_Comment_Based_Help` topic.

Using Write-* cmdlets

When writing PowerShell functions, it is often confusing to know exactly which cmdlet should be used to produce output. There are a number of cmdlets and methods that seem to do the same thing at first glance. The most important thing to remember in this context is that functions should always write objects to the output stream. In order to do this, there are several correct ways and one incorrect way that is frequently used.

Write-Host

PowerShell scripters who are beginners see the `Write-Host` cmdlet as a simple way to produce output. It is similar to a `PRINT` statement in many languages and if output to the console is the goal, it is a perfect fit. Unfortunately, the output is made solely to the console (or, in PowerShell terminology, the **host**). The following screenshot shows the main issue with `Write-Host`:

```
PS C:\Users\mike> function get-stuff{
>>     write-host "This is the stuff"
>> }
>>
PS C:\Users\mike> get-stuff
This is the stuff
PS C:\Users\mike> $stuff=get-stuff
This is the stuff
PS C:\Users\mike> $stuff
PS C:\Users\mike> _
```

Even though the function seems to output the string, attempting to capture the output in a variable shows that the value isn't actually output, but instead is simply text written to the host. Because of this, `Write-Host` is not a good fit for functions. Scenarios where `Write-Host` makes sense to use in a function are similar to those where formatting cmdlets are used (as discussed earlier in this chapter).

 `Write-Host` should only be used where output is to be read by a user and not ever by another function. This is one of the most universally accepted PowerShell best practices.

Output – the correct way

A cmdlet that at first glance looks similar to `Write-Host` is `Write-Output`. Rewriting the `get-stuff` function from the previous section using `Write-Output` produces the expected results, as shown in the following screenshot:

```
PS C:\Users\mike> function get-stuff{
>>     write-output "This is the stuff"
>> }
>>
PS C:\Users\mike> get-stuff
This is the stuff
PS C:\Users\mike> $stuff=get-stuff
PS C:\Users\mike> $stuff
This is the stuff
PS C:\Users\mike> _
```

Even though the output looks the same in the console, capturing the output in a variable is successful this time. The reason is that `Write-Output` writes the values of its parameters to the output stream rather than the host. Think back to the discussion about how a function returns values in *Chapter 1, PowerShell Primer,* and you might recall that there are several ways to return values from a function. All of these variations produce equivalent results:

```
function get-stuff{
    write-output "This is the stuff"
}
function get-stuff2{
    return "This is the stuff"
}
function get-stuff3{
    "This is the stuff"
}
function get-stuff4{
    "This is the stuff" | write-output
}
```

What about the other Write-* cmdlets?

Write-Host and Write-Output are only two of several Write-* cmdlets. The other core cmdlets are listed as follows:

- Write-Verbose
- Write-Warning
- Write-Debug
- Write-Progress
- Write-Error

The first four cmdlets (Write-Verbose, Write-Warning, Write-Debug, and Write-Progress) are intended to be used to provide optional information about code execution. The output from these cmdlets is controlled by a set of preference variables. Preference variables are predefined by the host and used to indicate what action should be taken when one of these cmdlets is executed. The following screenshot shows the list preference variables with the PSDrive mechanism . The full list of predefined preference variables can be seen along with their values by listing matching names from the variable:

```
PS C:\Users\mike> dir variable:*preference

Name                         Value
----                         -----
ConfirmPreference            High
DebugPreference              SilentlyContinue
ErrorActionPreference        Continue
ProgressPreference           Continue
VerbosePreference            SilentlyContinue
WarningPreference            Continue
WhatIfPreference             False
```

 PSDrives and **PSProviders** are mechanisms PowerShell uses to expose hierarchical storage. The FileSystem provider implements drives that match local and mapped drives. Other providers, such as the Variable and Function providers, give some visibility to PowerShell objects. In this example, we used the dir alias of Get-ChildItem to view a list of variables using the Variable: drive in the same way we would have looked at files in a folder.

We came across the `$errorActionPreference` variable in *Chapter 2, PowerShell Peculiarities*, in the context of error handling with non-terminating errors. The following shows an example of using `$VerbosePreference` to control the output from `Write-Verbose`:

```
PS C:\Users\mike> $VerbosePreference
SilentlyContinue
PS C:\Users\mike> write-verbose "This is a verbose message"
PS C:\Users\mike> $verbosePreference="Continue"
PS C:\Users\mike> write-verbose "This is a verbose message"
VERBOSE: This is a verbose message
PS C:\Users\mike> _
```

Since the value of `$VerbosePreference` was `SilentlyContinue`, no output was produced by the first invocation of the cmdlet. Changing the value to `Continue` allowed output from the second call. Note that the output is written to the host differently than output that comes from `Write-Host` or `Write-Output`. That is because `Write-Verbose` writes to its own stream. `Write-Debug`, `Write-Warning`, `Write-Error`, and `Write-Verbose` each have their own output streams, which are distinct from the standard object output stream.

Possible values for preference variables include: `Stop`, `Continue`, `SilentlyContinue`, `Ignore`, `Inquire`, and `Suspend`. Not all values are valid for all variables. The acceptable values are given in the following table:

Variable	Potential values (default values are shown with quotes)
`ErrorActionPreference`	`Stop`, `"Continue"`, `SilentlyContinue`, `Inquire`, and `Suspend`
`DebugPreference`	`Stop`, `Inquire`, `Continue`, and `"SilentlyContinue"`
`VerbosePreference`	`Stop`, `Inquire`, `Continue`, and `"SilentlyContinue"`
`WarningPreference`	`Stop`, `Inquire`, `"Continue"`, and `SilentlyContinue`
`ProgressPreference`	`Stop`, `Inquire`, `"Continue"`, and `SilentlyContinue`

`ConfirmPreference` and `WhatIfPreference` are not listed in the table because they deal with risk mitigation rather than output. Their usage will be explained in detail in *Chapter 7, Reactive Practices – Traditional Debugging*.

Preference variables are global in scope; that is, their value is used in all scopes unless they are overwritten in a local scope. Because of this, care should be given in changing these variables from their default values. Changing $ErrorActionPreference to Stop, for instance, might cause error handling in other functions or modules to stop working correctly.

Which Write should I use?

Except for Write-Output or its equivalents, which should always be used for function output, the precise use of the Write-* cmdlets is neither mandatory nor spelled out in the help content. The exact meaning of the verbose, warning, and debug streams is left to the user of the function or script. On the other hand, it is useful to have some guidelines for what kind of information should be communicated using these streams.

Write-Verbose

Verbose output should include non-technical information that will be valuable to the end user, enabling them to understand the functional processes that are taking place. For instance, using Write-Verbose to indicate when each step of a ten-step process is being started would be appropriate. If timing information is something that an end user might want to see, that might be included as well at a high level. It would probably not be usual practice to show timing information for individual iterations of a loop or low-level tasks. The following screenshot shows an example of built-in verbose output with import-module:

```
PS C:\Users\Mike> import-module adolib -verbose
VERBOSE: Importing function 'Invoke-Bulkcopy'.
VERBOSE: Importing function 'Invoke-Query'.
VERBOSE: Importing function 'Invoke-Sql'.
VERBOSE: Importing function 'Invoke-StoredProcedure'.
VERBOSE: Importing function 'New-Connection'.
VERBOSE: Importing function 'New-SQLCommand'.
```

Write-Debug

Debug output, as the name implies, is intended to be used to troubleshoot the code in question. Because of this, the content of debug output should provide insight into the implementation details of the operations. Unlike verbose output, which should be general information, debug output should be technical information including variable values, property values, counts, low-level timing information, and so on. The information provided in the debug stream should make what is happening in the code clear and why it is happening. Depending on the complexity of the function, the amount of debug information might be overwhelming, but the point is to provide enough details to help solve problems. Most end users will avoid turning on debug output unless they are working with the code, so the amount of output is not a problem.

Write-Warning

Warning output should always point out conditions that are not as expected, but are also not fatal. Some examples, depending on the operation, might be overwriting a file, no results from a query, stopping a service that is already stopped, or trying to delete a file that doesn't exist. None of these occurrences would necessarily mean that the code would need to stop, but might help the user correct something in the environment.

Write-Error

The error stream is for non-terminating errors. As discussed in *Chapter 2, PowerShell Peculiarities*, non-terminating errors indicate that something went wrong, but that the entire operation does not need to stop. By sending output to the error stream, a user could inspect the $Error collection to see the specifics about what needs to be followed up on or what results might be missing from the function output.

Write-Progress

The progress stream is where information about the process completion status is written. Operations that might take a long time to complete and have a known number of steps can send the completed percentage or other status information. The following screenshot shows an example using `Write-Progress` in the **Integrated Scripting Environment (ISE)**:

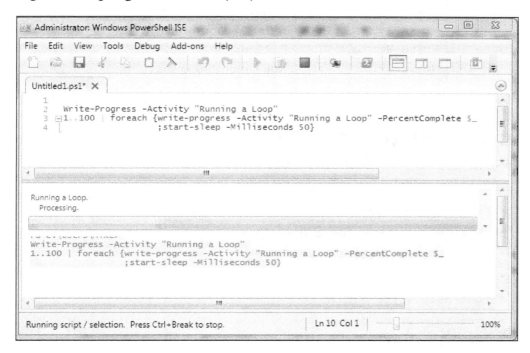

The following screenshot shows the output rendered in the console:

In summary, the following table gives the guidelines for when to use the different output `Write-*` cmdlets:

Cmdlet	Type of information
Write-Output	Objects
Write-Host	Formatted text
Write-Verbose	Nontechnical process information
Write-Debug	Technical implementation details
Write-Warning	Problems
Write-Error	Non-terminating errors
Write-Progress	Process completion information

Further reading

You can go through the following list of references for more information:

- get-help measure-command
- get-help out-default
- get-help about_comment_based_help
- get-help get-help
- get-help write-host
- get-help write-output
- get-help write-debug
- get-help write-warning
- get-help write-progress
- get-help write-verbose
- get-help write-error

Summary

This chapter dealt with practices that are specific to PowerShell. Filter left and format right are important principles to keep in mind in order to keep pipelines efficient and avoid losing properties that are needed. Comment-based help and the various `Write-*` cmdlets are crucial parts of the PowerShell environment that allow users to discover details about cmdlets and parameters and understand the operation of code.

The next chapter will introduce topics that, while common in development groups, might not be firmly established in the system administration groups. These *programming professionalism* topics include using naming standards, modularization, and unit testing.

4

PowerShell Professionalism

PowerShell scripters might not think of the process of writing a script as a development process, but some industry-standard development practices are appropriate to use with PowerShell, for example:

- Naming standards
- Source control
- Modularization (functional decomposition)
- Unit testing/mocking

Naming conventions

Naming conventions are not rocket science and they are certainly not unique to PowerShell. They are also not concrete rules that will cause your code to stop working if they are ignored. On the other hand, the designers of PowerShell began the language with a strong foundation of consistent naming which is one of the keys to its success. In the following sections, we will discuss several instances where naming conventions will improve your PowerShell experience.

Cmdlet and function naming

As discussed in *Chapter 1*, *PowerShell Primer*, built-in cmdlets are named with a verb-noun format using a verb from a predefined list of approved verbs. This format is not required for user-defined cmdlets, functions, advanced functions, or scripts, but is highly recommended. The only place where not having properly named functions will cause any kind of programmatic issue is when a module, including the code, is imported into a PowerShell session. A module exporting functions that are not correctly named will cause a warning when the module is imported. To disable the warning, the −DisableNameChecking switch can be used. −Verbose will allow us to see the individual function definitions being imported and will show which functions have issues with naming. The following function uses the verbose output to find incorrectly named functions:

```
function Get-InvalidFunction{
Param([string]$module)
if(Get-Module $module){
    Remove-Module $module -force
}
Import-Module $module -Force -Verbose *>&1 |
    Select-String "The '(.*)' command in the (.*)' module .*" |
    Where-Object {$_.Matches.Groups[2].Value -eq $module} |
    Foreach-Object { $_.matches.groups[1].Value}

}
```

When the Get-InvalidFunction function is used to find invalid function names in the SQLPS module, for instance, it shows two offending functions, shown as follows:

```
PS C:\> get-invalidfunction sqlps
Decode-SqlName
Encode-SqlName
```

A simple test shows that although PowerShell will warn about functions in modules that use improper verbs, it does not indicate a problem with functions that do not follow the verb-noun syntax. The following code snippet shows a function missing a dash, and a function to detect poorly named functions in modules:

```
function testnaming{
  Write-Host "No dash!"
}

function get-MissingDashFunction{
Param([string]$module)
```

```
if(get-module $module){
    Remove-Module $module -force
}

    Import-Module $module -force -Verbose *>&1 |
    Select-String "Importing function '(.*)'.*" |
    Where-Object {$_.Matches.Groups[1].Value -notlike "*-*"} |
    Foreach-Object { $_.matches.groups[1].Value}


}
```

The following screenshot illustrates the output showing the function that is missing the dash:

```
PS > get-MissingDashFunction testmodule
testnaming
```

A final thing to mention is that the convention for the noun in a function name is to be a singular noun. This sometimes leads to awkwardly named functions, such as get-MissingDashFunction in the previous example, but in order to stay consistent with delivered modules this is a convention that should be observed.

Parameter naming

There are no fixed rules for parameter naming, but we can learn from the authors of the built-in cmdlets and try to use their examples. For instance, looking at the parameters to the get-childitem cmdlet, we can see the following parameters (excluding common parameters):

- Path
- LiteralPath
- Filter
- Include
- Exclude
- Recurse (switch)
- Force (switch)
- Name (switch)
- Attributes
- Directory (switch)

- `File` (switch)
- `Hidden` (switch)
- `ReadOnly` (switch)
- `System` (switch)

The first thing to see is that `-Path` (and `-LiteralPath`) are the parameters to supply the identity of the child items. This is a good pattern to follow, instead of using other alternatives such as `$filename`, `$file`, `$inputfile`, and so on. Also note that like most of the `*-Item` cmdlets, the `Get-ChildItem` cmdlet provides parameter sets to allow both standard paths (including wildcards) and literal paths, which might include special characters that PowerShell would otherwise attempt to interpret. A final thing to see is that a number of switch parameters have been provided to make it simpler to get the specific results without requiring `Where-Object`. Obviously, not all possibilities are covered with switches, but most of the common cases have been addressed. Other filtering parameters include `-Filter`, `-Include`, and `-Exclude`.

As we write functions, we should try to think about using our functions and include parameters that make their use as fluid and effortless as possible. As we use our own functions (a practice known as **dogfooding**) we will invariably find things that don't flow quite as we'd like them to, so we will have an opportunity to improve them at that time.

Module naming

A survey of public PowerShell modules will reveal fairly quickly that there is no accepted naming convention for modules. Patterns include starting with Posh, starting with PS, using verb-noun formatting, or using single or compound words to name the module. With that out of the way, the following are a few guidelines that will help in this area:

- Use a company-specific prefix for private modules to avoid naming conflicts with public modules (for example, XYZActiveDirectory for a module of functions related to the ActiveDirectory implementation at company XYZ)

- Use a consistent naming scheme for your modules (for example, don't have some Posh modules and some verb-noun modules)

- Group functions into modules based on functionality (rather than project) and name the module according to that functionality

Following these simple guidelines will make your module names easier to remember and make it easier to find functions when you need to look at the source code.

Variable naming

Like modules, there is no accepted naming convention for variables. Again, some commonsense practices will help you keep your variable usage straight and less error-prone. The following is a list of some of these practices:

- Do not use a type prefix for variable names (for example, use `$FileName` instead of `$strFileName`).

- Do not overly abbreviate variable names. Tab completion makes using longer, descriptive variable names less painful.

- Do not reuse variables. PowerShell is garbage-collected, so any efficiency gained by avoiding new variables is miniscule compared to the risk of using a variable incorrectly.

- Avoid generic variable names like `$temp`, `$var`, `$obj`, and so on. Use the variable name to indicate what the variable is being used for or what is being stored.

- Use camel casing (initial capitals in each subsequent word contained in the variable name) to increase readability, for example, `$customerNumber`.

Modularization

Writing a script to accomplish a task can be a daunting process. For those of us that are administrators without any programming background, it might not be straightforward to even know where to start.

For very simple tasks, it might be possible to write the entire script in a single line-by-line flow. While this is possible for the shortest tasks, as we get more comfortable with scripting we will definitely be applying PowerShell to more complex problems. Writing complex scripts in a simple start-to-finish way is bound to cause difficulties. In the following sections, we will give some basic instruction on how to go from an idea to a workable script. We will use the task of copying a production database down to a development server as an example.

Breaking a process into subtasks

The first step is to break the task down into subtasks or steps. A common way to do this is to use a comment statement (starting with the hash character, #) for each step. For our example, it might look something like the following:

```
#Find the latest full backup file

#Figure out how much space is required to restore the database
```

```
#Make sure there is enough space for the restore

#Restore the database with _REFRESH suffix

#Wipe out database-level security on the _REFRESH database

#Export the original database's security as a sql statement

#Run the sql statement to assign the correct security to the _REFRESH
database

#Close all connections to the original database

#Rename the original database to _OLD

#Rename the _REFRESH database to drop the suffix

#Send an email to notify users of the completion
```

Describing a task in this kind of detail is a crucial step in automating. This level of information can be shared with users who might not be familiar with PowerShell for them to validate that what you are writing is going to accomplish the required result. More importantly, it gives us smaller items to work on writing so we can focus on very specific things rather than getting lost in the big picture.

Helper functions

One of the things we can do with this process outline is to look for obvious functions that we will need to write to help us accomplish the steps. In this example, it is clear that we are going to need to be able to communicate with the database. SQL Server comes with a PowerShell module called SQLPS. Using that module to do the low-level database communication, some examples of helper functions that might make sense are given as follows:

- Execute a SQL statement
- Get file sizes from a SQL backup file
- Restore a database

Note that these functions are going to help us write our script, but they are not limited in usefulness to our script alone. Because of this, it would make sense to have a module with these functions in it with a name like SQLServerTools. If we have identified common operations that we need to break out that were specific to this task, we might have helper functions embedded in the script. Remember, though, that reusability is a key benefit of scripting, so try to think in terms of writing more general-purpose functions.

Single responsibility principle

In programming, the single responsibility principle is one of the basic principles of object-oriented programming. This principle states that an object should have a single responsibility. PowerShell uses objects throughout, but most scripting is not considered to be object oriented. On the other hand, the principle can be applied to functions as well as objects. When we write a function, we should make sure that the function performs one operation. When it does more than one thing, it makes using the function difficult. What if we only want one of the things to be done? We could introduce switches to indicate which responsibilities we want to address, but this type of complexity is unnecessary. It is simpler to break the function into multiple functions, each with their own responsibility.

Don't repeat code

One of the keys to automation is that, ideally, anything that you might need to do more than once should be automated. When writing scripts, this principle can be extended to encompass code that is repeated. That is, any code that you might use more than once should be extracted into a function. The reason is that by doing this, you have isolated that operation. By isolating it, any changes to the operation need only be made in one place, rather than needing to find all of the places that we copied the code to.

In our example, we see that we are renaming databases twice, so that immediately indicates that we should have a function to handle that operation. To begin with, we don't need to actually write the function. Simply defining the function with its parameters is a good way to start. This can be done as follows:

```
function rename-Database{
Param($connection,
[string]$name,
[string]$newName)

#construct and invoke sql statement to rename the database

}
```

Since we identified the need to have a helper function to execute SQL statements, we can use that helper function in this function once it has been written. Another example of writing general purpose functions can be seen in the requirement to find the latest full backup. A first attempt at writing this might look like the following code snippet:

```
Function get-LatestFullBackup{
Param($SQLInstanceName,$DatabaseName)
    #look through the appropriate files and return the latest full
backup file
}
```

Although this does satisfy our requirement, it will only satisfy that specific requirement. A more general approach might look like the following code snippet:

```
Function get-BackupFiles{
Param($SQLInstance,
      $Database,
      [switch]$latest,
      [switch]$full)
    #get the backup files for the database in question
  #if $full was specified, use where-object to
      only include those files
  #if $latest was specified, use sort-object and
    select-object to only return the latest file
}
```

With this definition, we can possibly do other things with backup files, such as figure out how old our backups are on disk (what's the oldest full backup) or determine how much disk space is taken up by the backups of a specific database. It takes some thought to write functions with more general focus, but the time spent in designing them will pay off in the end.

Understanding the process

Once we have defined the steps in the task and written the appropriate helper functions, the next thing to do is to code each of the steps. At this point, we still might find some helper functions that need to be written. For instance, the following code snippet might be the start of the script:

```
#Find the latest full backup file
$backup=get-backupFiles -sqlinstance $source `
                        -database $DBName -latest -full
#figure out how much space is required to restore the database
```

```
$space=get-backupSize $backup

#Make sure there is enough space for the restore
If (-not (test-diskSpace -computername $dest `
-size $space)){
  Throw "$space bytes needed on $dest"
}
#Restore the database with _REFRESH suffix
Start-Restore -SQLInstance $dest -database "$DBName`_REFRESH" `
-path $backup
```

As you expand each step, you will probably realize that there is information that you need in order to execute the step. When this happens, simply insert a step to take care of it. That may involve writing more helper functions. Complex steps might be better broken down into smaller steps. One way to do this is to simply replace the step with the list of smaller steps. Another approach (which I prefer) is to write that step as a function, and include the smaller steps in it. You will need to be careful to pass all of the required information into the new function. Eventually, you will find that you have all of the steps coded and are ready to test your script!

Breaking your script into smaller sections is not a magic trick that makes it more reliable, but it does allow you to test the smaller portions (for example, the helper functions) independently of the whole process. Gaining confidence in the quality of your helper functions makes it possible to spend more time focusing on the business process, which means higher productivity. A big part of troubleshooting is knowing where to look for mistakes. Being able to eliminate large portions of your code will make a tremendous difference.

Version control

Source control, or version control, is for developers, right? Why would PowerShell scripters, who are mostly administrators of one flavor or other, need to use source control? Here are a few scenarios that will hopefully convince you.

You get a call at midnight that a mission-critical script is failing. You dial into the server and look at a thousand-line script with no indication of what the problem is. With source control you would at least be able to look at the history of the script and see if there were any changes made recently. Recent changes aren't always the culprit, but without anything else to go on, they are usually a good place to start. If you're lucky, the person who made the changes included a really good check-in comment about why the changes were made that will help you determine if it's relevant. If it sounds like it's the problem, a solution might be as simple as reverting the script to its previous version.

Let's take a look at a second scenario. The drive storing the scripts on your production server just bit the dust. You can kind of remember what the scripts on that server were doing, but do you have time to rewrite them? If you were using source control, you should be able to get the latest versions of all of the scripts.

Perhaps you have more than one administrator writing scripts. Having a central place to store scripts is a pretty straightforward result of using source control. Source control also allows more than one person to be working on a script and gives the ability to merge the changes together. This might seem somewhat far-fetched, but as more and more tasks in the Microsoft ecosystem are turning to PowerShell, the more likely this scenario is becoming. Once most admins are scripting the possibility of a collision ("Hey, I was editing that file! You just wiped out my changes!") is much greater.

With a software project, there's the idea of a project. It could be a website, a desktop application, a service, or a mobile app, but there is a definite grouping that makes sense to use when organizing a source code repository. With PowerShell, scripting generally involves building up a good selection of modules with helper functions related to the tasks you perform, and a bunch of scripts that use those modules. There's no "big thing" that stands out that will be a natural organization.

One way to organize a repository of PowerShell scripts is to have a folder of modules (which would each have its own subfolder) and a folder of scripts. This setup would mirror the `Documents\WindowsPowerShell` folder present in each Windows user profile. Another possibility is to organize the repository according to what server the scripts are going to be deployed on.

However you choose to organize your repository, the important thing is that you consistently commit code to the repository. Committing code is similar to making a backup. You know you can always go back to that point in time. Just as you wouldn't consider running a database without performing periodic backups, you should not write scripts without frequently committing those scripts. An important ingredient in a commit is a comment describing what changes were made and why. The system will take care keeping track of who made the changes, to what files, and when the changes were made.

Using version control with PowerShell

Since PowerShell runs on Windows systems, we have several good options for version control, including **Team Foundation Services (TFS)**, Subversion, Git, and Mercurial (hg). If we consider TFS Express edition, all of these are free of charge, so there is no financial reason to keep from implementing one. Each has its own advantages and disadvantages, so choose the one that's best suited to you. Your company might already have a standardized version control system, so ask around to see if the choice has been made for you.

All four of the version control systems mentioned have popular GUI frontends and extensions to Windows Explorer, so using them can be as simple as right-clicking on files and folders and selecting the appropriate operation in a context menu. With PowerShell, though, we have a couple of other possibilities. We can use the built-in command-line interfaces for these systems or we can use PowerShell cmdlets written to interface with them.

The specific details of how to use version control (that is, which commands perform which operations) are beyond the scope of this section. The important point for you to take away is that you need to be submitting your scripts to a version control system. How that happens is mostly a matter of preference. No matter what software you decide on, whatever workflow you chose to check code, the benefits will follow from consistent use.

Unit testing

Unit testing is the logical continuation of modularizing code. Once you have broken the problem into smaller pieces or units, the next step is to test those units. To perform unit testing means that we will write tests that exercise each unit with a variety of inputs that will ensure that the code is correct. One emphasis of unit testing is that the tests need to be automatic. That is, we're not reading a list of test cases off of a piece of paper and running the code with each to verify that the results are as expected. Unit tests are code and are just as important as the code being tested (and as such should be checked into your version control system). Developers are familiar with automated unit testing, but the use of unit tests by system administrators is growing. As system administration begins to involve more and more code, the knowledge that the code we use is correct is of utmost importance.

You might hear discussion of **Test Driven Development (TDD)**, which relies on a failing unit test in order to do any development, but for our purposes that is not necessary. Our emphasis will simply be on using unit tests to have confidence in our implementation.

Another important point is that unit tests only test the code in the function. They are not intended to test the entire environment (filesystem, network, database, and so on). End-to-end testing involving the entire infrastructure is called integration testing and is a separate subject.

Rolling your own unit tests

Let's consider a function that takes a list of computer names and a domain name as parameters and returns a list of **fully-qualified domain names (FQDN)**. An implementation might look like the following code snippet:

```
function get-fqdn{
Param([string[]]$computerName,
    [string]$domainName)
  $output=@()
  foreach($computer in $computerName){
    $output+=$computer+'.'+$domainName
  }
  return $output
}
```

At first, we might try to think of some things to test using the following list of conditions and their respective code:

- Pass two computer names and a domain name (base test):

  ```
  get-fqdn comp1,comp2 -domain test.com #Should
    be @("comp1.test.com","comp2.test.com")
  ```

- Pass a single computer name and a domain name:

  ```
  get-fqdn comp1 -domain test.com #Should be "comp1.test.com"
  ```

- Pass a single computer name and a domain name starting with a dot:

  ```
  get-fqdn comp1 -domain .test.com #Should be
    "comp1.test.com"
  ```

- Pass a FQDN (instead of a computer name) and a domain name:

  ```
  get-fqdn comp1.domain.com -domain .test.com #Should be
    "comp1.domain.com"
  ```

It's important to understand that writing unit tests is, in a way, writing the specification for your code. For instance, the third and fourth tests are logical, but they weren't in the description of the code. By writing these tests in code, we are expressing how our function is intended to be called as well as explaining what kind of output is expected. Unit tests that are kept up to date are an important kind of documentation. In fact, functioning unit tests are often the best documentation since written documentation (in the form of documents or comment-based help, for example) can get out of sync with the code. Unit tests that pass necessarily reflect the code as written or they wouldn't pass.

To test these conditions, you would probably need some helper functions. We will introduce an open source framework to simplify this later in the chapter, but at this point we will keep it simple. The following is a simple function that tests whether two arrays are equal:

```
function test-arraysEqual{
Param([array]$a,
[array]$b)
-not (compare-Object -ReferenceObject $a -DifferenceObject $b)
}
```

This works because the `Compare-Object` cmdlet returns the difference objects for objects in the list which are different. The –not changes the empty list from equal arrays into a $true and changes the list of objects for different lists (which is logically $true) into $false. With that function, we can express the previous list of tests using the following code snippet:

```
test-arraysEqual (get-fqdn comp1,comp2 -domain test.com )
    ("comp1.test.com","comp2.test.com")

test-arraysEqual (get-fqdn comp1  -domain test.com )
    ("comp1.test.com")

test-arraysEqual (get-fqdn comp1 -domain .test.com )
    ("comp1.test.com")

test-arraysEqual (get-fqdn comp1.domain.com -domain test.com )
    ("comp1.domain.com")
```

When we run that, we get the following disappointing, but not very surprising, results:

```
True
True
False
False
```

The two tests we hadn't thought about when writing the code didn't pass. Let's make a quick adjustment to the code to fix that:

```
function get-fqdn{
Param([string[]]$computerName,
      [string]$domainName)
    $output=@()
    if($domainName.StartsWith(".")){
        $domainName=$domainName.Substring(1)
    }
    Foreach($computer in $computerName){
        if($computer.Contains('.')){
            $output+=$computerName
        } else {
            $output+=$computer+'.'+$domainName
        }
    }
    return $output
}
```

Now, we get a clean set of results:

```
True
True
True
True
```

That's the rhythm of coding with unit tests. You write code, you test it. You fix the code so the tests pass. If you think of more things to test, you add tests and repeat.

A great thing about unit tests is that if you have an implementation with all passing tests, you can change the way you implement it and you can still know if the implementation is correct (with respect to the tests). In the following example, we could remove the use of the `$output` variable to hold the results and simply output the values directly to the pipeline instead:

```
function get-fqdn{
Param([string[]]$computerName,
     [string]$domainName)
    if($domainName.StartsWith(".")){
        $domainName=$domainName.Substring(1)
    }
    foreach($computer in $computerName){
        if($computer.Contains('.')){
            $computerName
        } else {
            $computer+'.'+$domainName
        }
    }
}
```

Seeing that the unit tests all still pass tells us that this was a valid change. If we had gotten any failures, we would know we still have some work to do.

If you find a bug in your code, a good thing to do is isolate that bug in a unit test before fixing the test. When you write the test first, you are making sure you understand what went wrong. You are saying "the code should have returned this" and instead you get a negative result. That doesn't seem like it's telling you anything, but once you've corrected the code you now have a test that should pass.

Why is PowerShell testing difficult?

Consider the following function:

```
function get-dayOfWeek{
    return (get-date).DayOfWeek
}
```

While this is a simple function that is not performing anything original, and we would probably not write tests for it, it is interesting to try to imagine how we would go about trying to test it. We could certainly test it manually by running it and looking at a calendar, but the fact that the output is dependent on the current date makes it difficult. Many typical PowerShell functions have many more dependencies than this.

Thinking back to our example in the section on modularization, you'll remember we had a function that renamed databases. Writing a unit test for that would not be nearly as straightforward as the tests we showed for get-fqdn in the previous section. For instance, it requires that there is an SQL Server instance with a database we can connect to. It would also require that we have permissions to rename the database and that there isn't a database with the new name on that SQL instance. Similarly, most PowerShell scripts deal with external entities: filesystems, servers, active directory, exchange, and so on. It's not reasonable to assume that there is a test environment available for testing scripts. Even if there was, there is no guarantee that it is configured like the live environment that our scripts will be running in. Furthermore, the logic of our function is what we want to test, not the behavior of the external system. To isolate our tests from external dependencies like this, we will turn to the concept of mocking and the Pester testing framework.

An introduction to Pester

The Pester framework (https://github.com/pester/Pester) gives us a more structured way to perform our unit tests. First of all, Pester has us create a fixture for our unit testing purposes with the new-fixture function. A fixture is simply a folder with two scripts in it. The first script has the function we are going to test. The second is where our tests will go. The test script files must be named with an extension of .Tests.PS1 in order for Pester to be able to find them. After copying the get-fqdn function into the first script, I have rewritten the tests in Pester's syntax. The vocabulary Pester uses is from the **behavior-driven development** (BDD) style of testing. The syntax might look strange because it doesn't follow the verb-noun format in tests. Instead, our tests are included in an It statement, and use the Should function and the Be assertion. Understanding exactly how the PowerShell works is interesting and I recommend reading through the Should function to help in this regard. For our purposes, though, it is enough to know that this is a simple and self-explanatory way to write tests, such as the following:

```
$here = Split-Path -Parent $MyInvocation.MyCommand.Path
$sut = (Split-Path -Leaf $MyInvocation.MyCommand.Path).Replace(".
Tests.", ".")
. "$here\$sut"
```

```
Describe "get-fqdn" {

    It "works with a list" {
      get-fqdn comp1,comp2 domain.com |
             Should Be 'comp1.domain.com','comp2.domain.com'
    }
    It "works with a single computername" {
      get-fqdn comp1 domain.com |
Should Be 'comp1.domain.com'
    }
    It "works with a leading dot in domainname" {
    get-fqdn comp1 .domain.com |
Should Be 'comp1.domain.com'
    }
    It "doesn't modify a specified fqdn" {
    get-fqdn comp1.domain2.com .domain.com |
Should Be 'comp1.domain2.com'
    }


}
```

Running the tests with the `Invoke-Pester` function gives us the following result which shows that all four tests passed:

```
Executing all tests in C:\Users\Mike\SkyDrive\Documents\
PowerShellTroubleshooting\ChapterDrafts\Chapter4_1stDraft\Code\get-
fqdn
Describing get-fqdn
  [+] works with a list 22ms
  [+] works with a single computername 2ms
  [+] works with a leading dot in domainname 24ms
  [+] doesn't modify a specified fqdn 2ms
Tests completed in 51ms
Passed: 4 Failed: 0
```

Mocking with Pester

One of the interesting features of the Pester framework is the ability to create mocks. In general, a mock is something that will be substituted for a dependency in a unit test. The mock is created so that it only has the behavior that we are interested in and gives predictable results. Testing the simple function we described earlier is fairly simple to accomplish with mocks. First, let's write the following function:

```
function get-dayOfWeek{
    return (get-date).DayOfWeek
}
```

Now, let's consider the following tests:

```
$here = Split-Path -Parent $MyInvocation.MyCommand.Path
$sut = (Split-Path -Leaf
  $MyInvocation.MyCommand.Path).Replace(".Tests.", ".")
. "$here\$sut"

Describe "DayOfWeek" {

    It "Returns Thursday for 6/26/2014" {
      Mock Get-Date {return [DateTime]'6/26/2014'}
          get-DayOfWeek | Should Be 'Thursday'
        }
    It "Returns Monday for 3/24/2014" {
        Mock Get-Date {return [DateTime]'3/24/2014'}
            get-DayOfWeek | Should Be 'Monday'
        }
```

Note that we used the Mock function to create versions of get-date that return specific dates. With those dates, it is trivial to check the day of the week against the return value. By using a mock, we have eliminated the dependency on the implementation of get-date and are free to concentrate on how the output of get-date is used.

A more complicated function allows us to use more of the functionality provided by Pester. The following is a function that restarts the current machine if it has been running for more than 30 days:

```
function restart-ServerAfter30Days {
   $lastBootTime=get-CIMInstance Win32_OperatingSystem |
select-object -expand LastBootUpTime
   $now=get-date
   if(($now - $lastBootTime).TotalDays -gt 30) {
```

```
        Restart-Computer -WhatIf
    }
}
```

To test this function, we first need to remove the dependency on Get-Date and Get-CIMInstance using mocks. We also need to mock Restart-computer because it would not be helpful for the computer running the test to restart during the test. We can use the Assert-MockCalled function to ensure that the Restart-Computer cmdlet was called (or not) in the correct situations. Finally, we have supplied a filter on the Get-CIMInstance mock so that it only applies if the Win32_OperatingSystem class name was passed as a parameter. In this case, the filter was not necessary, but it serves to illustrate the usage of filters. The following code snippet explains this:

```
$here = Split-Path -Parent $MyInvocation.MyCommand.Path
$sut = (Split-Path -Leaf $MyInvocation.MyCommand.Path).Replace(".
Tests.", ".")
. "$here\$sut"


Describe "restart-ServerAfter30Days" {
    Mock get-CIMInstance { new-object PSObject -prop @{LastBootUpTi
me=[Datetime] '2/1/2014'}}  -parameterFilter {$ClassName -eq 'Win32_
OperatingSystem'}
    Mock Restart-Computer {}
    Context "When restart date is more than 30 days old" {
        Mock get-date {return [Datetime]'4/1/2014'}
        restart-ServerAfter30Days
        It 'reboots' {
            Assert-MockCalled Restart-Computer -times 1
        }
    }
    Context "When restart date is less than 30 days old" {
        Mock get-date {return [DateTime]'2/15/2014'}
        restart-ServerAfter30Days
        It 'Does not reboot' {
            Assert-MockCalled Restart-Computer -times 0
        }
    }
}
```

Again, using `Invoke-Pester` shows us that the function passes both tests in the following code snippet:

```
Executing all tests in C:\Users\Mike\SkyDrive\Documents\
PowerShellTroubleshooting\ChapterDrafts\Chapter4_1stDraft\Code\
restartTest
Describing restart-ServerAfter30Days
    Context When restart date is more than 30 days old
      [+] reboots 4ms
    Context When restart date is less than 30 days old
      [+] Does not reboot 26ms
Tests completed in 30ms
Passed: 2 Failed: 0
```

Mocking is an important tool in the unit testing arsenal and allows us to test a number of things that would be difficult to test without them. On the other hand, as the mocking scenario gets more and more complex, there is a question about how tightly-coupled your code and the mock object are. Tightly-coupled code is a danger, as it makes changing code difficult. If you find yourself spending a lot of your time writing mocks, you might want to take a step back and re-evaluate.

Further reading

Take a look at the following references for more information:

- Naming conventions at `http://en.wikipedia.org/wiki/Naming_convention_%28programming%29`
- Dogfooding at `http://en.wikipedia.org/wiki/Eating_your_own_dog_food`
- Modularization at `http://en.wikipedia.org/wiki/Modular_programming`
- Unit testing at `http://en.wikipedia.org/wiki/Unit_testing`
- Pester at `https://github.com/pester/Pester`
- Mocking at `http://en.wikipedia.org/wiki/Mock_object`

Summary

In this chapter, we looked at several practices borrowed from traditional software development that will help your scripting look more professional. These practices include things like using naming conventions for different types of PowerShell entities, breaking scripts down into smaller units, using version control consistently, and finally unit testing and mocking.

In the next chapter, we will look at using some of the built-in features of PowerShell to proactively create more trouble-free programs. These features include error handling (`try` / `catch` vs trap), parameterization and pipeline input, parameter validation, parameter type transformation, and so on.

5
Proactive PowerShell

PowerShell includes capabilities to improve the quality of scripts that will prevent some of the problems that might be encountered in the scripting process. In this chapter, we'll cover the following topics:

- Error handling (`try`/`catch` versus `trap`)
- Parameterization and pipeline input
- Pipelines and function execution
- Parameter validation
- Parameter type transformation
- Strictmode/PSDebug
- #REQUIRES statements (version or administrator)
- CmdletBinding and common parameters

Error handling

Chapter 2, PowerShell Peculiarities introduced PowerShell's two error-handling mechanisms: the `trap` statement and the `try`, `catch`, and `finally` statements. That chapter explained how these statements function in PowerShell code. The following sections will give you some guidance on how to use them effectively and some techniques for writing error-handling code.

Error-handling guidelines

The first thing to mention is that although the `trap` statement can be effective for handling errors, its flow can be confusing, especially when considering the many ways to exit a trap statement. For this reason, it is a good idea to avoid the `trap` statement in most cases and use the `try` / `catch` / `finally` constructions instead. Since environments that only support PowerShell Version 1.0 are not very common, `try`, `catch`, and `finally` can be used almost everywhere. Also, the flow of `try` / `catch` / `finally` is much more linear, leading to less confusion about the flow of execution.

A second point is that when writing error-handling code (with either `try`/`catch`/ `finally`, or `trap`), we should avoid using empty error handlers. The following code is a bad example of handling errors:

```
#this is bad!
try {
    Start-Service MSSQLSERVER -Computer CORPSQL -errorAction Stop
} catch { }
```

The reason this is a poor practice is simple. If it doesn't matter whether the code had an error, the operation couldn't have been very important. If we don't need the code to succeed, or even to know what went wrong, we probably don't need to be executing the code in the first place. The same observation can be made for using the `Ignore` value for the `ErrorAction` common parameter or the `$ErrorActionPreference` variable. Since that setting instructs PowerShell to not only refrain from writing errors to the error stream but also to not record the error in the `$Error` collection, there is no way to know whether the operation succeeded or not, and there is no way to know what went wrong.

Error-handling techniques

First of all, let's state for the record that it is important to handle errors. That might sound obvious, but it is easy to get caught up in how powerful PowerShell is and then forget that even though PowerShell has the capability to do things, the world doesn't always cooperate with our plans. For instance, consider the following line of a script:

```
$service = Get-Service MSSQLServer -computername MYSERVER
```

While the expectation might be that the statement in question will always succeed, and in ordinary circumstances it will, there are clearly some ways in which things can go wrong. Scripters with a development background usually start the error-handling process with code like this:

```
Try{
    $service = Get-Service MSSQLServer -ComputerName MYSERVER
}
catch {
    #handle the error appropriately
}
```

In this case, this approach is not successful since the Get-Service cmdlet doesn't throw terminating errors but emits non-terminating errors instead. Even though we're trying to handle all errors here, the try / catch statements seem to have no effect.

Using a try / catch / finally construct in conjunction with the -ErrorAction STOP parameter gives us the ability to handle non-terminating errors. The code now looks like this:

```
Try {
$service = Get-Service MSSQLServer -computername MYSERVER -ErrorAction
Stop
} catch {
    #respond appropriately to the error condition.
}
```

Knowing what kinds of errors need to be handled can be accomplished by running some sample broken scripts:

```
#test a good computer name with a bad service name
Get-Service MSSQLSERVERZZZZ -ComputerName Localhost
#test a bad computer name with a good service name
Get-Service MSSQLSERVER -ComputerName NOSUCHCOMPUTER
```

This gives a good start for trying to figure out how to respond. Now, we need to determine whether these errors are terminating errors or non-terminating errors. Like we covered in *Chapter 2*, *PowerShell Peculiarities*, non-terminating errors aren't caught by a try / catch construction, so we can do something like the following:

```
Try {
    Get-Service MSSQLSERVERZZZZ -ComputerName Localhost
} catch {
  "An exception : ($_) happened"
}
```

In this case, the code indicates that an exception (that is, a terminating error) has not occurred, so we know that this particular error is a non-terminating error. To handle non-terminating errors, we need to use the -ErrorAction parameter with the value Stop:

```
Try {
    Get-Service MSSQLSERVERZZZZ -computername Localhost -ErrorAction
Stop
} catch {
  $err=$_
  "An exception : ($err) happened"
}
```

We are now able to handle this condition. By repeating this process with each kind of bad parameter, we can figure out how to structure the error-handling code.

Investigating cmdlet error behavior

Although the PowerShell language designers have worked very hard to create a scripting environment that is very consistent and have included many language features to help out in this direction, it can be dangerous to assume that different cmdlets will respond to errors in the same way. A couple of examples should indicate the danger of assuming cmdlets behave similarly.

First, have a look at the following script, which gets references to the Spooler service on two computers using Get-Service and Get-WMIObject:

```
$computers='localhost','NOSUCHCOMPUTER'
Get-Service Spooler -ComputerName $computers
Get-WMIObject Win32_Service -ComputerName
  $computers -Filter "Name='Spooler'"
```

The Get-Service cmdlet simply returns the localhost spooler with no indication of any error except for the delay in trying to resolve the nonexistent computer. The Get-WMIObject cmdlet, on the other hand, emits a non-terminating error about not being able to connect to the RPC service on NOSUCHCOMPUTER, which is the service responsible for WMI communication.

A second example concerns operations that require administrative privileges. In a PowerShell instance that is not running with administrative privileges, the Get-VM cmdlet simply returns no objects even if there are VMs configured on the system. On the other hand, stop-service BITS will emit a non-terminating error if it's run as a non-administrator.

Hopefully, these examples are sufficient to convince you that actually investigating the error responses for cmdlets is a valuable exercise. Being able to respond correctly to the error conditions is an important part of troubleshooting PowerShell code.

Catch and release

One last thing to mention about error handling is that error handling in a function or script does not necessarily need to respond to every possible error. This might seem to contradict the previous sections' emphasis on investigating error modes for cmdlets that you're using, but there is an important distinction. It really only makes sense to handle the errors that are related to the process that is being performed. For instance, code that deals with reading a performance counter should probably be expected to react to only a few kinds of errors:

- Missing performance counters
- Insufficient privileges to read the performance counter

What conditions are we not considering? What about the *Out of Memory* errors? What if the OS is shutting down? What if a non-terminating error is not one of the conditions that you have a response for? In cases such as these, it might make sense to either throw the exception again (in the case of a terminating error) or rewrite the error to the error stream, as shown in the following code snippet:

```
try {
   Get-Service BLAH -ErrorAction stop
} catch {
  if($_.Exception.Message -like 'Cannot find any service*'){
     #do something about the missing service
  } else {
    throw
  }
}
```

This is not always necessary, but it does allow system-level errors to be handled at the appropriate level.

CmdletBinding()

In PowerShell Version 1.0, the only way to write cmdlets was with managed code. Starting with Version 2.0, it became possible to write advanced functions that have all of the capabilities of managed cmdlets but are written in 100 percent PowerShell. The key to writing advanced functions (also sometimes called script cmdlets) is the CmdletBinding() attribute, which is added to the Param() statement. Since the attribute is tied to the Param() statement, advanced functions must have a Param() statement even if they have no parameters. In this case, an empty Param() statement can be used. The following is an example of a normal function and an advanced function, which are nominally the same:

```
#this is a normal function
function add-item{
param($x,$y)
    Write-Output $x+$y
}

#the same function as an advanced function
function add-itemAdv{
[CmdletBinding()]
param($x,$y)
    Write-Output $x+$y
}
```

Common parameter support

Although the two functions seem to be the same, Get-Help shows that there is a difference:

```
PS C:\WINDOWS\system32> get-help add-item

NAME
    add-item

SYNTAX
    add-item [[-x] <Object>] [[-y] <Object>]


ALIASES
    None


REMARKS
    None


PS C:\WINDOWS\system32> get-help add-itemadv

NAME
    add-itemAdv

SYNTAX
    add-itemAdv [[-x] <Object>] [[-y] <Object>]  [<CommonParameters>]


ALIASES
    None


REMARKS
    None
```

One of the benefits of writing advanced functions is the support for common parameters. From the about_CommonParameters help topic, we can see that the basic set of common parameters that are available to every advanced function or cmdlet (in PowerShell Version 4.0) include the following:

- -Debug
- -ErrorAction
- -ErrorVariable
- -OutVariable
- -OutBuffer

- -PipelineVariable
- -Verbose
- -WarningAction
- -WarningVariable

Supporting these parameters means that we don't have to do anything to make them work. For instance, we can use `Write-Verbose` throughout our advanced function and the verbose output will show up if the `-Verbose` switch is specified. Similarly, we can use `Write-Error` to emit non-terminating errors and the engine will convert them to exceptions if the caller specifies `-ErrorAction Stop`.

SupportsShouldProcess

Cmdlets whose execution changes the state of the system where some risk is involved should include risk mitigation parameters, which are the following:

- -WhatIf
- -Confirm

For an advanced function to use these parameters, the `SupportsShouldProcess` parameter of the `CmdletBinding` attribute should be given a value of `$true`. Portions of code that involve the risk should be guarded with the `$PSCmdlet.ShouldProcess()` method. This method returns `$true` unless the caller specified the `-WhatIf` switch or the `-Confirm` switch followed by a negative response:

```
function remove-something{
[CmdletBinding(SupportsShouldProcess=$true)]
Param($item)

    if ($PSCmdlet.ShouldProcess($item)){
        Write-Output "Removing $item"
    }

}
```

Here is some sample output from that advanced function showing the operation of the -Whatif and -Confirm switches:

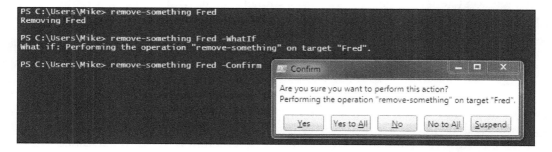

Parameter name validation

One important consequence of writing advanced functions (that is, using CmdletBinding) is that named parameters that are passed but do not exist in the function will cause the parameter binding to fail. The following code will help you understand this:

```
function f1{
Param($a,$b)
    Write-Host $a+$b
}

function f2{
[CmdletBinding()]
Param($a,$b)
    Write-Host $a+$b
}
```

Given these two functions, observe the following output:

```
PS C:\Users\Mike> f1 -a 5 -c 2
5+

PS C:\Users\Mike> f2 -a 5 -c 2
f2 : A parameter cannot be found that matches parameter name 'c'.
At line:1 char:9
+ f2 -a 5 -c 2
+         ~~
    + CategoryInfo          : InvalidArgument: (:) [f2], ParentContainsErrorRecordException
    + FullyQualifiedErrorId : NamedParameterNotFound,f2
```

Though this is a very simple example, and it doesn't seem like a big deal, parameter name checking is an essential ingredient in writing robust scripts. The reason is that we don't generally name parameters things such as A and B. Longer parameter names such as ConnectionString and ComputerName are much easier to mistype, and without this feature, parameter name typos will go unnoticed. Also, because the parser is checking parameter names, it is possible to abbreviate parameter names and the parser will be able to determine which parameter is being referenced.

This kind of mistake bit me early in my PowerShell experience when I was testing some code. I was trying to stop a demo system and "typoed" the name of the parameter that specified which system to stop. The code in question didn't do any sanity checking to make sure that reasonable parameters were supplied. Since this was PowerShell Version 1.0, which didn't have advanced functions, the function didn't receive any -System parameter and ignored the demo system name that I passed with the wrong parameter name. I shut down all relevant systems in my company. Oops! This is not the kind of mistake you want to make.

Parameter value validation

In addition to validating the names of parameters, using CmdletBinding() allows us to provide several types of validation rules for values of parameters. Validation rules enable us to provide checks that are performed by the parameter binding engine that specify when values are appropriate or not for the function. These parameter checking attributes can be divided into two groups: requirement validation and value checking. Requirement checking indicates whether the parameter is required or if various types of empty values are allowed. These attributes include the following:

- Mandatory
- AllowNull
- AllowEmptyString
- AllowEmptyCollection
- ValidateNotNull
- ValidateNotNullOrEmpty

Value checking attributes restrict the values that are allowed for a parameter. Value checking attributes include the following:

- `ValidateCount`
- `ValidateLength`
- `ValidatePattern`
- `ValidateRange`
- `ValidateScript`
- `ValidateSet`

Parameter attribute usage is illustrated in the following script:

```
Function test-validation{
[CmdletBinding()]
Param([ValidateLength(4,10)][string]$word)
Write-Output "the word was $word"
}
```

In this script, we have used the `ValidateLength` parameter attribute to ensure that values passed in for `$word` are strings between 4 and 10 characters in length. Passing invalid values (either longer or shorter) will cause this validation rule to fail and an error will be emitted without executing the function. We can fairly easily write code to validate the parameter without attributes like this:

```
Function test-validation{
[CmdletBinding()]
Param([string]$word)
  #Don't do this!
    If($word.Length -lt 4 -or $word.Length -gt 10){
    Throw "The value for $word has an invalid length"
    }
Write-Output "the word was $word"
}
```

There are several reasons this approach should be avoided. Some of them are listed as follows:

- It involves more manual coding
- The function is actually executing, so any errors in the parameter validation might end up with inadvertent results
- The parameter checking code is separated from the parameter definition
- Custom error messages will be inconsistent between different scripters (and often even with the same scripters)
- Custom error messages will not (in general) be localized, so they will appear in the scripter's language only

Pipeline input

The ability to accept pipeline input has been included in PowerShell since Version 1.0. There are three main ways to deal with the pipeline: `$input`, filters, and (fully specified) functions.

The `$input` automatic variable exposes an enumerator (think collection) of all the values passed in on the pipeline. An example using the `$input` automatic variable might look like this:

```
Function get-pipelineinput{
    $input | Foreach-Object {Write-Host "the object was $_"}
}
```

The second option, filters, are simply functions whose bodies are executed for each pipeline element. Filters use the `$_` symbol to represent the current pipeline element. Here is an example of a filter script:

```
Filter get-reverse{
    $_.ToString().Reverse()
}
```

Because there is no way to specify what types of values were available for pipeline input using the `$input` or `$_` variables, these are not good solutions for most production scripts. With PowerShell Version 2.0 and the introduction of `CmdletBinding()`, another more powerful option became available, using parameter attributes to indicate pipeline binding. Before illustrating these parameter attributes, we need to explain that the example functions presented in *Chapter 1, PowerShell Primer*, did not illustrate the full form of a function definition. When working with the pipeline we need to know that there are three possible sections in a function definition: `Begin`, `Process`, and `End`. If no named section is used, the (unnamed) function body is the end section. Here is the full form of a function:

```
Function <function name>{
[CmdletBinding()]
Param(<parameters>)
Begin {
        #<executed before processing pipeline items>
        }
Process {
          #<code executed for each pipeline item>
          }
End {
      #<executed after processing pipeline items>
        }
}
```

It should be clear from the outline that the begin block is executed at the beginning of the pipeline, before any items have been processed. The process block is then executed for each item received from the pipeline that can be accessed via the `$_` variable which is also used in filters or with parameters that have been designated to bind to pipeline items.

The `ValueFromPipeline` and `ValueFromPipelineByPropertyName` parameter attributes allow a function to indicate how specific parameters bind to items on the pipeline. `ValueFromPipeline` tells the engine to attempt to bind each pipeline item to a parameter as an object. The `ValueFromPipelineByPropertyName` attribute instructs the engine to examine each item on the pipeline and use the object properties whose names match the parameter name to populate the parameter. Unlike with `ValueFromPipeline`, more than one parameter can bind to a property name with the same pipeline object. This should be made clearer with the following example:

```
Function get-fileExtension{
[CmdletBinding()]
Param([Parameter(ValueFromPipeline=$true)]
```

```
        [System.IO.FileInfo]$file,
        [Parameter(ValueFromPipelineByPropertyName=$true)]
        [String]$extension)
    Process{
        Write-Output "The filename was $($file.Name)"
        Write-Output "the extension was $($file.Extension)"
        Write-Output "the extension is also $extension"
    }
}
```

In this example, the $file parameter is set to bind with the FileInfo objects in the pipeline. Likewise, the $extension parameter is set to bind with properties called Extension on objects in the pipeline. Note that folders are represented by the System.IO.DirectoryInfo class, so the $file parameter will not bind but since those objects have the Extension properties the $extension parameter will be populated. Here is an example of calling this function:

```
PS C:\temp> dir


    Directory: C:\temp


Mode                LastWriteTime       Length Name
----                -------------       ------ ----
d----         5/27/2014  12:54 PM              folder
d----         5/27/2014  12:53 PM              FolderWith.Extension
-a---          4/8/2014   7:33 PM        58272 cbh.txt
-a---         4/11/2014   5:04 PM            0 errors.txt
-a---         4/11/2014   8:40 PM      3328100 files.txt
-a---         3/11/2014   7:47 PM          115 get-powershellversionmessage.ps1
-a---         3/25/2014   8:10 PM            0 hello.txt
-a---         3/12/2014   7:37 PM        35376 keys.txt
-a---         3/11/2014   7:26 PM            0 test.txt
-a---         3/25/2014   8:23 PM            4 testout.txt


PS C:\temp> dir | select -first 3 | get-fileExtension
The filename was
the extension was
the extension is also
The filename was
the extension was
the extension is also .Extension
The filename was cbh.txt
the extension was .txt
the extension is also .txt
PS C:\temp>
```

The process block of a function is repeated for each object in the pipeline. However, if the user calls the function supplying the values for the parameters on the command line, we also need to make sure that our function will handle those seamlessly. Here is a useful pattern to handle pipeline and command-line input with the same parameter:

```
function get-value{
[CmdletBinding()]
Param([Parameter(ValueFromPipeline=$true)]
        [string[]]$computername)
begin {
  #initialize
}
process{
    Foreach ($computer in $computername){
    #process one value from the pipeline or commandline
    }
}
end {
  #finish up
}
}
```

The new features of this function are making the parameter an array and adding a loop in the process block. In this code, the process block will be executed once for each pipeline item and the foreach loop in it will execute once per item. For command-line input, the $computername parameter will have all of the values supplied (rather than one at a time) and the loop in the process block will loop through them. With command-line input, the process block will only execute once.

Pipelines and function execution

Although pipelines are written sequentially with each element following the previous one, function execution in a pipeline is somewhat different. In order to illustrate this, consider the following advanced functions that all allow pipeline input:

```
function A{
[CmdletBinding()]
Param([Parameter(ValueFromPipeline=$true)]$x)
  begin { Write-Host "A in begin"}
  process { Write-Host "A in Process{}"
          Write-Output $x }
  end { Write-Host "A in end"}
```

```
}
function B{
[CmdletBinding()]
Param([Parameter(ValueFromPipeline=$true)]$y)
  begin { Write-Host "B in begin"}
  process { Write-Host "B in Process{}"
          Write-Output $y }
  end { Write-Host "B in end"}
}
function C{
[CmdletBinding()]
Param([Parameter(ValueFromPipeline=$true)]$z)
  begin { Write-Host "C in begin"}
  process { Write-Host "C in Process{}"
          Write-Output $z }
  end { Write-Host "C in end"}
}
```

The only thing these functions do is display a message when one of the three
`Begin-Process-End` script blocks is run and output any objects that come in
from the pipeline. With this in mind, examine the output from the command line
`1,2,3 | A | B | C` in the following screenshot:

```
PS C:\Users\Mike> 1,2,3 | A | B | C
A in begin
B in begin
C in begin
A in Process{}
B in Process{}
C in Process{}
1
A in Process{}
B in Process{}
C in Process{}
2
A in Process{}
B in Process{}
C in Process{}
3
A in end
B in end
C in end
```

The sequence of execution should be clear:

1. The Begin block of each function in the pipeline is executed in sequence.
2. The Process block of the first function is passed the first item in the pipeline.
3. Since the first Process block outputs an object, it is passed to the second Process block, and so on.
4. After all of the pipeline objects have been processed, the End blocks are all called in sequence.

If we don't use Begin-Process-End blocks in a function, only the End block is called. In this case, the last value from the pipeline is still assigned to the parameter. To see this, have a look at the following simple function:

```
function D{
[CmdletBinding()]
Param([Parameter(ValueFromPipeline=$true)]$z)
  Write-Host "This is the only block in D and `$z is $z"
}
```

Now, observe the output in the following screenshot from 1,2,3 | A | B | D and compare it to the previous output:

```
PS C:\Users\Mike> 1,2,3 | A | B | D
A in begin
B in begin
A in Process{}
B in Process{}
A in Process{}
B in Process{}
A in Process{}
B in Process{}
A in end
B in end
This is the only block in D and $z is 3
```

Parameter type transformation

PowerShell allows us to ignore the idea of variable types in most situations and this is a tremendous productivity boost. When you consider all of the different Common Language Runtime (CLR) types that are used in a typical script it's easy to see why not worrying about naming the types saves a lot of time. Adding in all of the anonymous types (for instance, results of a select-object call), the need for a very liberal typing system is obvious. One example when specifying types is useful, or even critical, is when specifying parameters to a function:

```
function get-dayofweek{
param($date)
  Write-Output $date.DayOfWeek
}
```

This function seems like it would work well, but testing it shows that it's not quite right, as shown in the following screenshot:

```
PS C:\temp> get-dayofweek (get-date)
Tuesday

PS C:\temp> get-dayofweek '5/27/2014'

PS C:\temp>
```

Since we didn't specify what type the parameter was, the problem was that the constant string '5/27/2014' was passed into the parameter as is, that is, as a string. Since the string didn't have a DayOfWeek property, the output is $null. The solution, of course, is to include the type of the parameter as part of the definition, as shown in the following script:

```
function get-dayofweek{
param([datetime]$date)
  Write-Output $date.DayOfWeek
}
```

Now the function works as expected:

```
PS C:\temp> get-dayofweek (get-date)
Tuesday

PS C:\temp> get-dayofweek '5/27/2014'
Tuesday
```

It's important to include the type of your parameter because the PowerShell engine does a remarkable job to not only make sure that the type of object that is passed is the correct type, but it also tries to coerce the value into the correct type. This is how the `'5/27/2014'` string was changed into a `DateTime` object. PowerShell uses several different methods to try to convert the supplied value to the requested type. In this instance, it found a `Parse()` static method on the `DateTime` type with a single string parameter and passed `'5/27/2014'` to it to create the value that was accepted by the function.

Passing a value that does not correspond to a legitimate object of the correct type will result in an error as the engine attempts to bind the value to the parameter:

```
PS C:\temp> get-dayofweek "Hello World"
get-dayofweek : Cannot process argument transformation on parameter 'date'. Cannot convert value "Hello World" to type
"System.DateTime". Error: "The string was not recognized as a valid DateTime. There is an unknown word starting at index 0."
At line:1 char:15
+ get-dayofweek "Hello World"
+               ~~~~~~~~~~~~~
    + CategoryInfo          : InvalidData: (:) [get-dayofweek], ParameterBindingArgumentTransformationException
    + FullyQualifiedErrorId : ParameterArgumentTransformationError,get-dayofweek
```

PowerShell's method of automatic type conversion is almost always what is expected. On the other hand, some types have constructors, such as shown in the following screenshot, which we might not have considered:

```
PS C:\temp> get-dayofweek 100
Monday
```

While this doesn't seem to make sense, PowerShell pushed through and gave an answer. It turns out that the `DateTime` type has a constructor that takes a single integer parameter corresponding to the number of ticks (since the minimum `DateTime` value). It's probably not what we wanted, but it's the price we pay for the 99 percent of the time where PowerShell is silently converting values (for example, filename strings to `FileInfo` objects):

```
function get-extension{
param([System.io.fileinfo] $file)
   Write-Output $file.extension
}
```

Because the text value on the command-line was converted to a FileInfo object, we are able to refer to its extension property:

```
PS C:\temp> get-extension C:\temp\adv_event1.ps1
.ps1
```

The point to remember is that we can control what objects are accepted for parameters by specifying the type of the parameter. We can't control what conversions PowerShell will attempt to use to give us a correctly-typed object. We might get an unexpected value if PowerShell uses an unusual transformation, but we won't have to validate the type of the object we receive.

#REQUIRES statements

It's no secret that some code has prerequisites that need to be met in order for it to work. In PowerShell, certain types of requirements can be specified in scripts using a #REQUIRES statement. Although the #REQUIRES statement looks like a comment (that is, it starts with #), it is a statement to the engine that tells PowerShell not to run the script unless the requirements are met. As of PowerShell Version 4.0, the following options are available in a #REQUIRES statement:

Option	Parameters	Notes
-Version	N[.N] (for example, 4.0)	Required version of PowerShell engine
-PSSnapIn	PSSnapinName [-Version N[.N]]	Required Snapin (with optional minimum version #)
-Modules	ModuleName[,ModuleName] or Hashtable	Required modules to be loaded
-ShellID	ShellID	Required PowerShell Host (for example, Microsoft.PowerShellISE)
-RunAsAdministrator	none	Required session privileges

When the conditions of the #REQUIRES statement are not met, or cannot be met, the script will not load and will emit an error. With the following code in RequireAdministrator.ps1 and a PowerShell session not running as administrator, observe the error message that follows:

```
#Requires -RunAsAdministrator

Write-Host "hello world"
```

```
PS: >. .\RequireAdministrator.ps1
. . The script 'RequireAdministrator.ps1' cannot be run because it contains a "#requires" statement for running as
Administrator. The current Windows PowerShell session is not running as Administrator. Start Windows PowerShell by
using the Run as Administrator option, and then try running the script again.
At line:1 char:3
+ . .\RequireAdministrator.ps1
+   ~~~~~~~~~~~~~~~~~~~~~~~~~~~~
    + CategoryInfo          : PermissionDenied: (RequireAdministrator.ps1:String) [], ScriptRequiresException
    + FullyQualifiedErrorId : ScriptRequiresElevation

PS: >
```

Set-StrictMode and Set-PSDebug -strict

In addition to PowerShell not requiring a script to specify the type of a variable, it also doesn't require any kind of declaration prior to using the variable. If the first use of a variable is to assign a value to it, this relaxed attitude doesn't cause any harm. On the other hand, reading a variable that hasn't been written to is generally not what is intended.

There are two ways to ensure that reading from an uninitialized variable will cause an error. The first, introduced in PowerShell Version 1.0, was to use the -strict switch on the Set-PSDebug cmdlet. Once this has been issued in a PowerShell session, references to uninitialized variables (except in string substitution) will produce an error. References inside strings will resolve to $null. This is a global switch in the engine and is reversed by issuing Set-PSDebug with the -off switch. The following screenshot explains this:

```
PS C:\Users\mike> set-psdebug -strict
PS C:\Users\mike> $x = $blah + 5
The variable '$blah' cannot be retrieved because it has not been set.
At line:1 char:6
+ $x = $blah + 5
+      ~~~~~
    + CategoryInfo          : InvalidOperation: (blah:String) [], RuntimeException
    + FullyQualifiedErrorId : VariableIsUndefined

PS C:\Users\mike> "$blah + 5"
 + 5
PS C:\Users\mike> set-strictmode -off
PS C:\Users\mike> $x = $blah + 5
PS C:\Users\mike> $x
5
PS C:\Users\mike>
```

The second method, introduced in PowerShell Version 2.0, is to use Set-StrictMode and use the -Version parameter to specify the level of strictness. Set-Strictmode -Version 1.0 gives the same results as Set-PSDebug -strict. Set-StrictMode -Version 2.0 and causes the following conditions to result in an error:

- Referencing uninitialized variables in strings
- Referencing nonexistent properties of an object

- Calling a cmdlet using parentheses (as if it were an object method)
- Referencing a variable with no name (${})

The following screenshot illustrates the strict-mode errors:

```
PS C:\Users\mike> set-strictmode -version 2.0
PS C:\Users\mike>
PS C:\Users\mike> $blah
The variable '$blah' cannot be retrieved because it has not been set.
At line:1 char:1
+ $blah
+ ~~~~~
    + CategoryInfo          : InvalidOperation: (blah:String) [], RuntimeException
    + FullyQualifiedErrorId : VariableIsUndefined
PS C:\Users\mike> "$Blah"
The variable '$Blah' cannot be retrieved because it has not been set.
At line:1 char:2
+ "$Blah"
+  ~~~~~
    + CategoryInfo          : InvalidOperation: (Blah:String) [], RuntimeException
    + FullyQualifiedErrorId : VariableIsUndefined
PS C:\Users\mike> $x.Blah
The property 'Blah' cannot be found on this object. Verify that the property exists.
At line:1 char:1
+ $x.Blah
+ ~~~~~~~
    + CategoryInfo          : NotSpecified: (:) [], PropertyNotFoundException
    + FullyQualifiedErrorId : PropertyNotFoundStrict
PS C:\Users\mike> rename-item($oldname,$newname)
The function or command was called as if it were a method. Parameters should be separated by spaces. For information
about parameters, see the about_Parameters Help topic.
At line:1 char:1
+ rename-item($oldname,$newname)
+ ~~~~~~~~~~~~~~~~~~~~~~~~~~~~~~~
    + CategoryInfo          : InvalidOperation: (:) [], RuntimeException
    + FullyQualifiedErrorId : StrictModeFunctionCallWithParens
PS C:\Users\mike>
```

As of PowerShell 4.0, `-Version 2.0` is the most restrictive setting available. To ensure that code uses all possible restrictions for future versions as well, the value of Latest is available, which currently gives the same results as `-Version 2.0`.

One difference between `Set-PSDebug` and `Set-StrictMode` is that while `Set-PSDebug` is a session-level setting, `Set-StrictMode` is scoped, that is, the setting is changed in the current scope and its children. For this reason it can be used to guard against errors in a function, module, or script without concern that it will place restrictions on the session in general and is preferred over `Set-PSDebug` unless working in PowerShell Version 1.0.

```
PS C:\Users\mike> set-strictmode -off
PS C:\Users\mike> 5+$blah; & {set-strictmode -version 2.0;$blah};5+$blah
5
The variable '$blah' cannot be retrieved because it has not been set.
At line:1 char:41
+ 5+$blah; & {set-strictmode -version 2.0;$blah};5+$blah
+                                         ~~~~~
    + CategoryInfo          : InvalidOperation: (blah:String) [], RuntimeException
    + FullyQualifiedErrorId : VariableIsUndefined
5
PS C:\Users\mike>
```

`Set-Strictmode` is an important tool in our toolbox because the restrictions it makes are generally encountered in erroneous code. Referencing uninitialized variables usually happens when a variable is misspelled and similarly, with nonexistent property names. Calling functions or cmdlets using method syntax (parentheses and commas) is usually a mistake as it packages up the arguments as an array and passes that array to the first parameter, which is rarely intended.

Further reading

You can go to the following references for more information:

- `get-help about_try_catch_finally`
- `get-help about_functions_cmdletbinding_attribute`
- `get-help about_commonparameters`
- `get-help about_functions_advanced_methods`
- `get-help about_functions_advanced_parameters`
- `get-help about_functions`
- `get-help about_pipelines`
- Parameter Type Transformation at `http://blogs.msdn.com/b/ powershell/archive/2013/06/11/understanding-powershell-s-type- conversion-magic.aspx`
- `get-help about_requires`
- `get-help set-strictmode`
- `get-help set-psdebug`

Summary

This chapter has explored some really important PowerShell features in depth. We spent a lot of time talking about advanced functions, parameters, and the pipeline. The important `Set-StrictMode` cmdlet was introduced to show how to restrict the PowerShell language slightly in ways that will help us script more carefully. Hopefully, by employing some of these practices, you will be to write more powerful, flexible scripts and avoid some common errors.

In the next chapter, we will turn our thoughts to the environment that scripts run in. We will look at several ways to determine the characteristics of the environment in order to eliminate errors that lie outside of our scripts.

6

Preparing the Scripting Environment

Writing scripts carefully and leveraging the PowerShell language is important, but deploying those scripts into an uncertain environment can cause any number of headaches. Validating that the scripting environment is configured as expected will eliminate many of the potential errors that might otherwise occur. Several methods to check the existing configuration will be presented in this chapter. Many of these techniques are also useful for routine validation after maintenance (patching, upgrading, and so on). In this chapter, we will cover the following topics:

- Validating the operating system (OS) version and 32/64-bit
- Validating the service status
- Validating disk and memory availability
- Validating network connectivity

Validating operating system properties

Details about the installed operating system on a computer can have a tremendous impact on the operation of a script. In the following sections, we will examine the Win32_OperatingSystem class and build a function that provides us with the data we need to support our scripts. The class has over 60 properties, but a handful of them are all we will need. We will use the **Common Information Model (CIM)** cmdlets to retrieve the data, though using the **Windows Management Instrumentation (WMI)** cmdlets will work as well. To start off, let's retrieve the (only) instance of the class using the following script:

```
$os=get-CIMInstance –class Win32_OperatingSystem
```

There is a lot of confusion between WMI and CIM. The CIM cmdlets introduced in PowerShell Version 3.0 seem to provide the same functionality as the WMI cmdlets that have always been present. The main difference is that the CIM cmdlets use **Web Services Management (WSMAN)** by default instead of using DCOM like the WMI cmdlets. Also, CIM cmdlets allow you to use a session for multiple requests, which reduces the overhead. If your environment doesn't allow CIM cmdlets to be used, you should be able to use the corresponding WMI cmdlets.

Workstation/server version

The designation of the installed operating system as a workstation or server (or domain controller) is given by the ProductType property, which takes one of the following values:

Value	Meaning
1	Workstation
2	Domain controller
3	Server

Here, we see a computer that is running a workstation version of Windows:

```
PS C:\Users\mike> $os=get-CIMInstance -class Win32_OperatingSystem
PS C:\Users\mike> $os.ProductType
1
```

If we store these values in an array with a dummy entry, the indices will correspond with the product values:

```
$ProductTypes="Unused",
             "Workstation",
             "Domain Controller",
             "Server"
```

Operating system version

We can get other information from `Win32_OperatingSystem` about the specific version of the operating system that we have installed. The properties we will use are:

- `Caption`
- `ServicePackMajorVersion`
- `Version`

In the following screenshot, you can see the values my laptop shows for these properties:

```
PS C:\Users\Mike> get-CIMInstance Win32_OperatingSystem |
    select-object Caption,ServicePackMajorVersion,Version |
    format-list


Caption                   : Microsoft Windows 7 Home Premium
ServicePackMajorVersion   : 1
Version                   : 6.1.7601
```

The `Caption` property is clearly what a user will be familiar seeing, but it is going to be difficult to use that in a script. The `Version` property will be easier to use in a script, but the values aren't necessarily what would be expected by us. For instance, I would have expected Windows 7 to be Version 7. Here is a table of the values that are returned in this property and the corresponding operating system versions:

Version number	Operating system
5.1	Windows XP
5.2	Windows Server 2003
5.2.3	Windows Server 2003 R2
6.0	Windows Vista or Windows Server 2008
6.1	Windows 7 or Windows Server 2008 R2
6.2	Windows 8 or Windows Server 2012
6.3	Windows 8.1 or Windows Server 2012 R2

For versions 6.x we can use the ProductType to determine whether the OS is the desktop (workstation) or Server edition. One last piece of information that will come in handy is knowing whether the OS installation is a 32-bit or 64-bit installation. We can start with the OSArchitecture property, which shows my computer to be 64-bit, as shown in the following screenshot:

```
PS C:\Users\Mike> get-CIMInstance Win32_OperatingSystem |
    select-object OSArchitecture


OSArchitecture
--------------
64-bit
```

The OSArchitecture property does not exist in the WMI class definition delivered on Windows XP or Windows Server 2003, which exist in both 32-bit and 64-bit versions. There are other indicators of what architecture is present in hardware, like the SystemType property of the Win32_ComputerSystem class or the Architecture property of the Win32_Processor class, but those refer to the hardware rather than the installed operating system. Rather than digging through all of the possible WMI classes, a simpler approach is to simply look for the existence of a ProgramFiles(x86) environment variable. All 64-bit installations will include this environment variable, but 32-bit systems won't have it.

This gives us the following function to retrieve the architecture of the OS, which will work for all versions:

```
function get-OSArchitecture{
    if (test-path "env:programfiles(x86)"){
        "64-bit"
    } else {
        "32-bit"
    }
}
```

This code only works on the current machine because it uses ENV: drive. A more general solution involves accessing environment settings through the `Win32_Environment` class. Unfortunately, the `ProgramFiles(x86)` environment variable isn't available in that class as a property. Fortunately, there are some other environment variables we can use (in combination) if the `OSArchitecture` property is not present. We can use the following function to retrieve environment variables from remote machines:

```
Function Get-EnvironmentVariable{
Param(
[string]$name='%',
[string]$username='<SYSTEM>',
[parameter(ValueFromPipeline=$true,
  ValueFromPipelineByPropertyName=$true)]
[string[]]$computername='localhost')

    Process{
      $values=Get-WMIObject -class
        Win32_Environment -computerName $computerName
        -filter "Name like '$name' and UserName='$username'"
        if($name.Contains('%')){
            $values
        } else {
            $values | select-object -ExpandProperty VariableValue
        }
    }
}
```

I've written the function so that it will return the value of a single variable or the list of `Win32_Environment` objects if the name parameter contains a wildcard. This makes it simple to retrieve a single value if that's what is needed.

With the `Get-EnvironmentVariable` function, we can write the following script:

```
Function get-legacyOSArchitecture{
Param($computername)
    If((get-EnvironmentVariable -name 'PROCESSOR_ARCHITECTURE' -
computername $computername) -eq 'AMD64'){
        '64-bit'
    } else {
    If((get-EnvironmentVariable -name 'PROCESSOR_ARCHITEW6432'
        -computername $computername) -eq 'AMD64'){
            '64=bit'
        } else {
```

```
        '32-bit'
      }
    }
  }
```

If you don't have a Windows 2003 or XP system, I would recommend using the OSArchitecture property on Win32_OperatingSystem since there are several other properties that we will want to look at on that class. Since both of these operating systems are no longer supported, the need for a workaround should be short-lived.

Putting it all together

We can combine all of the research in the following sections into a flexible script which retrieves all of the operating system details that we're interested in. To start, our input will be a list of computer names. We should allow the parameter to be provided on the command line or from the pipeline (by value or from a property).

Troubleshooting tip

When including a ComputerName parameter, remember to allow the aliases of CN and MachineName. When populating the parameter from the pipeline by property name, this will enable input from Active Directory cmdlets as well as other sources.

The function looks like this:

```
function get-OperatingSystem{
[CmdletBinding()]
Param([Parameter(ValueFromPipeline=$true,
  ValueFromPipelineByPropertyName=$true)]
      [Alias('CN','MachineName')]
      [string[]]$computerName=$env:ComputerName)
begin {
$ProductTypes='Unused',
              'Workstation',
              'Domain Controller',
              'Server'
}
process {
  foreach($computer in $computerName){
    $output=@{ComputerName=$computer}
```

```
    $os=get-CIMInstance -computerName $computer
      -class Win32_OperatingSystem
    $output.OSDescription=$os.Caption
    $output.OSVersion=$os.Version
    $output.OSServicePack=$os.ServicePackMajorVersion
    $output.OSProductType=$ProductTypes[$os.ProductType]
    If($os | get-member OSArchitecture){
    $output.OSArchitecture=$os.OSArchitecture
          } else {
    $output.OSArchitecture=get-legacyOSArchitecture $computer
    }
    new-object PSObject -property $output
  }
 }
 }
```

As usual, we output objects from our function. Running this on my laptop yields the
following results:

```
PS C:\Users\Mike> get-OperatingSystem


OSDescription  : Microsoft Windows 7 Home Premium
ComputerName   : KYNDIG
OSProductType  : Workstation
OSVersion      : 6.1.7601
OSServicePack  : 1
OSArchitecture : 64-bit
```

Validating service status

One of the first things we learn to do with PowerShell is to inspect the services on a
computer. The Get-Service cmdlet with its -ComputerName parameter makes this a
simple task. For instance, if we had a list of computers that have SQL Server installed
in a variable called $servers, we could issue the following script to get the status of
the service running the default instance like this:

```
Get-service -name MSSQLSERVER -computername $server |
   Select-object -property Name,Status,MachineName
```

If our goal was simply to find out whether the service is running, this will do the trick. One piece of information that is missing from the objects output from the Get-Service cmdlet is the name of the account that is used to run the service, the run as account. To find that detail, we must turn to WMI. The class to use is Win32_Service, which contains the StartName property. The value of the StartName property is the name of the user account running the service. To find the run as user, as well as the service state for the list of computers in $servers, we could use the following command:

```
Get-WMIObject -class Win32_Service -filter "Name='mssqlserver'"
    -ComputerName $computer | select-object -Property
    Name,StartName,State
```

Validating disk and memory availability

Trying to run a script on a system that is out of memory or disk space is a frustrating experience. An important piece of preparation is to determine the amount of memory and disk space present as well as how much of each is unused. Retrieving these statistics with WMI is a simple matter, and with a bit of effort we can make the results more user-friendly.

We already encountered the Win32_OperatingSystem class in the first part of this chapter. Fortunately for us, there are two properties on this class that will tell us both the total amount and the free amount of memory.

```
Get-CIMInstance Win32_OperatingSystem |
    Select-object FreePhysicalMemory,TotalVisibleMemorySize
```

The output on my laptop is this:

```
FreePhysicalMemory TotalVisibleMemorySize
------------------ ----------------------
          1121880                3977596
```

Since we're going to probably want to see these in a different unit than kilobytes, we can use a trick recommended by Jeffery Hicks (Microsoft MVP in PowerShell) to add script properties to the class returned by get-CIMInstance:

```
Update-TypeData -TypeName Microsoft.Management.Infrastructure.
CimInstance#root/cimv2/Win32_OperatingSystem `
    -MemberType ScriptProperty -MemberName TotalMemoryInGB
      -Value {[math]::Round($this.TotalVisibleMemorySize/1MB,2)}
```

```
Update-TypeData -TypeName Microsoft.Management.Infrastructure.
CimInstance#root/cimv2/Win32_OperatingSystem `
    -MemberType ScriptProperty -MemberName FreeMemoryInGB
      -Value {[math]::Round($this.FreePhysicalMemory/1MB,2)}
```

The `Update-TypeData` cmdlet uses the extended type system in PowerShell to add metadata to the class definition. The actual .NET framework class involved is `Microsoft.Management.Infrastructure.CimInstance`, but PowerShell allows us to differentiate between different types of `CIMInstance` objects by appending the full WMI path to the type name, in this case, `#root/cimv2/Win32_OperatingSystem`. This is a very useful thing to do since the data in different types of WMI instances are very different. The results of the `Update-TypeData` cmdlet only affect the current session, but they do make the display a lot nicer. In the following script, I'm using a wildcard to select these properties from the object:

```
PS C:\> Get-CIMInstance win32_operatingsystem |select *inGB
```

The following screenshot shows the result:

```
TotalMemoryInGB FreeMemoryInGB
--------------- --------------
           3.79           1.06
```

A general purpose function to get memory statistics for a set of servers is as follows:

```
function get-ComputerMemory{
[CmdletBinding()]
Param([Parameter(ValueFromPipeline=$true,
  ValueFromPipelineByPropertyName=$true)]
      [Alias('CN','MachineName')]
      [string[]]$computerName=$env:ComputerName)
    process {
        Get-CIMInstance Win32_OperatingSystem
          -ComputerName $computerName |
            select PSComputerName,@{N='TotalMemoryInGB';
  E={[math]::Round($_.TotalVisibleMemorySize/1MB,2)}},
          @{N='FreeMemoryInGB';
  E={[math]::Round($_.FreePhysicalMemory/1MB,2)}}
    }
}
```

Here, I added the property conversions to gigabytes using expressions rather than adjusting the type data.

To find the total disk space and free disk space we need to use the Win32_LogicalDisk class. Fixed disks have DriveType of 3. The following command line is used to find the disk space:

```
PS C:\ > get-CimInstance win32_logicaldisk -filter 'DriveType=3' |
   select DeviceID,Size,FreeSpace
```

Looking at the disks on my laptop shows the following results:

DeviceID	Size	FreeSpace
C:	125027500032	6430572544
D:	354107752448	78328864768

A function to find this information for a group of computers is similar to the function to find memory statistics, as follows:

```
function get-DiskSpace{
[CmdletBinding()]
Param([Parameter(ValueFromPipeline=$true,ValueFromPipelineByPropertyN
ame=$true)]
      [Alias('CN','MachineName')]
      [string[]]$computerName=$env:ComputerName)
    process {
       get-CIMInstance Win32_LogicalDisk -filter 'DriveType=3'
-ComputerName $computerName |
          select PSComputerName,DeviceID,@{N='SizeInGB';
             E={[math]::Round($_.Size/1GB,2)}},
               @{N='FreeSpaceInGB';E={[math]::
                 Round($_.Freespace/1GB,2)}}
    }
}
```

The results of this function will look like this:

PSComputerName	DeviceID	SizeInGB	FreeSpaceInGB
KYNDIG	C:	116.44	5.99
KYNDIG	D:	329.79	72.95

Validating network connectivity

In a perfect world, every computer system would be able to connect to any other computer system that it needed to. In the real world, there are often complications that arise due to firewalls and IPSec rules. Making sure that all of the needed network connectivity is in place will help to eliminate a common source of script failure.

Using telnet

You may be familiar with using telnet to test TCP connections. To do this, you need to have telnet installed (it's not installed by default on recent server editions). Once you have it installed, you simply run `telnet` hostname port, where you replace the hostname and port with the appropriate values for your test. To see whether the box you're on can connect to DBSERVER01 on port 1433 (the default SQL Server port), run `telnet DBSERVER01 1433`. Since the port being tested is not necessarily a telnet server, the output isn't always clear, but in general, when a connection is successful, the screen is cleared. A failed connection will give an error message, as shown in the following screenshot:

```
C:\Users\Mike>telnet localhost 1500
Connecting To localhost...Could not open connection to the host, on port 1500: C
onnect failed
```

For one-off checking, telnet is pretty convenient. The main issue is that you'll need to have the telnet client installed on every machine you'll be testing. Since you probably don't need telnet otherwise, this can be a problem. This solution involves logging in to each machine and testing each port individually, so it doesn't work well for larger applications.

Before proceeding further, it is probably worth mentioning that there are products designed primarily to test network connectivity, such as nmap or netcat. If you have one of these at your disposal, or if you can get it approved by your IT team, these will save you some time and effort. If you would like to implement something of this nature using PowerShell, however, this section is for you.

Using Test-NetConnection

An alternative to telnet was introduced in Windows 8.1 and Server 2012 R2 with the `Test-NetConnection` cmdlet. On these versions of the operating system, the `Test-NetConnection` cmdlet can be used to test TCP communication on a port similar to how the telnet client does. The earlier test would be done with `Test-Netconnection`, as shown in the following script:

```
Test-NetConnection –computerName DBSERVER01 –port 1433
```

This will return a detailed report about the availability of the connection. To get a true/false result, append `-InformationLevel Quiet`. This is another convenient solution, but it does require a specific operating system to be useful. Also, this requires logging in to each machine in the environment, which might not be very practical.

Writing Test-NetConnection in downstream versions

Since we can't depend on `Test-NetConnection` being available everywhere, we can write our own using .Net classes. The crucial class we will use is the [`System.Net.Sockets.TCPClient`] class. Here is a somewhat flexible implementation:

```
function test-TCPConnection{
[CmdletBinding()]
Param([Parameter(ValueFromPipelineByPropertyName=$true)]
     [string]$computerName,
     [Parameter(ValueFromPipelineByPropertyName=$true)]
     [int]$port,
     [switch]$quiet)
process{
    try {
        $client=New-Object System.Net.Sockets.TCPClient
        $client.Connect($computerName,$port)
    $result=$true
    } catch {
      $result=$false
    } finally {
      $client.Close()
    }
    if($quiet){
  $result
    } else {
```

```
        New-Object PSObject -property @{
ComputerName=$ComputerName;
        Port=$port;
        Connected=$result}
        }
    }
}
```

There are several ways to use this function. The first and most straightforward way is to simply test a single connection via the `ComputerName` and `port` parameters, as shown in the following script:

```
Test-TCPConnection -computername DBServer01 -port 1433
```

This will return an object with the computer name, port, and the protocol (TCP) as well as a Boolean property called `connected` that indicates the success of the connection. If you just need a Boolean value for a test, like in an `if` statement, you can supply the `-quiet` switch:

```
Test-TCPConnection -computername DBServer01 -port 1433 -quiet
```

By including the `ValueFromPipelineByPropertyName` parameter attribute on both parameters, we can also easily consume input from a **comma-separated value (CSV)** file. For instance, if we have a CSV file called `Network.csv` with the following contents:

```
ComputerName,Port
DBServer01,1433
SMTPServer01,25
FTPServer01,22
```

We can then execute the following script:

```
Import-csv Networkcsv | test-TCPConnection
```

This will output a list of objects reporting the details of our connectivity. Note that we did not include the `ValueFromPipeline` attribute for either of the parameters because only one parameter at a time can receive pipeline input from an object, rather than from a property, and we really need the computer name / port pair for the parameter to make sense.

Testing UDP and ICMP connectivity

Network connectivity is not limited to TCP though. An almost identical function can be written to test for UDP connectivity, as follows:

```
function test-UDPConnection{
[CmdletBinding()]
Param([Parameter(ValueFromPipelineByPropertyName=$true)]
      [string]$computerName,
      [Parameter(ValueFromPipelineByPropertyName=$true)]
      [int]$port,
      [switch]$quiet)
process{
      try {
          $client=New-Object System.Net.Sockets.UDPClient
          $client.Connect($computerName,$port)
          $result=$true
      } catch {
      $result=$false
      } finally {
      $client.Close()
      }
      if($quiet){
      $result
      } else {
        new-object PSObject -property @{ComputerName=$ComputerName;
          Port=$port;
          Connected=$result}
      }
   }
}
```

A final kind of connectivity is ICMP or ping. There is a built-in cmdlet called `Test-Connection` introduced in PowerShell Version 2.0. We can write a wrapper function so the signatures of our connectivity-testing functions will match. Note that ICMP is not port-based, so the port parameter will be ignored. The following code snippet explains this:

```
function test-ICMPConnection{
[CmdletBinding()]
Param([Parameter(ValueFromPipelineByPropertyName=$true)]
      [string]$computerName,
      [Parameter(ValueFromPipelineByPropertyName=$true)]
      [switch]$quiet)
```

```
process{
    try {
    $result=test-connection -computerName $computerName -quiet
    } catch {
    $result=$false
    }
    if($quiet){
    $result
    } else {
      new-object PSObject -property @{ComputerName=$ComputerName;
        Port=-1;    #ICMP doesn't use a port
        Protocol='ICMP';
        Connected=$result}
    }
  }
}
}
```

Having function signatures that match will be helpful when we need to be able to test different connectivity types with the same code in a later section.

Validating connectivity prior to implementation

The previous functions work fine if the software being connected to has already been implemented. But how can you check whether a computer can connect to an SQL Server, for example, if SQL Server hasn't been installed yet? To handle this scenario, we can write a script that listens on the appropriate port and run that on the server we're trying to connect to. Since we don't want to accidentally leave a process listening on a port that a piece of software will eventually try to use, we can build in a timeout so that the listener will stop after a preset time interval. The following code snippet demonstrates this:

```
function Start-TCPListener{
param([System.Net.IPAddress]$IPAddress=[System.Net.IPAddress]
  '0.0.0.0',[int]$port,[int]$timeout=10)
    try {

        $listener = new-object
          System.Net.Sockets.TcpListener($IPAddress, $port)
        $listeningTimeout=(get-date).AddSeconds($timeout)
        $listener.Start()
        while ((get-date) -lt $listeningTimeout
          -and !$listener.Pending() ){
```

```
                        start-sleep -Milliseconds 50
        }
        if ($listener.Pending()){
          $client = $listener.AcceptTcpClient()
          Write-Output "Connected from
            $($client.Client.RemoteEndPoint)"
        } else {
          Write-Output "listener timed out after $timeout seconds"
        }
        $listener.Stop()
    } catch {
      write-Error "unable to start listener : $($_.Message)"
    }
}
```

Here, we're not interested in pipeline input because we're only going to start a single listener at a time that will block until it receives a request or the time-out is reached. By doing this, we can simulate the connectivity of the software that is going to be installed. To use this function in conjunction with the test-TCPConnection function from the previous section, follow these steps:

1. Open a PowerShell session on the listening computer
2. Open a PowerShell session on the calling computer
3. Run the Start-TCPListener function on the listening computer
4. Run the Test-TCPConnection function on the calling computer

With PowerShell remoting, you can open the sessions in remote PowerShell tabs in ISE and you do not have to use remote desktop to make this work.

Putting it all together

The previous sections showed how to check ports in a one-at-a-time way, and to check a number of remote connections from a single box as well as starting a TCP listener in case a piece of software hasn't been installed yet. Unfortunately, in anything but a simple system, the process of checking every kind of connectivity between every computer is going to be a very time-consuming process. Also, due to the number of combinations, it is going to be fraught with human error. To overcome these challenges, we can turn to PowerShell remoting and automate much of the process.

An assumption we're going to make is that you have a machine that can reliably connect to all of the computers in the environment using PowerShell remoting. With that in place, let's expand the input file we used for our TCPListener function to include a source computer, a protocol, and a flag to say whether we need to start a listener. Our sample input file might look like this:

```
Source,Destination,Port,Protocol,StartListener
Web01,DBServer01,1433,TCP,Y
Web02,DBServer02,1433,TCP,Y
Web01,SMTPServer01,25,TCP,N
Web01,NTPServer01,123,UDP,N
```

The function to test the ports would look something like this:

```
function Test-EnvironmentConnectivity{
Param([string]$path, [PSCredential]$Cred)

    $tests=import-csv $path
    if($Cred){
        $CredParam=@{Credential=$Cred}
    } else {
        $CredParam=@{}
    }
    $listeners=@{TCP=${function:start-tcpListener}}
    $testFunctions=@{TCP=${function:test-tcpConnection};
                     UDP=${function:test-udpConnection};
                     ICMP=${function:test-icmpConnection}}
    foreach($test in $tests){
        if($test.Startlistener -eq 'Y'){
            if(($listeners.ContainsKey($test.Protocol))){
                write-verbose "Starting $($test.Protocol)
                    listener on $($test.Destination)"
                $listenerjob=invoke-command -ScriptBlock
                    $listeners[$test.Protocol] -argumentList
                    $test.Port -ComputerName $test.Destination
                    @CredParam -AsJob
            }
        }
        try {
            $result=invoke-command -ScriptBlock
                $testFunctions[$test.Protocol] -ComputerName
                $test.Source -ArgumentList
                $test.Destination,$test.Port @CredParam
            if($result){
```

```
            write-output ("{0} connection from {1} to {2} on
               port {3} succeeded" -f
               $test.Protocol,$test.Source,
               $test.Destination,$test.Port)
         } else {
            write-output ("{0} connection from {1} to {2} on
               port {3} failed" -f
               $test.Protocol,$test.Source,
               $test.Destination,$test.Port)
         }
      } catch {
         write-output  ("{0} connection from {1} to {2}
            on port {3} failed" -f
            $test.Protocol,$test.Source,
            $test.Destination,$test.Port)
      } finally {
         if($test.StartListener -eq 'Y'){
            remove-job -job $listenerJob -Force
         }
      }
   }
}
```

Here's a sample input file with representative output:

```
Source,Destination,Port,Protocol,StartListener
Web01,DBServer01,1433,TCP,Y
Web02,DBServer02,1433,TCP,Y
Web01,SMTPServer01,25,TCP,N
Web01,FTPServer01,22,TCP,N
APP01,UDPServer,500,UDP,N
```

The following screenshot shows the corresponding output:

```
TCP connection from Web01to DBServer01 on port 1433 succeeded
VERBOSE: Starting TCP listener on DBServer01
TCP connection from Web02 to DBServer02 on port 5000 succeeded
TCP connection from Web01to SMTPServer01 on port 25 succeeded
TCP connection from Web01to FTPServer01on port 22 succeeded
UDP connection from APP01 to UDPServer on port 500 succeeded
```

When running this function, you will probably want to inform your network security group about your activities. Otherwise, they might think you're performing a port-scanning attack on the network.

Further reading

The following references will help you get more information on the topics covered in this chapter:

- Enabling telnet at `http://social.technet.microsoft.com/wiki/contents/articles/910.windows-7-enabling-telnet-client.aspx`
- `get-help get-CIMInstance`
- `get-help about_WMI`
- `get-help about_WMI_Cmdlets`
- `get-help get-WMIObject`
- `get-help get-service`
- `get-help Update-TypeData`
- `get-help about_Types.ps1xml`
- `NetCat and NMAP- http://nmap.org/`
- `get-help Test-NetConnection`
- `get-help New-Object`

Summary

This chapter focused on the environment that the script runs in, namely the operating system installed on the servers, the hardware of the servers, and the network connectivity between the servers. Making sure that all of these are accounted for will make your PowerShell troubleshooting much easier, as an unexpected result in one of these areas might make your script fail.

The next chapter will cover traditional troubleshooting techniques, including debugging scripts both at the command line and in the ISE, using risk-mitigation parameters, and other techniques that are unique to PowerShell.

7
Reactive Practices – Traditional Debugging

So far, we have focused on making the code easier to troubleshoot. This chapter will introduce the techniques used to troubleshoot the code while it's running. We will see that the investment we've put into the proper design and implementation of our code will make the job of troubleshooting much easier. The specific techniques that we will cover in this chapter are as follows:

- Reading error messages
- Using `Set-PSDebug`
- Debugging in the ISE (or other integrated environment)
- Debugging in the console
- Event logs
- The PSDiagnostics module
- Using `-confirm` and `-whatif`
- Reducing input size
- Using `Tee-Object`
- Replacing the `foreach` loop with the `foreach-object` cmdlet

Reading error messages

This section shouldn't be necessary for people who are serious about writing scripts, but in my experience it involves one of the simplest techniques of troubleshooting and, unfortunately, one of the techniques that is often overlooked. We have talked about how to handle errors using try / catch / finally, and about the difference between terminating and non-terminating errors, but we haven't spent any time talking about error messages themselves. The simple practice of carefully reading the error messages that occur can help to pinpoint not only the problem, but also where the problem occurred in the code. While that information isn't unique to error messages in PowerShell, I have seen countless occasions where it is overlooked.

The color problem

My personal opinion is that the default color scheme in the console and the ISE is part of the reason. Due to the default color scheme, errors in PowerShell look somewhat jarring and cause me, at least, to try to skip over them. If you're not familiar with this phenomenon, the following screenshot shows some example errors in the default schemes, first from the console:

The error-display interface in the ISE isn't very good in my opinion, as is shown in the following screenshot:

The red text on the dark blue background is hard to read (for me) and I know I have often received bug reports of some red text rather than a useful cut-and-paste of the error message. As a color-blind person, I don't tend to give advice on changing the colors in a program. In this case, though, I always recommend that the foreground and background color for error messages be changed.

Changing console colors

The configuration of the PowerShell console colors is done through the Get-Host cmdlet. This cmdlet returns an InternalHost object that has a property called PrivateData. The PrivateData property, in turn, has properties that describe the foreground and background colors used to display different items in the console. The list of colors is shown in the following screenshot:

Note the red foreground and black background for errors. To change these, simply set these properties to a more reasonable value. For instance, the following screenshot illustrates a red background and white foreground error display:

Now, the error messages in the console still show red, but they are much more readable.

Changing ISE colors

The process of changing the colors in the ISE is similar to changing the console colors, but it uses different objects. The ISE exposes its object model through the `$PsISE` variable, which lets us work with several different components in the ISE, as shown in the following screenshot:

```
PS C:\Users\Mike> $PSISE


CurrentPowerShellTab          : Microsoft.PowerShell.Host.ISE.PowerShellTab
CurrentFile                   : Microsoft.PowerShell.Host.ISE.ISEFile
CurrentVisibleHorizontalTool  :
CurrentVisibleVerticalTool    :
Options                       : Microsoft.PowerShell.Host.ISE.ISEOptions
PowerShellTabs                : {PowerShell 1}
```

For our purposes, we will use the `Options` property, which again shows a lot of potential places to customize the ISE:

```
PS C:\Users\Mike> $psISE.Options


SelectedScriptPaneState          : Top
ShowDefaultSnippets              : True
ShowToolBar                      : True
ShowOutlining                    : True
ShowLineNumbers                  : True
TokenColors                      : {[Attribute, #FF00BFFF], [Command, #FF0000FF], [Commar
ConsoleTokenColors               : {[Attribute, #FF00BFFF], [Command, #FF0000FF], [Commar
XmlTokenColors                   : {[Comment, #FF006400], [CommentDelimiter, #FF008000],
DefaultOptions                   : Microsoft.PowerShell.Host.ISE.ISEOptions
FontSize                         : 9
Zoom                             : 100
FontName                         : Lucida Console
ErrorForegroundColor             : #FFE50000
ErrorBackgroundColor             : #00FFFFFF
WarningForegroundColor           : #FFB26200
WarningBackgroundColor           : #00FFFFFF
VerboseForegroundColor           : #FF007F7F
VerboseBackgroundColor           : #00FFFFFF
DebugForegroundColor             : #FF007F7F
DebugBackgroundColor             : #00FFFFFF
ConsolePaneBackgroundColor       : #FFEAEAEA
ConsolePaneTextBackgroundColor   : #FFEAEAEA
ConsolePaneForegroundColor       : #FF626262
ScriptPaneBackgroundColor        : #FFFFFFFF
ScriptPaneForegroundColor        : #FF000000
ShowWarningForDuplicateFiles     : True
ShowWarningBeforeSavingOnRun     : False
```

The `ErrorForegroundColor` and `ErrorBackgroundColor` properties are clearly the properties that control the appearance of errors, so let's set them first and see what effect they have:

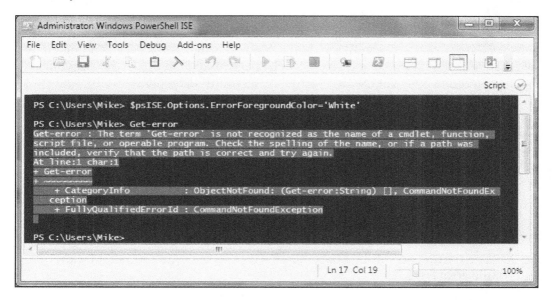

Remember that these changes will need to be made in each session. One way to make this happen all the time is to place them in a *profile*.

PowerShell profiles

Profiles are scripts that are run when a PowerShell session is started. Each PowerShell host has four possible profiles. The value of the $profile variable shows one of these. Note that just because $profile has a value, it doesn't mean that the file exists. The following screenshot shows the profile:

```
PS C:\Users\Mike> $profile
C:\Users\Mike\Documents\WindowsPowerShell\Microsoft.PowerShellISE_profile.ps1
```

To find the other three locations, we need to look at properties that have been added to the $profile variable. Since the property names all include the word Host, they are easy to isolate, as shown in the following screenshot:

```
PS C:\Users\Mike> $profile| select-object *Host* | format-list

AllUsersAllHosts        : C:\Windows\System32\WindowsPowerShell\v1.0\profile.ps1
AllUsersCurrentHost     : C:\Windows\System32\WindowsPowerShell\v1.0\Microsoft.PowerShellISE_profile.ps1
CurrentUserAllHosts     : C:\Users\Mike\Documents\WindowsPowerShell\profile.ps1
CurrentUserCurrentHost  : C:\Users\Mike\Documents\WindowsPowerShell\Microsoft.PowerShellISE_profile.ps1
```

The two AllHosts values point to scripts that will run no matter what host is running. The CurrentHost values point to profile scripts that are specific to the current host. Note that you can see PowerShellISE in the path of the output, so these will only run in the ISE. Since the code to change colors is different between the console and the ISE, either of the CurrentHost profiles would be an appropriate choice. Depending on whether you wanted the customizations to be present for all users, or just for yourself, would determine which of the two CurrentHost profiles you used.

Error message content

The content of the error messages is not particularly surprising. It contains the following items:

- The command (cmdlet, function, or script) where the error occurs
- The text of the error message
- The location of the error (line and column)
- The source code of the line where the error occurs (underlined to show the error)
- The category and full type name of the error

Although all of this information is expected, it is completely wasted if you don't read it. Reading it doesn't help, either, unless you look at the code where the error is and the error message itself to try to determine what is causing the problem. For instance, a common error message is that a property being referenced doesn't exist on the object in question. There are several reasons that might lead to that particular error, and some are listed as follows:

- Misspelling the name of the property
- Misspelling the name of the variable that has the property
- Using the wrong variable
- The variable isn't the expected type

Spending the time to analyze the error, and probably eliminating most of them, is definitely worth the effort. In this case, the first three should be simple to validate (for example, check the spelling and match the variable name). The fourth is a little trickier to determine. If you recall from *Chapter 1*, *PowerShell Primer*, the Get-Member cmdlet outputs the types of the objects that are piped to it, so it is often the first cmdlet that we turn to. Our attempt would look something like what is shown in the following screenshot:

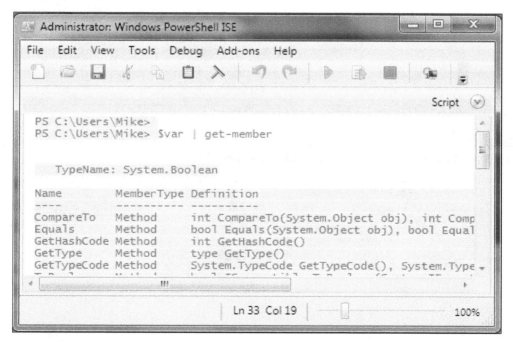

With this information in hand, we proceed with the information that our variable holds a Boolean value. The problem is that we're misusing Get-Member here. The purpose of Get-Member is to list the members of the distinct types of objects that it receives from the pipeline or the -InputObject parameter. By using the pipeline we have obscured the value of the variable. Using the -InputObject parameter gives us a different answer altogether, as shown in the following screenshot:

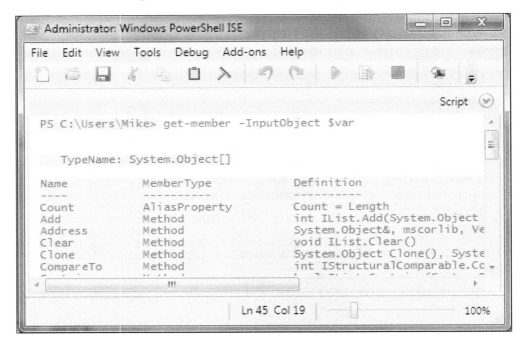

Here, we see that the variable actually contains an array of objects. We can see this as well by calling the GetType() method of the variable:

```
PS C:\Users\mike> $var.GetType()

IsPublic IsSerial Name                                     BaseType
-------- -------- ----                                     --------
True     True     Object[]                                 System.Array
```

To see the individual objects, we can check the count and index the items separately. What we will find is that $var is an array of a $null and $true value, as shown in the following screenshot:

```
PS C:\Users\mike> $var.count
2
PS C:\Users\mike> $var[0].gettype()
You cannot call a method on a null-valued expression.
At line:1 char:1
+ $var[0].gettype()
+ ~~~~~~~~~~~~~~~~~~
    + CategoryInfo          : InvalidOperation: (:) [], RuntimeException
    + FullyQualifiedErrorId : InvokeMethodOnNull

PS C:\Users\mike> $var[0] -eq $null
True
PS C:\Users\mike> $var[1]
True
PS C:\Users\mike>
```

The reason this is important is that when you are troubleshooting, knowing the types and values of variables is of the utmost importance. Using the pipeline to provide the input to Get-Member hid the value because the pipeline unrolls arrays and Get-Member saw a $null and a Boolean value. There's no object corresponding to $null, so it wasn't represented in the output. Given that it's possible to accidentally output more objects from a function than intended, this kind of investigation is something that you will probably be doing a lot, especially when the errors don't seem to make sense.

Using Set-PSDebug

We already met the Set-PSDebug cmdlet in *Chapter 5, Proactive PowerShell,* where we learned that the -Strict switch can be used to ensure that references to variables that haven't been assigned will cause an error. In the context of debugging, the Set-PSDebug cmdlet gives a very simple debugging experience at the command line using the -Trace parameter and the -Step switch. Let's use a simple script to illustrate this:

```
foreach ($i in 1..10){
    write-host $i
}
```

While there should be no confusion over what this script will do when executed, watch what happens when we run `Set-PSDebug -Trace 1` and then run the script:

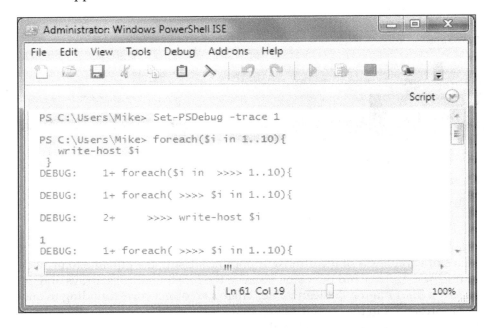

I've truncated the output, but it should be clear that the PowerShell engine is outputting debug messages (like we could with `Write-Debug`) for each line that is executed. The output shown is from the ISE, but the cmdlet works in the console as well, although the formatting is slightly different:

Changing the value of the trace parameter to 2 gives a more detailed result, as shown in the following screenshot:

```
PS C:\Users\Mike> Set-PSDebug -trace 2
DEBUG:     1+  >>>> Set-PSDebug -trace 2

PS C:\Users\Mike>  foreach($i in 1..10){
    write-host $i
}
DEBUG:     1+  foreach($i in  >>>> 1..10){

DEBUG:        ! CALL function '<ScriptBlock>'
DEBUG:        ! SET $foreach = 'IEnumerator'.
DEBUG:     1+  foreach( >>>> $i in 1..10){

DEBUG:        ! SET $i = '1'.
DEBUG:     2+        >>>> write-host $i

1
DEBUG:     1+  foreach( >>>> $i in 1..10){

DEBUG:        ! SET $i = '2'.
DEBUG:     2+        >>>> write-host $i

2
DEBUG:     1+  foreach( >>>> $i in 1..10){

DEBUG:        ! SET $i = '3'.
DEBUG:     2+        >>>> write-host $i
```

Now we see the (implied) assignment to the $i loop variable, as well as some bookkeeping done by PowerShell with the $foreach variable. Function calls, and calls to scripts, would also be called out by this trace level.

The final option with Set-PSDebug is the -Step switch. This switch causes the execution of code to be interrupted. Here, I've run the code with the -Step switch and clicked on the **Yes** button one time:

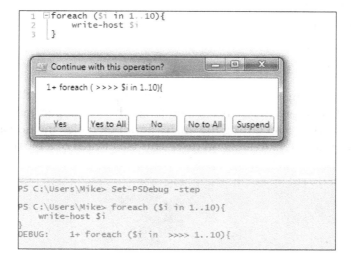

An interesting option with -Step is the ability to suspend. By suspending, a nested shell is started. Nested shells are essentially a new PowerShell instance running inside the current instance. You have access to all of the variables and functions from the outer shell and can investigate or modify the state of the system including changing variable values, importing modules, or whatever you wish. Once you are done, the exit keyword causes the nested shell to end and you are back at the Set-PSDebug prompt at the same line of code that you suspended. Once the -Trace parameter or -Step switch have been used, the -Off switch causes the Set-PSDebug cmdlet to stop outputting Debug statements and prompting at each line.

The Set-PSDebug cmdlet with the -Trace parameter and -Step switch applies to whatever code is running so you can't use them to set breakpoints. On the other hand, there is no reason that the Set-PSDebug cmdlet can't be included in a script. Setting the trace level to 1 or 2 before a critical section of code, and turning it off with the -Off switch, would allow you to get this level of debugging information for that section of code without needing to manually step through all of the code up until that point.

Debugging in the console

The Set-PSDebug cmdlet gives a good amount of detail, but getting to a particular point in the code requires you to add Set-PSDebug statements in the code (which you might not be able to do) or step through all of the code up until that point. Fortunately, there is another set of cmdlets that allows interactive debugging, the PSBreakPoint cmdlets:

- Set-PSBreakPoint
- Remove-PSBreakPoint
- Get-PSBreakPoint
- Enable-PSBreakPoint
- Disable-PSBreakPoint

With Set-PSBreakpoint, it is easy to create a breakpoint to cause the execution to be suspended when a certain line is reached using the -Line parameter. One caveat is that the parameter sets including the -Line parameter, also include a mandatory script parameter that refers to a file on disk. This isn't much of a barrier in the console since we would generally be working with a script file.

Here's another sample script:

```
Write-Host "Script starting"
Foreach ($i in 1..10){
    Write-Host $i
    Write-Host "Inside the loop"
}
```

With that script in `.\`, issuing `Set-PSBreakPoint -Line 4 -Script .\Set-PSBreakPointExample1.ps1` will cause the execution to stop if line 4 is reached. Note that the `Set-PSBreakPoint` cmdlet outputs an object that we could store if we needed to refer to it later, as shown in the following screenshot:

```
PS >Set-PSBreakpoint -line 4 -script .\set-psbreakpointExample1.ps1

ID Script                          Line Command Variable Action
-- ------                          ---- ------- -------- ------
 2 set-psbreakpointExample1.ps1      4
```

When we execute the code, it stops at the specified line, as shown in the following screenshot:

```
PS C:\temp> .\set-psbreakpointExample1.ps1
Script starting
1
Hit Line breakpoint on 'C:\temp\set-psbreakpointExample1.ps1:4'
[DBG]: PS C:\temp>>
```

Then, when a breakpoint is encountered, a nested shell is created exactly like what is used with `Set-PSDebug -Step` when the `Suspend` option is chosen. If we use the `Get-PSBreakPoint` cmdlet to see what breakpoints exist, and use `Format-List *` to show us all of the properties, we can see that there's a `HitCount` property on the breakpoint object that tells us how many times the breakpoint has been hit. The prompt also changes to indicate that you are now in debug mode. There are several commands you can enter at the prompt to control the debugging, as shown in the following table:

Command	Action
S, stepInto	Step to the next statement
V, stepOver	Step to the next statement in this scope (that is, don't step into function calls)
O, stepOut	Step out of the current function or script
C, Continue	Continue executing the script or function

Command	Action
K, Get-PSCallstack	Display the current call stack
L, List	Show the source code for the current script or function
Q, quit	Exit the debugger
<enter>	Repeat the last command
?, h	Display a list of possible commands

Troubleshooting tip

If you have customized your prompt function (that is, redefined it), you won't get an indication that you're in debug mode in the prompt. You will still get a message indicating that you're in debug mode.

There is a -Column parameter that can be used in conjunction with the -Line parameter to indicate that the breakpoint is only active if the execution hits the code in a particular column. This can be useful if code includes long pipelines.

Troubleshooting Tip

If your code is formatted so that each segment of a pipeline is on a separate code line, the -Column parameter is not needed.

A second way to use Set-PSBreakpoint is to cause the execution to be stopped when a variable is accessed. Since the focus with a variable breakpoint is not on a line of code, a script file is not required. The -variable parameter takes a list of variable names (without $) to be watched. The -Mode parameter allows us to specify what kind of variable activity triggers the breakpoint. The possible values are Read, Write (the default), and ReadWrite. With this example code, let's see what a variable breakpoint shows us:

```
write-host "Script starting"
foreach ($i in 1..10){
    write-host $i
    write-host "Inside the loop"
}
```

The execution is suspended as soon as the variable is referenced, as shown in the following screenshot:

```
PS C:\Users\mike> Set-PSBreakpoint -Variable i

  ID Script                          Line Command                  Variable
  -- ------                          ---- -------                  --------
   0      █                                                        i

PS C:\Users\mike> write-host "Script starting"
Script starting
PS C:\Users\mike> foreach ($i in 1..10){
>>      write-host $i
>>      write-host "Inside the loop"
>> }
>>
Entering debug mode. Use h or ? for help.

Hit Variable breakpoint on '$i' (Write access)

At line:1 char:10
+ foreach ($i in 1..10){
+         ~~
[DBG]: PS C:\Users\mike>> _
```

Setting a breakpoint on a variable can be very useful in troubleshooting, especially if a variable ends up with an unexpected value. A final way to set a breakpoint instructs the engine to stop when a particular command (function or cmdlet) is executed. This could be useful if you wanted to know where a built-in or binary cmdlet was being called. Since you wouldn't have the source code, a line-level breakpoint would not be possible. For example, if you knew that Get-CIMInstance was referenced at several points in a script, but didn't know which one was being called, you could issue the following command:

```
Set-PSBreakPoint -command get-CIMInstance
```

Then, when the script runs, anytime the `get-CIMInstance` cmdlet is invoked the script execution will stop at that point. Here are the results of that breakpoint using the `Get-DiskSpace` function we wrote in *Chapter 6, Preparing the Scripting Environment*:

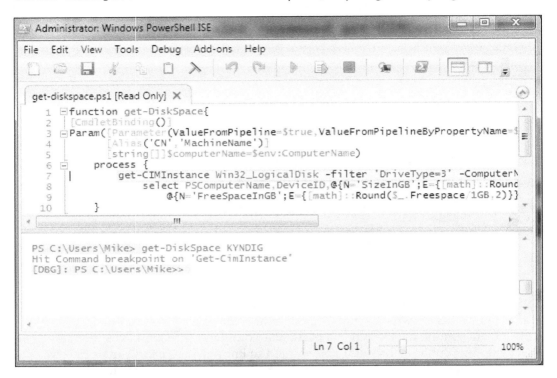

At this point, we could use the debug mode options to display the source code around where the breakpoint was set using the `List` or `L` command:

```
PS C:\Users\Mike> get-invalidVerbfunction SQLPS
Hit Line breakpoint on 'C:\Users\Mike\SkyDrive\Documents\PowerShellTroubleshooting\Chapte
[DBG]: PS C:\Users\Mike>> L

    3:  if(get-module $module){
    4:      remove-module $module -force
    5:  }
    6:  import-module $module -force -Verbose *>&1 |
    7:      select-string "The '(.*)' command in the (.*)' module .*" |
    8:*     where-object {$_.Matches.Groups[2].Value -eq $module} |
    9:      foreach-object { $_.matches.groups[1].Value}
   10:
   11:  }
   12:
```

To summarize, there are four different types of breakpoints that can be set using the `Set-PSBreakPoint` cmdlet:

- Line breakpoints (with the `-line` parameter)
- Column breakpoints (with the `-line` and `-column` parameters)
- Variable breakpoints (with the `-variable` parameter)
- Command breakpoints (with the `-command` parameter)

Debugging in the ISE

We've already discussed the use of `Set-PSDebug` in the ISE, so we know that we can use the `-Trace` and `-Step` parameters to get extra output and control options as the script runs in the ISE. As simple as using `Set-PSDebug` is, debugging in the ISE using the GUI is probably used more often than in the console. This is due to the simple point-and-click operation of the ISE. As in most development environments, a breakpoint can be set on a line of code by right-clicking on a line and selecting **Toggle Breakpoint** from the context menu:

Cut	Ctrl+X
Copy	Ctrl+C
Paste	Ctrl+V
Start Intellisense	Ctrl+Space
Start Snippets	Ctrl+J
Run Selection	F8
Toggle Breakpoint	F9

When a breakpoint has been set, the line will be highlighted in red, as shown in the following screenshot:

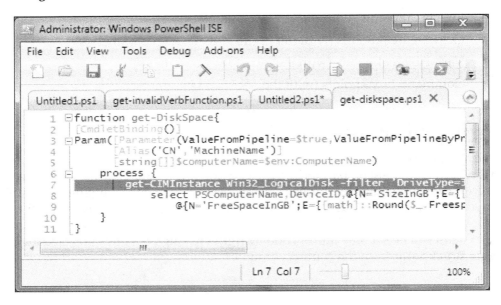

When a breakpoint is reached in the ISE, the script containing the breakpoint is loaded in the ISE if it isn't already loaded, and the cursor is placed at the position of the breakpoint. The current line is highlighted yellow, as shown in the following screenshot:

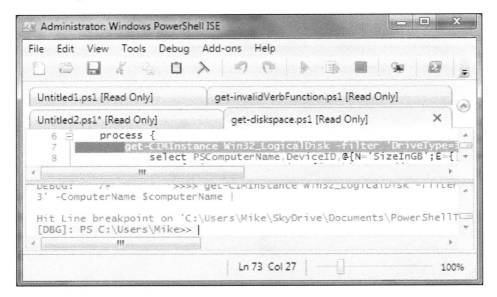

Once a breakpoint has been reached, the ISE has some additional features to help guide the debugging session. First, the **Step Into** (*F11*) command in the **Debug** menu will execute the current statement. If the current statement is a function call, execution will step into the function. Using the **Step Over** (*F10*) command, the next statement is also executed, but if it is a function call it will be considered a single statement and will not step into the function. Finally, the **Run/Continue** (*F5*) command will cause the execution to continue from the current line without breaking (until a breakpoint is reached, of course), and the **Stop Debugger** (*Shift +*
F5) command will halt the execution of the current script. The following screenshot shows the list of features in the **Debug** menu:

Debug	Add-ons	Help	
	Step Over	F10
	Step Into	F11
	Step Out	Shift+F11
	Run/Continue	F5
	Stop Debugger	Shift+F5
	Toggle Breakpoint	F9
	Remove All Breakpoints	Ctrl+Shift+F9
	Enable All Breakpoints	
	Disable All Breakpoints	
	List Breakpoints	Ctrl+Shift+L
	Display Call Stack	Ctrl+Shift+D

Event logs

If you've ever spent time troubleshooting a Windows system, you have probably dealt with event logs. Windows writes the details of several kinds of activities into two different kinds of logs. The first is called *classic* because this type of log has been present since the early days of Windows. The classic logs called **Application**, **Security**, **Setup**, and **System** are found on all systems. There can also be a classic log called **Forwarded Events** if you have subscribed to events from a remote computer. There may be other classic logs present on your system depending on what software, roles, and features you have installed.

The following screenshot shows the features of the classic log:

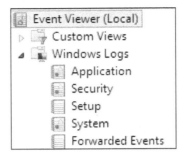

The newer type of event logs are an XML-based system introduced in Windows Vista and have the (not very helpful) name of Windows Event Log technology. We will call them WEL for short since Windows Event Log sounds like it could refer to either type of log. These WEL event logs are listed in a section called **Applications and Services Logs**. Each WEL log can have a subtype of a log called **Admin**, **Operational**, **Analytic**, and **Debug**. Here is a view of **Event Viewer** displaying a few of the hundreds of WEL logs on a computer:

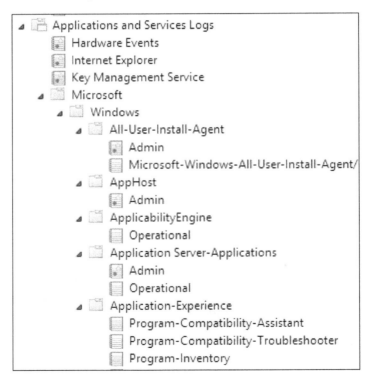

Listing event logs

PowerShell Version 1.0 only included cmdlet support for classic event logs. The Get-EventLog cmdlet includes a -List switch that causes it to list the classic event logs present on a computer. There is also a -ComputerName parameter that allows the cmdlet to target a list of computers. The output of Get-EventLog -list will look similar to this:

```
PS C:\Users\Mike> get-eventlog -List

  Max(K) Retain OverflowAction          Entries Log
  ------ ------ --------------          ------- ---
  20,480      0 OverwriteAsNeeded        36,656 Application
  20,480      0 OverwriteAsNeeded             0 HardwareEvents
     512      7 OverwriteOlder                0 Internet Explorer
  20,480      0 OverwriteAsNeeded             0 Key Management Service
   8,192      0 OverwriteAsNeeded         3,555 Media Center
     128      0 OverwriteAsNeeded           245 OAlerts
  20,480      0 OverwriteAsNeeded        32,853 Security
  20,480      0 OverwriteAsNeeded        62,193 System
     512      7 OverwriteOlder                0 Windows Azure
  15,360      0 OverwriteAsNeeded        18,374 Windows PowerShell
```

PowerShell Version 2.0 introduced the Get-WinEvent cmdlet, which is able to access both classic and WEL logs. It is also capable of reading the files generated by **Event Tracing for Windows** (**ETW**) which can, for instance, be recorded with the Performance Monitor application. The parameter to get the list of logs using Get-WinEvent is called -ListLog, and unlike with Get-EventLog, -ListLog is not a switch. The -ListLog takes an array of strings, so in order to get a complete list of logs on a system with Get-WinEvent, you would issue the Get-WinEvent -listlog * command. On my system, the output starts:

```
PS C:\Users\Mike> get-winevent -ListLog *

LogMode    MaximumSizeInBytes RecordCount LogName
-------    ------------------ ----------- -------
Circular             20971520       36656 Application
Circular             20971520           0 HardwareEvents
Circular              1052672           0 Internet Explorer
Circular             20971520           0 Key Management Service
Circular              8388608        3555 Media Center
Circular              1052672         245 OAlerts
Circular             20971520       32853 Security
Circular             20971520       62193 System
Circular              1052672           0 Windows Azure
Circular             15728640       18374 Windows PowerShell
Circular              1052672             Cisco-EAP-FAST/Debug
Circular              1052672             Cisco-EAP-LEAP/Debug
Circular              1052672             Cisco-EAP-PEAP/Debug
Circular              1052672           0 ConnectionInfo
Circular              1052672             Debug
Circular              1052672           0 Error
Circular             20971520             ForwardedEvents
Circular              1052672             Info
Circular              1052672             Microsoft-IIS-Configuration/Administrative
Circular              1052672             Microsoft-IIS-Configuration/Operational
Circular            104857600        6347 Microsoft-Team Foundation Server/Debug
```

I have truncated the output because it runs for several pages. To see just how many logs are shown, we can use the `Measure-Object` cmdlet, as shown in the following screenshot:

```
PS C:\Users\Mike> get-winevent -ListLog * | measure-object


Count    : 175
Average  :
```

You might also see errors corresponding to logs that don't exist on your system. I get an error on this machine about the `Microsoft-Windows-DxpTaskRingtone/Analytic` log, which does not have a valid path set. For what it's worth, I get an error trying to view the log using **Event Viewer** as well.

Reading event logs

Although both `Get-EventLog` and `Get-WinEvent` allow you to read event logs, `Get-EventLog` can only work with the classic logs. To get entries from a classic log using `Get-EventLog`, you will use the `-LogName` parameter to specify which log to read and you will generally include one or more parameters to narrow down which log messages are required. Some of the more useful filtering parameters for `Get-EventLog` are:

Parameter	Meaning
-Index	The numerical index of the log entry
-EntryType	Includes `Error`, `Information`, `FailureAudit`, `SuccessAudit`, and `Warning`
-Message	Filter by the contents of the message (allows wildcards)
-Source	Include messages written to the log by certain sources
-Before and -After	Filter based on the time the message was written
-Newest	Only retrieve the latest log entries
-UserName	Include messages associated with certain usernames

For instance, to read the most recent five entries in the **Application** event log, you would use the following command:

```
Get-EventLog -LogName Application -newest 5
```

The results are as expected:

```
Index Time              EntryType    Source                  InstanceID Message
----- ----              ---------    ------                  ---------- -------
120332 Oct 23 21:26     Information  gupdate                          0 The des...
120331 Oct 23 21:26     Information  Windows Error Rep...          1001 Fault b...
120330 Oct 23 21:26     Information  Windows Error Rep...          1001 Fault b...
120329 Oct 23 21:26     Information  Windows Error Rep...          1001 Fault b...
120328 Oct 23 18:38     Information  Windows Error Rep...          1001 Fault b...
```

Reading event logs with `Get-WinEvent` uses a `-LogName` parameter to indicate which log we want to look at, but now we have the option of listing more than one event log and are allowed to use wildcards. Given the large number of logs accessible by using `Get-WinEvent`, that flexibility is important. The filtering parameters for `Get-WinEvent` are given as follows:

Parameter	Purpose
`-FilterXPath`	Uses an XPath expression to filter the log entries
`-FilterHashTable`	Uses a hashtable of keys and values to filter the log entries
`-FilterXML`	Uses a structured XML query to filter the log entries
`-MaxEvents`	Limits the number of entries returned
`-Oldest (switch)`	Forces retrieval of oldest entries first instead of the default (newest first)

The first thing to note is that there aren't parameters to filter by specific properties of the entries. One reason for this is the large number of properties exposed by the new log format. The `-FilterXPath`, `-FilterXML`, and `-FilterHashTable` parameters allow us to filter by multiple properties at the same time. The second thing to note is that the `-LogName` parameter is not in the same parameter set as any of these three filtering parameters, so the name of the log will have to be specified in in the hashtable, XPath, or XML query.

For instance, finding the most recent five events in the **System** event log with `EventID` of `6013` (uptime messages) could be achieved with the `-FilterHashTable` parameter using the following command:

```
Get-WinEvent -FilterHashtable @{LogName='System';Id=6013} -MaxEvents 5
```

It is important to realize that there have been some terminology changes between some of the parameter names. For instance, with `Get-EventLog` you can only limit the number of events with the `–Newest` parameter. With `Get-WinEvent`, you can use `–MaxEvents` to find the most recent events, or add the `–Oldest` switch to find the earliest events. Also, some of the parameters for `Get-EventLog` have corresponding entries in the `–FilterHashtable` parameter for `Get-WinEvent` with different names. The following table lists such parameters:

Get-EventLog parameter	Get-WinEvent Hashtable entry
`-Source`	`Provider`
`-EventID`	`InstanceID`

It should be clear that there is quite a difference in using the `Get-EventLog` and `Get-WinEvent` cmdlets. Deciding which to use in a given situation can be tricky. Since `Get-EventLog` only works with classic logs, that might be the deciding factor if you need to work with a log that's in the newer WEL format. On the other hand, if you need to work with a classic log, you might find the filtering options provided by `Get-EventLog` to be more convenient. Remembering the filter left principle from *Chapter 3, PowerShell Practices*, the greater range of filtering parameters for `Get-WinEvent` will probably tip the balance if you are querying event logs on multiple machines or reading very large event logs. Whatever your situation, try to do some experiments to see which cmdlet gives you the best balance of performance and ease of use. Only you can decide what the correct choice is.

Writing to event logs

Writing to classic event logs is accomplished via the `Write-Eventlog` cmdlet. Each entry in a classic log has an associated source that is a required item when trying to write an entry. A very simple example using an existing log and source is as follows:

```
Write-EventLog -LogName Application -Source msiInstaller
  -message "hello, world" -EventId 0
```

Here, we've used the `msiInstaller` source and a dummy value of `0` for `EventID`. Event IDs correspond to resources in a `.dll` file, so we have some options for how to proceed:

- Simply use 0 (or some other constant) for all of our messages
- Create a convention that maps values to messages
- Create our own `.dll` file to contain message resources

Since the first two will both show errors in **Event Viewer** as there's not a resource for all of the event IDs we would be using, and the third option is beyond the scope of this book, I will choose to use 0 for all of my entries.

Another issue with this sample is that we used the value of `msiInstaller` even though we are clearly not an installer. We really should use a different source to distinguish our events from any others. Unfortunately, an attempt to do this fails, as shown in the following screenshot:

```
PS C:\Users\Mike> Write-EventLog -LogName Application -Source PoshTrouble -message "hello, world" -EventId 0
Write-EventLog : The source name "PoshTrouble" does not exist on computer "localhost".
At line:1 char:1
```

To overcome this error we need to use the `New-EventLog` cmdlet. The obvious use case for `New-EventLog` is to create a completely new classic event log. It can also be used to add a new source (or sources) to an existing event log, as shown in the following screenshot:

```
PS C:\Users\Mike> new-eventlog -LogName Application -Source PoshTrouble

PS C:\Users\Mike> Write-EventLog -LogName Application -Source PoshTrouble -message "hello, world" -EventId 0
```

Once we've added the new source to the existing event log, the `Write-EventLog` cmdlet is able to use that source. Creating a custom event log with `New-EventLog` uses the same syntax as we used to create the new source. Also, we can add more than one source at the same time, which is convenient, as shown in the following code snippet:

```
New-EventLog -LogName PowerShelTroubleShooting -Source
    Script,Text,Chapters,Images
```

Note that the event log won't show up in the results of `Get-EventLog`, `Get-WinEvent`, or in **Event Viewer** until an entry has been written to the log.

The PSDiagnostics module

PowerShell Version 2.0 is shipped with a new module called PSDiagnostics, which has some interesting capabilities. One drawback to the PSDiagnostics module is that it contains no documentation of any kind except for a single comment at the beginning of the `.psm1` file, as shown in the following screenshot:

```
<#
    Windows PowerShell Diagnostics Module
    This module contains a set of wrapper scripts that
    enable a user to use ETW tracing in Windows
    PowerShell.
#>
```

ETW provides, among other things, the capability to trace system and application activity and write the triggered events to a logfile. The simplest functions in the module are the `Enable-PSTrace` and `Disable-PSTrace` functions that turn the **Analytic** and **Debug** logs for the Microsoft/Windows/PowerShell log on (or off). Since the functions eventually call the command-line `wevutil.exe` application that requires input, you will want to use the `–Force` switch if you are running the ISE since it doesn't handle console input well. Enabling these logs will clear them if they already exist, so make sure that's what you want to do.

There are similar functions that start and stop a tracing session involving WS-Man (`Enable-WSManTrace` and `Disable-WSManTrace`) or that involve both WS-Man and PowerShell (`Enable-PSWSManCombinedTrace` and `Disable-PSWSManCombinedTrace`). Note that the verbs are inconsistent: `Enable-PSTrace` simply enables the logfiles, it does not start a tracing session, but the other two enabling cmdlets start tracing sessions.

WS-Man is the protocol implemented by WinRM and is the basis for the CIM cmdlets. PowerShell remoting is also based on WinRM, so troubleshooting issues involving CIM and remoting will definitely benefit from using the combined trace that is generated by `Enable-PSWSManCombinedTrace`. A thorough walk-through of this functionality can be found at the following links:

- `http://windowsitpro.com/blog/troubleshooting-winrm-and-powershell-remoting-part-1`
- `http://windowsitpro.com/blog/tools-troubleshooting-powershell-remoting-and-winrm-part-2`

Using –confirm and –whatif

We've already covered what the `–confirm` and `–whatif` risk mitigation parameters do. We've also seen how it's not difficult to include support for these parameters in your functions. It is now time to think about how to use them in a troubleshooting session. We will focus on `–whatif`, but the discussion applies to `–confirm` in exactly the same way. Obviously, if you are trying to troubleshoot a single function that includes support for `–whatif`, you can add `–whatif` to be sure that any system changes that the function would have made are skipped, while finding out what those would have been. This ability is incredibly beneficial to testing because we don't need to worry about the negative effects of running the code.

The way that the risk mitigation parameters (as well as the output preference parameters) work is something like the following. If you specify –whatif in a function call, as the function enters scope, the $whatifpreference variable is set to $true. The $PSCmdlet.ShouldProcess function uses the value of this variable to know whether it should output the string representing the task that would have been performed and return $false (skipping the task) or if it should return $true.

Besides calling a function and specifying the –whatif switch, there are a couple of other ways to activate the functionality. First, you can explicitly set the $whatifpreference variable to $true and reset it to its original state after the end of the code you want to be able to avoid running. The following code snippet is an example of –whatif:

```
function update-MyProcess{
[CmdletBinding(SupportsShouldProcess=$true)]
Param()

    # do something "safe"
    # do something "safe"
    write-host "whatif=$whatifpreference"
    $whatifpreference=$true
    write-host "whatif=$whatifpreference"
    # do something I don't want to do at this time
    $whatifpreference=$PSBoundParameters.ContainsKey('Whatif')
    write-host "whatif=$whatifpreference"
}
```

I used the $PSBoundParameters hashtable to check whether –whatif was specified on the command line in order to set the value back. Another approach would be to store the original value in a variable.

A final way to force the whatif functionality is to use the $PSDefaultParameterValues hashtable to set the whatif parameter to $true for the functions where you want –whatif to always be applied. For instance, if you want to be sure never to run the restart-computer cmdlet, you could run this command:

$PSDefaultParameterValues['restart-computer:whatif']=$True

The key to the $PSDefaultParameterValues hashtable is the name of the cmdlet (wildcards are allowed) followed by a colon (:) and the name of the parameter. The value associated with the key will be supplied for the parameter for that function or set of functions if no value is explicitly passed. So it would not keep the Restart-Computer –whatif:$false command from executing, but that kind of thing is not likely to happen.

Reducing input set

It's often easy when debugging, or trying to understand what has happened in a script, to be overwhelmed by the sheer volume of output. One simple strategy to help troubleshoot a script is to reduce the number of objects or input being considered in the script in order to be able to focus more clearly on what is being done.

The first way I do this is to only consider a data point or set of points that I understand really well. So instead of having the script pull in all of the servers from a CSV file, I might use a smaller CSV file or use a different parameter to have it look at a specific server. For instance, consider the following script:

```
function generate-bigreport{
[CmdletBinding()]
Param([Parameter(ValueFromPipeline=$true,
  ValueFromPipelineByPropertyName=$true)]
    [Alias('CN','MachineName')]
    [string[]]$computerName=$env:ComputerName)
  #do lots of interesting and complicated stuff here
}
```

Instead of piping in all of the computers in my active directory, I would run the function with a constant input using a known computer name. For instance, consider the following script:

```
'TESTSRV01' | generate-bigreport
```

By doing this, I have accomplished several things. First of all, I should know exactly what the output will look like. If I don't, data points for a single computer might not be very hard to validate manually. Secondly, the execution of the script will undoubtedly be much quicker than if I had run it against hundreds of computers. Thirdly, if I do need to step through the code in the debugger, I won't have to trace through several iterations to get to the end of the function.

If the issue I'm troubleshooting in a script involves the interaction between data points, you can try using pairs or other sets of known computer names (or whatever kind of input is required). Using a CSV file for these types of input might be natural. For example, the following screenshot shows the contents of TestComputers.csv:

```
TestComputers.csv  X

1   ComputerName,Description
2   WEBSERV01,Public Web Server
3   WEBSERV02,Intranet Web Server
4   SQLSERV01,Department SQL Server
```

With that, we can run the function in the preceding screenshot using the following script:

```
Import-csv .\TestComputers.csv | generate-bigreport
```

If, you are thinking that this is just common sense, remember that some administrators have never done any kind of programming. While this kind of thought process comes naturally to some people, it is generally learned as part of training in programming. Administrators aren't always wired the same way as developers (which is a good thing) and might need a nudge in areas where developers wouldn't necessarily.

If the function gathers its input internally, it might be possible to make slight changes (with the original source checked into source control, right?) in order to shorten the process. As an example, if we had a function called get-computer that returned all of the computers we managed, the code in a function might look like this:

```
function generate-bigreport{
    [Array]$computers=get-computer
    #do lots of interesting and complicated stuff here
}
```

Changing the assignment statement to be a pipeline with some filtering can have the same effect as limiting the input. The following script shows some possible options:

```
[Array]$computers=get-computer | select -first 1    #or 2
[Array]$computers=get-computer | where ComputerName -in
    'TESTSERV01','TESTSERV02'
```

Using select-object -first n on the output of a function is useful at times as well, when the output is lengthy. In this case, we would need to include enough output to be able to tell whether the function seems to be working properly, but not so much that it would not be practical to check each output object.

Using Tee-Object to see intermediate results

Debugging long pipelines can be tricky. While it is possible to split a pipeline over several source lines in order to set a breakpoint on a particular segment of a pipeline, it is often the cumulative results of the pipeline that are important. In cases where the end result is not what is expected, it can be helpful to be able to see what the intermediate results are in the pipeline. For instance, consider the following (incorrect) code to find the largest items in a folder structure:

```
#find largest 5 items in the directory tree
dir -recurse |
  sort-object Length |
  select-object -last 5
```

Since the output is incorrect, we can insert `Tee-Object` commands into the pipeline to save the intermediate results (after `dir` and after `sort`) into variables or files for our convenience. First, let's look at how to get the results into files using the following code:

```
#find largest 5 items in the directory tree
dir -recurse |
  tee-object -FilePath c:\temp\files.txt |
  sort-object Length |
  tee-object -FilePath c:\temp\sortedFiles.txt |
  select-object -last 5
```

The `Tee-Object` cmdlet with the `-FilePath` parameter works in a similar way to `Out-File`, in that it takes all of the objects coming in from the pipeline and outputs them to a text file. However, unlike `Out-File`, it also writes those same objects back to the pipeline for the next pipeline element to process. Saving the output to variables is easy as well, with one step that's important to remember. The following code shows the use of the `Tee-Object` cmdlet:

```
#find largest 5 items in the directory tree
dir -recurse |
  tee-object -Variable Files |
  sort-object Length |
  tee-object -Variable SortedFiles |
  select-object -last 5
```

The thing to remember when specifying variables in `Tee-Object` is that you only want the name of the variable (that is, without the dollar sign ($)). If you include the dollar sign, the objects will be placed in a variable whose name is the value of the variable. If those variables have not been set, the `Tee-Object` cmdlet will fail because the `-Variable` parameter is `$null`. This common error is illustrated in the following screenshot:

```
PS C:\Users\Mike> get-service | tee-object -Variable $ServiceList

Tee-Object : Cannot bind argument to parameter 'Variable' because it is null.
At line:1 char:36
+ get-service | tee-object -Variable $ServiceList
+                                    ~~~~~~~~~~~~~
    + CategoryInfo          : InvalidData: (:) [Tee-Object], ParameterBindingValida
   tionException
    + FullyQualifiedErrorId : ParameterArgumentValidationErrorNullNotAllowed,Micros
   oft.PowerShell.Commands.TeeObjectCommand
```

The correct `-Variable` parameter would be `ServiceList` (without the $), as shown in the following screenshot:

```
[DBG]: PS C:\Users\Mike>> get-service | tee-object -Variable ServiceList

Status   Name                DisplayName
------   ----                -----------
Running  AdobeARMservice     Adobe Acrobat Update Service
Stopped  AdobeFlashPlaye...  Adobe Flash Player Update Service
Stopped  ADSMService         ADSM Service
Running  AeLookupSvc         Application Experience
Running  AFBAgent            AFBAgent
Stopped  ALG                 Application Layer Gateway Service
Running  AppHostSvc          Application Host Helper Service
Stopped  AppIDSvc            Application Identity
Stopped  Appinfo             Application Information
Stopped  aspnet_state        ASP.NET State Service
Running  AudioEndpointBu...  Windows Audio Endpoint Builder
Running  AudioSrv            Windows Audio
```

Replacing the foreach loop with the foreach-object cmdlet

When you write a function to process a file, a typical approach might look like this:

```
function process-file{
param($filename)

    $contents=get-content $filename
    foreach($line in $contents){
        # do something interesting
    }
}
```

This pattern works well for small files, but for really large files this kind of processing will perform very badly and possibly crash with an out of memory exception. For instance, running this function against a 500 MB text file on my laptop took over five seconds despite the fact that the loop doesn't actually do anything. To determine the time it takes to run, we can use the measure-command cmdlet, as shown in the following screenshot:

```
PS D:\temp> measure-command {process-file -filename .\big_file500MB.txt}


Days              : 0
Hours             : 0
Minutes           : 0
Seconds           : 5
Milliseconds      : 692
Ticks             : 56923059
TotalDays         : 6.58831701388889E-05
TotalHours        : 0.00158119608333333
TotalMinutes      : 0.094871765
TotalSeconds      : 5.6923059
TotalMilliseconds : 5692.3059
```

Note that the result is a Timespan object and the TotalSeconds object has the value we are looking for. You might not have any large files handy, so I wrote the following quick function to create large text files that are approximately the size you ask for:

```
function new-bigfile{
param([string]$path,
      [int]$sizeInMB)
    if(test-path $path){
      remove-item $path
    }
    new-item -ItemType File -Path $path | out-null
    $line='A'*78
    $page="$line`r`n"*1280000
    1..($sizeInMB/100) | foreach {$page | out-file $path -Append
      -Encoding ascii}
}
```

The code works by creating a large string using string multiplication, which can be handy in situations like this. It then writes the string to the file the appropriate number of times that are necessary. The files come out pretty close to the requested size if the size is over 100 MB, but they are not exact. Fortunately, we aren't really concerned about the exact size, but rather just that the files are very large.

A better approach would be to utilize the streaming functionality of the pipeline and use the ForEach-Object cmdlet instead of reading the contents into a variable. Since objects are output from Get-Content as they are being read, processing them one at a time allows us to process the file without ever reading it all into memory at one time. An example that is similar to the previous code is this:

```
function process-file2{
param($filename)
    get-content $filename | foreach-object{
        $line=$_
        # do something interesting
    }
}
```

Note that since we're using the ForEach-Object cmdlet instead of the foreach loop we have to use the $_ automatic variable to refer to the current object. By assigning that immediately to a variable, we can use exactly the same code as we would have in the foreach loop example (in place of the #do something interesting comment). In PowerShell Version 4.0, we could use the -PipelineVariable common parameter to simplify this code. As with all parameters where you supply the name of a variable, you don't use the dollar sign:

```
function process-file3{
param($filename)
    get-content $filename -PipelineVariable line | foreach-object{
        # do something interesting
    }
}
```

With either of these constructions, I have been able to process files of any length without any noticeable memory usage. One way to measure memory usage (without simply watching the process monitor) is to use the Get-Process cmdlet to find the current process and report on the WorkingSet64 property. It is important to use the 64-bit version rather than the WorkingSet property or its alias: WS. A function to get the current shell's memory usage looks like this:

```
function get-shellmemory{
    (get-process -id $pid| select -expand WorkingSet64)/1MB
}
new-alias mem get-shellmemory
```

I've included an alias (mem) for this function to make it quicker to call on the command line. I try to avoid using aliases in scripts as a practice because they can make code harder to understand, but for command line use, aliases really are a time-saver. Here's an example of using get-shellmemory via its alias, mem:

```
PS C:\temp> mem;process-file3 D:\temp\big_file500MB.txt;mem
193.90625
197.21875
```

This shows that although the function processed a 500 MB file, it only used a little over 3 MB of memory in doing so. Combining the function to determine memory usage with measure-command gives us a general purpose function to measure time and memory usage:

```
function get-performance{
param([scriptblock]$block);
    $pre_mem=get-shellmemory
    $elapsedTime=measure-command -Expression $block
    $post_mem=get-shellmemory
    write-output "the process took $($elapsedTime.TotalSeconds)
seconds"
    write-output "the process used $($post_mem - $pre_mem) megabytes
of memory"
}
new-alias perf get-performance
```

One thing to note about measuring memory this way is that since the PowerShell host is a .NET process that is garbage-collected, it is possible that a garbage-collection operation has occurred during the time the process is running. If that happens, the process may end up using less memory than it was when it started. Because of this, memory usage statistics are only guidelines, not absolute indicators. Adding an explicit call to the garbage collector to tell it to collect will make it less likely that the memory readings will be unusual, but the situation is in the hands of the .NET framework, not ours.

You will find that the memory used by a particular function will vary quite a bit, but the general performance characteristics are the important thing. In this section, we're concerned about whether the memory usage grows proportionally with the size of the input file. Using the first version of the code that used the foreach loop, the memory use did grow with the size of the input file, which limits the usefulness of that technique.

For reference, a summary of the performance on my computer using the `foreach` loop and the `ForEach-Object` cmdlet is given in the following table:

Input size	Loop time	Loop memory	Cmdlet time	Cmdlet memory
100 MB	1.1s	158 MB	1.5s	1.5 MB
500 MB	6.1s	979 MB	8.7s	12.9 MB
1 GB	38.5s	1987 MB	16.7s	7.4 MB
2 GB	Failed		51.2s	8.6 MB
4 GB	Failed		132s	12.7 MB

While these specific numbers are highly dependent on the specific hardware and software configuration on my computer, the takeaway is that by using the `ForEach-Object` cmdlet you can avoid the high memory usage that is involved in reading large files into memory.

Although the discussion here has been around the `get-content` cmdlet, the same is true about any cmdlet that returns objects in a streaming fashion. For example, `Import-CSV` can have exactly the same performance characteristics as `Get-Content`. The following code is a typical approach to reading CSV files, which works very well for small files:

```
function process-CSVfile{
param($filename)
    $objects=import-CSV $filename
    foreach($object in $objects){
        # do something interesting
    }
}
```

To see the performance, we will need some large CSV files to work with. Here's a simple function that creates CSV files with approximately the right size that will be appropriate to test. Note that the multipliers used in the function were determined using trial and error, but they give a reasonable 10-column CSV file that is close to the requested size:

```
function new-bigCSVfile{
param([string]$path,
      [int]$sizeInMB)
    if(test-path $path){
      remove-item $path
    }
    new-item -ItemType File -Path $path | out-null
    $header="Column1"
```

```
    2..10 | foreach {$header+=",Column$_"}
    $header+="`r`n"
    $header | out-file $path -encoding Ascii
    $page=$header*12500

    1..($sizeInMB) | foreach {$page | out-file $path -
      Append -Encoding ascii}
}
```

Rewriting the `process-CSVfile` function to use the streaming property of the pipeline looks similar to the rewritten `get-content` example, as follows:

```
function process-CSVfile2{
param($filename)
    import-CSV $filename |
        foreach-object -pipelinevariable object{
        # do something interesting
        }
}
```

Now that we have the `Get-Performance` function, we can easily construct a table of results for the two implementations:

Input size	Loop time	Loop memory	Cmdlet time	Cmdlet memory
10 MB	9.4s	278 MB	20.9s	4.1 MB
50 MB	62.4s	1335 MB	116.4s	10.3 MB
100 MB	165.5s	2529 MB	361.0s	21.5 MB
200 MB	Failed		761.8s	25.8 MB

It's clear to see that trying to load the entire file into memory is not a scalable operation. In this case, the memory usage is even higher and the times much slower than with `get-content`. It would be simple to construct poorly executing examples with cmdlets such as `Get-EventLog` and `Get-WinEvent`, and replacing the `foreach` loop with the `ForEach-Object` cmdlet will have the same kinds of results in these as well. Having tools like the `Get-Performance` and `Get-ShellMemory` functions can be a great help to diagnosing memory scaling problems like this. Another thing to note is that using the pipeline is slower than using the loop, so if you know that the input file sizes are small the loop might be a better choice.

Further reading

For more information on the topics covered in this chapter, you can go through the following references:

- `get-help get-host`
- `get-help about_profiles`
- `get-help get-member`
- `get-help set-psdebug`
- `get-help about_prompts`
- `get-help get-eventlog`
- `get-help get-winevent`
- `get-help measure-object`
- `get-help write-eventlog`
- `get-help new-eventlog`
- `get-help about_commonparameters`
- `get-help about_preference_variables`
- `get-help about_functions_advanced`
- `get-help about_parameters_default_values`
- `get-help import-csv`
- `get-help select-object`
- `get-help tee-object`
- `get-help measure-command`
- `get-help foreach-object`
- `get-help about_foreach`
- `get-help get-content`
- `get-help new-alias`

Summary

This chapter has focused on things that you can do when running the program, including traditional debugging in both the ISE and the console. We spent some time looking at error messages and how to make them more readable in order to help us take the time to look carefully at all of the information contained in them. We also looked at a couple of issues involving large input sets, namely, how to more easily debug a process by reducing the input and also how to alleviate memory issues with large file input by effectively using the pipeline.

In the next chapter, we will explore some things to look out for in your code that might indicate an opportunity to clean the code up in some way. Some of these red flags, known as *code smells*, are common among programming languages, but some are very specific to PowerShell code.

8

PowerShell Code Smells

No code is ever perfect, and we must realize that throughout the act of writing code we will be making choices continually. As we mature as developers or scripters, we become more confident in our choices and will tend to make decisions that are more well-informed and lead to better, more stable solutions. As we look back on scripts that we wrote in the past, we will almost certainly find opportunities for improvement. Depending on the source, we might also find the same kinds of issues in code that we obtain from other sources such as the Internet. In this chapter, we will consider some of the things to look for in code that might indicate some improvements may be applicable. In particular, we will discuss the following:

- What are code smells?
- Language-agnostic code smells
- Why are there PowerShell-specific code smells?
- Missing `Param()` statements
- Homegrown common parameters
- Unapproved verbs
- Accumulating output objects
- Sequences of assignment statements
- Using untyped or `[object]` parameters
- Static analysis tools (ScriptCop and Script Analyzer)

Code smells

A **code smell** is a feature of code that indicates something may need to be rewritten. Just as a smell in the refrigerator or pantry gives us a clue that something may have gone bad, a code smell tells us that the code may not be written as well as it perhaps should have been. Code smells are not errors as such, in that they don't mean the code functions incorrectly. Instead, they are indicators that the code might not be as flexible or easy to maintain as it could be, or even that it doesn't take advantage of language features that would make the code easier to understand and perform better. As I mentioned in the introduction to the chapter, all coding involves choices, and the choice to address a code smell is not always cut-and-dry. It may be that the code in question has needed no maintenance and is used infrequently, resulting in a questionable return on investment for fixing the code. It may be that the design of the code was specifically non-standard for some reason, whether that was a business requirement or other requirement.

Another source of code smells is the continual progress of language releases. For example, programs that were written in C# 1.0 wouldn't have been able to take advantage of features added to the language in later versions. Similarly, scripts written in PowerShell 1.0 may have included code to implement features added to the PowerShell language in more recent versions. When we view or review old code, we might find that they "smell old."

Code smells, best practices, antipatterns, and technical debt

Three other code-related observations are best practices, antipatterns, and technical debt. A best practice is an industry standard, recognized pattern that has been shown to be the best way to accomplish something in code. Examples of a best practice are using meaningful variable names and making code modular. An antipattern is a common way of performing an operation or structuring code that is likely to cause problems, especially where there is a best practice or set of best practices that are applicable. A typical antipattern is to construct an SQL statement which includes user input using string concatenation rather than using parameterized SQL statements. Technical debt is a term that describes the effort needed to change an implementation into what would be considered a proper, complete implementation. Technical debt can include outdated frameworks or language versions, poorly documented code, tightly-coupled modules, and a number of other things. Code smells, best practices, and antipatterns are clearly similar and their meanings overlap quite a bit. Debt is a good metaphor because the longer the debt is unaddressed, the larger the debt becomes, similar to how interest accumulates. The following list introduces the idea of each observation:

- Best practices are how the industry says it should be done

- Antipatterns are how it should not be done
- Code smells say that it might be wrong
- Technical debt is how hard it will be to fix

Language-agnostic code smells

Some things look wrong no matter what language they're written in. For instance, if you have 200 lines of code in a block, it's always going to be a sign that some effort might pay off in terms of rewriting it using smaller, more modular code. Also, if you see several blocks of code that are identical, or even very similar, it will probably be worthwhile from a maintenance standpoint to factor that code out into a function. Some other code smells that are very common are:

- A very large parameter list
- Overly short identifiers
- Extremely long identifiers
- Deeply-nested loops or conditionals
- Multiple-personality functions (that is, functions that do more than one thing)

One thing that is worthwhile to point out is that these are all somewhat subjective. For instance, what is a large parameter list? Some PowerShell cmdlets have dozens of parameters. Do they smell? Everyone will have their own perception of when that line has been crossed. Even when a usage isn't excessive, the fact that the question is asked may lead to useful refactoring or rewriting.

PowerShell-specific code smells

As you have learned throughout this book, PowerShell is an interesting creation. It is a powerful scripting language that can be used to write complex solutions as well as short and quick scripts. The language design is also somewhat unique because of the PowerShell pipeline, which is a central feature. Finally, the scope of the PowerShell language has grown tremendously over the course of the last seven or eight years, so code that was written early on will probably look primitive in light of the latest version. Here some of the large changes to the language and environment that have occurred in the various PowerShell versions:

- Introduced in Version 1.0:
  - Functions, filters, scripts, and pipeline

- Introduced in Version 2.0:
  - Modules
  - PowerShell remoting
  - PowerShell ISE
  - Advanced functions
  - Background jobs
  - Eventing

- Introduced in Version 3.0:
  - Workflows
  - Scheduled jobs
  - CIM cmdlets
  - Updateable help
  - Simplified `Where-Object` syntax

- Introduced in Version 4.0:
  - Desired state configuration
  - The `PipelineVariable` parameter
  - The `$PSItem` automatic variable
  - The `.Where()` and `.ForEach()` methods

Missing Param() statements

Parameters to functions in PowerShell can be defined in two ways: either as a list following the name of the function or in a `Param()` statement. In Version 1.0 of PowerShell, there was no compelling reason to use a `Param()` statement in a function, although `Param()` statements were required to define parameters to scripts and scriptblocks. Since most programming languages use a parameter list following the function name, it was natural at that time to skip the use of `Param()` statements in functions. With the introduction of advanced functions in PowerShell Version 2.0, there was suddenly a reason to use a `Param()` statement, as the `CmdletBinding()` attribute binds to the `Param()` statement. That is, in order to include the `CmdletBinding()` attribute, you needed to include a `Param()` statement.

It is not necessary that all functions be advanced functions, but the effort required to make the change is trivial compared to the advantages. Common parameters, parameter checking, validation, and risk mitigation support are straightforward implementations given an advanced function. The only change required to make an advanced function is to replace the following code snippet:

```
function Get-Something($thing){
#get the thing
}
```

It should be replaced with:

```
function Get-Something{
[CmdletBinding()]
Param($thing)
#get the thing
}
```

When I see functions like the first code snippet, missing a `Param()` statement, my first thought is that the code was written back in the days of PowerShell Version 1.0. The process of moving the list of parameters into a `Param()` statement and (usually) adding the `CmdletBinding()` attribute is straightforward and almost always correct. Be aware that if you are using the `$args` automatic variable, the code will need to be rewritten to be an advanced function, as `$args` lists the undeclared parameters passed in and advanced functions do not allow undeclared parameters. An option to replace `$args` would be to use the `ValueFromRemainingArguments` parameter. Consider a case where the original function looked like this:

```
function Get-Args{
$args
}
```

The rewritten function could look like this:

```
function Get-Args2{
[CmdletBinding()]
Param([Parameter(ValueFromRemainingArguments=$true)]
     $myargs)
$myargs
}
```

Homegrown common parameters

Also in the time of PowerShell Version 1.0, the only way to get native support for common parameters (for example, -Verbose and -ErrorAction) was to write a cmdlet using managed code. Since scripters, in general, are not C# or VB.NET programmers, there was a tendency at that time to manually implement the common parameters. For instance, it wasn't uncommon to find code like this:

```
function Get-Stuff{
Param($stuffID, [switch]$help)

    if($help){
      write-host "Usage: get-stuff [-stuffID] ID"
      write-host "Retrieves a list of stuff which matches"
      write-host "the given stuffID"
      return
    }
    #get the stuff
}
```

This was not an unapproved method in fact. Here is a blog post from Jeffery Snover advocating implementing the -whatif, -Confirm, and -Verbose parameters in script:

http://blogs.msdn.com/b/powershell/archive/2007/02/25/supporting-whatif-confirm-verbose-in-scripts.aspx#10555359

The post even contains a note explaining how important this method is:

> <This is a super-important issue so you should definitely start using this in your scripts that you share with others (that have side effects on the system).
> Please try it out and blog about it to others so that it becomes a community norm.
> Thanks-jps>

Mr. Snover made a very good point, which was crucial during the early days of PowerShell, about the goal of script cmdlets being as powerful as cmdlets written in managed code. He also did a great job of illustrating how to use [ref] parameters in PowerShell. I certainly won't contradict the creator of PowerShell, whereas this was clearly a promoted practice in Version 1.0 of PowerShell, it has become a code smell starting with Version 2.0.

With the language changes introduced in PowerShell 2.0, we know that we can use [CmdletBinding()] by itself to allow access to the common parameters. We have also seen that adding SupportsShouldProcess=$true to the CmdletBinding() attribute gives us the additional risk mitigation parameters of -Whatif and -Confirm. Finally, we know that help in a function should be created using comment-based help.

You might ask yourself what the risk of implementing your own parameters is or what problems might arise from this practice. There are a few good principles that should be mentioned:

- Code that you can omit is code that you don't have to troubleshoot
- Code written by the PowerShell team is documented and maintained by Microsoft
- Delivered code is always available on a given machine

With these principles in mind, it should be clear that you shouldn't try to implement features of PowerShell yourself. In instances where a feature you have implemented is added to the PowerShell language, you should consider refactoring to use the delivered feature instead.

Unapproved verbs

In *Chapter 1, PowerShell Primer*, and *Chapter 4, PowerShell Professionalism*, we discussed the approved list of verbs and how the module system will issue a warning when a module exports a function with an unapproved verb. We saw that there was a switch called -DisableNameChecking that suppressed the warning. Not seeing the warning is acceptable if we don't have access to the source code (as is the case with the SQLPS module discussed in *Chapter 4, PowerShell Professionalism*), but in our own code we are able to be more careful. In situations where we are creating a new module, consideration can be made for what functions are performed. By consulting the list of approved verbs provided by Get-Verb, we should have no issues creating an appropriately named set of functions.

The instance where we are bound to run into an issue, as is the case with most of the code smells we are discussing, is where we find code that is already in use and that violates this principle. Given a well-organized codebase, it is possible that we could simply rename the offending functions throughout every script in which they appear. In reality, however, there is a risk involved in this kind of operation. What if there was a file that was missed, or if a server was offline for maintenance that contained scripts that use the functions? In these situations, a different approach is usually preferable.

The solution to this problem is to rename the function with a proper verb in the module and create an alias for the function that has the original name. For instance, this code uses the unapproved verb "perform":

```
function perform-operation{
    #legacy code
}
```

The replacement for this function would look something like this:

```
function invoke-operation{
    #legacy code
}
new-alias -name perform-operation -value invoke-operation
Export-ModuleMember -Alias perform-operation
```

The function now uses the approved verb "invoke", and we have created an alias with the original name, perform-operation so that existing code will be able to access the function. It is crucial that an Export-ModuleMember function call be added to the module to export the alias, as aliases are not exported from a module by default. Assuming that this was the only improperly named function in the module, the module will now import with no warnings.

Accumulating output objects

In Chapter 7, *Reactive Practices – Traditional Debugging*, we spent a lot of time discussing replacing the foreach keyword (loop) with the ForEach-Object cmdlet. In that section, we were concerned with reading a large amount of data from a file into memory rather than processing it one line at a time. In this section, we will consider the converse, that is, functions that accumulate the objects they are going to output in a container such as an array.

The pipeline is a very powerful and unique feature of the PowerShell language. Executing the cmdlets in the pipeline at the same time as input is available to them, instead of running them sequentially, allows PowerShell scripts to deal with huge amounts of data without incurring a heavy memory footprint. However, we need to be careful if we are going to take advantage of this. Consider the following somewhat contrived function to retrieve the list of services running on a list of computers:

```
function get-RunningServices{
Param([string[]]$computerName)

    $RunningServices=@()
    foreach($computer in $computername){
        $RunningServices+=
            [array](get-service -ComputerName $computer |
                where Status -eq 'Running')
    }
    return $RunningServices
}
```

While a list of services is probably not going to become a memory issue unless we are processing a list of thousands of computers, it is clear that there is no need to hold these objects in memory. Another consideration is that as written, no objects will be available downstream in the pipeline until all of the computers have been processed. If the pipeline contains `select-object -first 5`, for instance, the code will waste a lot of time retrieving services from every computer rather than stopping after the first five service objects have been emitted. Rewriting the function to take advantage of the pipeline could look like this:

```
function get-RunningServices2{
Param([string[]]$computerName)

    foreach($computer in $computername){
            get-service -ComputerName $computer |
                    where Status -eq 'Running'
    }
}
```

It is instructive to note that the rewriting here only involved removing code. As mentioned in the *Homegrown common parameters* section, code that you can omit is code that you don't have to troubleshoot. So in addition to performing much faster and working with downstream cmdlets, it should require less troubleshooting.

Sequences of assignment statements

As I have mentioned several times, scripting in PowerShell is somewhat different than programming in other languages. A programmer who isn't comfortable with the pipeline might easily fall into the trap of writing code in a style that matches the imperative programming language that he is most familiar with. For instance, filtering and sorting a list of files in a directory could easily be seen as a sequence of operations, as follows:

1. Get the list of files.
2. Filter the list of files to match the given criteria.
3. Sort the remaining list of files.

This thought process could lead to a PowerShell script that looks like this:

```
function get-sortedFilteredList{
Param($folder,$extension)

    $files = dir $folder
    $matchingFiles = where-object -InputObject $files -
      FilterScript {$_.Extension -eq $extension}
```

```
        $sortedMatches = sort-object -InputObject $matchingFiles -
          Property Name

        return $sortedMatches
}
```

While this is a correct solution to the problem in some senses, it is certainly not how the problem would be solved in idiomatic PowerShell. A more typical solution would look like this:

```
function get-sortedFilteredList2{
Param($folder,$extension)
    dir $folder |
      where-object {$_.Extension -eq $extension} |
      sort-object -Property Name
}
```

The PowerShell-style solution is not only shorter, but also contains no local variables (which is worth noting). Because it doesn't contain any variables, it is much less likely that there will be a problem with a typo of a variable name or a type mismatch in an assignment statement. Again, by removing code we have less to worry about.

There are times when a pipeline needs to be broken up for readability purposes, and it's also possible that in a complex pipeline, it might be preferable to have discrete steps in order to simplify debugging. In general though, using pipelines will allow you to code more quickly and with fewer errors.

Using untyped or [object] parameters

When writing a function with flexibility in mind, we might be tempted to omit a type on a parameter in order to allow the user to supply different kinds of objects as arguments. PowerShell definitely allows for this, and in PowerShell Version 1.0 this was a common practice. With PowerShell Version 2.0, and with the introduction of advanced functions and parameter sets, we have a better option.

Recall that PowerShell doesn't allow the overloading of functions, where multiple function definitions exist with distinct signatures. If it did, some built-in cmdlets would have over a dozen different definitions. Instead, the concept of parameter sets, or mutually exclusive sets of parameters, is provided. Each parameter set corresponds to a usage pattern of the function or cmdlet. For instance, the help for Rename-Item shows two parameter sets:

- Using a standard path
- Using a literal path

The following screenshot shows the name, synopsis, and syntax of `Rename-Item`:

```
NAME
    Rename-Item

SYNOPSIS
    Renames an item in a Windows PowerShell provider namespace.

SYNTAX
    Rename-Item [-Path] <String> [-NewName] <String> [-Credential <PSCredential>] [-Force] [-PassTh
    [<CommonParameters>]

    Rename-Item [-NewName] <String> [-Credential <PSCredential>] [-Force] [-PassThru] -LiteralPath
    [<CommonParameters>]
```

Trying to determine which parameters are unique to each parameter set can be very frustrating. Looking at the command in the `show-command` window in the ISE gives a graphical view of the two parameter sets, each represented in a tab. I find this to be a good way of trying to figure out what the parameter sets mean. The following screenshot shows the two parameter sets of `Rename-Item`:

We can also find the parameter sets programmatically by inspecting the command metadata, as shown in the following script:

```
get-command rename-item|
    select-object -expand ParameterSets |
    select-object Name
```

As expected, the results match the labels on the tabs in the show-command example, as shown in the following screenshot:

```
Name
----
ByPath
ByLiteralPath
```

Using parameter sets gives the user an idea of how the function is intended to be used. In this case, the -Path and -LiteralPath parameters are supplying the same information (a location), but in slightly different ways.

Compare this to the following parameter declarations from a function in an open source project. I'm not picking on the developer because it's a project that I've been associated with for a long time.

```
function Get-SqlDatabase
{
    param(
    [Parameter(Position=0, Mandatory=$true)] $sqlserver,
    [Parameter(Position=1, Mandatory=$false)] [string]$dbname,
    [Parameter(Position=2, Mandatory=$false)] [switch]$force
    )
```

Because the $sqlserver parameter is declared as mandatory, you have to pass it in. Unfortunately, there is no guidance on what type of object is expected to be supplied, as is the case with the $dbname and $force parameters. Inspecting the body of the function gives us some insight into how the $sqlserver parameter is used:

```
switch ($sqlserver.GetType().Name)
    {
        'String' { $server = Get-SqlServer $sqlserver }
        'Server' { $server = $sqlserver }
        default { throw 'Get-SqlDatabase:Param `$sqlserver must be a
String or Server object.' }
    }
```

From this we can see that we're expected to supply either a string or a `Server` object, and that anything else will cause an exception to be thrown. We're missing a few good opportunities here by using parameter sets and specifically-typed parameters:

- We don't get any guidance when we use `Get-Help` on what type of objects to pass
- We can't tell from the parameter list that there are two different ways to call the function
- We bypass PowerShell's extensive type-conversion facilities
- The error message is not a standard error message and is not localized

In this case, the server class (`[Microsoft.SqlServer.Management.Smo.Server]`) contains a constructor that takes a single string argument naming the server, so one option we would have is to simply use the default parameter set (that is, not specify any parameter sets) and specify that the parameter is of this specific type. If a string was passed, the engine would instantiate a `Server` object using the string and the function would have had a correctly-typed object. However, this code is using a separate function (`get-sqlserver`) to convert from a string to a `Server` object, so we will need to use parameter sets to reproduce the functionality. We need to create a `$sqlserverName` parameter and assign the `$sqlserver` and `$sqlserverName` parameters to different parameter sets. Then, in the function body, we check `$PSCmdlet.ParameterSetName` to determine whether a server name was passed rather than a server object and call the conversion function, as shown in the following code snippet:

```
function Get-SqlDatabase
{
    param(
    [Parameter(Position=0, Mandatory=$true,ParameterSet='Server')]
      $sqlserver,
    [Parameter(Position=0,
      Mandatory=$true,ParameterSet='ServerName')] $sqlserverName,
    [Parameter(Position=1,
      Mandatory=$false,ParameterSet='ServerName')]
        [string]$dbname,
    [Parameter(Position=2, Mandatory=$false)] [switch]$force
    )

if ($PsCmdlet.ParameterSetName -eq 'ServerName'){
  $sqlserver=get-sqlserver $sqlserverName
}
```

With that change, we have changed the function so that we can leverage PowerShell's parameter handling capabilities to give type guidance, type checking, and documentation in the form of a more useful help display.

Using parameter sets is a powerful technique that gives a lot of control over the way parameters are passed into a function. Giving up this control by using [object] or untyped parameters inevitably leads to more code and frustrated users.

Static analysis tools – ScriptCop and Script Analyzer

This chapter has focused on things that we can see when we look at code in a code review situation. Such observations are necessarily somewhat subjective and open to disagreement. Another approach to the problem of analyzing code is to use a static analysis tool. Static analysis tools read the source code and apply a set of rules to determine places that the rules are broken. A report from such a tool gives very quick input into the quality of the code.

Some languages have a long history of static analysis tools. The C language, for example, has lint. If you're using C#, you have probably heard of StyleCop and FxCop. PowerShell has two static analysis tools: ScriptCop and Script Analyzer.

ScriptCop

ScriptCop is a tool created by Start-Automating.com in 2011 and can be found at `http://scriptcop.start-automating.com`. It can be used to test a function or module either online, through a web form, or through a cmdlet interface. ScriptCop defines a number of rules that can be tested as well as groups of rules, which it calls *patrols*. The web form is simple to use: copy the code into the form, select the rules or patrols to execute, and optionally a rule to exclude, and click on the **Test Command** button, as shown in the following screenshot:

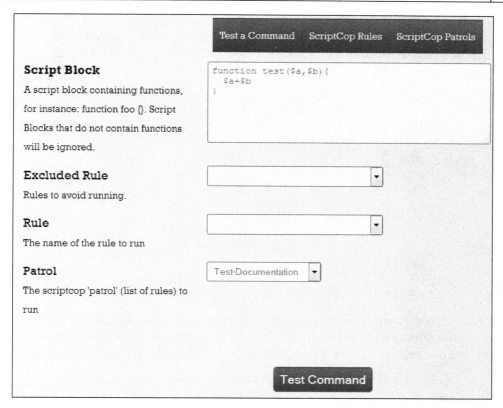

Here, I am passing in a simple function and running the `Test-Documentation` patrol against it. As expected, this example turns up a number of problems:

Problem	ItemWithProblem
test does not have examples	test
Not all parameters in test have help. Parameters without help: a b	test
No command is an island. Please add at least one .LINK .	test
Code is sparsely documented (Only 0 % comments).	test
test does not define any #regions	test

The cmdlet interface is through a module called ScriptCop that defines the rules as functions and also exports a function called `Test-Command`. We can easily use this function to reproduce the result we got on the website, as shown in the following screenshot:

```
PS C:\Users\Mike> test-command -ScriptBlock {function test($a,$b){ $a+$b}} -Patrol Test-Documentation


   Rule: Test-Help

Problem                                      ItemWithProblem
-------                                      ---------------
test does not have examples                  test
Not all parameters in test have help.        test
Parameters without help: a b
No command is an island.  Please add at      test
least one .LINK .


   Rule: Test-DocumentationQuality

Problem                                      ItemWithProblem
-------                                      ---------------
Code is sparsely documented (Only 0 %        test
comments).
test does not define any #regions            test
```

ScriptCop defines a number of rules (currently 14 for functions and 3 for modules) and includes source code for them. The rules are advanced functions that inspect the command metadata and a list of tokens provided by the PowerShell parser.

There are a number of really strong points for ScriptCop. First, the large number of rules means that the analysis is more thorough. Second, the fact that rules and patrols are written in PowerShell means that you can write your own, or you can customize the delivered rules and patrols to match your preferences. Third, ScriptCop has a PowerShell interface, so it could be applied automatically to a library of functions and modules.

Script Analyzer

Script Analyzer is a recent arrival in the PowerShell world, showing up on TechNet in May 2014 along with the Script Browser. Script Analyzer is a PowerShell ISE add-on, that is, a graphical pane that can be installed into ISE and can interact with the ISE. The download link for the Script Browser and Script Analyzer is `http://www.microsoft.com/en-us/download/details.aspx?id=42525`. The download is an installer, which includes a note about execution policies as well as this interesting page:

Microsoft Script Browser Setup Wizard

By default, this installer updates your Windows PowerShell ISE profile in order to make sure that Script Browser will be loaded automatically later. However, you can run Enable-ScriptBrowser in Windows PowerShell ISE console pane to enable Script Browser add-on manually. Please uncheck this checkbox if you don't want to update the existing Windows PowerShell ISE profile.

☑ Allow the installer to update Windows PowerShell ISE profile.

After the installation is complete, starting the ISE shows two new add-ons, as shown in the following screenshot:

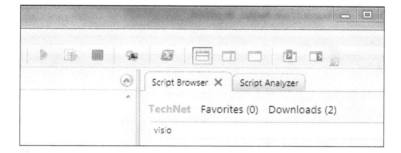

The Script Browser gives an interesting searchable interface to the TechNet PowerShell gallery, but we're interested in the **Script Analyzer** tab. It features a button labeled **Scan Script**, a gear button for options, and a grid for results. Typing the same function we used in the ScriptCop section into the ISE and pressing the scan button, unfortunately, doesn't give us any results, as shown in the following screenshot:

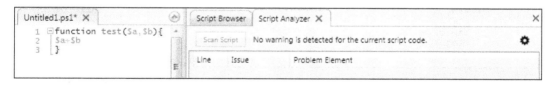

Clicking on the gear to see the options shows us the reason for this, namely that there aren't many rules implemented by the analyzer at this point.

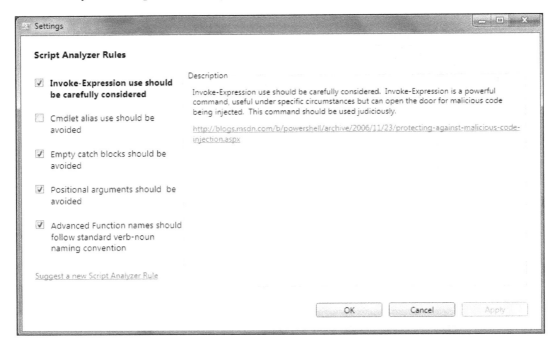

Looking through the rules, we can create a more complex example function that triggers some of the rules, as shown in the following screenshot:

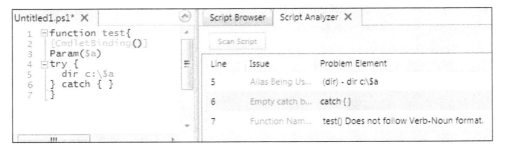

The tool caught three of the rules, but apparently missed the positional argument in line 5. It is good to note that on the options page there is a link to suggest new rules. The forum that the link points to already has 14 suggestions for rules, so there's hope that the script analyzer will mature into a more detailed tool. The same forum can be used to report bugs, as I have for the positional parameter being missed in the script as illustrated in the preceding screenshot.

The installation procedure asked about modifying the ISE profile, so let's take a look at those changes. First, the ISE profile is called Microsoft.PowerShellISE_profile.ps1 and is found in the WindowsPowerShell folder under the MyDocuments folder. Looking in that file, we find the following lines:

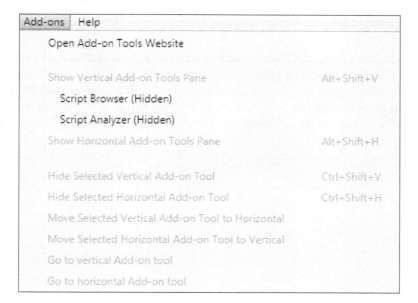

The code simply pulls in the .dll files associated with the add-on and then uses the $psISE variable to add the add-ons to the interface and make them visible. Once they are installed, we can also turn them on and off with the **Add-Ons** menu, as shown in the following screenshot:

Further reading

For more information on the topics covered in this chapter, take a look at the following references:

- Code smells at http://en.wikipedia.org/wiki/Code_smell
- Antipatterns at http://en.wikipedia.org/wiki/Anti-pattern

- Best practices at `http://en.wikipedia.org/wiki/Best_practice`
- Technical debt at `http://en.wikipedia.org/wiki/Technical_debt`
- `get-help about_parameters`
- `get-help out-gridview`
- `get-help about_functions_cmdletbindingattribute`
- `get-help get-verb`
- `get-help export-modulemember`
- `get-help about_pipelines`
- `get-help about_functions_advanced_parameters`
- ScriptCop at `http://scriptcop.start-automating.com`
- Script Browser and Script Analyzer at `http://www.microsoft.com/en-us/download/details.aspx?id=42525`

Summary

In this chapter, we examined the concept of code smells, which are related to best practices and antipatterns. We looked at several code smells that are found in most programming languages and then looked in-depth at code smells that are specific to PowerShell scripts due to the unique nature of PowerShell. Finally, we examined the state of static script analysis in PowerShell, reviewing the functionality of ScriptCop and the Script Analyzer add-on.

Index

Symbols

A

B

C

D

ISE colors, error message
   changing 132-134

L

language-agnostic code smells 169

M

Measure-Command cmdlet 46
memory
   availability, validating 116-118
mocking
   URL 82
modularization
   about 67
   process 70, 71
   process, breaking into subtasks 67, 68
   single responsibility principle 69
   URL 82
module naming 66
modules 21, 22
Monad Manifesto
   URL 22

N

naming conventions
   about 63
   cmdlet 64, 65
   function naming 64, 65
   module naming 66
   parameter naming 65, 66
   URL 82
   variable naming 67
network connectivity
   validating 119
   working 124
network connectivity, validating
   ICMP connectivity, testing 122, 123
   implementation, prior to 123, 124
   telnet used 119
   Test-NetConnection used 120
   UDP connectivity, testing 122, 123
non-terminating error 40-42

O

operating system properties
   validating 109, 110
   version 111-113
   working 114
   workstation/server version 110
operating system version 111-113
output objects
   accumulating 174, 175

P

parameter naming 65, 66
parameters
   about 172, 173
   blog post, URL 172
   name, validating 93, 94
   value, validating 94, 95
parameter type transformation
   about 102-104
   URL 107
Param() statements
   about 90
   missing 170, 171
Pester
   about 78, 79
   mocking with 80-82
   URL 82
pipelines
   about 15-19
   and function execution 99, 101
   input 96-99
   processing 32-36
PowerShell. *See also* **Windows PowerShell**
PowerShell
   error handling 37
   pipeline, processing 32-36
   strings 25, 26
   string substitution 26-28
   testing 77, 78
   version control, using with 73
PowerShell profiles, error message 134

Thank you for buying
PowerShell Troubleshooting Guide

About Packt Publishing

Packt, pronounced 'packed', published its first book "*Mastering phpMyAdmin for Effective MySQL Management*" in April 2004 and subsequently continued to specialize in publishing highly focused books on specific technologies and solutions.

Our books and publications share the experiences of your fellow IT professionals in adapting and customizing today's systems, applications, and frameworks. Our solution based books give you the knowledge and power to customize the software and technologies you're using to get the job done. Packt books are more specific and less general than the IT books you have seen in the past. Our unique business model allows us to bring you more focused information, giving you more of what you need to know, and less of what you don't.

Packt is a modern, yet unique publishing company, which focuses on producing quality, cutting-edge books for communities of developers, administrators, and newbies alike. For more information, please visit our website: www.packtpub.com.

About Packt Enterprise

In 2010, Packt launched two new brands, Packt Enterprise and Packt Open Source, in order to continue its focus on specialization. This book is part of the Packt Enterprise brand, home to books published on enterprise software – software created by major vendors, including (but not limited to) IBM, Microsoft and Oracle, often for use in other corporations. Its titles will offer information relevant to a range of users of this software, including administrators, developers, architects, and end users.

Writing for Packt

We welcome all inquiries from people who are interested in authoring. Book proposals should be sent to author@packtpub.com. If your book idea is still at an early stage and you would like to discuss it first before writing a formal book proposal, contact us; one of our commissioning editors will get in touch with you.

We're not just looking for published authors; if you have strong technical skills but no writing experience, our experienced editors can help you develop a writing career, or simply get some additional reward for your expertise.

Windows PowerShell 4.0 for .NET Developers

ISBN: 978-1-84968-876-5   Paperback: 140 pages

A fast-paced PowerShell guide, enabling you to efficiently administer and maintain your development environment

1. Enables developers to start adopting Windows PowerShell in their own application to extend its capabilities and manageability.

2. Introduces beginners to the basics, progressing on to advanced level topics and techniques for professional PowerShell scripting and programming.

Citrix® XenDesktop® 7 Cookbook

ISBN: 978-1-78217-746-3   Paperback: 410 pages

Over 35 recipes to help you implement a fully featured XenDesktop® 7 architecture with a rich and powerful VDI experience

1. Implement the XenDesktop® 7 architecture and its satellite components.

2. Learn how to publish desktops and applications to the end-user devices, optimizing their performance and increasing the general security.

3. Designed in a manner which will allow you to progress gradually from one chapter to another or to implement a single component only referring to the specific topic.

Please check **www.PacktPub.com** for information on our titles

Citrix® XenApp® 6.5 Expert Cookbook

ISBN: 978-1-84968-522-1   Paperback: 420 pages

Over 125 recipes that enable you to configure, administer, and troubleshoot a XenApp® infrastructure for effective application virtualization

1. Create installation scripts for Citrix® XenApp®, License Servers, Web Interface, and StoreFront.

2. Use PowerShell scripts to configure and administer the XenApp's® infrastructure components.

3. Discover Citrix® and community-written tools to maintain a Citrix® XenApp® infrastructure.

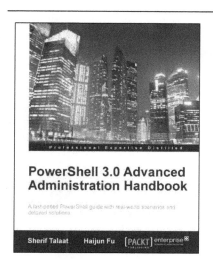

PowerShell 3.0 Advanced Administration Handbook

ISBN: 978-1-84968-642-6   Paperback: 370 pages

A fast-paced PowerShell guide with real-world scenarios and detailed solutions

1. Discover and understand the concept of Windows PowerShell 3.0.

2. Learn the advanced topics and techniques for a professional PowerShell scripting.

3. Explore the secret of building custom PowerShell snap-ins and modules.

Please check **www.PacktPub.com** for information on our titles

Securing Cloud PCs and Azure Virtual Desktop

Start implementing and optimizing security for Windows 365 and AVD infrastructure

Dominiek Verham

Johan Vanneuville

Securing Cloud PCs and Azure Virtual Desktop

Group Product Manager: Pavan Ramchandani
Publishing Product Manager: Prachi Sawant
Book Project Manager: Ashwini C
Senior Editor: Roshan Ravi Kumar
Technical Editor: Rajat Sharma
Copy Editor: Safis Editing
Proofreader: Roshan Ravi Kumar
Indexer: Hemangini Bari
Production Designer: Shankar Kalbhor and Aparna Bhagat
Senior DevRel Marketing Executive: Marylou De Mello

First published: June 2024

Production reference: 1310524

Published by Packt Publishing Ltd.
Grosvenor House
11 St Paul's Square
Birmingham
B3 1RB, UK

ISBN 978-1-83546-025-2

www.packtpub.com

I would like to thank my wife, Myrna, and my beautiful daughter, Mila, for allowing me to pursue my passion for writing this book and my various community efforts. It was a lot of fun writing this book, even though it took a lot of work and dedication. I truly hope that you will have a lot of fun reading it and that it will help you in any way possible!

– Dominiek Verham

A special thanks to my two kids, Mats and Paulien, for their support in this journey. Writing a book requires a lot of dedication and hard work but I loved every step of the way. I hope you will enjoy reading this book and that it will help you.

– Johan Vanneuville

Foreword 1

Let's begin with a brief history lesson. In 1975, Microsoft had a vision of there being "a computer on every desk and in every home." At the time, this seemed like an impossible feat, but now we know better. Windows has evolved over time, and since the 90s, its operating systems have been accessible remotely. In 1994, Microsoft introduced the Remote Desktop Protocol (RDP 4.0) in Windows NT4, revolutionizing the way IT administrators managed servers remotely. This allowed us to connect to server operating systems without physically being in front of them. A year later, Windows NT introduced the UI that gave us the start menu and taskbar in Windows 95, which still facilitates billions of users today.

Windows virtualization continued to evolve with the introduction of Remote Desktop Services (RDS). However, this still required a control plane that included a web server, gateway, and broker, along with the session host for user sessions. This model continued until the launch of Microsoft Azure in 2012, which brought new opportunities such as hosting RDS on Azure via Infrastructure as a Service (IaaS).

This led to the control plane becoming a cloud-based service, called Windows Virtual Desktop (now Azure Virtual Desktop), as well as the acquisition of FSLogix in 2018, the same year I joined Microsoft. As the virtualization and cloud industry evolved, virtualization-specific skills became standard in every business. As applications shifted to Software-as-a-Service models, becoming easier to buy as a subscription model, easy to maintain, and scalable, cloud virtualization lagged in simplicity. Virtualization needed something completely turnkey, like the transition from Office to Office 365.

Thus, Windows 365 was created as a new vision for the future of Windows, a cloud service with Cloud PC as the endpoint managed by Microsoft—a new revolution. The release of Windows 365 and Azure Virtual Desktop was key, positioning us as a leader in virtualization, recognized by Gartner in 2023's Magic Quadrant for Desktop-as-a-Service—just 4.5 years with Azure Virtual Desktop and 2.5 years with Windows 365 (at the time of writing).

Windows 365 sparked a computing revolution, moving PCs to the cloud while maintaining "like-local" experiences, manageable via Microsoft Intune without needing specialized skills. This principle guides Windows 365's latest end user experience features, such as Boot and Switch, allowing anyone familiar with Windows to log on effortlessly, unlike traditional VDI, which often requires manuals and assistance.

I also want to welcome everyone into the new era of AI. Returning to Microsoft's early vision of "a computer on every desk…," the innovation around Client + Cloud + AI will continue to revolutionize our Windows experiences. End users and IT pros will leverage new tools that accelerate their productivity and creativity.

With Microsoft Copilot joining Windows, the cloud and AI will come together. We are entering a new era where the cloud and client converge, and hardware will no longer be the boundary for end users that determines their experience—offering endless possibilities in the next generation of AI PCs and cloud computing. Enjoy the ride, as we are just getting started. This book will give you superpowers for this exciting journey. Dominiek and Johan have done an excellent job of demystifying Azure Virtual Desktop and Windows 365, with a focus on security. This book will support anyone's Windows in the cloud journey.

By Christiaan Brinkhoff, Principal Product Manager and Community Director, Windows 365 and Azure Virtual Desktop

Foreword 2

Virtualization solutions in today's market offer a rich set of options and tools for savvy admins to deploy complex environments for their end-users. These admins invest in staying up-to-date with the evolving virtualization landscape and the various compute and storage solutions that host end-user workloads. Admins have numerous options for on-premises and cloud-based virtualization infrastructure to manage hybrid workloads. They can choose where to host these workloads, whether with one of the ever-growing list of public cloud providers or on the long list of server-class on-premises hardware. Once the infrastructure and hardware are defined, admins must navigate through myriad operating systems, app virtualization, user profile technologies, and other virtualization software solutions. They also need to manage hypervisors, user density, security, high availability, disaster recovery, and all other requirements for a robust virtualization solution. There are thousands of knobs and dials with thousands of settings, creating millions of possible configurations.

I equate the challenge a virtualization admin faces in defining, deploying, and managing a virtualization environment to the challenge a pilot faces while learning to fly a commercial airliner. All the knobs, dials, and switches allow a pilot to effectively fly a 350,000-pound tube through the sky at 500 knots. Even though there are approximately 300,000 commercial pilots in the world today who have been certified to take on this complex task, there are far more passengers who have found their way onto a plane to get from point A to point B.

So, what does flying a plane have to do with virtualization?

Some customers want full control of the virtualization environment to reduce costs or fine-tune the experience to meet their specific needs. Traditional VDI admins have developed the equivalent skills of flying a commercial airplane, building a VDI environment that is cost-effective and provides an optimal user experience. There has been a steadily growing adoption of traditional VDI, but overall penetration in the commercial market is still relatively small due to the complexity and perceived costs.

A new era of computing is upon us – the era of the Cloud PC introduced in 2021 with the announcement of Windows 365™. Windows 365 provides a purchase and management solution on par with traditional end-user computing (EUC) tools and workflows, without requiring admins to have any VDI knowledge or experience. For end-users, a Cloud PC is a Personal Computer in the Cloud, offering an experience more consistent with a traditional computing model. For admins and users, the Cloud PC provides a ticket to ride to a modern computing paradigm delivered from the cloud.

Through Dominiek and Johan's book, you can experience this journey and equip yourself with the tools and confidence to tackle the most pressing virtualization challenges.

This book serves as your essential guide to effectively implementing and maintaining secure virtualized systems. It provides a comprehensive understanding of Microsoft virtual endpoints, covering everything from the fundamentals of Windows 365 and Azure Virtual Desktop to advanced security measures. You will learn how to adeptly secure, manage, and optimize virtualized environments in line with contemporary cybersecurity challenges.

In addition to covering the essential aspects of virtualization security, this book emphasizes the importance of staying ahead in the rapidly evolving tech landscape. As virtual environments become more complex and integral to business operations, the ability to anticipate and mitigate potential security threats is crucial. This book not only provides the technical knowledge needed but also encourages a proactive mindset towards continuous learning and adaptation.

Moreover, the book highlights best practices for integrating virtualized systems within existing IT frameworks, ensuring seamless interoperability and minimal disruption to business processes. It also addresses compliance with industry standards and regulations, offering strategies to meet these requirements without compromising on security or efficiency.

I hope you enjoy reading this book, and I wish you all the best in the new era of computing.

By Scott Manchester, VP of Product, Windows 365 and Azure Virtual Desktop

Contributors

About the authors

Dominiek Verham lives in the Netherlands. He has over 20 years of experience in IT, working in all kinds of technical roles focused on Microsoft products. Nowadays, he works primarily with Microsoft cloud products, such as Windows 365, Microsoft Intune, AVD, and related products, such as Nerdio. He is passionate about sharing his knowledge and personal experiences with the community via his personal blog, various presentations, and communities such as the Windows 365 community and the Cloud Experts Community. Dominiek has been a Microsoft MVP for Windows 365 as well as a Nerdio NVP since 2022.

Johan Vanneuville lives in Belgium together with his two children. He started in IT on a helpdesk and since then has taken multiple technical roles focusing on Azure and Azure Virtual Desktop and Nerdio. He loves to share his knowledge with the community on his personal blog and with the AVD community but also as a Microsoft Certified Trainer. Johan currently also holds the prestigious Microsoft MVP award for his contributions to the AVD community since 2022. Alongside that, he also is a Nerdio NVP.

About the reviewers

As a Microsoft MVP, **Micha Wets** enjoys talking about all Azure and Azure Virtual Desktop (AVD) topics and has spoken at Microsoft conferences, international (User Group) events, and Microsoft-hosted webinars and Workshops. He has over 15 years of experience as an Azure and DevOps engineer and has in-depth knowledge of private, hybrid, and public clouds. Today, Micha mainly focuses on Azure, DevOps, Windows 365, and AVD environments and is particularly knowledgeable about migrating those environments to Azure. Micha is a freelance Azure architect and works with Microsoft on Azure, Windows 365, and AVD.

Wim Matthyssen, based in Belgium, is a Microsoft Azure MVP with over 15 years of expertise in Microsoft technology. He specializes in guiding companies through their transition to the cloud and leveraging various Microsoft hybrid cloud services.

Alongside his role as an Azure technical advisor and trainer, Wim is deeply passionate about community work. He shares his knowledge and experiences through blogs and speaking engagements, actively contributing to the community. Additionally, he serves as a board member of the MC2MC user group, further highlighting his commitment to community engagement.

I want to express my sincere gratitude to my wife and son for their unwavering support, which allows me to dedicate a significant amount of our personal time to community activities. Additionally, I extend my heartfelt thanks to Johan Vanneuville and Dominiek Verham, the authors of this book, for giving me the opportunity to review their work. It has been an incredible honor and a truly enriching experience.

Sune Thomsen is a Windows 365 MVP based in Denmark with over 19 years of experience in the IT industry. He has spent at least a decade specializing in client management via Microsoft Configuration Manager and Intune, and he's currently helping enterprise customers with their cloud journey. Sune works as a consultant for a consulting company called Mindcore. Prior to joining Mindcore, Sune gained 10 years of experience in the engineering industry, managing and deploying various Microsoft solutions and projects. He's passionate about community work. Besides blogging and speaking at tech events, he's also an official contributor within the Windows 365 community and the Modern Endpoint Management LinkedIn group.

First, I'd like to thank Dominiek and Johan for giving me the opportunity to review the book. It has been a great honor and an educational journey to be part of! Last but not least, I want to take a moment to express my deepest gratitude to my lovely family (Annie, Carl, and Lucas). Your support and understanding have allowed me to dedicate significant time to the community. I am truly blessed to have you by my side. With all my love, Sune.

Jitesh Kumar is based in India, and he's a Windows 365 (Windows and Devices for IT) and Microsoft Intune MVP with over 8 years of IT experience. He focuses mainly on Microsoft device management technologies, and managing devices via Microsoft Configuration Manager and Microsoft Intune, and he loves to help customers and community members with their cloud journey.

He actively contributes to the tech community by writing insightful articles explaining concepts and providing insights into Microsoft Technology and tech information by writing insightful step-by-step guides. Being a tech enthusiast, he loves to keep tabs on new trends and advancements in the digital workplace tech space.

I'd like to thank my family, friends, and beloved community members who understand the time and commitment it takes to help grow the community. Working in tech would not be possible without the supportive tech community that has developed over the last several years. Reviewing this book has been a tremendous honor and an exciting opportunity for learning. Thank you, Dominiek and Johan, for the opportunity.

Table of Contents

Part 3: Security Controls for W365 and AVD

6

Update Management Strategies   97

7

Threat Detection and Prevention   161

10

Securing Azure Virtual Desktop   261

11

Securing Azure Infrastructure   309

Part 5: Use Cases

12

13

Preface

Windows 365 and Azure Virtual Desktop are Microsoft cloud solutions that allow companies to use virtual desktops. There are key differences between both solutions. This book will provide a short introduction to the worlds of Windows 365 and Azure Virtual Desktop and it will discuss various use cases.

But the real journey this book will take you on is about securing virtual desktops, no matter whether they are deployed using Windows 365 or Azure Virtual Desktop. Our goal is to give you a better understanding of what security controls can be used to secure Windows 365, Azure Virtual Desktop, and Azure infrastructure for both existing and new environments.

We hope that you will enjoy this book!

Who this book is for

This book is for IT decision-makers, IT consultants and engineers, security professionals, and students who want to learn more about security implications for desktops and the security controls that can be used to prevent cyberattacks or data leakage.

We will cover many topics. Some are introductory and other topics will go in depth. Some working knowledge about Windows 365, Azure Virtual Desktop, and Azure infrastructure will help to understand these chapters.

What this book covers

Chapter 1, Introducing Windows 365 and Azure Virtual Desktop, provides an introduction to the worlds of Windows 365 and **Azure Virtual Desktop** (AVD). It will cover the Windows 365-only features and editions. Licensing for Windows 365 works differently compared to AVD. Want to learn more? This chapter has got you covered! As an added bonus, we included the new Windows app as well!

Chapter 2, Importance of Securing Your Desktop, explains why securing a desktop is a very important task. The desktop tends to be the heart of the workspace. It's used to access company data and, while doing so, data can be stored on that desktop. What kind of consequences are there if something were to happen to that data? Even worse, what happens when desktops are lost or stolen? What controls do you, as an admin or company, have?

Chapter 3, Modern Security Risks, takes you on a journey to learn about bad actors and cyberattacks. What kind of cyberattacks are there and how do they relate to the desktop? How can a company recover from a cyberattack? How can virtual desktops help in the recovery process?

Chapter 4, Securing User Sessions, describes various security controls that can be used to protect access to the virtual desktop.

Chapter 5, Preventing Data Leakage from Desktops, introduces you to security controls to prevent data leakage from the desktop. We'll look at screen capture protection along with watermarking and how various screen locking options help to provide a secure environment.

Chapter 6, Update Management Strategies, discusses various strategies to keep your desktops up to date. Learn more about Windows Update for Business and the extra benefit of using Windows Autopatch. Did you know that you can build a template for AVD with customizations and let Azure Image Builder do the actual building of the image? Or perhaps you want to learn more about creating your own custom image manually? This chapter has got you covered on all of these solutions!

Chapter 7, Threat Detection and Prevention, covers how to use Microsoft Defender for Endpoint to protect your Cloud PCs and desktops in AVD against malware. But how do you make sure that all required components are running? Learn how tamper protection does exactly that! BitLocker is commonly used to encrypt the local drive of a desktop. But did you know that Cloud PCs do not support BitLocker? Learn more about the encryption of Cloud PCs and AVD in this chapter.

Chapter 8, Configuring Access Control, explores the world of role-based access control. It covers other access control solutions such as Azure Bastion, just-in-time virtual machine access, Microsoft Entra Privileged Identity Management, and the new Windows LAPS for Windows 365 and AVD.

Chapter 9, Securing Windows 365, covers specific security controls for Windows 365. Did you know that Microsoft has an advanced deployment guide to help you get started the right way? Or security guidelines, specifically for Windows 365? We will extensively cover Endpoint Privilege Management, a technique to run privileged actions with a standard user account. We will also learn how to create and export a Cloud PC restore point. We will end this chapter with some tips and tricks from the field.

Chapter 10, Securing Azure Virtual Desktop, covers specific security controls for AVD. We will learn about backups and securing your AVD environment with private endpoints, and how to use confidential computing or restrict apps that can be executed using AppLocker. **Active Directory Domain Services (AD DS)** is an important part of managing AVD, so we will learn more about the AD DS structure and security in this chapter.

Chapter 11, Securing Azure Infrastructure, takes you on a journey to secure the infrastructure that is needed for AVD. We will talk about storage, and network security with Azure Firewall, NSGs, and Azure VPN Gateway. We will also learn more about deploying AVD on dedicated hosts and how to configure Defender for Cloud for an AVD subscription.

Chapter 12, Windows 365 Use Cases, gives examples of when to implement Windows 365 for your company. These use cases can help if you already implemented Windows 365 or if you are looking at a new solution to deploy desktops. Are you thinking about replacing an existing VDI infrastructure or using Windows 365 for contractors? Or what about using a Cloud PC as a Privileged access workstation? Learn all about these topics in this chapter.

Chapter 13, Azure Virtual Desktop Use Cases, gives you examples of when to implement AVD for your company.

To get the most out of this book

To get the most out of this book, we recommend having a base-level understanding of the following technologies:

- Windows 365

- Microsoft Intune

- Entra ID

- Active Directory Domain Services

- Azure Virtual Desktop

- Azure infrastructure

Conventions used

There are a number of text conventions used throughout this book.

`Code in text`: Indicates code words in text, database table names, folder names, filenames, file extensions, pathnames, dummy URLs, user input, and Twitter handles. Here is an example: " Type `azure virtual desktop` in the search bar or search for the `9cdead84-a844-4324-93f2-b2e6bb768d07` app ID"

A block of code is set as follows:

```
{
    "properties": {
        "roleName": "Custom - AzureImageBuilder",
        "description": "Permissions for Azure Image Builder",
        "assignableScopes": [
            "/subscriptions/00000000-0000-0000-0000-000000000000/
resourceGroups/RG-MVP-AIB"
        ],

    . . .
```

Any command-line input or output is written as follows:

```
New-AzUserAssignedIdentity -ResourceGroupName <RESOURCEGROUP> -Name
<USER ASSIGNED IDENTITY NAME> -Location <LOCATION>
```

Bold: Indicates a new term, an important word, or words that you see onscreen. For instance, words in menus or dialog boxes appear in **bold**. Here is an example: "IT admins can use a device action called **Locate device**."

> **Tips or important notes**
> Appears like this.

Get in touch

Feedback from our readers is always welcome.

General feedback: If you have questions about any aspect of this book, email us at customercare@packtpub.com and mention the book title in the subject of your message.

Errata: Although we have taken every care to ensure the accuracy of our content, mistakes do happen. If you have found a mistake in this book, we would be grateful if you would report this to us. Please visit www.packtpub.com/support/errata and fill in the form.

Piracy: If you come across any illegal copies of our works in any form on the internet, we would be grateful if you would provide us with the location address or website name. Please contact us at copyright@packt.com with a link to the material.

If you are interested in becoming an author: If there is a topic that you have expertise in and you are interested in either writing or contributing to a book, please visit authors.packtpub.com.

Share Your Thoughts

Once you've read *Securing Cloud PCs and Azure Virtual Desktop*, we'd love to hear your thoughts! Scan the QR code below to go straight to the Amazon review page for this book and share your feedback.

https://packt.link/r/1-835-46025-9

Your review is important to us and the tech community and will help us make sure we're delivering excellent quality content.

Download a free PDF copy of this book

Thanks for purchasing this book!

Do you like to read on the go but are unable to carry your print books everywhere?

Is your eBook purchase not compatible with the device of your choice?

Don't worry, now with every Packt book you get a DRM-free PDF version of that book at no cost.

Read anywhere, any place, on any device. Search, copy, and paste code from your favorite technical books directly into your application.

The perks don't stop there, you can get exclusive access to discounts, newsletters, and great free content in your inbox daily

Follow these simple steps to get the benefits:

1. Scan the QR code or visit the link below

https://packt.link/free-ebook/9781835460252

2. Submit your proof of purchase
3. That's it! We'll send your free PDF and other benefits to your email directly

Part 1: An Introduction to Microsoft Virtual Desktops

This part of the book provides an introduction to Windows 365 and Azure Virtual Desktop solutions by Microsoft. While both solutions provide the ability to deploy large numbers of virtual desktops, they are different solutions with their own unique advantages, which are highlighted in key topics, such as Windows 365-only features, the editions of Windows 365, and how to license Windows 365 or Azure Virtual Desktop. By the end of this part, you will have gained a comprehensive understanding of Windows 365 and Azure Virtual Desktop and their features.

This part contains the following chapter:

- *Chapter 1, Introducing Windows 365 and Azure Virtual Desktop*

1

Introducing Windows 365 and Azure Virtual Desktop

We would like to welcome you to our book, *Securing Cloud PCs and Azure Virtual Desktop*! Thank you for joining us on a journey that takes us through many security-related topics about Microsoft virtual desktops. We hope you find the book informative and use it as a source of knowledge for your own journey, no matter whether it be for business or personal growth.

The workplace of the user has evolved a lot over the last few decades. It all started with physical desktops and laptops, and it changed into server-based computing. Nowadays we see physical desktops being used and managed in a modern way. But the evolution continues as Windows 365 and Azure Virtual Desktop bring even more features and use cases. With all these great modern options on offer, we hope to be your guide in securing these solutions.

In this chapter, we will take you on a journey into the world of Microsoft-based desktops. We will learn about the advantages that virtual desktops have compared to physical desktops, and we will guide you to choose the correct solution to securely deploy virtual desktops via Windows 365 and Azure Virtual Desktop.

This chapter covers the following topics:

- Advantages of using a virtual desktop
- Introducing Windows 365
- Windows 365 editions
- Introducing Azure Virtual Desktop
- Licensing Windows 365 and Azure Virtual Desktop
- Bonus – introducing the Windows app

Advantages of using a virtual desktop

Desktops are an important part of your IT infrastructure. Companies can choose to use either virtual and physical desktops or use both approaches. Each approach has its own strengths and drawbacks. Here are some advantages of using a virtual desktop compared to a physical desktop:

- **Flexibility and scalability**: Virtual desktops can easily be provisioned or de-provisioned, meaning that the number of desktops can be scaled up or down depending on the needs of the organization. Distributing a virtual desktop to an end user is a fast process since a virtual desktop can be accessed remotely.

  Scaling up using physical desktops often involves buying additional hardware or implementing a strategy to keep stock of certain hardware. This hardware needs to be configured before handing over the desktop to the user, which can take up more time.

- **Resource utilization**: Virtual desktops can run together on a physical machine, which allows for better resource utilization. Companies who use Azure Virtual Desktop have to plan for and maintain resource planning since Azure Virtual Desktop is a Platform-as-a-Service offering. Windows 365 simplifies this process by providing an isolated VM with a fixed number of vCPUs, RAM, and disk on a per-user/per-month license. IT admins can easily upgrade or downgrade the license by assigning a different SKU.

  Physical desktops are often dedicated to one user or used as a shared desktop by a group of users.

- **Isolation and security**: Virtualization solutions have the ability to use isolation technology. This means each physical host machine can run multiple virtual machines. These virtual machines cannot interact with each other. So if one virtual machine becomes compromised or crashes, it will most likely not impact other virtual machines.

  Physical machines have no need for isolation unless you are a developer and use virtualization software. However, there are some other security concerns when using a physical machine. This could be anything from losing a laptop to the theft of devices. If the correct security measures aren't in place, such as BitLocker, it could lead to data leakage.

- **Cost savings**: Using virtual desktops can lead to cost savings. Windows 365 has a per-user/per-month license that companies can increase or decrease in bulk. This is especially useful when companies need to onboard a very large number of users. Simply adding licenses is a really easy and fast process compared to ordering a large amount of physical desktops. Azure Virtual Desktop offers flexibility in providing virtual desktops and because of that, it's possible to implement cost-saving solutions in Azure Virtual Desktop. We will not go into detail about these options in this book.

- **Fast deployment**: The flexibility of using virtual desktops makes it easy for companies to adapt to changing business requirements such as the rapid increase (or decrease) of secure desktops. The process of deploying physical desktops takes up more time due to the need to order new hardware. The installation and configuration process can be accelerated using technologies such as Windows Autopilot.

There are other use cases for fast deployments, such as testing and development. If your organization employs developers, they will most likely want the ability to spin up additional desktops or quickly remove desktops that they do not need anymore. Companies can use Windows 365 or Azure Virtual Desktop to better support their developers. Or even better, they can use the Microsoft Dev Box solution, which is specifically geared towards developers and their way of working.

Microsoft has two great solutions to provide virtual desktops. Let's get acquainted with Windows 365 and Azure Virtual Desktop!

Figure 1.1 – Introducing Windows 365 and Azure Virtual Desktop

Introducing Windows 365

Windows 365 enables companies to stream a full desktop from the Microsoft cloud to the desktop of the user. Users can perform their daily tasks including accessing their company applications and data from the desktop in the Microsoft cloud, also referred to as a Cloud PC.

There are a lot of advantages to using Windows 365 when compared to a modern managed physical or virtual desktop for both IT admins and end users. Here are some key advantages:

- **Advantages for IT admins:**

    - Windows 365 is a **Software-as-a-Service (SaaS)** offering, which means that Microsoft takes care of a lot of complex tasks. IT admins do not need as much technical knowledge when compared to other VDI solutions.

    - Another advantage of SaaS is that it uses a per-user/per-month licensing model. Licenses can easily be scaled to company needs by adding or removing them.

    - IT admins can easily determine the total cost of licenses on a per user basis.

    - IT admins can use Microsoft Intune to manage Windows 365, which greatly simplifies the management of Cloud PCs.

    - IT admins can easily upgrade or downgrade virtual machines' hardware to improve or reduce performance as needed.

    - Windows 365 has great reporting options for IT admins. These reports let IT admins know if and what problems have occurred.

- Windows 365 is a great solution for bring-your-own-device scenarios. For example, contractors would benefit as they would be able to use their own laptops and connect to their Cloud PCs securely.

- Windows 365 enables users to perform basic management tasks such as rebooting their Cloud PC. This in turn can reduce the number of incidents reported to the service desk.

- IT admins can make sure that company data does not leave the Cloud PC.

- **Advantages for end users:**

  - End users have access to the basic management tasks to troubleshoot basic problems themselves. For example, users can reboot their Cloud PC when they are unable to sign in, and they can restore the Cloud PC to a previous state (point-in-time restore).

  - End users can use their own desktop to connect to the company's Cloud PCs.

  - End users can connect to their Cloud PCs from anywhere using any local client if they have internet available and a modern browser.

  - A Cloud PC uses Windows 11 (or 10) as the operating system, which feels more familiar to users than using a server operating system with a user environment manager.

Features of Windows 365

Windows 365 has great features that really set it apart from traditional virtual desktop infrastructure (**VDI**) or Cloud VDI. These features greatly improve the user experience or security aspects of using a desktop. Let us look into some of the features of Windows 365.

Windows 365 app

The **Windows 365 app** is a Windows app that can be downloaded from the Microsoft Store or published via Microsoft Intune if users work on a company-managed desktop. Since it's a Microsoft Store app, it will automatically update to the latest version, making the life of the IT admin just a little bit easier.

Users can sign in to the Windows 365 app and connect to their Cloud PCs. They will have access to their self-servicing options as well as the built-in troubleshooter. Users can pin their Cloud PC to the Windows taskbar or attach the Cloud PC to the Task View to enable Windows 365 Switch. Users can even configure a light or dark theme if they want to.

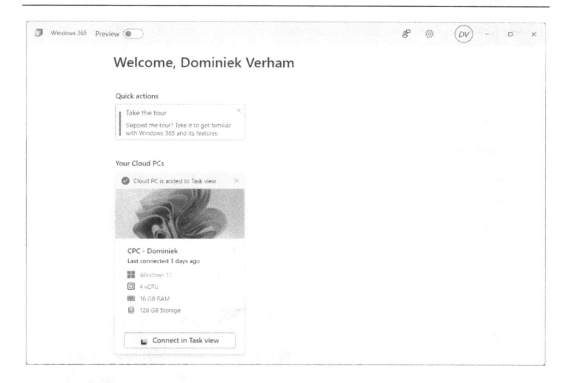

Figure 1.2 – Screenshot of the Windows 365 app

Windows 365 Boot

IT admins can transform a Microsoft Intune-enrolled desktop into a secure local desktop that users can use to sign into their Cloud PC without any data being stored locally on the desktop. Windows 365 Boot can be run in two device modes:

- **Dedicated device mode**: This mode presents a sign-in screen to the end users that closely resembles the default Windows 11 sign-in screen. It shows the picture of the user and supports passwordless sign-in using Windows Hello. For instance, think about signing in using a PIN or a security key.

- **Shared device mode**: This mode presents a sign-in screen that is not tailored to a specific user. Instead, it is meant to be used by a variety of users. Instead of showing the user's picture, the sign-in screen can instead be customized using either of the following:

  - A company background
  - The name of the company

After some recent improvements, it's also now possible to configure local device settings for Cloud PCs. This way, the user can configure a multimonitor configuration or audio settings.

Users cannot access the local device once it is configured with Windows 365 Boot. This means that no data is stored locally and features such as the local Task Manager cannot be used, making this a very secure desktop. The local device is fully managed using Microsoft Intune, which means that IT admins have the option to remotely redeploy the device using **Autopilot Reset**.

The only administrative tasks that users can perform on the local desktop are as follows:

- Changing the keyboard layout
- Accessibility options
- Connecting to a Wi-Fi network
- Accessing the power options

Users will see the following screen when they access their Cloud PC using a device configured as a dedicated Windows Boot device.

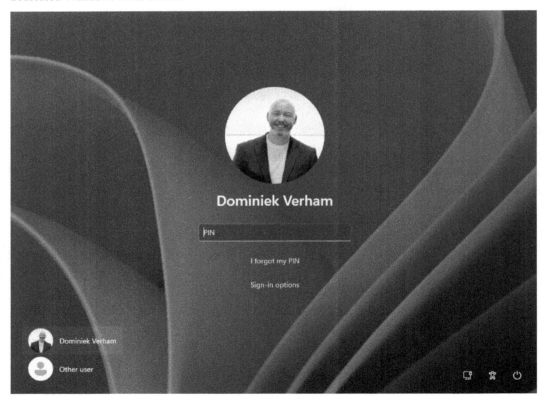

Figure 1.3 – Screenshot of a device in Windows 365 Boot dedicated device mode

Windows 365 Switch

Windows 365 Switch integrates with the Task View button in the Windows taskbar on devices running Windows 11. Imagine being able to click the Task View button and quickly switch to the Cloud PC and vice-versa. The local desktop doesn't need to be enrolled in the tenant of the company, which makes it a great solution for a bring-your-own-device scenario.

Users will need to sign into the Cloud PC the first time after their desktop boots up, after which they are then free to switch between their local desktop and the Cloud PC. Users will have to sign in again if the local desktop reboots or if the connection to the Cloud PC times out.

Let's take a look at how to use Windows 365 Switch:

- The following shows the Task View on the local desktop and the Cloud PC (the desktop on the right side).

Figure 1.4 – Windows 365 Switch on the local desktop

- The following shows the Task View on the Cloud PC with the option to switch back to the local desktop (the desktop on the left side):

Figure 1.5 – Windows 365 Switch on the Cloud PC

Windows 365 Offline

Windows 365 Offline was announced back in 2022. This feature boasts the capability of making it possible to continue to work on a Cloud PC even if the internet connection is lost so that users can stay productive. Windows 365 Offline is not yet available at the time of writing this book.

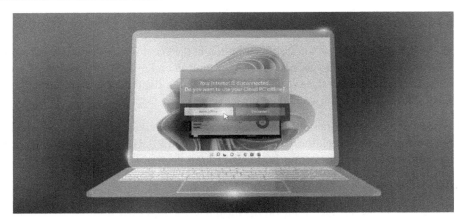

Figure 1.6 – Windows 365 Boot demonstration from Microsoft

We hope you like these features that make Windows 365 a unique solution. But did you know that there are a couple of different editions of Windows 365? Join me in the next section for an overview of these editions!

Windows 365 editions

In this section, we will introduce you to the different editions of **Windows 365** and explain the differences between them. In the following diagram, you can see the editions and the key aspects that differentiate them.

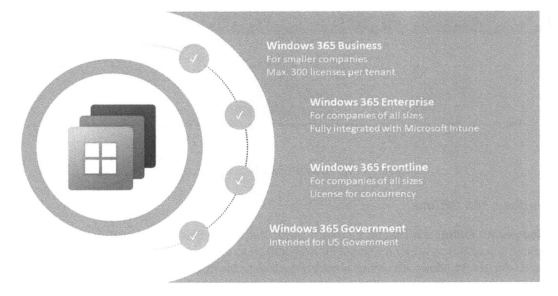

Figure 1.7 – Overview of Windows 365 editions

Windows 365 Business

The **Business** edition is meant for smaller companies who want to access a Cloud PC from anywhere without the administrative overhead. The Business edition allows the creation of a personal Cloud PC with Windows 11 (or 10) Business that is powered 24/7. Administration is primarily performed from `https://windows365.microsoft.com` or using the Microsoft Intune admin center if the option has been enabled. Keep in mind this will also require a Microsoft Intune and Entra ID P1 license. In this case, only the business features of Windows can be managed from Microsoft Intune.

The Business edition does have some limitations:

- Customers can have a maximum amount of 300 licenses
- Customers cannot use an **Azure Network Connection** (**ANC**) to connect to an existing corporate network
- Limited support for Microsoft Intune

If your company needs Microsoft Intune or Entra ID P1 licenses, the IT admin can add them in the Office 365 admin center using the Marketplace, or you can ask your preferred Microsoft license reseller to handle it.

Windows 365 Enterprise

The **Enterprise** edition is meant for companies of all sizes. Smaller companies can use Windows 365 Enterprise as well if they want to use the full management capabilities provided by Microsoft Intune. Once a Cloud PC has been assigned and deployed, the user will gain access to the Cloud PC that is always on and available.

Administration is performed using the Microsoft Intune admin center.

Windows 365 Enterprise does not have the limitations that Windows 365 Business has. Enterprise also has support for the following:

- Custom images and image management
- Universal print
- Policy management (either via Intune or GPO)
- Security baseline

Windows 365 Frontline

The **Frontline** edition is meant for companies who already decided to implement Windows 365 for their workforce. But instead of licensing every user, this edition allows licensing on a concurrency basis. Each license that is added to the tenant will give the company access to three Frontline Cloud

PCs and one connection. For example, 30 licenses will give the company access to 90 Cloud PCs and 30 users will be able to sign into the Windows 365 service at the same time.

Frontline Cloud PCs have almost all the features that Windows 365 Enterprise has, but there are some key differences:

- Frontline Cloud PCs will be turned off once users sign out.

- Signing in to the Frontline Cloud PC takes a bit longer compared to Enterprise Cloud PCs because Frontline Cloud PCs need to boot before users can sign in.

- Frontline Cloud PCs are licensed on a per-group instead of a per-user basis. Make sure to implement RDP timeout to free up licenses from disconnected sessions.

- Frontline Cloud PCs reboot before they are turned off. This makes sure that pending operations are completed before the Frontline Cloud PC turns off.

   Let's consider an example of how this works. Let's say a Frontline Cloud PC installs updates and needs to reboot to complete the installation of the update. By performing the reboot Microsoft ensures that the update is completed before the Frontline Cloud PC is turned off. The user does not have to wait for this process when they sign in the next time. Cloud PCs that have not been used for 7 days will automatically be turned on by the Windows 365 service. Outstanding updates will be installed, and pending reboots will be executed so that the user can then sign in without any delays.

Windows 365 Government

Windows 365 Government is an edition specifically designed to be used by the US government. The service spans across the regulated GCC and public-facing cloud. Windows 365 Government customers are usually government agencies or public entities that qualify to use services hosted in GCC or GCC High.

Now that we have introduced Windows 365, it's time to shift focus and take a look at Azure Virtual Desktop.

Introducing Azure Virtual Desktop

Azure Virtual Desktop is a Cloud VDI and offered as a **Platform as a Service** (**PaaS**). This means that companies can leverage all the scalability and flexibility that the Microsoft cloud provides. Using Azure Virtual Desktop has additional benefits such as running a multi-session operating system where multiple users can sign in to the same session host at the same time or provide a RemoteApp instance instead of a full desktop. A big advantage compared to the traditional Remote Desktop Services is that Microsoft manages the backend infrastructure, such as gateways and licensing.

The following diagram shows the components that Microsoft manages, and which components in turn need to be managed by the customer.

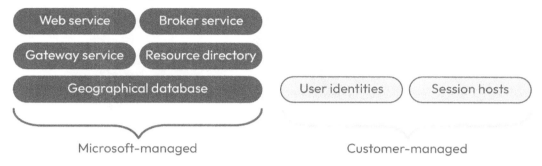

Figure 1.8 – Components managed by Microsoft and by the customer

The only component that we don't see in the preceding diagram is *security*. You can leverage the default security that Microsoft offers on the various AVD resources, but you can also take extra steps as we'll see later in *Chapters 9, 10,* and *11*, where we will take a further look at how to implement more advanced security on Windows 365, Azure Virtual Desktop, and the Azure infrastructure.

Using Azure Virtual Desktop instead of using a physical device brings a lot of advantages for both IT admins and users.

The key advantages for IT admins are as follows:

- Easily scale up or down in case of user demand
- Use the complete security stack of the cloud to ensure data security
- Give users access under a Bring-Your-Own-Device policy
- Azure Virtual Desktop can be very cost-effective when implemented correctly thanks to its scalability options, ephemeral disks, and reserved instances
- The Azure Virtual Desktop infrastructure can be monitored using Azure Monitor and Insights
- Hardware costs are reduced because IT admins don't need to buy and manage physical devices
- Easily keep all Azure Virtual Desktop session hosts patched and up-to-date

A major benefit for end users is that they can connect to their Azure Virtual Desktop resources from any device and from anywhere in the world in a secure manner.

Azure Virtual Desktop is also an ideal solution to provide users with a personal desktop. Users who need to install software can benefit from having a personal machine.

Connecting to resources in Azure Virtual Desktop can be achieved in multiple ways. Users have the following options:

- Use the Remote Desktop application provided by Microsoft

- Use their favorite browser

- Use the new Windows app that is in preview at the time of writing

The following screenshot shows an example of the Remote Desktop client.

Figure 1.9 – The AVD Remote Desktop client

The following screenshot shows an example of connecting via the browser to the Azure Virtual Desktop client (`https://client.wvd.microsoft.com/arm/webclient/`):

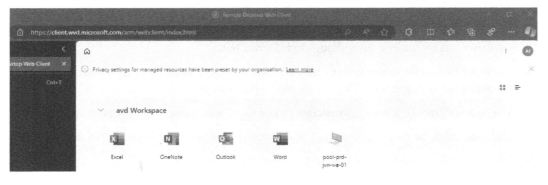

Figure 1.10 – Screenshot of the AVD web portal

This concludes the introduction of both technologies. Now let's take a look at the licensing part.

Licensing Windows 365 and Azure Virtual Desktop

Licensing Windows 365 works differently than that for Azure Virtual Desktop. Let's start with Windows 365!

Licensing Windows 365

Windows 365 Business does not have any prerequisites and licenses are assigned on a per-user/per-month basis.

Windows 365 Enterprise does have the following prerequisites:

- Windows 10/11 Enterprise
- Microsoft Intune
- Microsoft Entra ID P1

Chances are that companies already have these prerequisites covered if they are using a Microsoft 365 bundle license. For example, the Microsoft 365 E3 (or higher), Microsoft A3 (or higher), and the Microsoft 365 Business Premium bundles already have these prerequisites included.

Windows 365 Enterprise licenses are assigned on a per-user/per-month basis.

Windows 365 Frontline has the same prerequisites as Windows 365 Enterprise. Licenses are assigned to a group instead of on a per-user basis. This group will be assigned to a provisioning policy, which in turn will instruct the Windows 365 service to provision the required Cloud PCs. A huge advantage of Windows 365 Frontline is that an organization will be able to license based on concurrency, which is a great idea if the organization has shift workers, part-time workers, or employees that work remotely.

Each Frontline license will grant three Cloud PCs and one connection to a Cloud PC.

> **Note**
> Windows 365 licenses do not cover other Microsoft 365 licenses. Your organization will need to get the according licenses if it wants to use Cloud PCs with the Office 365 suite.

Licensing Azure Virtual Desktop

Let's continue with licensing Azure Virtual Desktop!

To be eligible to work with Azure Virtual Desktop, the end user needs to be assigned a license. There are multiple choices available, and it will most likely depend on the specific use case which license you assign to a given user.

Any of the following licenses will work:

- Microsoft 365 E3/E5

- Microsoft 365 A3/A5/Student Use Benefits

- Microsoft 365 F3

- Microsoft 365 Business Premium

- Windows 10 Enterprise E3/E5

- Windows 10 Education A3/A5

- Windows 10 VDA per user

Unlike Windows 365, there isn't a license check before you connect with the service.

It is possible to use Windows Server operating systems in Azure Virtual Desktop. In that case, the following license requirements apply:

- Remote Desktop Server CAL with Software Assurance

- RDS user subscription licenses

Besides these licenses, there is another way to make sure that you can provide users with a desktop or remote app.

Per-user pricing

With per-user pricing, you can pay for access to Azure Virtual Desktop resources for your external users. The benefit of this pricing model is that you only pay for the users who connected to the service during the last billing period.

Although this pricing model looks ideal for external users, the use of external identities is not currently supported. This means that the IT admin will have to create an identity for all the users that use the per-user pricing model.

You can enroll in per-user pricing by going to the **Azure Virtual Desktop** blade and selecting the correct subscription.

In the following screenshot, you can see where to enable the feature by going to the AVD portal and selecting **Per-user access pricing** on the left blade. The next step is to select the correct subscription and click on **Enroll** or **Unenroll**. When you do this, you will see the status change.

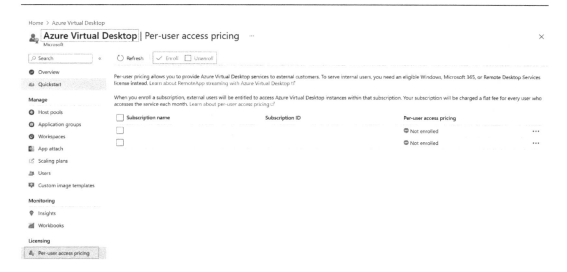

Figure 1.11 – Example of AVD per-user access pricing

Per-user access pricing comes in two tiers:

- **Apps:** This is a price for each user who accesses a remote app and no desktop application groups

- **Apps and Desktop:** This tier covers users accessing at least one desktop application group

If you plan to give access to users who have a license assigned to them, it's better to create a dedicated subscription for them. If you don't, then you will end up paying twice. In an ideal scenario, the IT admins would use a separate subscription when adopting this pricing model.

After looking at the licensing for both technologies, it's time to take a look at the newly introduced Windows app.

Introducing Windows App

Earlier in this chapter, we talked about the Windows 365 app, which is a great way to connect to your Cloud PC and provide users with self-service capabilities. One drawback of the app is that it is specifically for Windows 365. It cannot connect to desktops hosted in Azure Virtual Desktop. That's where the new Windows App comes in. This modern app is installed via the Microsoft Store, or by using Microsoft Intune for managed devices, which means it will automatically be updated without any action required from the IT admins.

The new Windows App provides a unified experience to connect to Microsoft-based virtual desktops. In the following table, you can see which platforms and virtual desktops are supported.

Figure 1.12 – The platforms and solutions to which Windows App can connect

Windows App has two sections that users can open via the sidebar. The top icon and default section that opens is named **Home**. Users can pin their favorite desktops to this overview, which is especially helpful when they have multiple desktops assigned to their accounts.

The second section is named **Devices**. This section provides an overview of all of the assigned desktops. Each desktop has its own solution-specific options. A Cloud PC will give you all of the Cloud PC management tasks, from rebooting to configuring some settings. A desktop that lives in Azure Virtual Desktop will understandably have fewer options available, such as pinning your favorite Cloud PCs or AVD session hosts to the **Home** section of the app or settings.

Compared to the Windows 365 and Remote Desktop app, the new Windows App does have a lot of new features. For example, the new Windows App supports the following:

- Dark/light modes
- Fast sign-in with other accounts
- Select the default Cloud PC to connect to from a Windows 365 Boot-enabled device

The following screenshot shows an example of Windows App.

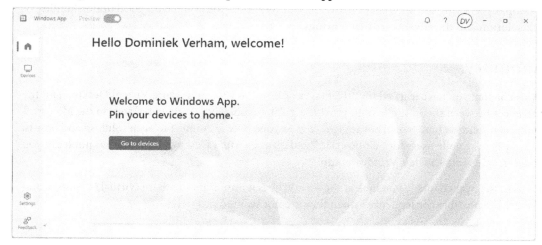

Figure 1.13 – Screenshot of the new Windows App

The new Windows App also has an updated web client that users can access via `https://windows.cloud.microsoft`.

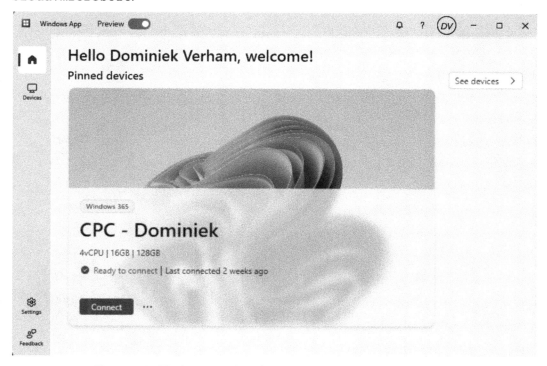

Figure 1.14 – The home section of Windows App with a pinned Cloud PC

With that, we conclude the introductory chapter into the world of Windows 365 and Azure Virtual Desktop. By learning the differences between both solutions, you will have a good understanding of each solution and the advantages that it brings.

Summary

In this chapter, you have learned the advantages of Windows 365 and Azure Virtual Desktop and the differences between them. While both provide a great way to deploy virtual desktops in the Microsoft cloud, each solution has its own advantages. You learned how to connect to each solution and how to properly license your users for Windows 365 and Azure Virtual Desktop. And last but not least, you gained insights into the new Windows App.

Join us in the next chapter as we look at the *why*. Why is it important to secure (virtual) desktops, and what are the possible consequences when they are not secured properly?

Part 2:
Why Is Endpoint
Security Important?

The second part of the book is dedicated to answering the question "*why is endpoint security important?*" It covers the role of the desktop as a whole and the security implications for companies when bad actors gain access to desktops and their data. This part continues with modern and popular cyberattacks and how they are related to desktops. By the end of this part, you will have gained a deeper understanding of the necessity to secure your desktops.

This part contains the following chapters:

- *Chapter 2, Importance of Securing Your Desktops*
- *Chapter 3, Modern Security Risks*

2
Importance of Securing Your Desktops

In this chapter, you will learn about the importance of securing your desktops and the implications of what happens if there is a security incident, such as a data breach. By the end of this chapter, you will understand the security implications that desktops pose to the security posture of your company. You will gain knowledge on the security implications of company data on a physical desktop, which increases when multiple users sign into a single desktop and the impact when a physical desktop is lost or stolen.

In this chapter, we will cover the following topics;

- A desktop at the heart of a user's workspace
- Multiple users on a single desktop
- What happens when a physical desktop is lost or stolen?
- What can IT admins do to prevent data leakage?

A desktop at the heart of a user's workspace

A company-owned desktop is the heart of a user's workspace. A modern workspace empowers the user to be productive at any time and from any location. It provides access to company-owned resources such as data and applications, as well as collaborative and communication tools for colleagues and external users alike.

While a modern workspace provides a lot of benefits to companies and their users, it also provides a big security risk if the workspace has not been secured correctly. Here are some examples of severe implications should the workspace of the user become compromised:

- **Legal consequences**: Companies should be aware of any legal consequences and responsibilities if any sensitive data becomes compromised or leaked.

- **Financial consequences**: Companies should be aware of the financial impact of any breaches. These consequences could be anything from investigating costs to legal fees, from fines to compensating affected individuals or companies.

- **Reputation consequences**: Even though countries might have different laws about data protection, it's highly likely that companies have to report data breaches to authorities. The European Union has the **General Data Protection Regulation** (**GDPR**), which states that companies have to report breaches within 72 hours to authorities after they become aware of a breach. Notifying the world about a breach can have a significant reputation impact on a company.

There are other things to take into consideration with regard to desktops;

- Since desktops have access to company apps and data, it's very likely that desktops have sensitive data stored on them.

- Desktops are vulnerable to malware and cyberattacks. Security should be planned accordingly.

- There's an impact on IT admins and the user should a desktop become compromised, which leads to less productivity.

Another thing to take into account is that desktops can be shared by a group of users. Let's take a look at that scenario next.

Multiple users on a single desktop

When a user signs into a modern desktop, Windows loads the personal profile. This profile contains user-specific elements such as desktop preferences, screen configurations, and themes. Additionally, it stores the user's documents, desktop, videos, and downloads folders. These locations are typically used by the user to store work-related documents.

The user profile also hosts a folder named `AppData`, which stores application-specific data. This could be anything from application settings to temporary documents.

Modern desktops use collaboration applications that synchronize data with cloud-based services. The Microsoft 365 Apps suite is a great collaborative solution. Another great collaborative tool from Microsoft is Teams, which has the ability to hold meetings, make calls, present notifications, and store work-related data. The data is usually stored in a team channel, which uses Microsoft SharePoint Online to store the data online. The Teams client has the feature to synchronize this data with the local drive, which is especially useful when users sometimes have to work offline. Windows 10/11 has a built-in OneDrive client, enabling seamless access to personal cloud storage with the Microsoft cloud. Similar to Teams, OneDrive has a feature that permits users to synchronize data in the cloud to the local drive.

These are basic examples where company data is stored on a desktop when a single user signs into a desktop. Physical desktops can be shared easily with other users, which will result in storing multiple profiles on the disk. Even though current desktops tend to have enough disk capacity, this could result in storing a lot of company data on a physical disk.

What happens when a physical desktop is lost or stolen?

The more devices a company owns, the higher the chances are that, at some point in time, a device will get lost or, even worse, stolen. Luckily, modern managed devices have a variety of options that IT admins can use in case the device is lost or stolen.

IT admins can use a device action called **Locate device**. This device action is supported on the following Windows platforms:

- Windows 10
- Version 20H2 (10.0.19042.789) or later
- Version 2004 (10.0.19041.789) or later
- Version 1909 (10.0.18363.1350) or later
- Version 1809 (10.0.17763.1728) or later
- Windows 11

> **Note**
>
> Make sure that the location services are enabled during the out-of-box experience, or use the `LetAppsAccessLocation` CSP.

To use the **Locate device** action, sign into the **Microsoft Intune admin center** > **Devices** > **All devices**. Select the device that is missing or stolen. Click the three dots on the menu at the top and select **Locate device**.

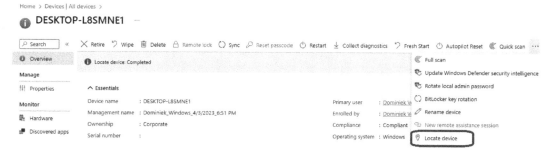

Figure 2.1 – The Locate device action in the Microsoft Intune admin center

The following notification will appear:

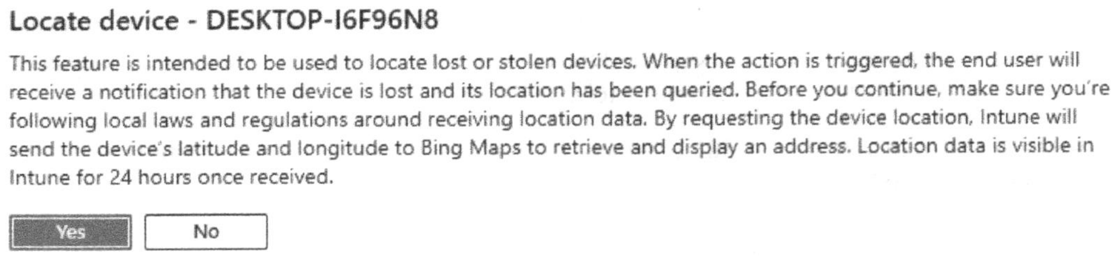
Locate device - DESKTOP-I6F96N8
This feature is intended to be used to locate lost or stolen devices. When the action is triggered, the end user will receive a notification that the device is lost and its location has been queried. Before you continue, make sure you're following local laws and regulations around receiving location data. By requesting the device location, Intune will send the device's latitude and longitude to Bing Maps to retrieve and display an address. Location data is visible in Intune for 24 hours once received.
Yes
No

Figure 2.2 – The notifications that IT admins get when using the Locate device action

Click **Yes** to query the location of the device. Microsoft Intune will show a world map and query the location:

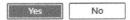

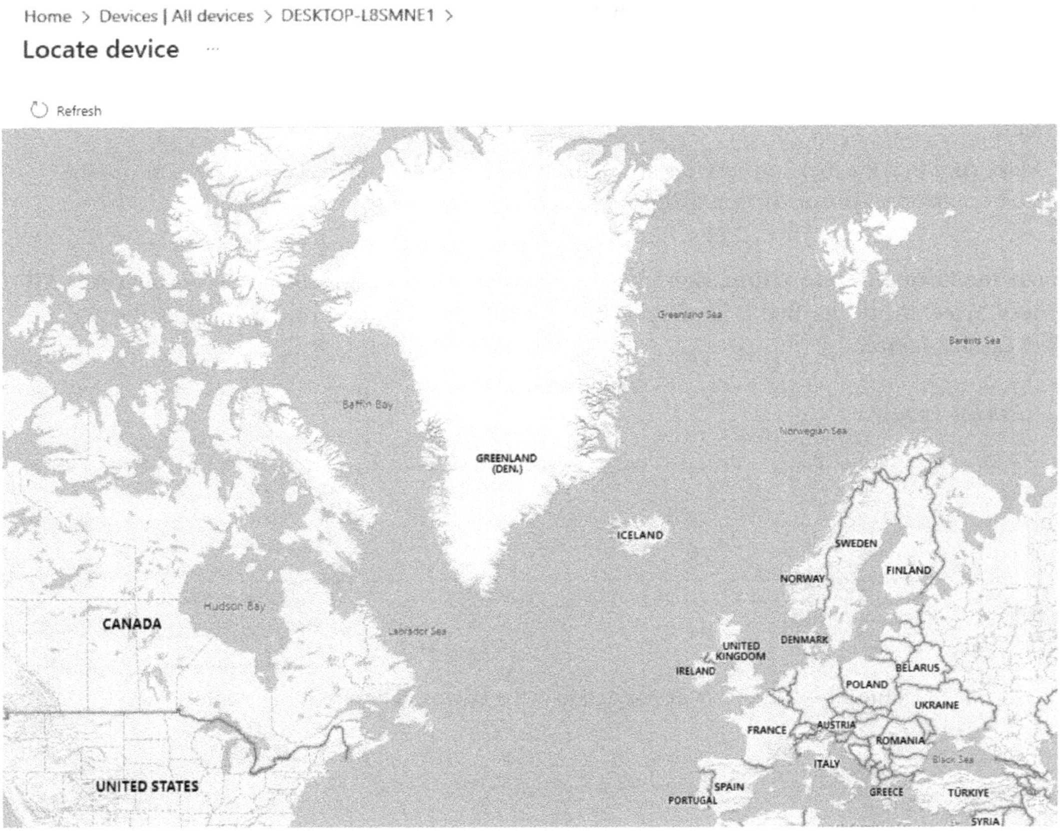
Home > Devices | All devices > DESKTOP-L8SMNE1 >
Locate device
Refresh
GREENLAND (DEN.)
ICELAND
SWEDEN
NORWAY
FINLAND
CANADA
UNITED KINGDOM
DENMARK
IRELAND
BELARUS
POLAND
UKRAINE
FRANCE
AUSTRIA
ROMANIA
ITALY
SPAIN
PORTUGAL
GREECE
TÜRKIYE
SYRIA
UNITED STATES

Figure 2.3 – The world map in Microsoft Intune while locating the device

Users will receive a similar message via **Notifications**:

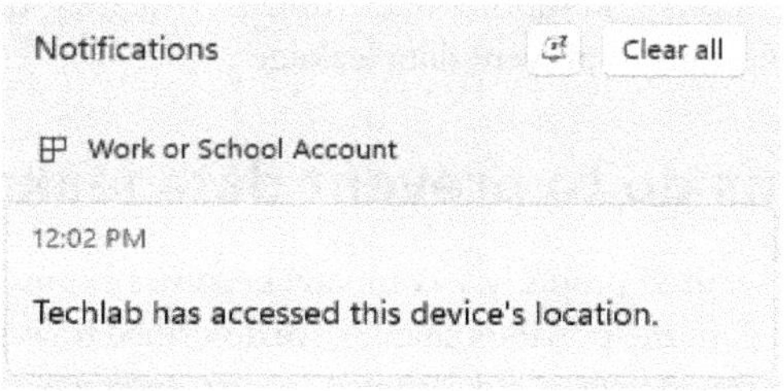

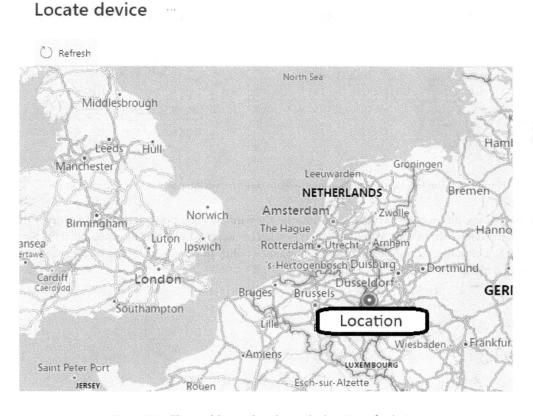

Figure 2.4 – The toast notification in Windows 11 that users will receive

Once the location is known, IT admins can view the location on the map. The location has the full address. The map allows you to zoom in and zoom out.

Figure 2.5 – The world map that shows the location of a device

Locate device is a great way to locate devices that are lost. However, this only works when such a device connects to Microsoft Intune and reports back in. Unfortunately, this is not always the case. So, let's take a look at other solutions to prevent data leakage.

What can IT admins do to prevent data leakage?

When a physical desktop isn't secured properly, a company becomes exposed to a security incident if sensitive company data is leaked. In the previous chapter, we described how easy it is to store company data on a desktop. But what happens when a desktop is lost or, even worse, gets stolen? Bad actors can remove the disk drive from the endpoint and connect it to a different endpoint, gaining access to the data that is stored on the disk.

IT admins can use **BitLocker**, a disk encryption feature built into modern Windows versions to make sure that data cannot be read once the disk is attached to a different computer. IT admins can make use of a variety of tools to configure and maintain BitLocker on managed desktops, such as group policies or Microsoft Intune policies, by navigating to **Endpoint security > Disk encryption**.

Figure 2.6 – The location where IT admins create disk encryption policies in Microsoft Intune

In most cases, BitLocker will successfully pick up the configuration policy and start to encrypt the local drive. However, in some cases, BitLocker will fail to encrypt the local disk, especially if the local device is a bit older. Admins can create a compliance policy in Microsoft Intune to easily identify when a desktop does not use BitLocker:

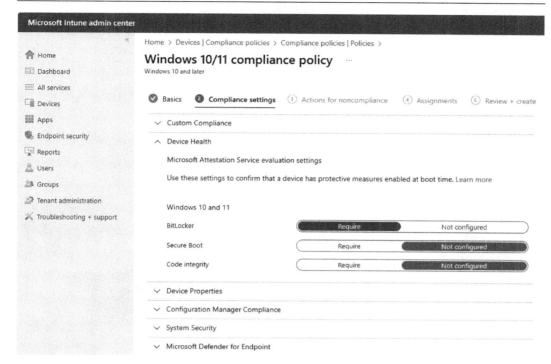

Figure 2.7 – An example of a disk encryption policy

Additionally, IT admins can use Microsoft Intune to remove company data from a lost or stolen device. To do so, sign into the Microsoft Intune admin center and go to **Devices** > **All devices**. Select the compromised device and then the **Wipe** device action.

Figure 2.8 – The Wipe device action in the Microsoft Intune admin center

Wiping the device will present the following screenshot. By default, a full wipe will be initiated, but there are two options that IT admins can check:

Are you sure you want to wipe DESKTOP-50JFDLI

Factory reset returns the device to its default settings. This removes all personal and company data and settings from this device. You can choose whether to keep the device enrolled and the user account associated with this device. You cannot revert this action. Are you sure you want to reset this device?

☐ Wipe device, but keep enrollment state and associated user account

☐ Wipe device, and continue to wipe even if device loses power. If you select this option, please be aware that it might prevent some devices running Windows 10 and later from starting up again.

[Wipe]   [Cancel]

Figure 2.9 – Administrative choices for the Wipe device action

The first option is **Wipe device, but keep enrollment state and associated user account**.

Select this option if you want to retain the following configurations:

- User accounts that are associated with the device
- Machine state (device joined to a domain or joined to Entra ID)
- MDM enrollment
- OEM-installed apps (both Store and Win32 apps)
- User profile
- User data outside of the profile
- User auto-login

It's best to leave this option deselected when a device is lost or stolen.

The second option is **Wipe device, and continue to wipe even if device loses power. If you select this option, please be aware that it might prevent some devices running Windows 10 and later from starting up again.**

By selecting this option, the device will try to execute the **Wipe** device action until it successfully completes it. The device will even continue the **Wipe** device action if it is forced to shut down.

It's best to select this option if the device is lost or stolen.

It takes up to 15 minutes before the device action propagates to the selected device. Remember that the device needs internet access to receive this device action.

Another device action that IT admins can perform is named **Retire**.

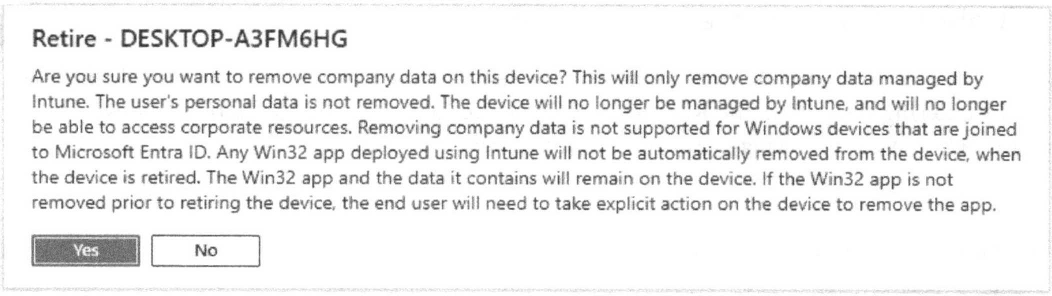

Retire - DESKTOP-A3FM6HG

Are you sure you want to remove company data on this device? This will only remove company data managed by Intune. The user's personal data is not removed. The device will no longer be managed by Intune, and will no longer be able to access corporate resources. Removing company data is not supported for Windows devices that are joined to Microsoft Entra ID. Any Win32 app deployed using Intune will not be automatically removed from the device, when the device is retired. The Win32 app and the data it contains will remain on the device. If the Win32 app is not removed prior to retiring the device, the end user will need to take explicit action on the device to remove the app.

> [Yes]   [No]

Figure 2.10 – The administrative notification of the Retire device action

The **Retire** device action retains the personal data but removes company data from the device, and it removes the record from Microsoft Entra ID.

The following are performed by the **Retire** device action:

- Apps that are installed via Microsoft Intune will be uninstalled.
- The Microsoft 365 Apps will remain installed on the device running Windows 10 build 1709 and higher.
- Sideloading apps means that IT admins can install apps from unofficial sources. This is particularly useful if a company creates its own app. A prerequisite for this to work is to enable sideloading. The retire device action will remove the sideloading configuration from the device.
- Win32 apps that are created by the Win32 content prep tool, that are managed by Microsoft Intune will not be removed from unenrolled devices.
- Configurations set by an Intune policy are no longer enforced, which means that users can change the settings.
- Wi-Fi and VPN profile settings are removed.
- Certificates are removed and revoked.
- Removes emails that are EFS-enabled, including emails and attachments in the Mail app for Windows. Removes mail accounts provisioned by Intune.
- The Microsoft Entra ID record is removed.
- For Windows 10 devices that join Microsoft Entra ID during the initial setup (**Out of Box Experience (OOBE)**), the **Retire** command will remove all Microsoft Entra accounts from the device.

It's best to use the **Wipe** device action instead of the **Retire** device action if the device is lost or stolen. With the **Wipe** device action, IT admins can make sure that the device resets and removes all data from the device, whereas the **Retire** device action still leaves the device in a usable state and does not remove the user's data from the device.

What about the Remote lock device action?

The **Remote lock** device action makes sure that the selected device(s) locks. It can be unlocked by a user by entering their PIN. The **Remote lock** device action is not supported by Windows 10 or Windows 11; only the following platforms are supported:

- Android
- Android Enterprise kiosk devices
- Android Enterprise work profile devices
- Android Enterprise fully managed devices
- Android Enterprise corporate-owned with work profile devices
- **Android Open Source Project** (**AOSP**) devices
- iOS
- macOS

These supported devices need to have a PIN configured; otherwise, the device will not lock.

Windows 10/11 devices have the **Remote lock** device action grayed out in the Microsoft Intune admin center.

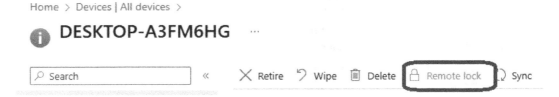

Figure 2.11 – The location of the Remote lock device action

This concludes this chapter; let's summarize what we have learned.

Summary

In this chapter, you learned about the security implications of the desktop, how easy it is for company data to be stored on local disk drives of physical machines, and the implications that occur when a physical machine is lost or stolen, as well as the modern device actions that you as an IT admin can use to safeguard your company data.

In the next chapter, we will move on from desktops to the security challenges that companies currently face.

3
Modern Security Risks

In this chapter, we will take a look at the modern security risks and challenges that companies face in today's world. Some risks are related directly to desktops, while other risks are related indirectly to them. Keep in mind that a desktop provides a great platform for a bad actor to start their attack on IT infrastructure, especially if that desktop is located in the corporate network.

By the end of this chapter, you will have a deeper understanding of the different kinds of cyberattacks that can take place and what steps a company can take to resolve and recover from an attack. You will also learn what an incident response plan is, why an organization needs it, and how virtual desktops can come to the rescue.

In this chapter, we will cover the following topics:

- What are bad actors?
- Types of cyberattacks and how to mitigate them
- Recovering from a cyberattack
- Virtual desktops to the rescue

What are bad actors?

Before we dive into the rest of this chapter and learn more about all the different types of cyberattacks and how virtual desktops can help, let's first focus a bit on the people who launch those attacks.

Cyberattacks are carried out by people who are often called **bad actors**. This type of person in the context of a cyberattack can be an individual or group that has malicious intent. They are engaged in getting unauthorized access and disrupting and exploiting computer systems, networks, or data. Typically, their goal is to cause harm by gaining unauthorized access to sensitive information and selling it to the highest bidder, or simply to cause chaos.

Types of cyberattacks

Cyberattacks are an important part of security challenges for companies. Cyberattacks come in many forms, and to make things more difficult, they tend to evolve at a very high pace. AI is a tool that evolves at a very high pace. Bad actors use AI to perform complex attacks on companies, while IT admins use Microsoft and other third-party solutions to protect companies and their IT infrastructure.

Let's focus more on cyberattacks and have some fun at the same time. Here are the top eight cyberattacks according to ChatGPT:

- Phishing attacks
- Ransomware
- Distributed denial of service
- Man-in-the-middle attacks
- SQL injection
- Cross-site scripting
- Zero-day exploits
- Social engineering attacks

Let's take a deeper look at these cyberattacks, what they are, and possible solutions that can be used to protect against them.

Phishing attack

A **phishing attack** is used to trick people into sharing sensitive or personal information, also known as **Personally Identifiable Information (PII)**. This can be banking information, personal information, or login credentials. There are a few methods that can be used, such as fraudulent emails, phone calls, SMS, or even websites that trick people into downloading malicious software or providing sensitive information. These attacks often lead to identity theft or data breaches and, ultimately, financial losses or other damage. Most of the time, it's difficult to tell whether an email is legitimate or not. Here are some ways users can identify a phishing mail:

- An urgent demand to take action
- Spelling errors and poor grammar
- Inconsistencies in the email address and domain names
- Requests for login information, payment details, or sensitive data

Protecting against this form of attack is not easy. Nowadays, a lot of companies tend to have internal campaigns to train end users to recognize phishing emails.

Ransomware

A **ransomware** attack is a type of attack that is designed to infect a device and keep the data hostage until a fee or ransom is paid. The result of typical ransomware is that data on a desktop or a network share is encrypted. Be aware that backups are a good way to protect your data, but keep in mind that modern ransomware attacks target backups as well. Attacks such as these can lead to permanent data loss, and they can be very harmful for all types of companies.

A ransomware attack can occur through various methods:

- Phishing emails
- Visiting corrupted websites
- Downloading infected files
- Vulnerabilities on a system and network
- An attack through the **Remote Desktop Protocol (RDP)** protocol

IT admins, or security specialists, are tasked to protect a company and its infrastructure to prevent ransomware attacks. Let's have a look at some methods that can be used to achieve this:

- Make sure that company data is stored in offline or off-site storage. Use immutable storage if possible. Immutable storage makes sure that data is stored once and cannot be modified or erased once the backup has finished. An example of immutable storage is using Azure Blob storage and storing data in a **write once, read many (WORM)** states.
- Ensure that updates and patches are installed for all applicable operating systems and software. This is also true for firmware on used hardware.
- Make sure to protect desktops against all sorts of malware by installing an antivirus application such as Microsoft Defender for Endpoint.
- Ensure that desktops are not directly connected to the internet. Instead, make sure that desktops are protected by a firewall. It does not matter whether these devices are physically at a location or virtually stored in a data center.
- Make sure that an organization's network is segmented so that you can limit the spread of the ransomware.

Distributed denial of service

A **distributed denial of service (DDoS)** attack creates and sends a massive amount of connections from many compromised devices (botnet) to a single resource. The desired result of this attack is to overload the specific resource or network that the specific resource uses so that it becomes unusable.

The symptoms of a DDoS attack could be one or more of the following:

- Unusual slowness on the network

- A resource not being available

- A massive increase in incoming spam mail, also known as a mailbomb

Let's take a look at how companies can protect against DDoS attacks. A lot can be done at the network level. Here are some key examples.

Once a DDoS attack commences, it's key to prevent the spread of the attack. A great way to prevent the spread is by enforcing a zero-trust segmentation on the network. In *Chapter 11, Securing Azure Infrastructure*, we will guide you on how to use solutions such as **Network Security Groups** (**NSGs**) and Azure Firewall to limit network access by blocking unused ports and protocols.

Another way to mitigate the spread of DDoS attacks is by patching network devices. If a network device has a vulnerability that is not patched, it makes it susceptible to misuse and potentially starting a DDoS attack.

Repeat this mantra: *"Do not directly connect a desktop to the internet."* Always make sure to keep desktops safe on the network by securing them behind a firewall solution. It does not matter whether the desktop runs in the local data center or Azure data center.

There are some really good solutions on the market to protect your environment from a DDoS attack. Microsoft has Azure DDoS Protection. Other third-party solutions are provided by Cloudflare and Big-IP, for example.

We recommend limiting the use of public IPs to systems that absolutely need to have one. An example would be to use a public IP for a firewall while using only private IPs for other endpoints, such as desktops, servers, and network devices. Keep in mind that Azure Bastion is a great solution to provide access to servers and desktops without directly connecting to a public IP.

Man in the middle attacks

A **man in the middle** (**MiTM**) attack is a kind of attack in which the attacker secretly intercepts and relays communication between two parties. The attacker makes the two parties believe that they are talking to each other. Using this method, the bad actor can manipulate people to provide sensitive information such as login credentials and bank details.

An attack like this usually involves the installation of a packet sniffer in the network. This could either be a hardware device or a software application that is installed. Using this packet sniffer, the bad actor will look for any unsecured traffic that uses the **Hyper Text Transfer Protocol** (**HTTP**) or a non-secure public Wi-Fi hotspot. An example would be when a user logs on to a malicious website and the attacker can retrieve the user's information or credentials, redirecting them to a fake website.

Like any other method, there are ways to protect an organization from this kind of attack. When browsing, a user should only visit websites that show HTTPS. The lock icon before the URL indicates that the website is secure.

A great way to prevent this type of attack is by using a **Virtual Private Network** (**VPN**) connection. A VPN encrypts the connection and all of the traffic that is sent across. This makes it a lot harder for bad actors to interfere or intercept network traffic and gain access to important data.

> Tip
>
> Make sure to read *Chapter 11, Securing Azure Infrastructure*. It will show how a VPN connection is used to secure the Azure Virtual Desktop environment.

SQL injections

SQL injections are designed to run commands on connected databases, with the intent to access or manipulate information. The impact of a successful SQL injection depends on the type of attack and the commands that have been executed. An example of an SQL injection is when a bad actor changes the text in the URL bar of the browser so that the web app runs a query on the database, possibly revealing PII information.

An SQL injection attack can have multiple purposes; the bad actor can use it to view or change the data in a database or even delete the entire database.

Here are some key actions to prevent SQL injections:

- Make sure that SQL servers are patched to reduce the danger of a vulnerability
- Limit privileges and access to the database with the use of least privileged access
- Use a **Web Application Firewall** (**WAF**) to monitor and filter traffic
- Use network segmentation to limit network access to a database

SQL injections do not target desktops specifically but keep in mind that bad actors have a great platform at their disposal if they gain access to a desktop, especially if it's a desktop in the company's network.

Cross-site scripting

Cross-site scripting (**XSS**) is a method of attack that manipulates scripts to disclose information to the bad actor, such as infecting the login files of a website so that the bad actor can gain control of the user's account. The technique can be done by injecting a malicious script into what appears to be a friendly website and using it to retrieve information.

Companies have the option to protect against XSS attacks by implementing an Azure **Web Application Firewall** (**WAF**). Combine the Azure WAF with Microsoft Sentinel and Azure Playbooks to detect and block the XSS attack.

Zero-day exploits

Some attacks can be aimed at desktops. An example of a **zero-day exploit** is when a bug is found in an operating system or application while there is no solution from the vendor to fix the issue. The best way to protect against these types of attacks is by running security software that checks the behavior of users and applications, automatically blocking applications when they perform unwanted actions. Only expose systems to the internet directly if they require internet access, and protect systems behind a firewall. Make sure to patch your operating system and applications as soon as security updates become available. We will discuss patching more in-depth later on in this book in *Chapter 6, Update Management Strategies*.

Social engineering attacks

A **social engineering attack** is based on gaining information and establishing trust with a user. This does not only happen virtually but also in person. An in-person example would be when a bad actor shows up on a doorstep and claims to belong to a bank, needing access to the user's banking details to solve a mysterious issue.

There are multiple ways that somebody can prevent this kind of attack from happening. Some important ways of preventing this are as follows:

- Using multi-factor authentication
- Using strong passwords and storing them in a password manager
- Using passwordless authentication
- Not sharing personal information with people you don't know
- Never leaving your device unguarded in public
- Not letting strangers connect to your private Wi-Fi network

In this section, we have not only taken a look at the different kinds of cyberattacks that are commonly used but also how IT admins are able to prevent them from doing damage. In the next part, we will talk about what an organization can do to recover from a cyberattack.

Recovering from a cyberattack

During the last couple of years, we have seen a lot of news articles about companies that have been hit by a cyberattack. Most of the time, these attacks are intended to cripple or extort an organization. Some examples of cyberattacks in the last couple of years are as follows:

- Attacks on national institutes using a DDoS attack, with the purpose of bringing down websites

- Ransomware attacks targeting hospitals to make sure that they can't treat patients anymore

It's nearly impossible to create an IT environment that cannot be compromised. So, let's assume the worst. What options do companies have to recover from a cybersecurity attack? The good news is that there are standards and protocols that help companies to respond in the correct manner after a cyberattack. Some examples are as follows:

- Microsoft has **incident response playbooks** for phishing, password spraying, app consent grantx, and compromised and malicious applications.

- **Microsoft DART** ransomware approach and best practices.

- Microsoft has a service called **Microsoft Incident Response**. This service encompasses a global team of security experts that help companies recover after a cyberattack.

- The **National Institute of Standards and Technology Incident Response Framework**. We will elaborate on this in the *A cyber incident response plan* section.

- The **Microsoft Azure Well Architected Framework** contains security guidelines to define an incident response plan. The incident response plan outlines the steps to be taken when an attack was successfully executed. Here are key recommendations:

  - **Logging and notifications**: Make sure that the correct roles and employees are notified, and make sure to keep an audit trail.

  - **Recover from the incident**: Use the recovery mechanism that is described in the incident recovery plan to recover safely.

  - **Learn from the incident**: Make sure to evaluate the incident and the recovery process. This will provide valuable feedback that can be used to improve the security posture and the incident response plan.

  - **Communication**: Communicate with the internal stakeholders about the root cause of the incident, the remediation, and further improvements.

A cyber incident response plan

The **National Institute of Standards and Technology (NIST)** has guidelines on how to create a cyber incident response plan. The reason for this plan is so that companies can react more quickly to cyber and security incidents. The goal of the plan is to minimize the time needed to react and resolve an incident, reducing its impact.

Let's take a look at these guidelines.

The first thing that a company needs to do before making a response plan is to *determine the response policy*. This policy includes different sections such as the following:

- The classification of a cyber or security incident
- Defining what assets are protected
- The different roles and responsibilities
- Determining who will respond to an incident
- Determining who is responsible for creating documentation

The classification of a cyber or security incident

This step is to determine which kind of security incident can happen and which events can trigger this response plan. Depending on the severity of the incident other teams might be needed to solve the incident. For example, if there was a phishing mail that nobody responded to, there is no need for a response plan.

Defining what assets are protected

An important aspect of the response plan is to determine what assets need to be protected, the level of importance, and where the asset is located.

The different roles and responsibilities

Determine which teams need to be involved, depending on the type and severity of the incident. It's imperative to react as fast as possible if there is an incident. A great way to improve reaction time is by determining the roles and responsibilities of each team.

Here are some examples of teams that can be involved in the incident response plan:

- Networking teams
- Threat researchers
- Security analysts

Define a role with the sole task of coordinating between the teams that are involved in responding to an incident, such as an incident response manager.

Determining who will respond to an incident

The size of a company plays a major factor in who will respond to an incident. Smaller companies can have a single team to respond to incidents, while large companies can have multiple response teams spread out over different locations over the world. These response teams should be coordinated by the incident response manager.

Determining who is responsible for creating documentation

A crucial part of a response plan is to create documentation. This documentation should ask questions such as the following:

- What kind of incident has happened?
- Which incident response teams have been involved?
- What steps and measures have been taken by the incident response teams?

Use this documentation to evaluate the process and determine possible improvements to make sure the incident cannot happen again. The responsibility of creating the documentation depends on who participated in resolving the incident. With this, we conclude the section about the types and recovery processes of a cyberattack. Now, it's time to return back to desktops. Let's take a look at how virtual desktops can be used to increase the recovery time after a cyberattack.

Virtual desktops to the rescue

What if desktops have become compromised? Recovery times can take a lot of time to complete, especially in the case of laptops that travel with their users to different locations. Recovery tasks may include the following steps:

1. Gain access to the device. The user might need to bring the device to the IT department.
2. Clean the device of any malware using an antivirus solution.
3. Reinstall the device.

These steps are time-consuming but not a big problem when only one or a couple of desktops need to be cleaned or reinstalled. But what happens when malware has spread throughout a lot of desktops, rendering most or all useless?

One big advantage of services such as Windows 365 and Azure Virtual Desktop is that companies can spin up large amounts of desktops that the workforce can use to sign into and resume their work. Both solutions are very flexible and scalable, giving a company the choice to either keep the virtual desktop or return to the physical desktop once an incident has been resolved and reviewed.

The option to deploy virtual desktops if there is an incident should be considered in advance and described in the incident response plan. This will help incident response teams to follow the correct steps in the correct order.

> **Tip**
> Make sure that your environment is ready to deploy virtual desktops if your company has determined to deploy them if there is an incident. The preparation includes determining which type of virtual desktop should be deployed and which preparation steps need to be performed for a particular solution. This reduces the time needed to deploy desktops in a recovery scenario.

Summary

In this chapter, you learned about modern cyberattacks and how to protect against these attacks. It's almost impossible to provide a 100% safe environment for a company and its users. You learned about the Microsoft solutions and guidelines as well as NIST and how an incident response plan should be followed if an incident has taken place. Lastly, you learned how virtual desktops, using the power and flexibility of the Microsoft Cloud, can be used to speed up the recovery process if existing desktops have become compromised.

The connection from a local device to a virtual desktop is called a session. In the next chapter, we will discuss the security controls that IT admins can leverage to secure user sessions.

Part 3:
Security Controls for
W365 and AVD

The third part of the book discusses security controls that are available for both Windows 365 and Azure Virtual Desktop. It explains how to secure user sessions by using controls such as Conditional Access and MFA and how to prevent data leakage from a desktop using screen capture protection and watermarking. It also covers Microsoft's cloud-based update solutions, such as Windows Update for Business, Windows Autopatch, and Custom Image Templates. But there is more to keeping company data safe on a desktop. Make sure to use solutions such as Defender for Endpoint with tamper protection and encryption to detect and prevent threats. This part concludes with configuring access control, where you'll learn about RBAC, Microsoft Entra PIM, and the new Windows LAPS. By the end of this part, you will have learned how to keep your data and desktop safe using modern security controls that can be used for both Windows 365 as well as Azure Virtual Desktop.

This part contains the following chapters:

- *Chapter 4, Securing User Sessions*
- *Chapter 5, Preventing Data Leakage from the Desktops*
- *Chapter 6, Update Management Strategies*
- *Chapter 7, Threat Detection and Prevention*
- *Chapter 8, Configuring Access Control*

4

Securing User Sessions

This chapter will cover various security controls that can be used to secure **user sessions** for both Windows 365 and Azure Virtual Desktop. The reader will learn how to configure **multifactor authentication (MFA)** using different methods such as per-user MFA, security defaults, and **conditional access (CA)**. The chapter will also cover the configuration of RDP devices and resource redirections for both Windows 365 and Azure Virtual Desktop and RDP session time limits.

By the end of this chapter, you will have a good understanding of why it's so important to configure these security controls to make your virtual desktops more secure.

In this chapter, we will cover the following topics:

- CA and MFA
- RDP device and resource redirections for Windows 365
- RDP properties for Azure Virtual Desktop
- RDP session time limits

CA and MFA

Let's start this chapter by taking a look at CA and MFA and why this is an important subject. In the past, it was common practice to have an account on a website with only a password to protect it. In the last decade, it has become a security best practice to use a second factor as an extra means to authenticate yourself.

One common reason that a user account is breached is because there isn't a second-factor authentication configured. By adding a second factor, we can increase the security of the user account by 99.9%. As you can see in *Figure 4.1*, there are various methods of verification that a user can add by logging on to their user profile at `https://myprofile.microsoft.com/`.

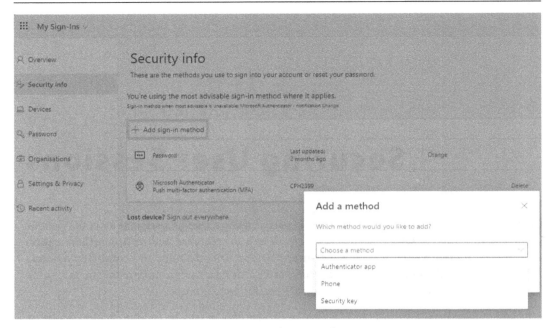

Figure 4.1 – Security info

Not all authentication options are available to the users unless the IT admins enable them. This can be done in the Microsoft Entra portal (`https://entra.microsoft.com`) in the **Protection** menu, as shown in *Figure 4.2*. You can enable the methods for all users or limit the methods by using Active Directory security groups that are synced to Entra ID using Entra ID Connect.

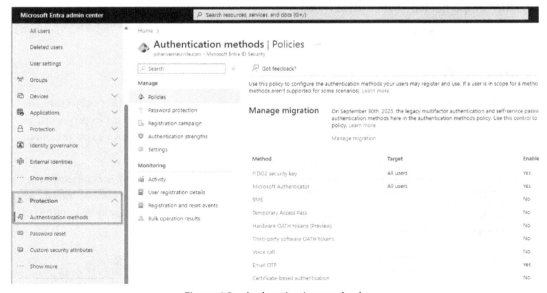

Figure 4.2 – Authentication methods

The IT admin has different options for configuring MFA. MFA adds an additional layer of authentication to the user's login. A method that is used often is the Microsoft Authenticator app, which can be downloaded and installed from either the Apple App Store or Google Play Store. Each has its advantages. Let's have a look at how these options are configured:

- Security defaults
- Per-user MFA
- CA policy (recommended)

Security defaults

Microsoft introduced **security defaults** as a default security setting in 2023. According to Microsoft, security defaults were introduced as a way to improve the security of organizations who want to increase their security posture, but are new to Microsoft Entra. The other reason is for organizations that are using the free tier of Entra ID or don't have Microsoft Entra ID licenses.

To activate or deactivate this setting, the IT admin needs to go to `https://entra.microsoft.com` and then **Identity** > **Overview** > **Properties** > **Manage security defaults** and set **Security defaults** to **Enabled** or **Disabled** and hit **Save**.

Figure 4.3 – Enabling security defaults in the Entra portal

After enabling security defaults, the IT admin should also revoke all existing tokens. This way, all users will be required to register for MFA. This step can be done using the `Revoke-AzureADUserAllRefreshToken` PowerShell command.

The user has 14 days to register using the Microsoft Authenticator app or any other supporting OATH TOTP. After 14 days, the user will be forced to register.

When the user has completed the MFA registration and tries to log on, they will get the following screen.

Figure 4.4 – MFA request with number matching

Per-user MFA

In case a company isn't eligible for using CA or doesn't want to use security defaults, they can still enable MFA on a per-user basis.

To enable this feature, the IT admin will need to complete the following steps:

1. The IT admin will need to go to `https://entra.microsoft.com` and then **Identity** > **Users** > **All users** and select **Per-user MFA**.

Figure 4.5 – Per-user MFA

2.   The IT admin will then need to verify the login credentials and they will see the following screen.

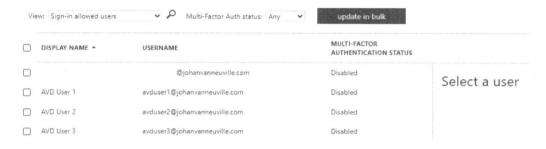

Figure 4.6 – Per-user MFA portal

3.   The IT admin has three different MFA options for the users.

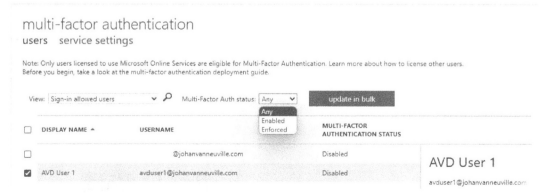

Figure 4.7 – Per-user MFA options

Let's have a look at the definitions of all the options:

- **Any** means when filtering on **Any**, the IT admin will be able to see all users and their current status.

- **Enabled** means that per-user is active for the user, but the user can still authenticate using their password for legacy authentication. The user will be prompted to register an MFA method the next time they sign in using, for example, a browser or an office application such as Outlook.

- **Enforced** means that the user is enrolled for MFA and will be asked to register an MFA method the next time they log on using a browser and modern authentication. The user's state will also automatically be changed to **Enforced** when a user completes the registration while in the **Enabled** state.

To change the MFA status, the IT admin needs to select the user and select Enable, and the state will change, as shown in *Figure 4.8*.

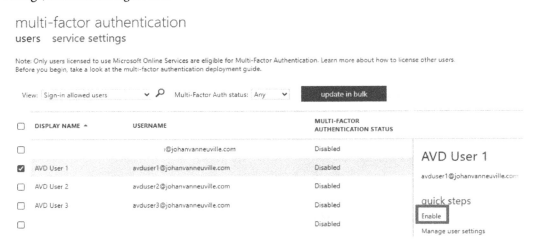

Figure 4.8 – Enable per-user MFA

The admin will be prompted, and the user will be enabled for MFA after this step.

Figure 4.9 – Enable per-user MFA message

To conclude this section about per-user MFA, this method of activating MFA is not recommended when using Entra ID joined session hosts, as explained in the following link: `https://learn.microsoft.com/azure/virtual-desktop/set-up-mfa?WT.mc_id=EM-MVP-5003320#microsoft-entra-joined-session-host-vms`.

CA policy

If a company wants to manage MFA centrally and add more conditions to it, it will have to use **CA policies**. CA works with *if-then* statements. *If* a user wants to access a resource, *then* the user must complete an action before they are allowed access to the resource.

However, before starting, the IT admin will have to make sure that the organization is compliant with Microsoft licensing. To use CA, one of the following licenses is required:

- Microsoft Entra ID P1 or P2
- Microsoft Enterprise Mobility & Security E3 or E5
- Microsoft 365 E3 or E5
- Microsoft 365 Business Premium

Let's have a look at how we can create a CA policy specifically to access Windows 365 and Azure Virtual Desktop. It's recommended to create separate policies for both technologies.

CA policy – Azure Virtual Desktop

A CA policy for Azure Virtual Desktop can be created in multiple portals. The IT admin can use the Azure portal or the Entra portal. Let's take a look at the configuration in the Entra portal.

Before configuring the policy, the IT admin needs to disable the security defaults.

Go to `https://entra.microsoft.com`, then **Protection** > **Conditional Access**, and select **Create new policy**.

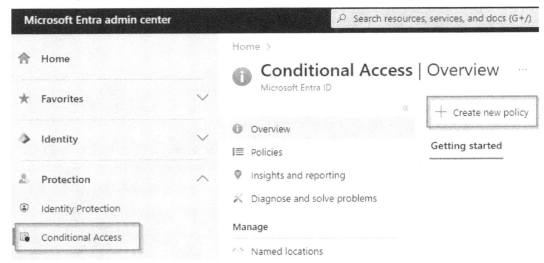

Figure 4.10 – Create a CA policy in the Entra portal

First of all, we need to give the new policy a name. It's possible that the company has a strict naming convention to follow for governance purposes. An example of a policy name can be found in the following image.

Figure 4.11 – Example of a name of policy

It's important to know that when we were creating a policy for Azure Virtual Desktop and Windows 365, there was a name change from *Windows Virtual Desktop* to *Azure Virtual Desktop*. Depending on when in time, meaning before or after the name change, the IT admin has registered *the Microsoft. DesktopVirtualization* provider on the subscription, the name of the app in your policy will be different. However, the ID of the app will be the same for both apps. The two possible names of the app are as follows:

- Windows Virtual Desktop
- Azure Virtual Desktop

It is important to know that both apps have the same app ID, which is `9cdead84-a844-4324-93f2-b2e6bb768d07`.

To register the provider, the IT admin goes to **AVD subscription** > **Resource providers** and searches for `desktop`. The following image shows us the provider with the status of **Registered** as a registration state. If the provider is not registered yet, the IT admin can select the provider and click **Register**. The process of registering the provider can take a couple of minutes.

hub-jvn-management-01

⋮≡ sub-hub-jvn-management-01 | Resource providers   ☆   ⋯
Subscription

| 🔍 Search | ⟳ « | ⊂ Register   ⟲ Unregister   ⟳ Refresh   ⟲ Feedback |

🔍 desktop

🎈 Overview		
🗄 Activity log		
🗝 Access control (IAM)	**Provider ↑**	**Status**
🏷 Tags		
✘ Diagnose and solve problems	◯ Microsoft.DesktopVirtualization ⋯	✅ Registered

Figure 4.12 – A registered DesktopVirtualisation provider

Of course, we need to assign this policy to users. We could assign the policy to all the users in the organization, but this is not recommended. It could be that not all the users in the organization need to be given access if they don't use it. In this example, the IT admin selects a security group of users that can have access.

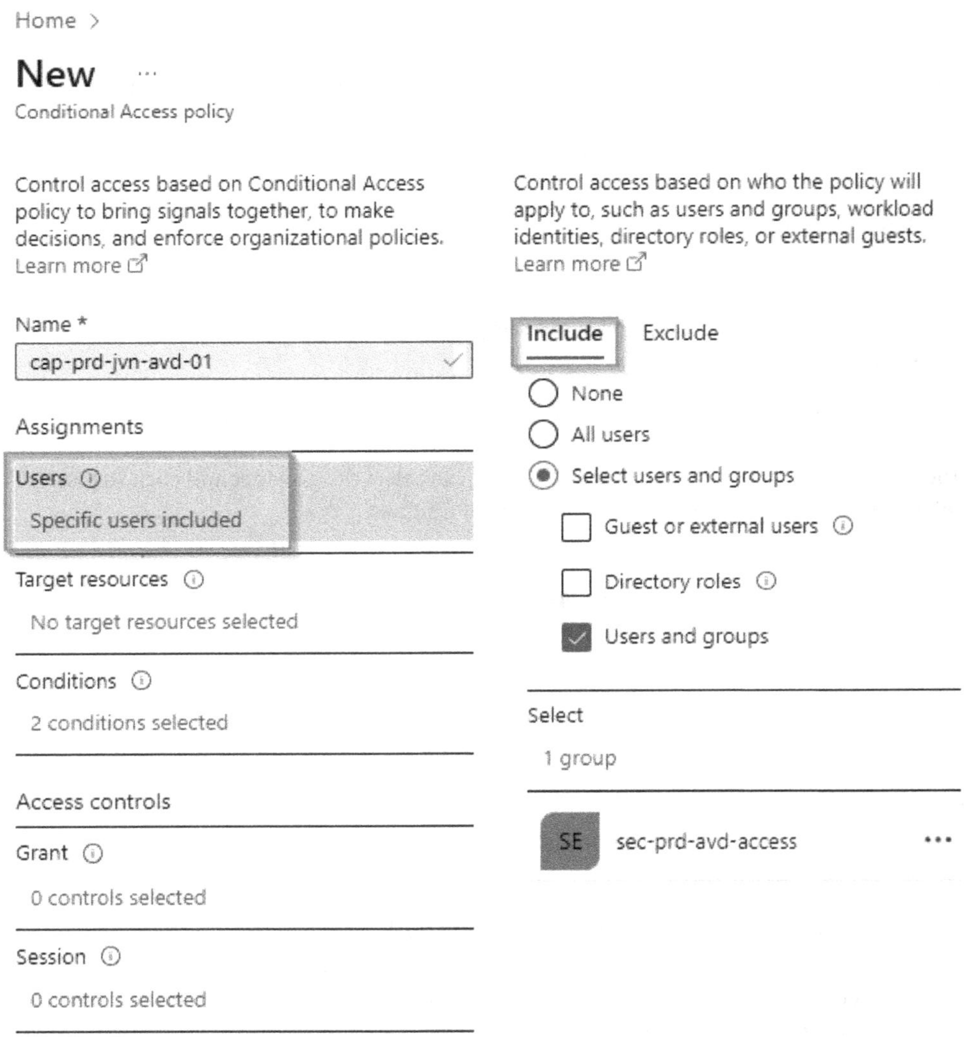

Home >

New   ···

Conditional Access policy

Control access based on Conditional Access policy to bring signals together, to make decisions, and enforce organizational policies. Learn more ☐

Control access based on who the policy will apply to, such as users and groups, workload identities, directory roles, or external guests. Learn more ☐

Name *

cap-prd-jvn-avd-01   ✓

Assignments

Users ⓘ

Specific users included

Target resources ⓘ

No target resources selected

Conditions ⓘ

2 conditions selected

Access controls

Grant ⓘ

0 controls selected

Session ⓘ

0 controls selected

Include   Exclude

◯ None

◯ All users

◉ Select users and groups

☐ Guest or external users ⓘ

☐ Directory roles ⓘ

☑ Users and groups

Select

1 group

[SE] sec-prd-avd-access   •••

Figure 4.13 – Security group for access to Azure Virtual Desktop

Another very important point is that you should also make an exclusion, for any groups or users that don't need to be assigned to this policy. For security reasons, it's important to exclude the **break-glass accounts** in case there is an outage with MFA. The break-glass accounts are accounts with the global admin roles assigned to them but without MFA. In case there is an issue and MFA is unavailable, the IT admin can still log in using these accounts.

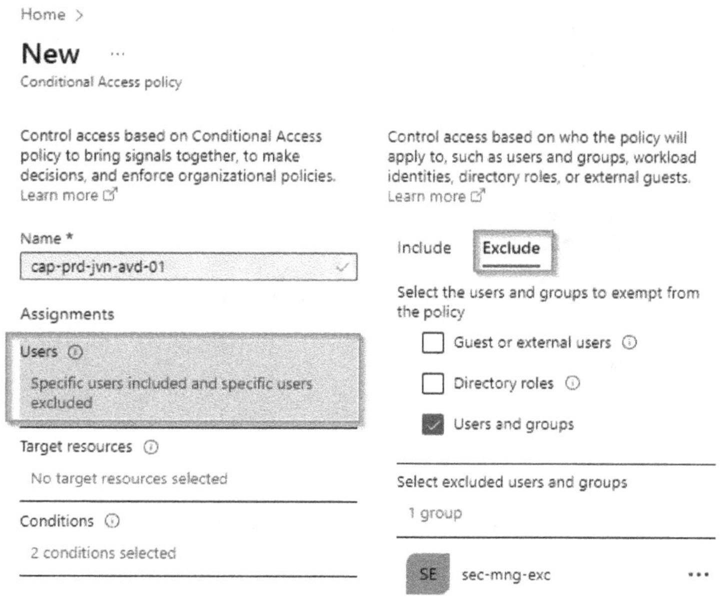

Home >

New ...
Conditional Access policy

Control access based on Conditional Access policy to bring signals together, to make decisions, and enforce organizational policies. Learn more

Control access based on who the policy will apply to, such as users and groups, workload identities, directory roles, or external guests. Learn more

Name *

cap-prd-jvn-avd-01

Assignments

Users ⓘ

Specific users included and specific users excluded

Target resources ⓘ

No target resources selected

Conditions ⓘ

2 conditions selected

Include   **Exclude**

Select the users and groups to exempt from the policy

☐ Guest or external users ⓘ

☐ Directory roles ⓘ

☑ Users and groups

Select excluded users and groups

1 group

SE   sec-mng-exc   ...

Figure 4.14 – Exclude break-glass accounts from policy

Now that the provider is registered, the IT admin can select the target resource.

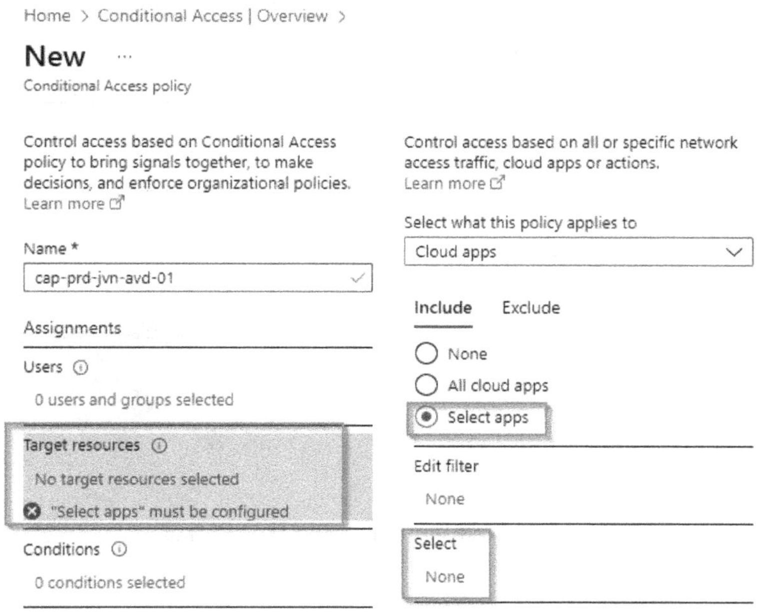

Home > Conditional Access | Overview >

New ...
Conditional Access policy

Control access based on Conditional Access policy to bring signals together, to make decisions, and enforce organizational policies. Learn more

Control access based on all or specific network access traffic, cloud apps or actions. Learn more

Name *

cap-prd-jvn-avd-01

Assignments

Users ⓘ

0 users and groups selected

Target resources ⓘ

No target resources selected
❌ "Select apps" must be configured

Conditions ⓘ

0 conditions selected

Select what this policy applies to

Cloud apps ▾

Include   Exclude

○ None

○ All cloud apps

● Select apps

Edit filter

None

Select

None

Figure 4.15 – Selecting the target resource app

Type `azure virtual desktop` in the search bar or search for the `9cdead84-a844-4324-93f2-b2e6bb768d07` app ID.

Figure 4.16 – Azure Virtual Desktop app ID

Home > Conditional Access | Overview >

New   ...
Conditional Access policy

Control access based on Conditional Access policy to bring signals together, to make decisions, and enforce organizational policies. Learn more ☐

Name *

| cap-prd-jvn-avd-01 | ✓ |

Assignments

Users ⓘ

0 users and groups selected

Target resources ⓘ

1 app included

Conditions ⓘ

0 conditions selected

Access controls

Grant ⓘ

0 controls selected

Session ⓘ

0 controls selected

Control access based on all or specific network access traffic, cloud apps or actions. Learn more ☐

Select what this policy applies to

| Cloud apps | ∨ |

Include   Exclude

○ None
○ All cloud apps
◉ Select apps

Edit filter

None

Select

Azure Virtual Desktop

| AV | Azure Virtual Desktop
9cdead84-a844-4324-93f2-b2e6bb768d07 | ... |

Figure 4.17 – Azure Virtual Desktop app selected

In the next step, IT admins can configure several conditions that all have the purpose of increasing the security of the CA policy. Some of them are necessary to configure for Azure Virtual Desktop.

The first setting the IT admin will need to change is **Client apps condition**. The IT admin will configure this to **Browser > Mobile and desktop clients**. Configuring this setting will make sure that the users have to use MFA when connecting from any browser or desktop client.

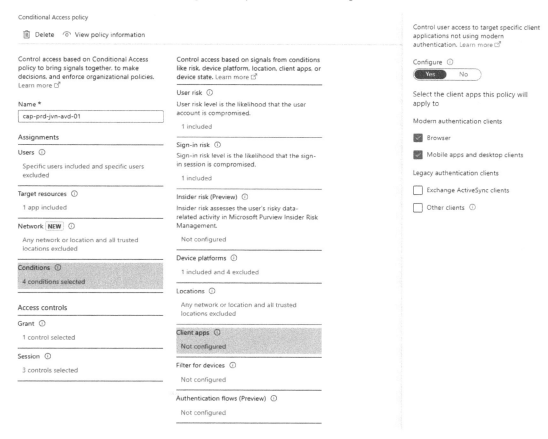

Figure 4.18 – Client apps selected

Some organizations don't want to burden users by doing MFA in the office. The IT admin can configure this in **Locations condition**. For example, the IPs from the organization's office can be excluded from the policy.

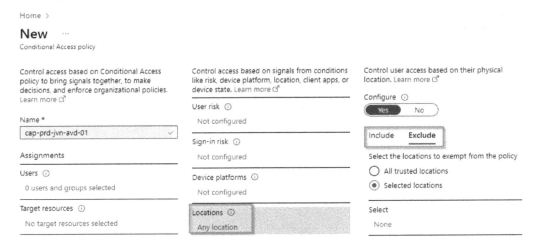

Figure 4.19 – MFA policy excludes locations

The next set of important settings are **Access controls**. This set of controls will determine whether a user will be blocked or granted access. In this example, the IT admin grants access to the Azure Virtual Desktop environment but only when the user does MFA.

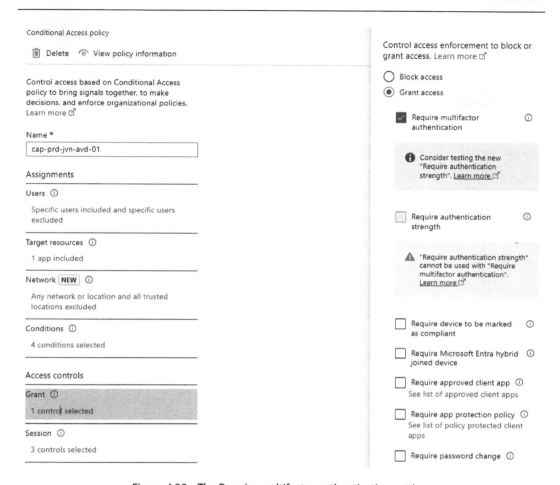

Figure 4.20 – The Require multifactor authentication setting

The last setting that is important is the *session controls*. Here, the IT admin can decide how often a user needs to use MFA. The default from Microsoft is every 90 days unless a user gets blocked or resets the account's password. To make the account more secure, the IT admin can set the sign-in frequency at 8 hours or to any amount of time that is agreed in the organization.

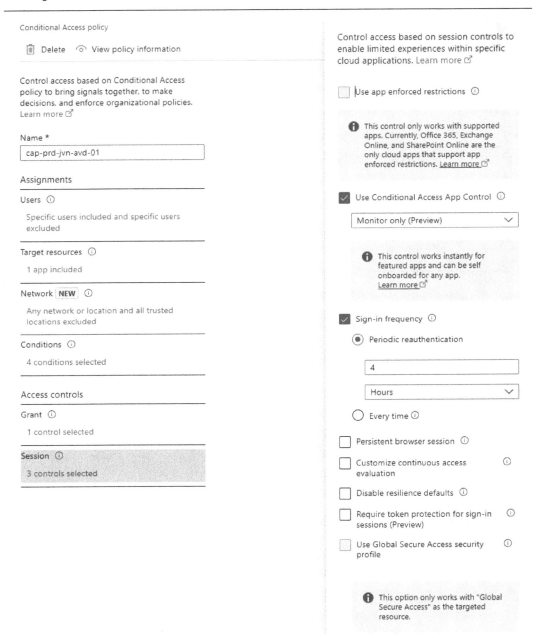

Figure 4.21 – The Sign-in frequency configuration

After all these steps, enable the policy by putting the slider on **status on** and pressing the **Create** button.

Now that we have a policy for Azure Virtual Desktop, the IT admin will create one for Windows 365.

CA policy – Windows 365

To create the policy for Windows 365 or, as they are also called, Cloud PCs, the IT admin can use multiple portals. There is the Azure portal, Entra portal, and the Intune admin center. In this example, the IT admin uses the Intune portal.

The IT admin goes to `https://intune.microsoft.com`, then **Endpoint security** > **Conditional access**, and selects **Create a new policy**.

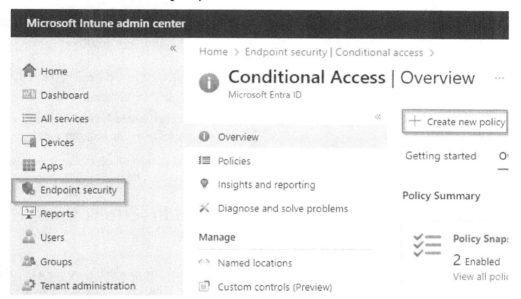

Figure 4.22 – Create a new policy for Windows 365

The steps that the IT admin needs to take are almost the same as with the Azure Virtual Desktop policy, so let's take a look at the differences between both.

The difference is between the apps in **Target resource**. For Windows 365, there are four apps that can be used. The first ones are Windows 365 and Azure Virtual Desktop. These apps are used for actions such as retrieving the list of resources for the user and with Cloud PC restarts.

Figure 4.23 – Windows 365 app ID

The other apps are shown in the following image when the IT admin configures a single sign-on in the Windows 365 provisioning policy. The recommendation from Microsoft is also to create a matching policy for these apps.

Figure 4.24 – The Microsoft Remote Desktop and Windows Cloud Login app IDs

Now that we have all the apps selected that we need, the IT admin can configure the rest of the policy like with Azure Virtual Desktop.

With these policies in place, the IT admin has already made sure that every user who wants to connect to their virtual desktop will need to perform MFA. This will already increase the security a lot.

Now that the user has learned the benefits of configuring CA, it's time to take a look at how to further secure the virtual desktop resources with RDP device and resource redirections.

Configuring RDP device and resource redirections for Windows 365

Especially after the COVID-19 pandemic, hybrid work has become the new standard for a lot of organizations. The device and resource redirections that will be explained in this topic will help IT admins foresee a safe working environment for the users, which also prevents data leakage. Let's take a closer look at each of them to see what the added value is.

To add more security to Windows 365, IT admins can configure RDP device and resource redirections for Cloud PCs. This can be configured in multiple ways with the help of the Intune admin center or with a **Group Policy Object (GPO)**.

Both of these methods have their benefits and requirements for Cloud PCs:

- Intune settings catalog is for Cloud PCs that are Entra joined and hybrid joined
- Active Directory GPO is for Entra hybrid joined

Device and resource redirections with Intune

The first way to configure these settings is through the Intune admin center. This is done using a configuration profile that the IT admin can create as shown in *Figure 4.25* by going to https:// intune.microsoft.com and then **Devices > Windows > Configuration profiles > + Create > + New Policy > Windows 10 and later > Settings catalog**.

The first step in creating the policy is to give it a name as shown in *Figure 4.25*. As with all items that need to be created, check whether you are compliant with any naming convention policy that the organization might have.

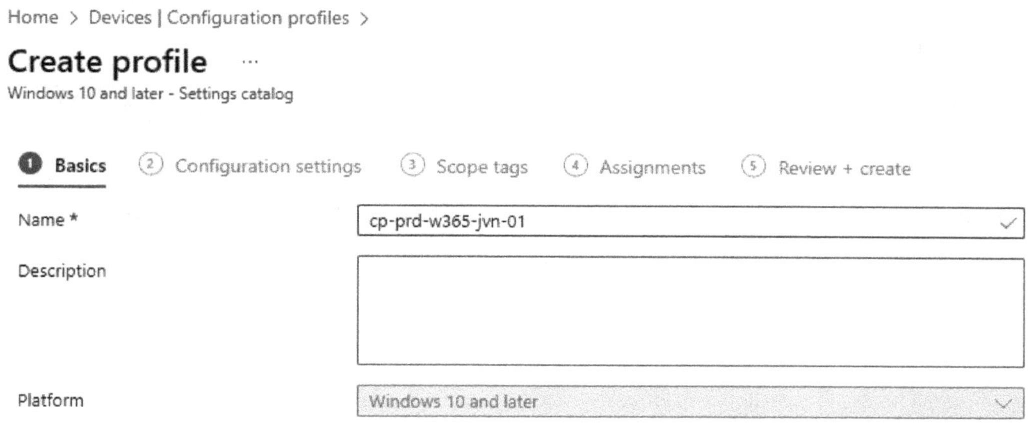

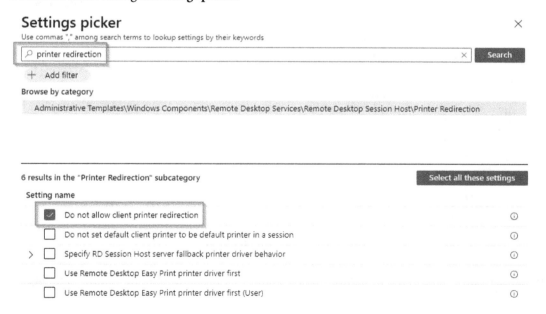

Figure 4.25 – Example policy name

After choosing the correct name for the policy, the IT admin searches for the correct `printer redirection` setting in **Settings picker**.

Figure 4.26 – Printer redirection

After choosing the correct printer settings, the IT admin will need to search for `Device and Resource Redirection` to get the other options that can be configured.

In the following example, the IT admin will block all redirections to comply with the company policy.

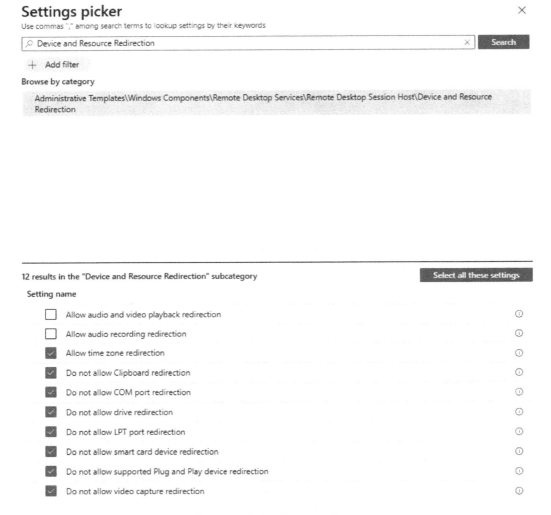

Figure 4.27 – Device redirections

After the IT admin selects all the settings, the settings need to be enabled. By selecting all these settings, you can block all these devices from being used.

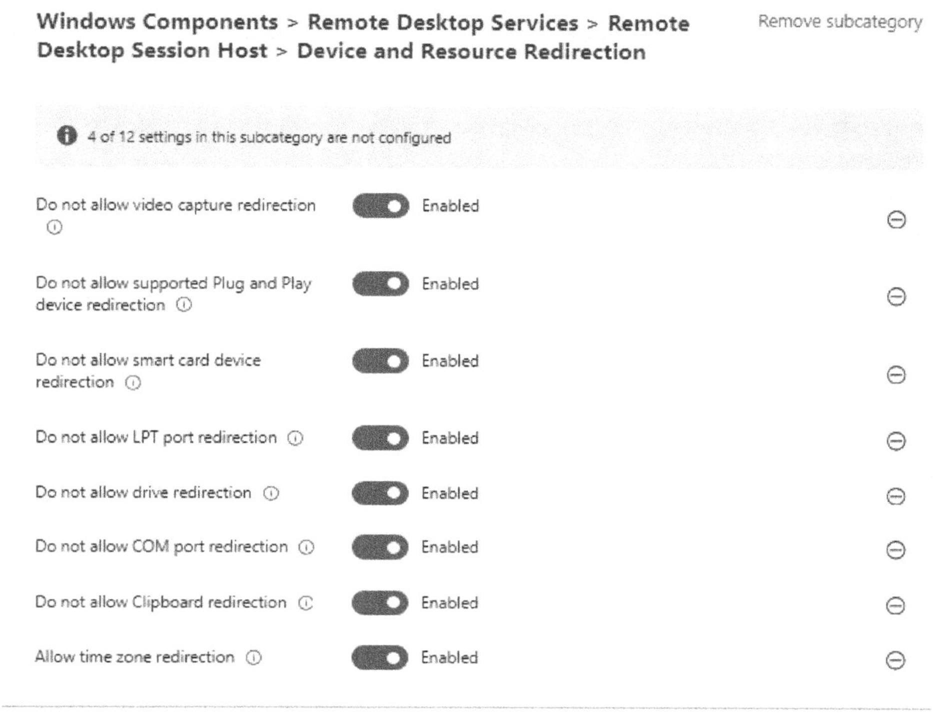

Windows Components > Remote Desktop Services > Remote Desktop Session Host > Device and Resource Redirection

Remove subcategory

🛈 4 of 12 settings in this subcategory are not configured

Do not allow video capture redirection ⓘ	⬤ Enabled	⊖
Do not allow supported Plug and Play device redirection ⓘ	⬤ Enabled	⊖
Do not allow smart card device redirection ⓘ	⬤ Enabled	⊖
Do not allow LPT port redirection ⓘ	⬤ Enabled	⊖
Do not allow drive redirection ⓘ	⬤ Enabled	⊖
Do not allow COM port redirection ⓘ	⬤ Enabled	⊖
Do not allow Clipboard redirection ⓒ	⬤ Enabled	⊖
Allow time zone redirection ⓘ	⬤ Enabled	⊖

Figure 4.28 – Enabling device redirections

The last step is to scope the policy based on a device filter for Cloud PCs, as you can see in *Figure 4.29*.

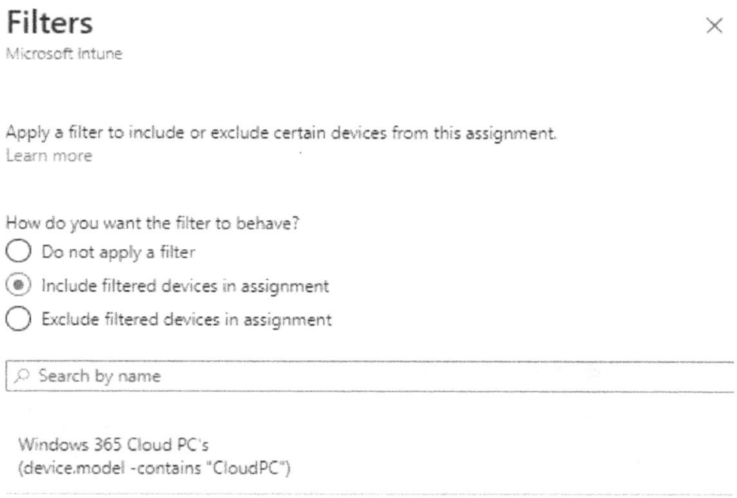

Filters   ✕

Microsoft Intune

Apply a filter to include or exclude certain devices from this assignment.
Learn more

How do you want the filter to behave?
◯ Do not apply a filter
◉ Include filtered devices in assignment
◯ Exclude filtered devices in assignment

🔍 Search by name

Windows 365 Cloud PC's
(device.model -contains "CloudPC")

Figure 4.29 – Intune device filter for Cloud PCs

The IT admin can review all the settings before creating the policy, making sure that all settings are correct.

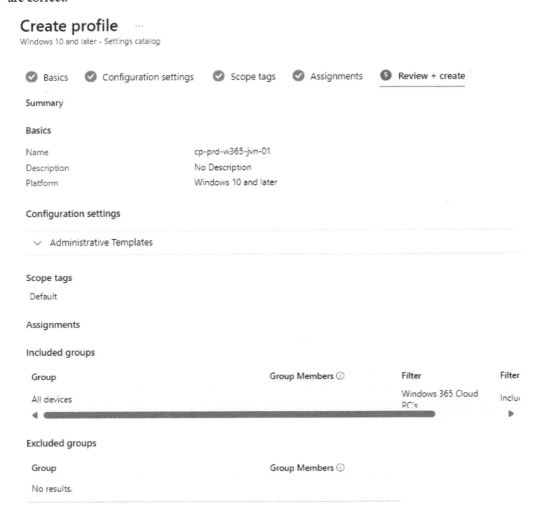

Figure 4.30 – Review profile settings

Device and resource redirections with group policy

Now that you know how to configure the device and resource redirections using Intune, it's time to check the other method using a GPO. This method only works if the Cloud PCs are *Entra hybrid joined*.

The IT admin needs a GPO with the following settings.

Navigate to **Computer Configuration > Administrative Templates > Windows Components > Remote Desktop Services > Remote Desktop Session Host > Device and Resource Redirection.**

Device and Resource Redirection			
Select an item to view its description.	Setting	State	Comment
	Do not allow video capture redirection	Enabled	No
	Allow audio and video playback redirection	Enabled	No
	Allow audio recording redirection	Enabled	No
	Limit audio playback quality	Not configured	No
	Do not allow Clipboard redirection	Enabled	No
	Do not allow COM port redirection	Enabled	No
	Do not allow drive redirection	Enabled	No
	Do not allow LPT port redirection	Enabled	No
	Do not allow supported Plug and Play device redirection	Enabled	No
	Do not allow smart card device redirection	Enabled	No
	Allow time zone redirection	Not configured	No
	Do not allow WebAuthn redirection	Not configured	No

Figure 4.31 – GPO device redirection

With this GPO configured, you will now be able to configure the device and resource redirections for Windows 365. Let's continue and see how these settings are applied to Azure Virtual Desktop host pools.

Configuring RDP properties for Azure Virtual Desktop

RDP device redirections are a great way to customize an Azure Virtual Desktop host pool. Because these settings are per host pool, you can set different redirections depending on the use case of the host pool. The IT admin can configure settings such as camera, speaker, and microphone redirection but also settings that can increase the security of the host pool. These settings are as follows:

- Drive and storage redirection
- Clipboard redirection
- COM ports redirection
- Printer redirection
- Smartcard redirection
- USB redirection

As with Windows 365, the RDP properties for Azure Virtual Desktop can also be configured using the GPO option, but now the IT admin will use the RDP properties option in the Azure portal. These settings can be found when searching for Azure Virtual Desktop in the Azure portal and going to **Host pools** > **RDP Properties** > **Device redirection**, as seen in the following figure.

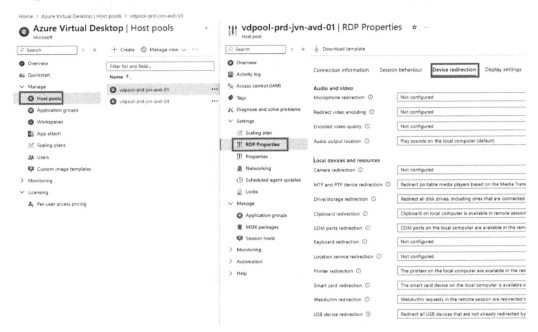

Figure 4.32 – Device redirection location

The following settings are available on a per-host-pool level.

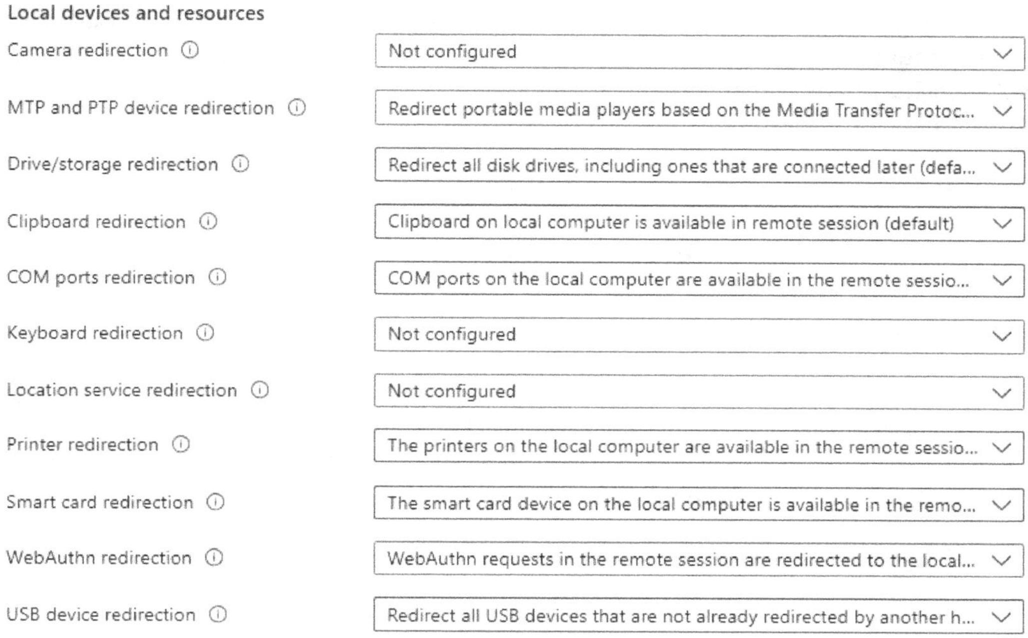

Local devices and resources

Camera redirection ⓘ	Not configured ⌄
MTP and PTP device redirection ⓘ	Redirect portable media players based on the Media Transfer Protoc... ⌄
Drive/storage redirection ⓘ	Redirect all disk drives, including ones that are connected later (defa... ⌄
Clipboard redirection ⓘ	Clipboard on local computer is available in remote session (default) ⌄
COM ports redirection ⓘ	COM ports on the local computer are available in the remote sessio... ⌄
Keyboard redirection ⓘ	Not configured ⌄
Location service redirection ⓘ	Not configured ⌄
Printer redirection ⓘ	The printers on the local computer are available in the remote sessio... ⌄
Smart card redirection ⓘ	The smart card device on the local computer is available in the remo... ⌄
WebAuthn redirection ⓘ	WebAuthn requests in the remote session are redirected to the local... ⌄
USB device redirection ⓘ	Redirect all USB devices that are not already redirected by another h... ⌄

Figure 4.33 – Device redirections

Drive and storage redirection

When a user connects from their own device and the **Drive/storage redirection** option is active, the user will be able to access the local drive on the virtual desktop. This is not ideal, especially if clipboard redirection is active. This is why it's recommended to configure this setting so that no drives are redirected, as seen in the following image.

Figure 4.34 – Drive/storage redirection

Clipboard redirection

One of the things users do all the time when working on a device is using the copy-paste feature. It's a very useful feature that can save a lot of time. However, when the users are working remotely and data may not leave the organization, it can be dangerous to allow this. When you disable this feature, users won't be able to copy text or files anymore to or from their local device.

Figure 4.35 – Clipboard redirection

COM port redirection

A lot of times, a COM port or a serial port is used to manage devices that are used in warehouses or for industrial automation. These devices are often in a different network for security reasons. If the IT admin needs to provision a host pool to manage these devices, it's recommended to only configure the COM port redirection on this host pool.

Figure 4.36 – COM port redirection

Printer redirection

Users need to be able to print out documents. However, this is also a potential source for a data breach. It's a benefit that these settings can be done per host pool. If a user works from home, it's not always recommended to allow them to print on that printer.

Figure 4.37 – Printer redirection

Smartcard redirection

Certain applications that a user needs might require the use of a smartcard device. The use of these devices can be limited to certain host pools.

Figure 4.38 – Smartcard redirection

USB device redirection

USB devices can be dangerous when it comes to data. When USB devices that are connected to the local device are allowed in the remote session, users can easily transfer data when the clipboard redirection is also active. The other reason why blocking USB devices can be important is because these devices can have malware or other viruses on them. For these reasons, the IT admin can block these devices.

Figure 4.39 – USB redirection

The other option to configure all these settings is through the **Advanced** blade of **RDP Properties**. When the IT admin deploys the host pools with infra as code, they can add these properties in the deployment.

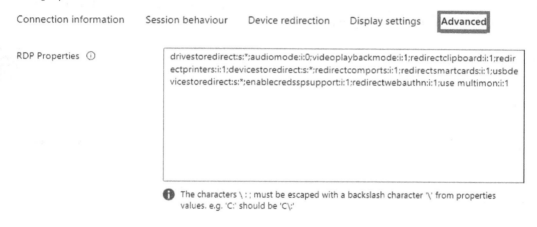

Figure 4.40 – RDP Properties | Advanced

Now that the reader knows how to implement the RDP properties for Azure Virtual Desktop, it's time to take a look at another security control. It's time to learn how to configure RDP session limit timeouts.

RDP session limit timeouts

Configuring session limit timeouts is not only needed to reduce the cost of the virtual desktops but also a good way to add more security. When a user's session is disconnected, these settings will make sure that the session will be logged off without any user or admin interaction. In this part, the reader will learn to configure these settings using a GPO through an Intune device configuration profile and the expected behavior from these settings.

The first option an IT admin has is to configure these settings using a GPO.

The two important settings are located in **Computer Configuration > Policies > Administrative Templates > Windows Components > Remote Desktop Services > Remote Desktop Session Host > Session Time Limits**.

Figure 4.41 – Session Time Limits

When correctly configured, the user will be disconnected when there is no input in the user session. In the Azure Virtual Desktop portal, you can see that there is a disconnected session. The amount of time configured in these settings depends on the organization.

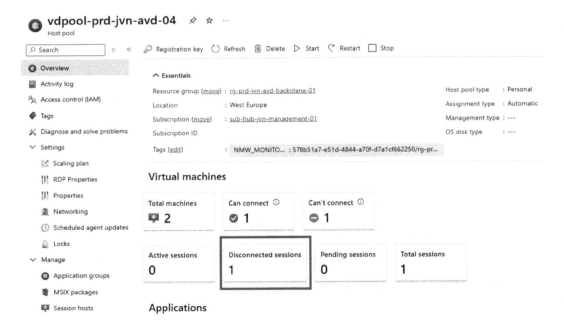

Figure 4.42 – Azure Virtual Desktop – the Disconnected sessions count

The last settings that the IT admin can set are the session time limits using the settings catalog from Intune. This setting can be found when typing `idle` in the search field.

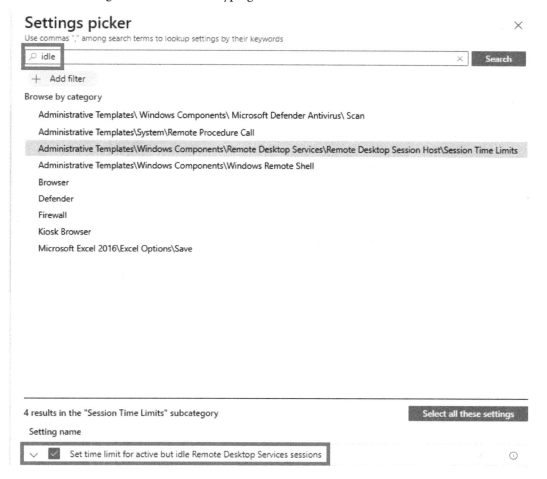

Figure 4.43 – Session time limit search in Intune

After selecting the correct setting, the IT admin needs to determine the amount of minutes before a session becomes disconnected.

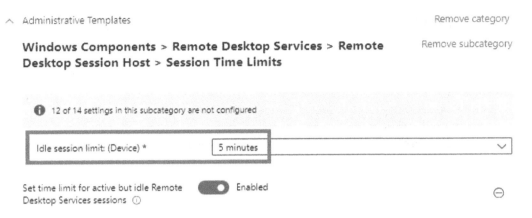

Figure 4.44 – Idle session limit minutes

With this setting configured and scoped to the Cloud PC's or Azure Virtual Desktop session hosts, the IT admin has created a more secure working environment for the users.

Summary

In this chapter, you have learned how to configure these shared security controls for virtual desktops. Not only do these controls add more security for the user accounts, but they also add an extra level of security to the virtual desktops in this new hybrid way of working.

Let's continue securing virtual desktops in *Chapter 5, Preventing Data Leakage from Desktops,* and take a look at how IT admins can prevent data leakage from the endpoint with technologies such as watermarking and screen capture protection.

Preventing Data Leakage from Desktops

This chapter will cover various security controls that IT admins can use for both Windows 365 and Azure Virtual Desktop to prevent data leaking from desktops. We will cover the topics of screen capture protection and watermarking and demonstrate how to configure and use these solutions. Last but not least, we will cover some more basic security controls implemented in Windows 10/11 to assist users in preventing data leakage.

By the end of this chapter, you will have a good understanding of screen capture protection and how it's complemented with watermarking. You will be able to resolve these watermark QR codes on Windows 365 Cloud PCs or resolve user sessions on Azure Virtual Desktop.

This chapter covers the following topics:

- Preventing screen captures
- Introducing and configuring watermarking
- Configuring screen locks

Preventing screen captures

By default, users have the ability to take screenshots of the virtual desktop. All they have to do is open their favorite screen capture utility, such as Snipping Tool, and take the screenshot. While this is perfectly OK in most situations, this might not be the desired behavior when users work with sensitive data such as personally identifiable data or important research data. In such cases, IT admins have the ability to prevent screen captures.

IT admins can configure screen capture protection for desktops running Windows 10/11. It does not matter whether they are physical, such as a desktop or laptop, or running in a virtualized environment such as Windows 365 or Azure Virtual Desktop. There are a few ways to enable the screen capture protection feature. IT admins can use either of the following:

- A device configuration profile in Microsoft Intune
- A Group Policy Object
- A local group policy

We recommend using a device configuration profile in **Microsoft Intune** for Windows 365 Cloud PCs. IT admins can also use a **Group Policy Object** (**GPO**) to enable the screen capture protection feature, depending on the design of the Azure Virtual Desktop infrastructure.

> **Tip**
> Make sure that end users use a supported sign-in method for the screen capture protection to work. At the time of writing, the web client is not supported. Users connecting to their virtual desktop with the screen capture protection enabled will be denied the ability to sign on.

Enabling screen capture protection for Windows 365

To enable the screen capture protection feature in Microsoft Intune, complete the following steps:

1. Go to **Devices** > **Windows** > **Configuration profiles** > **+ Create** > **+ New Policy**. Select **Windows 10 and later** as the platform and **Settings catalog** as the profile type.

Enter a name and a description, as shown in the following screenshot:

Home > Devices | Windows > Windows | Configuration profiles >

Create profile   ⋯
Windows 10 and later - Settings catalog

| **1** Basics | ② Configuration settings | ③ Scope tags | ④ Assignments | ⑤ Review + create |

Name *	Techlab	Enable screen capture protection on Cloud PCs ✓
Description	This configuration profile enables the screen capture protection.
Platform	Windows 10 and later ⌄

Figure 5.1 – Creating a configuration profile

2. Click + **Add settings** and search for `screen capture protection`. Select the result in the **Browse by category** window. Check the box next to **Enable screen capture protection** to add the settings to the configuration profile:

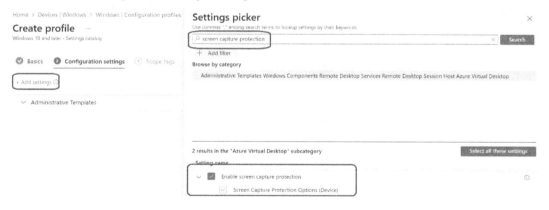

Figure 5.2 – Adding settings using the Settings picker tool

Once the switch is set to **Enabled**, the screen capture protection feature will be enabled for the client (the local machine that is used to connect to the virtual desktop).

3. IT admins can change the default behavior to prevent using screen capture utilities on the virtual desktop by toggling **Screen Capture Protection Options (Device)** to **Enabled**. In this case, the screen capture protection feature will work on the physical and virtual desktop:

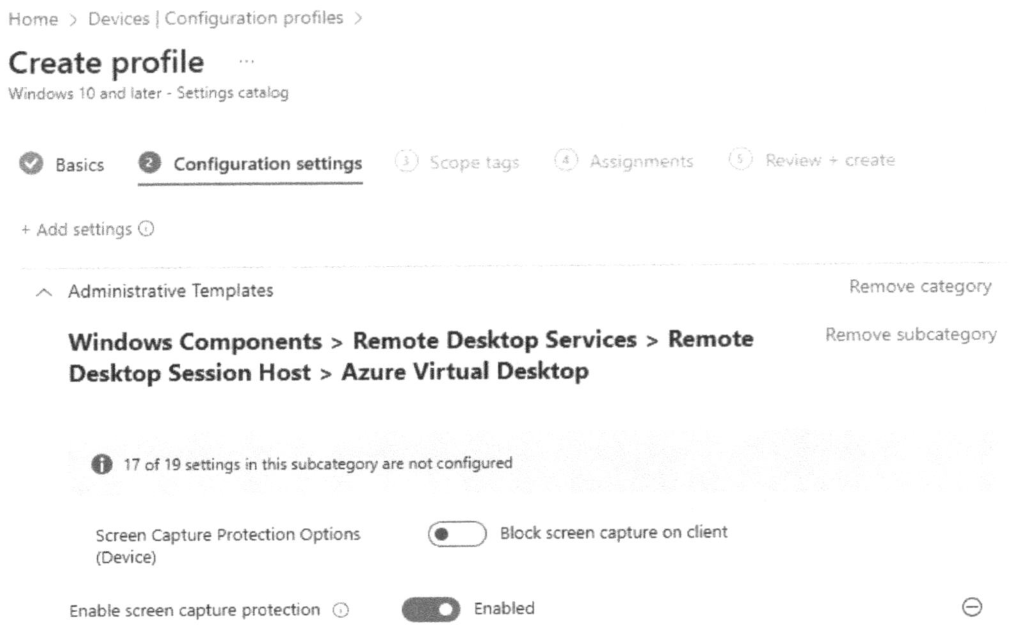

Home > Devices | Configuration profiles >

Create profile   ...
Windows 10 and later - Settings catalog

✅ Basics   ② **Configuration settings**   ③ Scope tags   ④ Assignments   ⑤ Review + create

+ Add settings ⓘ

⌄ Administrative Templates   Remove category

**Windows Components > Remote Desktop Services > Remote   Remove subcategory
Desktop Session Host > Azure Virtual Desktop**

ⓘ 17 of 19 settings in this subcategory are not configured

Screen Capture Protection Options   ◉▬   Block screen capture on client
(Device)

Enable screen capture protection ⓘ   ▬◉ Enabled   ⊖

Figure 5.3 – Configuring the options

4.   Add scope tags if you want to continue to the next step to assign the configuration profile to
     a group with the desired devices. **Scope tags** are part of role-based access controls and can be
     used to determine which objects an IT admin can see.

     The following screenshot shows the assignment of the configuration profile to a Microsoft Entra
     group called **Techlab – My personal Cloud PC**, which contains the Cloud PCs that will need
     to use the screen capture protection feature:

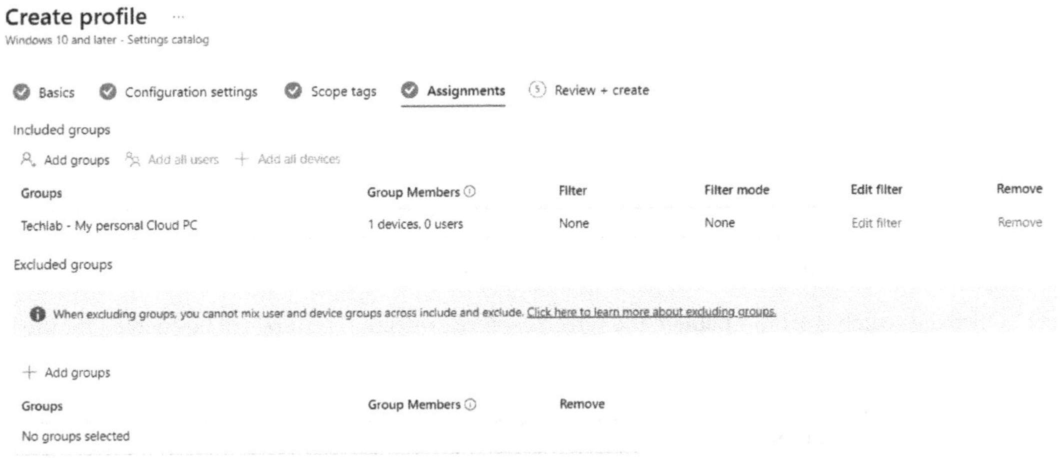

Create profile   ...
Windows 10 and later - Settings catalog

✅ Basics   ✅ Configuration settings   ✅ Scope tags   ✅ **Assignments**   ⑤ Review + create

Included groups

🧑 Add groups   🧑 Add all users   + Add all devices

Groups	Group Members ⓘ	Filter	Filter mode	Edit filter	Remove
Techlab - My personal Cloud PC	1 devices, 0 users	None	None	Edit filter	Remove

Excluded groups

ⓘ When excluding groups, you cannot mix user and device groups across include and exclude. Click here to learn more about excluding groups.

+ Add groups

Groups	Group Members ⓘ	Remove
No groups selected		

Figure 5.4 – Assigning the configuration profile

5. The last step provides an overview of the settings and assignments. Click the **Create** button to create the device configuration profile:

Home > Devices | Configuration profiles >

Create profile ...
Windows 10 and later - Settings catalog

✓ Basics   ✓ Configuration settings   ✓ Scope tags   ✓ Assignments   ⑤ Review + create

Summary

Basics

Name	Techlab | Enable screen capture protection on Cloud PCs
Description	This configuration profile enables the screen capture protection.
Platform	Windows 10 and later

Configuration settings

∧ Administrative Templates

Windows Components > Remote Desktop Services > Remote Desktop Session Host > Azure Virtual Desktop

Screen Capture Protection Options (Device)	Block screen capture on client and server
Enable screen capture protection ⓘ	Enabled

Scope tags

Default

Assignments

Included groups

Group	Group Members ⓘ	Filter	Filter
VER - CPC Dominiek	1 devices, 0 users	None	None

Excluded groups

Group	Group Members ⓘ
No results.	

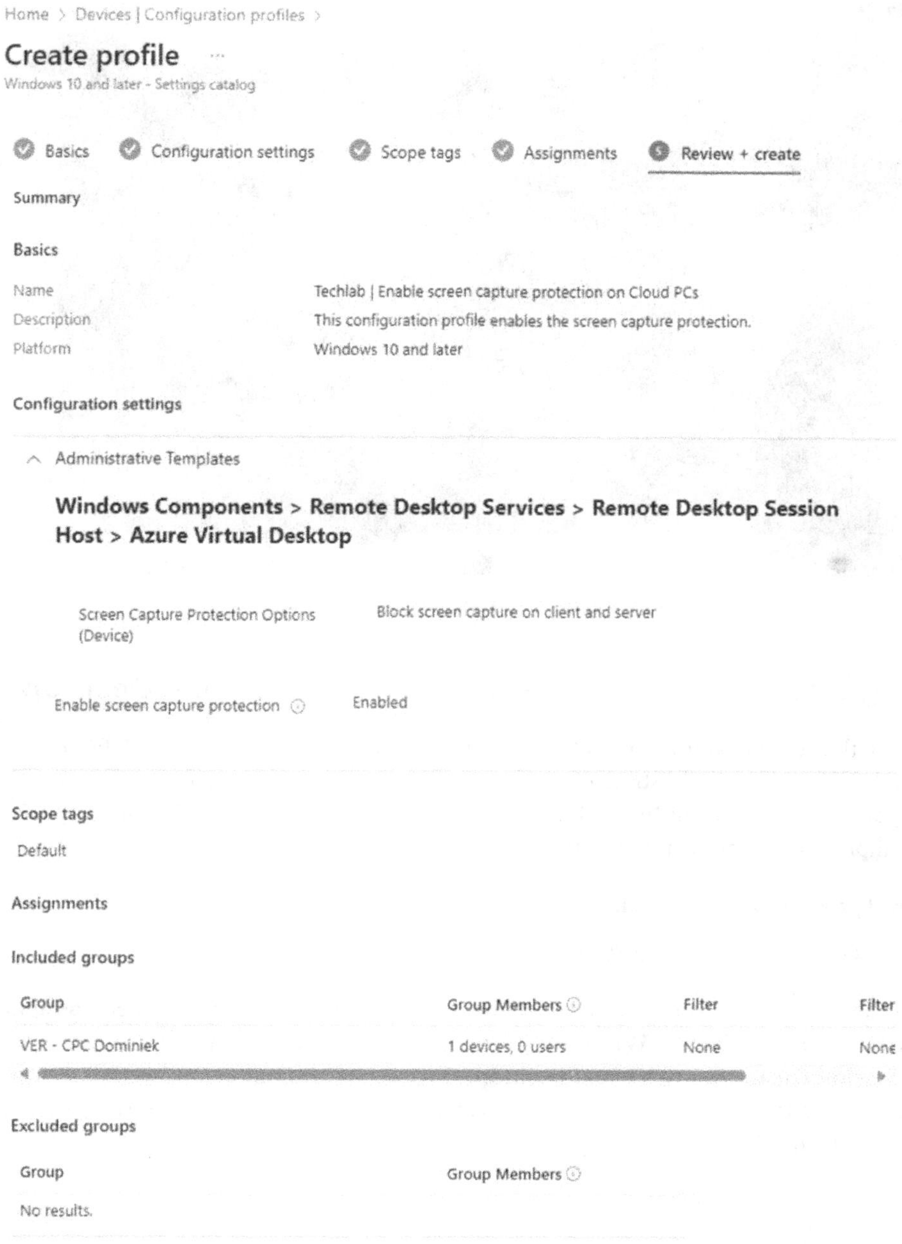

Figure 5.5 – Reviewing the configuration profile

Once the settings are applied to the Cloud PCs, users cannot create screenshots of the virtual desktop. Instead, the screen capture utility (or screen recording utility) will display a black screen:

Figure 5.6 – Screenshot attempts will result in a black screen

Enabling screen capture protection for Azure Virtual Desktop

Configuring the screen capture protection feature via a local group policy or a GPO requires IT admins to download the administrative template for Azure Virtual Desktop from `https://aka.ms/avdgpo`, or use Microsoft Intune if the desktops in AVD are Entra hybrid joined. Unpack and save the template to one of the following:

- **Local group policy**: `C:\Windows\PolicyDefinitions\`
- **GPO**: Group Policy Central Store

IT admins can enable the screen capture protection feature by navigating to **Computer Configuration > Administrative Templates > Windows Components > Remote Desktop Services > Remote Desktop Session Host > Azure Virtual Desktop**. Once the screen capture protection feature is set to **Enabled**, IT admins can select to block screen captures on either the client or the client and server, depending on the needs of the company.

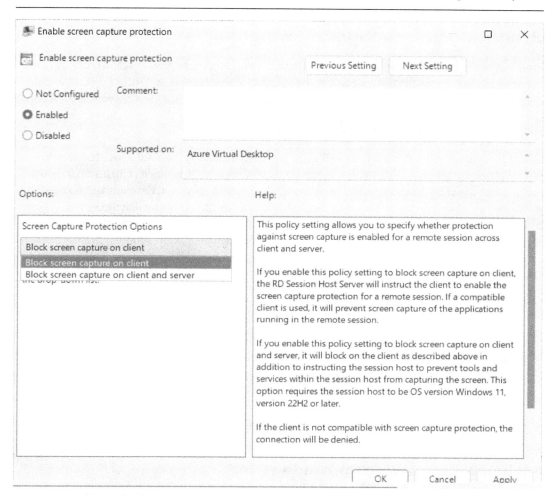

Figure 5.7 – Configuring screen capture protection via a GPO

Once the settings in the GPO are applied, users will automatically have screen capture protection enabled, which means that every attempt to create a screenshot will result in a black screen. This feature is easy to configure and has almost no impact on the user experience. Another security feature that IT admins can implement to safeguard sensitive company data on desktops is watermarking. Did you know that screen capture protection and watermarking can be combined to provide even better protection against data leakage? Let's get acquainted with watermarking next.

Introducing and configuring watermarking

Watermarking is a great security control that IT admins can leverage to protect against data leakage. The screen capture protection feature prevents the usage of screen capture and recording utilities, but it does not protect against taking pictures. That is where the watermarking feature comes in. When enabled, it adds a QR code to the desktop of the user. This QR code has the connection ID or device ID embedded in it, which can easily be traced back to the user.

This feature works for Windows 365 as well as Azure Virtual Desktop. The difference between both solutions is that the QR code will contain a device ID on Windows 365, whereas it contains a connection ID on Azure Virtual Desktop. Windows 365 Cloud PCs are always personal desktops and no one but the assigned user can sign in. By resolving the device ID, IT admins can immediately see which user is assigned to the Cloud PC. When compared to Azure Virtual Desktop, it perfectly makes sense to use a connection ID instead of a device ID since Azure Virtual Desktop supports multiple users on a single session host. IT admins have a lot of information when the connection ID is examined, including who signed in and at what time, for example.

Organizations can use the watermarking feature at the same time as the screen capture protection feature. It's fully supported.

The process of enabling watermarking for Windows 365 and Azure Virtual Desktop is largely the same as enabling the screen capture protection feature. IT admins can use one of the following:

- A device configuration profile in Microsoft Intune
- A GPO
- A local group policy

Enabling watermarking for Windows 365

To enable watermarking for Windows 365, IT admins can sign in to **Microsoft Intune admin center** and then go to **Devices** > **Windows** > **Configuration profiles** > **+ Create** > **+ New Policy**. Select **Windows 10 and later** as the platform and **Settings catalog** as the profile type.

Add a name and a description to the profile:

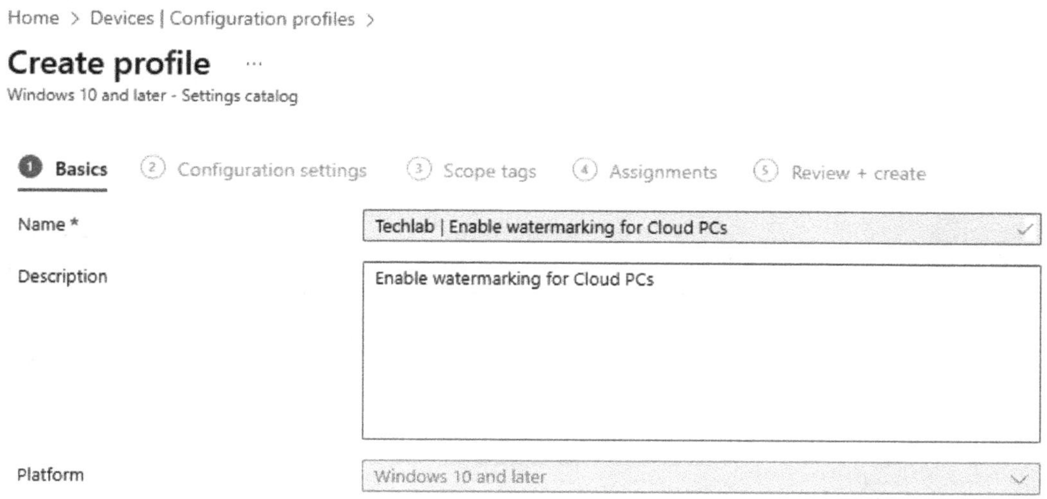

Home > Devices | Configuration profiles >

Create profile ···
Windows 10 and later - Settings catalog

1 Basics   ② Configuration settings   ③ Scope tags   ④ Assignments   ⑤ Review + create

Name *	Techlab	Enable watermarking for Cloud PCs ✓
Description	Enable watermarking for Cloud PCs
Platform	Windows 10 and later ⌄

Figure 5.8 – Creating a profile for watermarking

Click **+ Add settings** and search for `watermarking`. Double-click on the result in the **Browse by category** window. Make sure to check the box next to **Enable watermarking** to add the settings to the device configuration profile.

> **Warning**
> Do not use the deprecated version as this version does not have the setting to embed the device ID into the QR code.

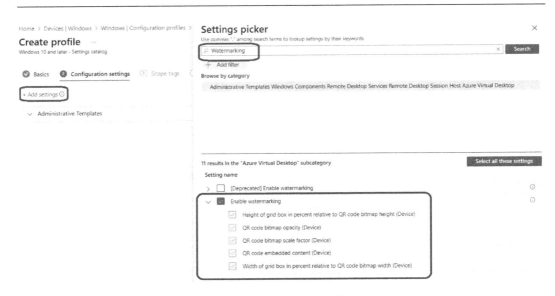

Figure 5.9 – Using the Settings picker tool to add watermarking settings

Toggle the **Enable watermarking** switch to **Enabled**. This will reveal the individual settings that IT admins can configure:

- **Height of grid box in percent relative to the QR code bitmap height**: Change this value to increase or decrease the space (height) of the QR code on the desktop.

- **QR code bitmap opacity**: Change this value to fade the QR code to the background. By using opacity, IT admins can make sure to make the QR codes less intrusive for the users.

- **QR code bitmap scale factor**: Change this value to increase the size of the pixels per square dot.

- **QR code embedded content**: Windows 365 only supports **Device ID**, so make sure to select **Device ID**; otherwise, IT admins will not be able to resolve the QR codes.

- **Width of grid box in percent relative to QR code bitmap width**: Change this value to increase or decrease the space (width) of the QR code on the desktop.

The following screenshot is an example of the watermarking settings:

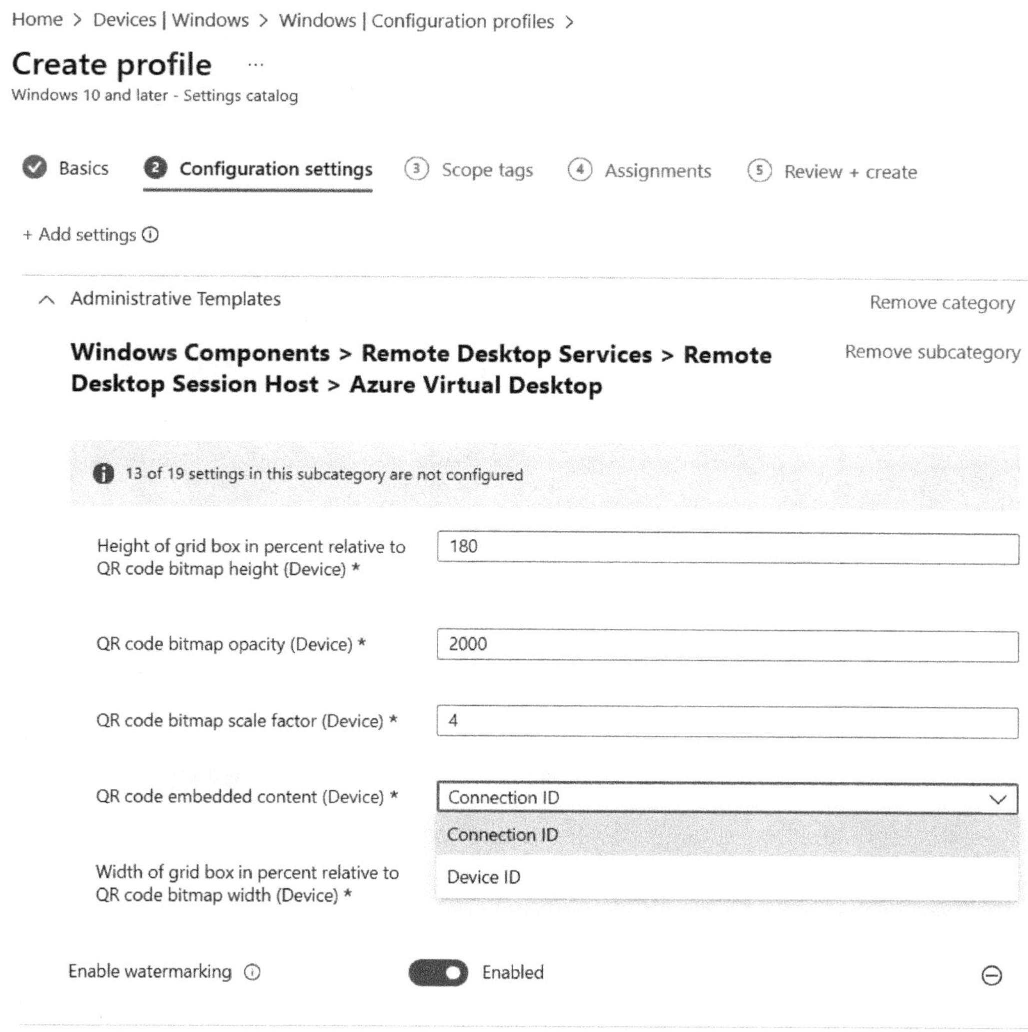

Home > Devices | Windows > Windows | Configuration profiles >

Create profile   ...
Windows 10 and later - Settings catalog

✓ Basics   ② **Configuration settings**   ③ Scope tags   ④ Assignments   ⑤ Review + create

+ Add settings ⓘ

∧ Administrative Templates   Remove category

Windows Components > Remote Desktop Services > Remote   Remove subcategory
Desktop Session Host > Azure Virtual Desktop

ⓘ 13 of 19 settings in this subcategory are not configured

Height of grid box in percent relative to QR code bitmap height (Device) *	180
QR code bitmap opacity (Device) *	2000
QR code bitmap scale factor (Device) *	4
QR code embedded content (Device) *	Connection ID ⌄
	Connection ID
Width of grid box in percent relative to QR code bitmap width (Device) *	Device ID

Enable watermarking ⓘ   ⬤ Enabled   ⊖

Figure 5.10 – Choosing which data should be embedded in the QR code

Add scope tags if necessary and assign the device configuration profile to a group containing the relevant devices:

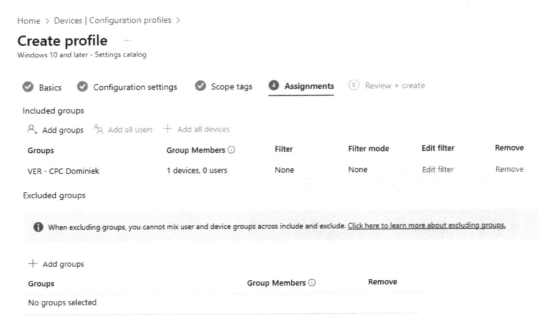

Figure 5.11 – Assigning the configuration policy

Review the settings in the **Review + create** overview and create the device configuration profile:

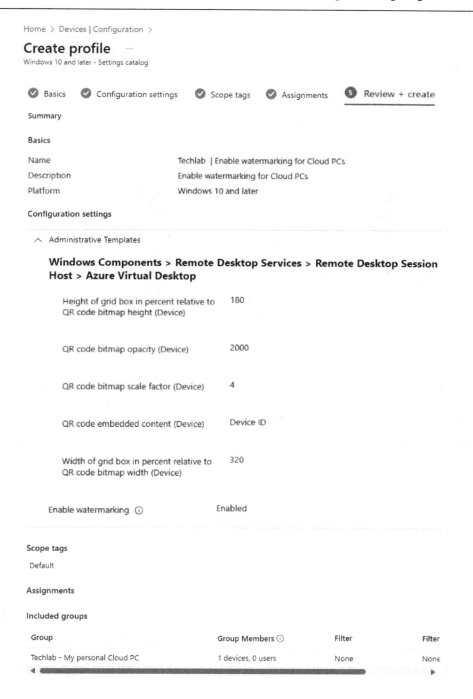

Figure 5.12 – Reviewing the watermarking settings

Once the device configuration profile is created and the settings have been applied to the Cloud PC, users will see the QR codes on their desktops. In the following figure, my device ID is shown at the bottom of the screen.

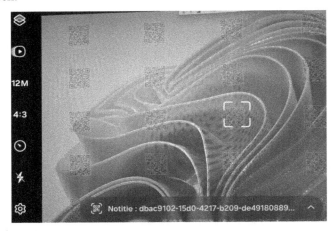

Figure 5.13 – A screenshot of a phone app that resolves the QR code

Resolving information in QR codes

IT admins can resolve the device ID for Windows 365 Cloud PCs in the Microsoft Intune admin center or the Microsoft Entra ID portal. The first step is to get the device ID. Current smartphones have a QR code scanner built into the Camera app but there are other QR code scanner apps out there.

Go to **Microsoft Intune admin center** > **Devices** > **All devices**. Use the search bar to search for the device ID.

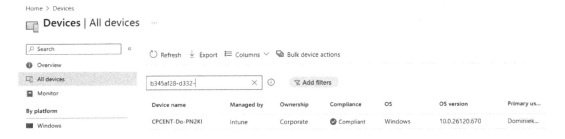

Figure 5.14 – Searching for the device ID in the Microsoft Intune admin center

IT admins can also use the Microsoft Entra ID portal. Go to **Devices** > **All devices** and search for the full device ID. This search does not support partial device IDs.

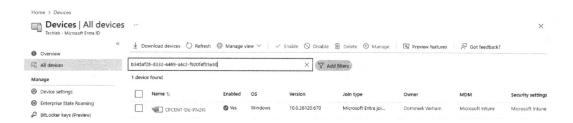

Figure 5.15 – Searching for the device ID in the Microsoft Entra portal

Enabling watermarking for Azure Virtual Desktop

Configuring the watermarking feature on Azure Virtual Desktop works a bit differently when compared to Windows 365. The watermarking feature only supports full desktops; it is not supported for RemoteApp connections. Make sure to use connection IDs instead of device IDs for Azure Virtual Desktop.

Depending on the design of the Azure Virtual Desktop infrastructure, IT admins can use Microsoft Intune, a GPO, or a local group policy to configure this feature. The process in Microsoft Intune is basically the same as Cloud PCs, except for the connection IDs. To configure watermarking using a GPO or a local group policy, navigate to **Computer Configuration** > **Policies** > **Administrative Templates** > **Windows Components** > **Remote Desktop Services** > **Remote Desktop Session Host** > **Azure Virtual Desktop**. Double-click on **Enable watermarking** and configure the settings:

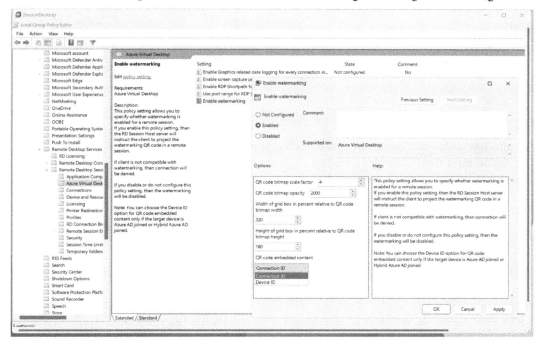

Figure 5.16 – Configuring the connection ID setting using a GPO

The process to resolve the connection ID to a specific user is completely different compared to Windows 365. Sign in to the Azure portal and go to **Azure Virtual Desktop** > **Monitoring** > **Insights**:

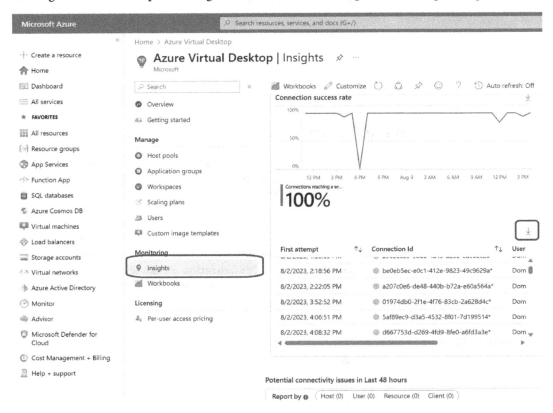

Figure 5.17 – Resolving the connection ID using AVD Insights

IT admins can search for the connection ID in this window, but a better way would be to click the downward-facing arrow to download the data and import the data into Microsoft Excel. Use the search function in Excel to find the connection ID:

2023-08-03T13:57:40.3574458Z	c6397b0b-1d99-4fc1-87e4-58c54a31 Dominiek(	1
2023-08-03T14:04:14.1920981Z	e359d03f-abff-49d1-9f20-64b34cbd' Dominiek(	3
2023-08-03T14:17:30.6306769Z	543bcde1-4057-4643-9db3-290a85d Dominiek(	1

Figure 5.18 – Searching for the connection ID using Microsoft Excel

Another method that more experienced IT admins use is to run a Kusto query against the Log Analytics workspace. To do so, open the Azure portal and go to **Log Analytics workspaces**, then open the workspace that is connected to your environment and go to **Logs**.

Customize the default Kusto query with the correct connection ID and click the **Run** button. You will see the following:

```
WVDConnections
| where CorrelationId contains "<connection ID>"
```

The result will be as shown in the following window:

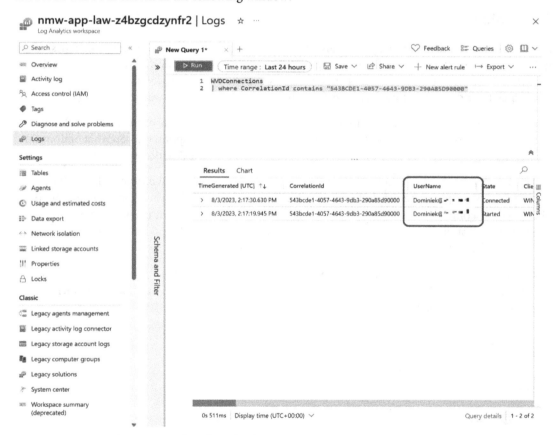

Figure 5.19 – Searching for the connection ID using a Kusto query

It does not matter which method the IT admin uses; every method will guide the IT admin to the user who signed in and leaked the data.

The screen capture protection and watermarking features are some of the newer security features that an IT admin can use to prevent data leakage on the desktop. Let's take a look at more basic ways to make sure the desktop is safe.

Configuring screen locks

Windows has some great built-in security features that help to keep the desktop secure. While some are configured on the desktop itself, others can be managed using Microsoft Intune as well. Join us while we explore the built-in security options of Windows.

Dynamic locking

A user has access to their company's apps and data once they have signed in to their personal desktop. It doesn't really matter whether their workspace is on their local device or a virtual desktop such as Windows 365 or Azure Virtual Desktop. In an ideal world, all of the users would hit the *Windows* key + *L* to lock their desktop before they leave for a short while. But what happens if they forget?

The workspace will be unlocked and access to corporate apps and potentially sensitive data will remain available. Bad actors have an opportunity to access data they are not supposed to. So what options do IT admins have to limit the time that the workspace is unlocked in a situation such as this?

Physical desktops running Windows 10 or later can use a feature called **dynamic locking**. The idea is to connect your phone to the desktop using Bluetooth. If users walk away from the desktop, the phone will disconnect, which functions as a trigger to lock the desktop. It takes about one minute from the moment that the Bluetooth connection is lost before the desktop locks. Keep in mind that some devices have better Bluetooth connectivity than others.

To configure dynamic locking, open the **Windows Settings** app > **Accounts** > **Sign-in options**. Search for `Dynamic locking` and check the box labeled **Allow Windows to automatically lock your device when you're away**.

Figure 5.20 – Dynamic lock settings with a connected phone

Users have to sign in again to unlock the desktop when they return.

Screen savers

What happens when users work on shared desktops or have a personal desktop but do not have their phone connected to the desktop? In this case, IT admins can configure a setting to automatically trigger a screen saver after a time of inactivity and make sure that the user has to sign in after the screen saver is triggered. The screen saver can be configured on the desktop itself, as well as via different management tools. We can use a device configuration profile in the Microsoft Intune admin center, for example. To do so, sign in to **Microsoft Intune admin center** and go to **Devices** > **Windows** > **Configuration profile** > **+ Create**. Follow the well-known steps to create the policy. On the **Configuration settings** tab, use the settings picker to search for `screen saver`. Add the relevant screen saver settings to the configuration policy:

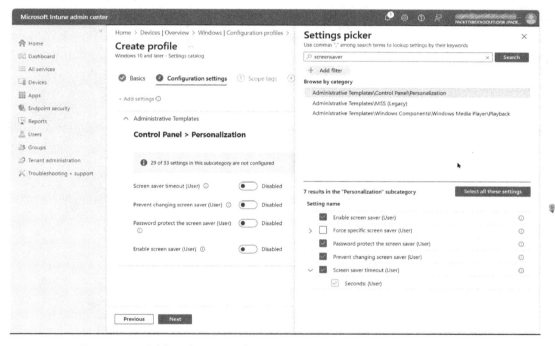

Figure 5.21 – Adding the personalization settings using the Settings picker tool

The IT admin can do the following:

- Enable the screen saver on the desktop
- Make sure that the user cannot change the screen saver
- Define the screen saver timeout in seconds
- Make sure that the user has to sign in again once the screen saver is activated
- Select a specific screen saver

Smart cards

Smart cards provide a secure method to sign in to the desktop. Using smart cards enables IT admins to configure security controls that determine what happens once a user removes the smart card from the desktop. The following options can be chosen:

- **No Action**
- **Lock Workstation**
- **Force Logoff**
- **Disconnect Remote Desktop Session**

These settings can be configured via Microsoft Intune or Group Policies. Let's start with Microsoft Intune. Go to **Devices > Windows > Configuration profiles > + Create**. Make sure to select **Settings catalog** as the profile type. In the **Configuration settings** tab, use the settings picker to add the **Interactive Logon Smart Card Removal Behavior** setting to the configuration profile. Select **Lock Workstation** as the action:

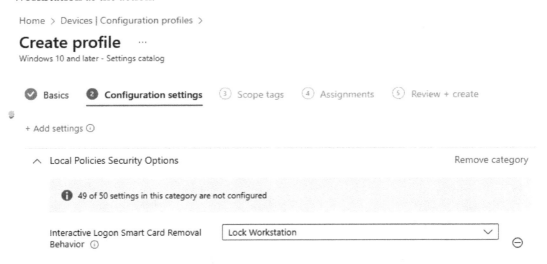

Figure 5.22 – Configuring what to do when the smart card is removed using Microsoft Intune

For Group Policies, navigate to **Computer Configuration > Windows Settings > Security Settings > Local Policies > Security Options**:

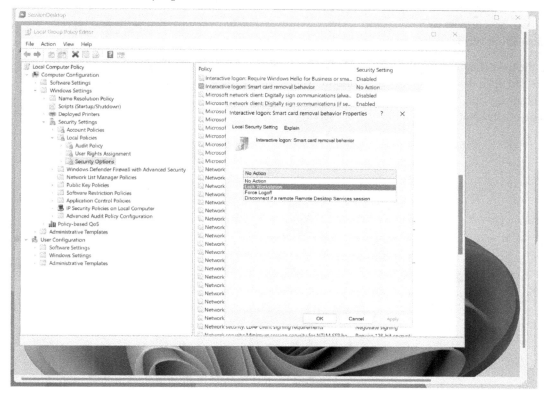

Figure 5.23 – Configuring what to do when the smart card is removed using a GPO

Session time limits

The previous security controls work great for physical desktops. But what controls do IT admins have for virtual desktops? IT admins can configure a setting called **Set time limit for active but idle Remote Desktop Services sessions**. This setting will configure a time limit before an active but idle Remote Desktop Services session gets disconnected. RDP session time limits are extensively described in *Chapter 4, Securing User Sessions*.

This concludes this chapter; let's summarize what we have learned.

Summary

In this chapter, you've learned how to prevent data leakage from the desktop. After reading this chapter, you can now protect yourself against screen captures and pictures being taken of the desktop, and you know about various solutions on how to lock the desktop to assist the user.

In the next chapter, we will focus on Update Management strategies to keep your operating system safe and up to date. We will discuss Windows Update for Business and how Windows Autopatch adds additional value. We will cover how to create a custom image using custom image templates and how to manually create a custom image from scratch.

6
Update Management Strategies

Microsoft provides various on-premises and cloud-based update services. In this chapter, we will discuss the cloud-based update services that organizations can use to update their desktops. We will start by introducing Windows Update for Business, which is arguably the most well-known solution covered in this book. We will continue this chapter with Windows Autopatch and walk you through all the various aspects of this great solution. Then, we will discuss custom image templates and how this solution assists IT admins to greatly simplify the creation of custom images. Did you know that custom image templates heavily rely on Azure Image Builder? There'll be more on that later in this chapter. We will also cover manually creating images and applying updates for both Windows 365 and Azure Virtual Desktop. By the end of this chapter, you will have a good understanding of the different updated solutions, when one solution is a better fit for the needs of your company, and how to use these solutions.

This chapter covers the following topics:

- Windows Update for Business
- Windows Autopatch
- Managing updates using custom image templates
- Manually creating custom images

The following figure gives an overview of the possibilities of each solution:

Windows Update for Business	Windows Autopatch	Custom Image Templates	Manual create custom images
Windows 10 Windows 11	Windows 10 Windows 11	Windows 10 Windows 11	Windows 10 Windows 11
Multi-session OS support	Windows 365 Cloud PCs	Multi-session OS support	Multi-session OS support
Windows 365 Cloud PCs	AVD personal host pools	AVD personal and pooled host pools	Windows 365 Cloud PCs
AVD personal and pooled host pools			AVD personal and pooled host pools

Figure 6.1 – An overview of the possibilities for each solution

Windows Update for Business

The first update management solution in this book is **Windows Update for Business (WUfB)**. WUfB is a modern solution to keep Windows-based desktops up to date and even upgrade outdated Windows builds to current and supported builds. Since its introduction, it has quickly become a popular and well-known solution to manage updates. For this reason, we will just offer a brief introduction, as most IT admins already have a good understanding of WUfB.

IT admins have to create update rings in the Microsoft Intune admin center and configure various settings specific to the goal of each update ring. It's recommended to use multiple update rings to make sure that a faulty update does not impact all of a company's devices.

Here is an example:

- A pilot group
- Production ring 1
- Production ring 2
- Broad deployment

In this example, all of the devices will be divided into four groups. The **pilot group** is the first group to receive the newest updates, followed by **production ring 1** and **production ring 2**. The **broad deployment** ring is targeted to most of the companies devices and is the last group to receive updates. The following schedule shows an example of when each group receives the updates:

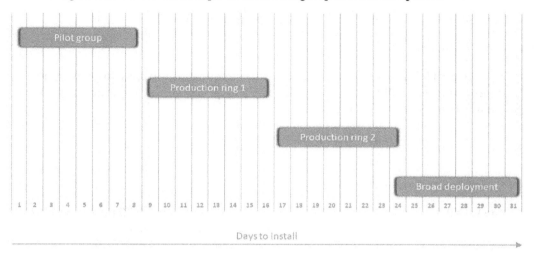

Figure 6.2 – An example of an update schedule

WUfB supports the following types of updates:

- **Feature updates**: Feature updates typically contain major updates for the operating system, along with security and quality revisions. Note that feature updates are not supported for long-term service release versions of Windows.

- **Quality updates**: Quality updates are traditional OS updates. They are usually released on the second Tuesday of the month, even though they can be released at any time. These updates include security updates, critical updates, and driver updates.

- **Driver updates**: Driver updates contain drivers for non-Microsoft devices. IT admins can disable driver updates using WUfB policies. By default, driver updates are turned on.

- **Microsoft product updates**: Microsoft product updates contain updates for other supported Microsoft applications, such as the MSI version of Microsoft Office.

WUfB supports the following versions of Windows 10 and 11:

- Pro, including Pro for Workstations
- Education
- Enterprise, including Enterprise LTSC, IoT Enterprise, and IoT Enterprise LTCS

Other services within the WUfB family are as follows:

- **WUfB reports**: This cloud-based solution provides information about Microsoft Entra-joined devices' compliance with Windows updates and is accessible via the Azure portal. IT admins can use these reports to do the following:

  - Monitor security, quality, driver, and feature updates for supported OSes
  - Show devices that are not compliant
  - Help analyze your updated data

- **The WUfB deployment service**: This service works with existing WUfB policies and WUfB reports. IT admins can use the deployment service for additional control over the approval, scheduling, and safeguarding of updates delivered from Windows Update.

WUfB is a modern and flexible solution to manage updates. Did you know that Microsoft has a solution that builds on top of these capabilities, designed to make the life of an IT admin a lot easier? At least for managing updates, that is! Let's find out more about Windows Autopatch!

Windows Autopatch

What if Microsoft could take away the burden of managing updates from your IT department? Well, that's exactly what **Windows Autopatch** can do for your company! This cloud-based service builds on top of WUfB, as it automates the planning and deployment of the following updates:

- Windows 10 and 11
- Microsoft 365 Apps
- Microsoft Teams
- The Microsoft Edge browser

It also supports Azure Virtual Desktop workloads for personal persistent virtual machines. It does not support multi-session hosts, pooled non-persistent virtual machines, or remote app streaming.

There are some requirements that have to be met before companies can make use of Windows Autopatch. The devices that use it need to be managed via Microsoft Intune or co-managed. This automatically means that bring-your-own-device scenarios are not supported. User accounts have to live in Entra ID or synchronized from a local Active Directory Domain Services domain using Microsoft Entra Connect. This service is a licensed feature. Which license would you need? Let's find out.

Licensing Windows Autopatch

Let's take a look at the license requirements for Windows Autopatch. This service requires a Windows 10/11 Enterprise license to work. It also requires Microsoft Entra ID P1 or higher and Microsoft Intune.

The good news is that companies might already have the required licenses in place if they use one of the following license offerings:

- Microsoft 365 E3
- Microsoft 365 E5
- Microsoft 365 F3

Enrolling into Windows Autopatch

We have already learned about Windows Autopatch and the license requirements. Now, it's time to configure Windows Autopatch and see the magic in action!

Enrolling into Windows Autopatch is a five-step process:

1. Register the service.
2. Run the assessment tool.
3. Review the status of the readiness checks.
4. Allow administrator access to Microsoft.
5. Provide admin contact details.

Registering the service

The first step is to register the Windows Autopatch service in the Microsoft tenant. To do so, sign into the Microsoft Intune admin center portal and navigate to **Tenant Administration** >**Windows Autopatch** >**Tenant enrollment**.

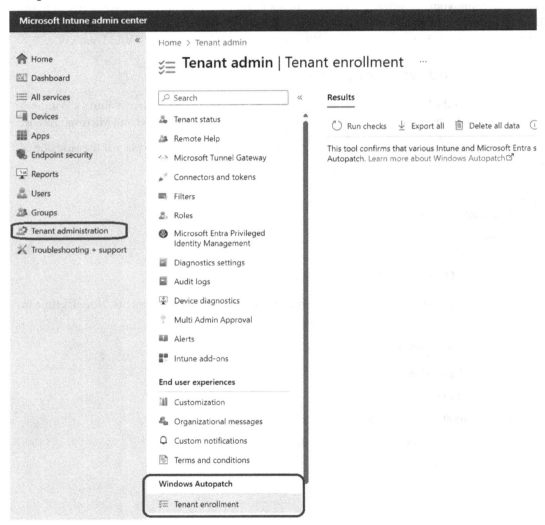

Figure 6.3 – Enroll the Microsoft tenant with Windows Autopatch

Running the assessment tool

The enrollment process starts by running the readiness assessment tool. This tool runs checks to make sure that the tenant is suitable to use Windows Autopatch. This process will store the readiness data. The first step is to accept the terms to allow Microsoft to assess and store results:

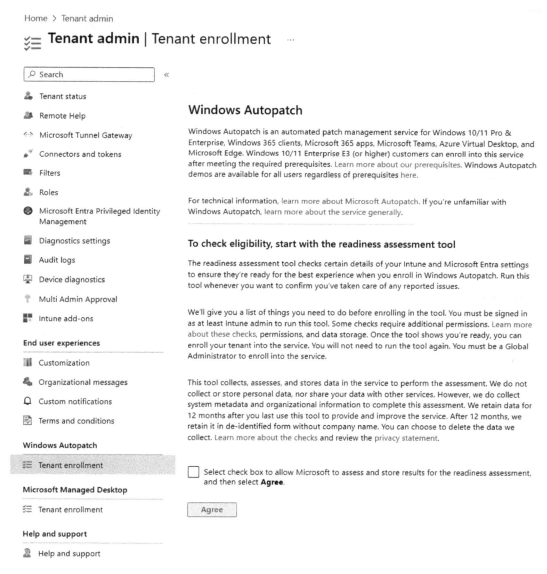

Home > Tenant admin

✓= **Tenant admin** | Tenant enrollment   ...

🔍 Search   «

🙎 Tenant status

🙎 Remote Help

<·> Microsoft Tunnel Gateway

🖋 Connectors and tokens

📠 Filters

🙎 Roles

🌐 Microsoft Entra Privileged Identity Management

🖼 Diagnostics settings

🖥 Audit logs

🖳 Device diagnostics

🏻 Multi Admin Approval

📇 Intune add-ons

End user experiences

📶 Customization

🛍 Organizational messages

🔔 Custom notifications

🗒 Terms and conditions

Windows Autopatch

✓= Tenant enrollment

Microsoft Managed Desktop

✓= Tenant enrollment

Help and support

🙎 Help and support

Windows Autopatch

Windows Autopatch is an automated patch management service for Windows 10/11 Pro & Enterprise, Windows 365 clients, Microsoft 365 apps, Microsoft Teams, Azure Virtual Desktop, and Microsoft Edge. Windows 10/11 Enterprise E3 (or higher) customers can enroll into this service after meeting the required prerequisites. Learn more about our prerequisites. Windows Autopatch demos are available for all users regardless of prerequisites here.

For technical information, learn more about Microsoft Autopatch. If you're unfamiliar with Windows Autopatch, learn more about the service generally.

To check eligibility, start with the readiness assessment tool

The readiness assessment tool checks certain details of your Intune and Microsoft Entra settings to ensure they're ready for the best experience when you enroll in Windows Autopatch. Run this tool whenever you want to confirm you've taken care of any reported issues.

We'll give you a list of things you need to do before enrolling in the tool. You must be signed in as at least Intune admin to run this tool. Some checks require additional permissions. Learn more about these checks, permissions, and data storage. Once the tool shows you're ready, you can enroll your tenant into the service. You will not need to run the tool again. You must be a Global Administrator to enroll into the service.

This tool collects, assesses, and stores data in the service to perform the assessment. We do not collect or store personal data, nor share your data with other services. However, we do collect system metadata and organizational information to complete this assessment. We retain data for 12 months after you last use this tool to provide and improve the service. After 12 months, we retain it in de-identified form without company name. You can choose to delete the data we collect. Learn more about the checks and review the privacy statement.

☐ Select check box to allow Microsoft to assess and store results for the readiness assessment, and then select **Agree**.

[Agree]

Figure 6.4 – The agreement to assess the tenant

These checks only take seconds to complete, and the following result will be shown:

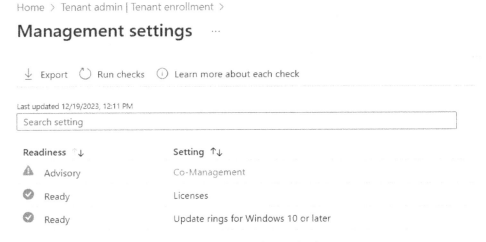

Figure 6.5 – The results of the readiness checks

Reviewing the status of the readiness checks

IT admins can click the View Details button to get more information if something went wrong or learn more about the checks that are performed:

Home > Tenant admin | Tenant enrollment >

Management settings   ...

↓ Export   ◌ Run checks   ⓘ Learn more about each check

Last updated 12/19/2023, 12:11 PM

Search setting

Readiness ↑↓	Setting ↑↓
⚠ Advisory	Co-Management
✓ Ready	Licenses
✓ Ready	Update rings for Windows 10 or later

Figure 6.6 – The readiness checks

These checks can have the following results:

- **Ready**: The check is completed successfully, and no errors or advisory issues have been found.

- **Advisory**: It's worth reviewing the advisory status to make sure that this issue does not have a negative impact on the enrollment process. IT admins can continue with the enrollment if a check has the **Advisory** status.

- **Not ready**: These issues need to be addressed before IT admins can continue the enrollment process.

- **Error**: The account of the IT admin does not have the correct Microsoft Entra role, or the tenant is not licensed for Microsoft Intune.

In the next example, we have a situation where the license check failed, with a **Not ready** status. IT admins can click on the name of the check, **Licenses**, to get a more detailed description of the error:

Figure 6.7 – An example where the tenant does not have the required licenses

The solution in this case would be to review the available licenses and make sure that the license requirements are met.

Let's continue the enrollment process. Previously, we had a tenant who passed the readiness checks. Click the **Enroll** button to start the enrollment process.

Allowing administrator access to Microsoft

Windows Autopatch relies on various components to perform its intended work. In this step, Microsoft will ask permission to set these components up. This is done by giving Microsoft permission on behalf of the organization. Make sure to check the box to continue to the next step:

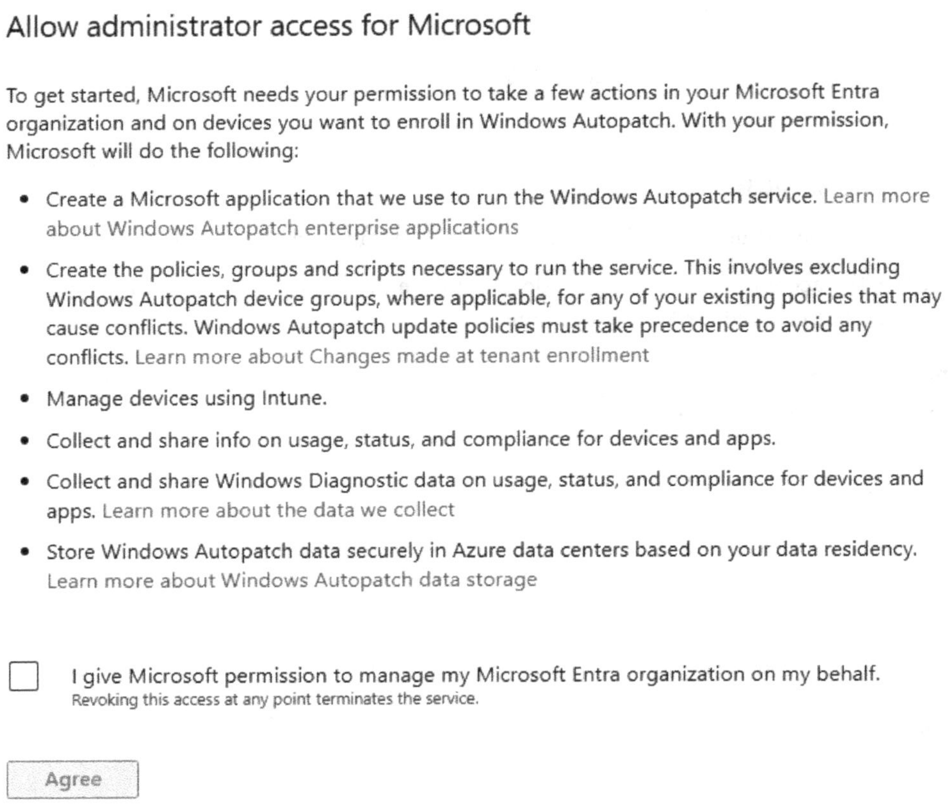

Allow administrator access for Microsoft

To get started, Microsoft needs your permission to take a few actions in your Microsoft Entra organization and on devices you want to enroll in Windows Autopatch. With your permission, Microsoft will do the following:

- Create a Microsoft application that we use to run the Windows Autopatch service. Learn more about Windows Autopatch enterprise applications

- Create the policies, groups and scripts necessary to run the service. This involves excluding Windows Autopatch device groups, where applicable, for any of your existing policies that may cause conflicts. Windows Autopatch update policies must take precedence to avoid any conflicts. Learn more about Changes made at tenant enrollment

- Manage devices using Intune.

- Collect and share info on usage, status, and compliance for devices and apps.

- Collect and share Windows Diagnostic data on usage, status, and compliance for devices and apps. Learn more about the data we collect

- Store Windows Autopatch data securely in Azure data centers based on your data residency. Learn more about Windows Autopatch data storage

☐ I give Microsoft permission to manage my Microsoft Entra organization on my behalf.
Revoking this access at any point terminates the service.

[Agree]

Figure 6.8 – Permit Microsoft to manage components in the tenant

Provide admin contact details

Once these permissions have been given, the IT admin will need to provide credentials for the primary and secondary admin. Both admins are mandatory.

Home >

Windows Autopatch   ...

Welcome to Windows Autopatch

We need some contacts in your organization for people that Windows Autopatch Operations can work with to help you with issues that are outside the scope of your own IT operations.

We might have to contact this contact at any time, so choose contacts you're sure will be available. Microsoft Privacy statement

1 **Primary Admin**   2   Secondary Admin

Provide contact info for your organization's Windows Autopatch admin.

Phone number *	
Email *	
First Name *	
Last Name *	
Preferred Language * ⓘ	English ∨

Figure 6.9 – Provide the information for the primary and secondary admin

It will take a couple of minutes before the setup of Windows Autopatch completes.

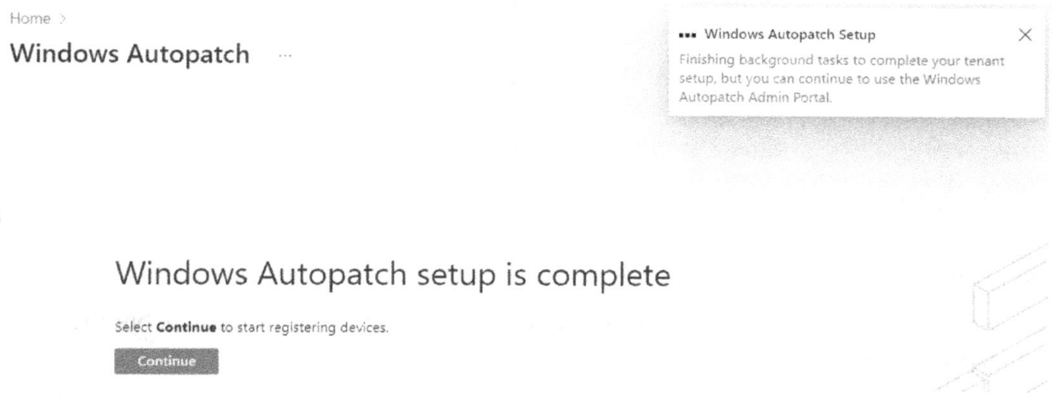

Home >

Windows Autopatch   ...

••• Windows Autopatch Setup   ✕

Finishing background tasks to complete your tenant setup, but you can continue to use the Windows Autopatch Admin Portal.

Windows Autopatch setup is complete

Select **Continue** to start registering devices.

Continue

Figure 6.10 – Setting up Windows Autopatch

The enrollment process is now complete! The next step is to register the devices.

Registering devices to Windows Autopatch

Devices need to be registered to Windows Autopatch before they will start to receive updates and follow the update settings.

Registering devices to Windows Autopatch is a two-step process:

1. Add devices to the Windows Autopatch Device registration group.

2. Optimize the automatic group assignment.

We can start the registration process right where we left off in the previous step; all we need to do is click the **Continue** button. This will bring you to the Windows Autopatch dashboard:

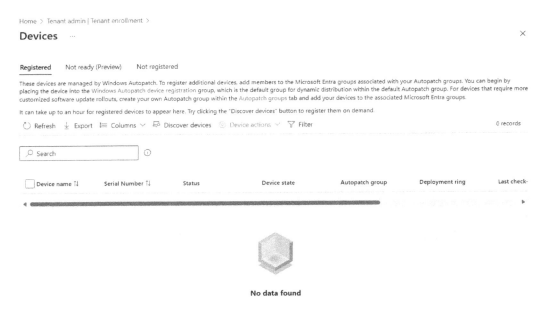

Figure 6.11 – The Windows Autopatch dashboard

There are three tabs in the menu on top:

- **Registered**: Devices in this overview are managed by Windows Autopatch

- **Not ready**: Devices in this overview are registered to Windows Autopatch, but they are experiencing issues

- **Not registered**: Devices in this overview did not register correctly to Windows Autopatch

Add devices to the Windows Autopatch Device registration group

The first step is to make sure that the devices are members of a group called **Windows Autopatch Device Registration**. This group was automatically created during the enrollment process. From the **Groups** tab, search for the group and add devices by clicking the + **Add members** button in the ribbon:

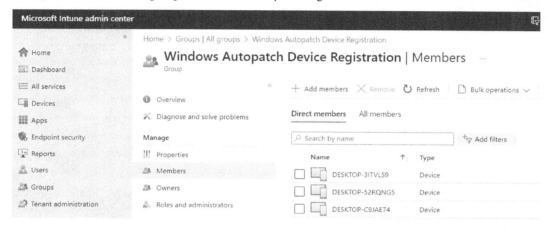

Figure 6.12 – Add members to the device registration group

It can take up to an hour before the discovery process starts, but the good news is that IT admins can speed up this process. To do so, go to **Devices** >**Windows Autopatch** >**Devices**, and click on the **Discover devices** action under the **Registered** tab.

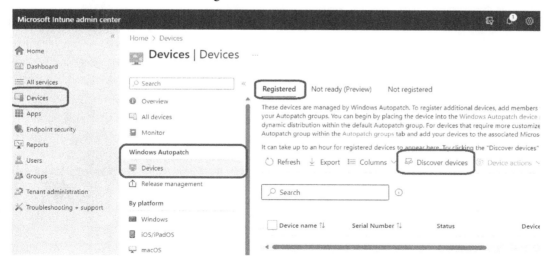

Figure 6.13 – Manually start the discovery process

It can take up to an hour before the discovery process is completed. The registered devices will appear in the **Registered** tab in the **Windows Autopatch** blade. The registered devices will be automatically distributed across the default deployment rings. The following is a screenshot of the registered devices:

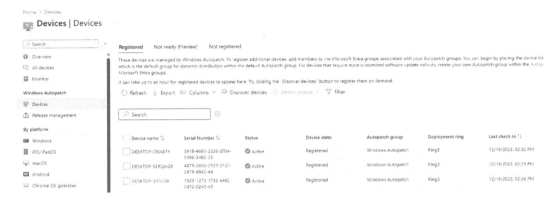

Figure 6.14 – An overview of devices that are registered correctly

Optimizing the automatic group assignment

It is possible to manually override the deployment ring assignment by selecting the device(s) and clicking **Device actions** >**Assign ring**:

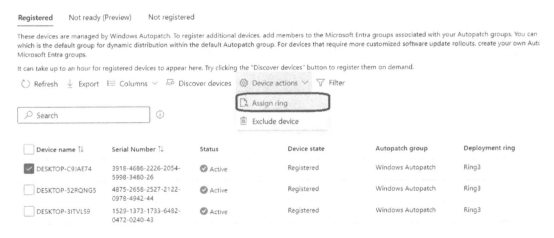

Figure 6.15 – Perform a manual assignment

Select the desired deployment ring and click the **Save** button.

Figure 6.16 – Select the desired deployment ring

Let's change the deployment ring to **Test**. It takes a couple of minutes for this change to take effect:

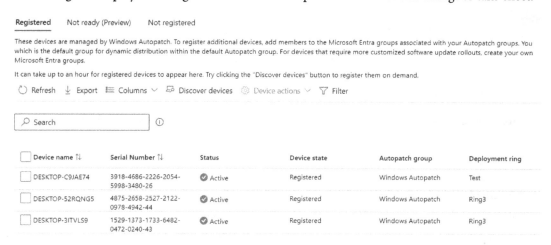

Figure 6.17 – The first device changed the deployment ring to Test

This concludes how Windows Autopatch is set up and devices are registered to the service. Let's continue to the next section, where we will cover everything related to release management such as release schedules, release announcements, release settings, Autopatch groups, and of course, the deployment rings.

Release management in Windows Autopatch

The next topic in Windows Autopatch is called **release management**. IT admins can access release management using the **Microsoft Intune admin center** >**Devices** >**Windows Autopatch** >**Release management**.

Figure 6.18 – Accessing release management

Release management provides access to four key areas;

- **Release schedule**: This allows IT admins to manage both Windows quality updates as well as Windows feature updates.

- **Release announcements**: This provides IT admins insights about newly released quality updates by Microsoft. These announcements provide a direct link to the Microsoft release notes for the specified quality update.

- **Release settings**: This allows more granular control to IT admins in relation to expediting quality updates, Microsoft 365 Apps updates, and Windows driver updates.

- **Autopatch groups**: This overview provides IT admins with information about the current Windows Autopatch deployment. It shows the default Windows Autopatch group with additional information about the number of deployment rings, the number of registered devices, the distribution type, and a link to get information about the configured Microsoft Entra group. More information about updates can be found under **Release schedule**.

Release schedule

IT admins can use this blade to view and manage Windows quality updates and Windows feature updates. The overview looks like this:

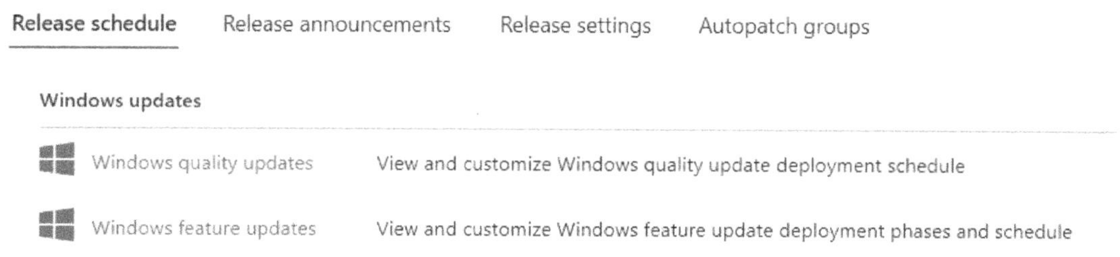

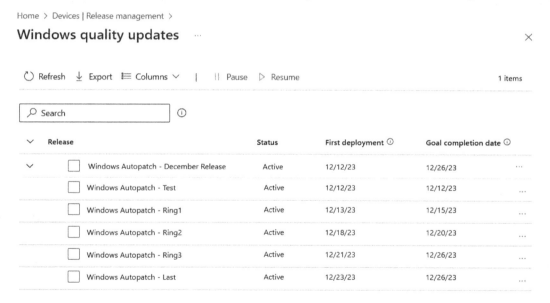

Figure 6.19 – Release schedule

Let's start with the Windows quality updates by clicking on the quality updates. This overview shows the default update rings and groups them together as a monthly release. It provides a great insight into when quality updates will be installed and when they should be installed on the targeted devices.

Figure 6.20 – An overview of Windows quality updates

IT admins can pause specific update rings by clicking on the three dots and selecting **Pause**. Resuming an update ring works the same way.

Figure 6.21 – Administrative options for an update ring

Monthly releases can be paused and resumed as well. It's also possible to edit the Autopatch group.

Figure 6.22 – Administrative options for a monthly release

Just like the Windows quality updates, Windows feature updates have their own overview. Feature updates are rolled out in phases. These phases, along with the start and end date, the version to deploy, and the status, are visible in the overview.

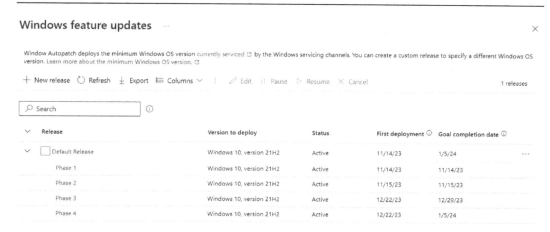

Figure 6.23 – An overview of Windows feature updates

It's possible to click on a specific phase to get more information. A blade on the right-hand side of the screen appears. In this example, we can see more detailed information about **Phase 2**. It uses the same Microsoft Entra group that deployment rings use.

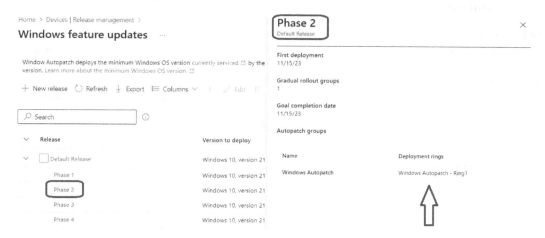

Figure 6.24 – Detailed information about Phase 2

> **Note**
> Note that **Phase 2** uses **Windows Autopatch - Ring1**. This is because **Phase 1** uses the **Windows Autopatch - Test** group.

There aren't any administrative tasks in the phases, but IT admins can edit, pause, resume, or cancel the default release.

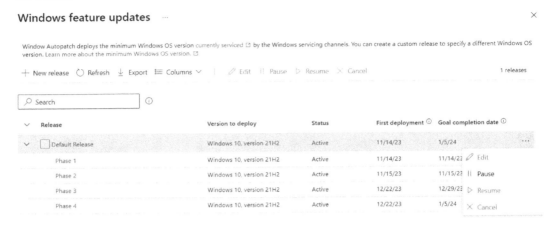

Figure 6.25 – Administrative tasks for a feature update release

Release announcements

The **Release announcements** tab provides an interactive overview of current and older Windows quality updates. IT admins have the option to follow the link of each quality update to access the release notes.

Figure 6.26 – An overview of Windows quality updates

Release settings

The **Release settings** tab allows IT admins to set specific settings regarding updates. Currently, the following settings are available:

- **Expedited quality updates**: By default, this setting is set to allow. The Windows Autopatch service evaluates the threat and vulnerability information of each revision of a Windows quality update. If the services determine that the quality update is critical for security, it will accelerate the deployment.

- **Microsoft 365 Apps**: By default, this setting is set to allow. When set to allow, the Windows Autopatch service will update the Microsoft 365 Apps. By switching to **block**, IT admins will have to take care of updating the Microsoft 365 Apps in another way.

- **Windows driver updates**: By default, this setting is set to allow, in which case, Windows Autopatch will take care of driver updates.

Autopatch groups

Let's start with the question, what is an Autopatch group? Think of it as a logical way to group several components together. For example, these groups contain information about relevant Microsoft Entra groups, update policies, and update rings. The benefit of having Autopatch groups is that companies have the flexibility to utilize different update strategies to meet their update demands.

The **Autopatch groups** tab provides an overview of the default group, called **Windows Autopatch**, as well as other custom-made groups. Per group, the tab shows the number of deployment rings, the registered devices, the distribution type, and the configured Microsoft Entra groups.

Here is a screenshot of **Autopatch groups**:

Release schedule	Release announcements	Release settings	Autopatch groups

ⓘ If you have questions about the Autopatch groups, submit a support request ticket.   ✕

Autopatch groups allow you to better control how software updates are rolled out to your devices. Learn more about Autopatch groups ▢.

+ Create   ○ Refresh   ↓ Export   ☰ Columns ∨   1 records

🔍 Search   ⓘ

Name ↑↓	Deployment rings ↑↓	Devices registered ↑↓	Distribution type ↑↓	Microsoft Entra groups
Windows Autopatch (default)	5	3	Dynamic	View details · · ·

Figure 6.27 – An overview of Autopatch groups

A Windows Autopatch group is assigned to a dynamic distribution group. This dynamic group contains the devices that will be registered to Windows Autopatch, and they will be automatically assigned to the deployment rings that are available in the group, based on the dynamic distribution group logic.

It also displays information about the Windows update settings, as shown in the following screenshot. Specifically, it will show each deployment ring with the following information:

- **Cadence type**: The cadence type determines how the updates are installed. It can be deadline-driven by specifying the deferral, deadline, and grace period. Alternatively, use a scheduled install to make sure that devices install updates on the configured schedule.

- **Deferral period**: Specify the number of days before an update is available to the targeted device.

- **Deadline**: Specify the number of days that a device has to install the update after the deferral period.

- **Grace period**: Specify the number of days that a device has to complete a pending restart due to an update.

The following screenshot shows the settings of the default **Windows Autopatch** group:

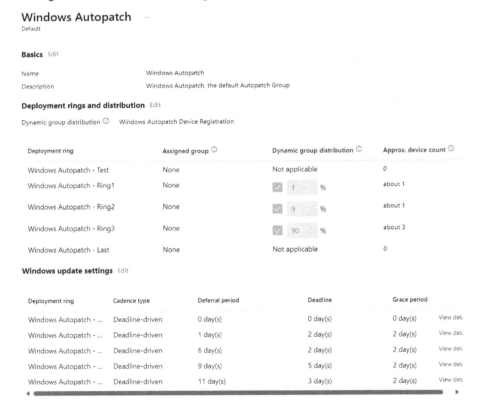

Figure 6.28 – An overview of the default Windows Autopatch group

As you can see in the preceding screenshot, IT departments can choose to use other scaling logic or even create their custom Autopatch group. To change the scaling logic, select the **Edit** option next to **Deployment rings and distribution**. The percentages are now available to edit:

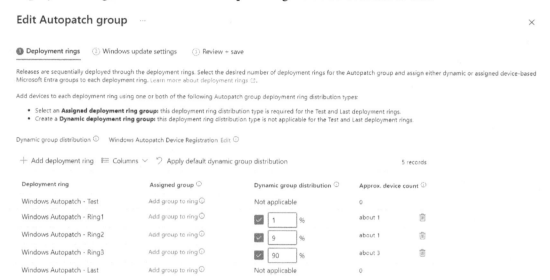

Figure 6.29 – Editing the default Windows Autopatch group

Creating a custom Autopatch group is done on the **Autopatch groups** tab and by selecting the **+ Create** button in the ribbon. Creating a new Autopatch group involves the following steps:

1. Determine the number of deployment rings and Windows update settings.

2. Create the necessary Microsoft Entra groups.

3. Create the Autopatch group by filling in the following details:

    -   **Basics**: Provide a name and description.

    -   **Deployment rings**: Select the dynamic distribution group and add the desired number of deployment rings. Assign the rings to the Microsoft Entra groups that were created in the previous step.

    -   **Windows update settings**: Validate the design by checking the cadence type, deferral period, deadline, and grace period.

The following screenshot shows what the deployment settings look like:

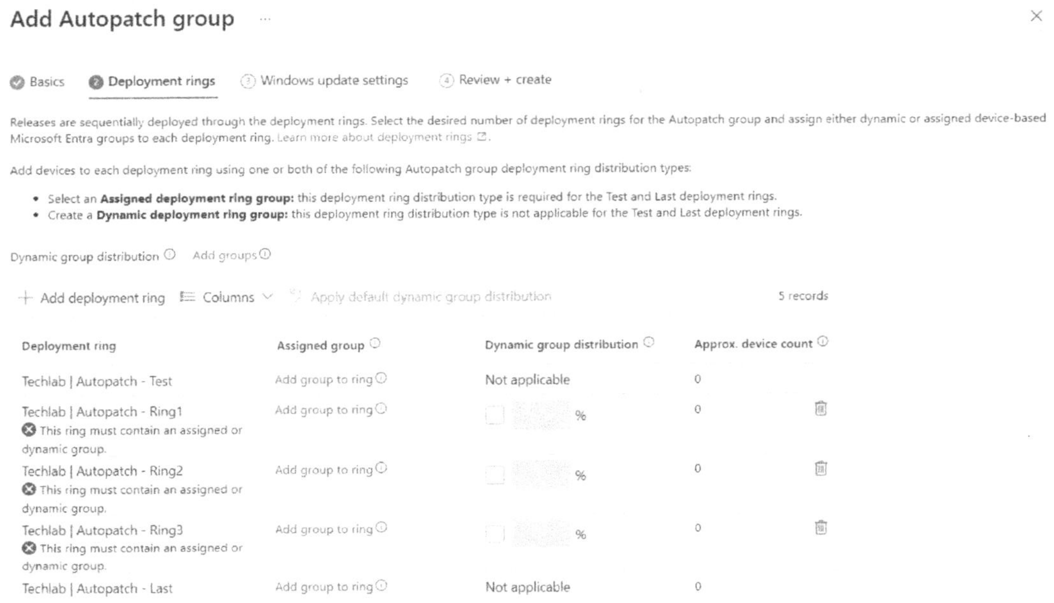

Figure 6.30 – Adding the deployment rings to the Autopatch group

Managing the Windows Autopatch service

It's time to circle back to other administrative options now that Windows Autopatch is all set up and devices are being updated. In the **Microsoft Intune admin center**, select **Tenant administration >Windows Autopatch**. IT admins have the following controls:

- **Messages**: This blade shows notifications published by Microsoft. These notifications are about a variety of topics. It could be anything from new features to planned maintenance. This blade also provides access to the **Service Health** dashboard, which shows current information or advice about the Windows Autopatch service if applicable.

- **Admin contacts**: This blade allows administrators to manage admin contacts used by Windows Autopatch.

- **Support requests**: This is your go-to blade when you need to create a support ticket for Microsoft regarding Windows Autopatch.

- **Tenant management**: This blade informs admin department when additional administrative tasks should be performed if the service has changed.

Let's zoom in on the admin contacts, since they tend to change over time:

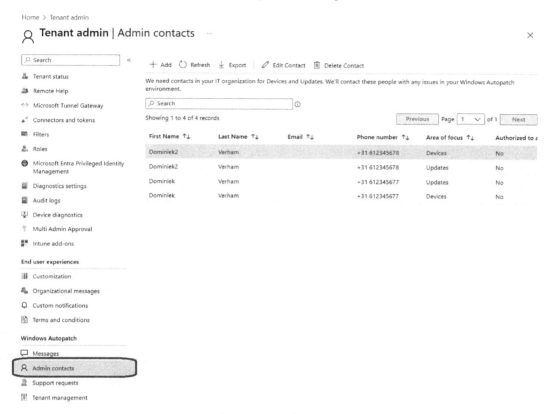

Figure 6.31 – Admin contacts for Windows Autopatch

Admin contacts are employees of the company who will be contacted by the Microsoft Autopatch service engineering team to assist when a support ticket is created.

Each admin contact is assigned to an area of focus. There are two areas:

- **Devices**: This area includes device registration and device health

- **Updates**: This area includes Windows quality and feature updates, Microsoft 365 Apps updates, Microsoft Edge updates, and Microsoft Teams updates

The admin contacts can be managed via the **Microsoft Intune admin center** > **Tenant administration** > **Windows Autopatch** > the **Admin contacts** blade. Each contact has the following options:

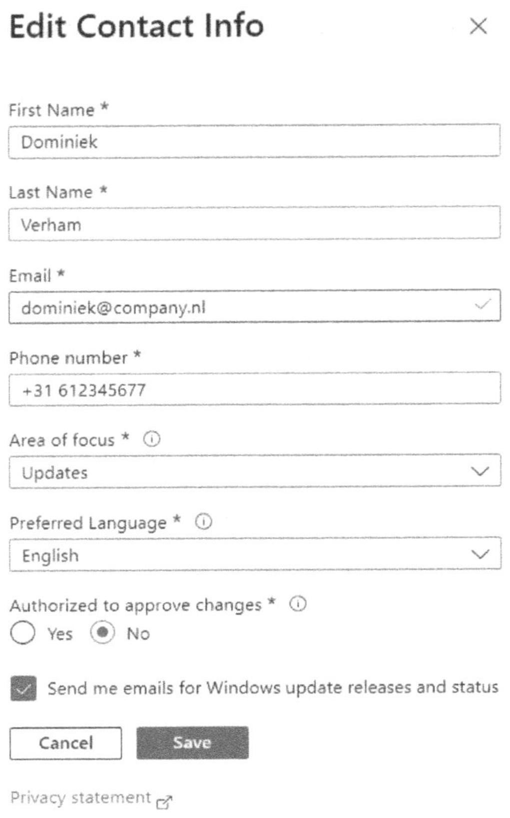

Figure 6.32 – An example of an admin contact

It's possible to add more than two contact admins and maintain control over which admin can approve changes that are recommended by Windows Autopatch operations. The default setting to approve changes is set to **No**.

But enough about Windows Autopatch. It's time to take a look at another great way to manage updates, using something that's called custom image templates.

Managing updates using custom image templates

In this section, we will cover **custom image templates**. This feature is designed to assist IT admins in creating custom images for Azure Virtual Desktop. Installing updates is an important part of creating a custom image. The service allows IT admins to reuse a configuration that was previously used, which makes it a breeze to create a new, up-to-date custom image and deploy it to your AVD session hosts.

Introducing custom image templates

IT admins that create a new custom image follow a two-step process:

1. Create a custom image template that contains all of the settings that will be applied in the custom image.

2. The newly created custom image template is submitted to **Azure Image Builder**, a service that reads the configuration of the template and proceeds to deploy a virtual machine, install the OS, and customize it according to the settings in the template. Once completed, it will capture and store the newly built custom image so that it can be deployed to the Azure Virtual Desktop session hosts.

Preparing for custom image templates

The upside of using custom image templates is that it is a powerful tool for creating custom images, as it makes the life of an IT admin a lot easier. The only downside is that it does require some steps before IT admins can use the service. But have no fear – we will walk you through the following steps:

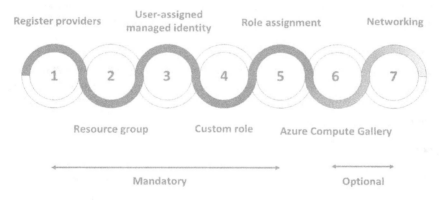

Figure 6.33 – Custom image templates prerequisites

Step 1 – register resource providers on the Azure subscription

Sign in to the Azure portal and search for **Subscriptions**. Click on the desired subscription. Go to **Settings** > **Resource providers**. Use the search bar to search for the following resource providers:

- `Microsoft.DesktopVirtualization`
- `Microsoft.VirtualMachineImages`
- `Microsoft.Storage`
- `Microsoft.Compute`

- `Microsoft.Network`

- `Microsoft.KeyVault`

Make sure that the status for each resource provider is **Registered**. If the status is *NotRegistered*, click the **Register** button. Allow this process a bit of time and check that the status changes to **Registered**:

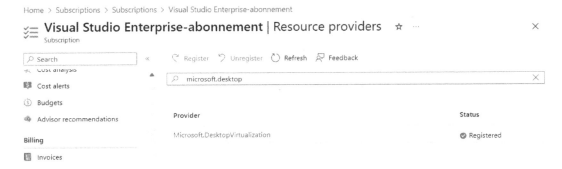

Figure 6.34 – The Microsoft.DesktopVirtualization resource provider is registered

Step 2 – prepare a resource group

IT admins can choose to create a new resource group that Azure Image Builder will use. Make sure that this resource group is empty. Resource groups can be created using different methods. The easiest way is using the Azure portal and searching for `Resource groups`. Click the **+ Create** button to create a new resource group.

Step 3 – create a user-assigned managed identity

A managed identity is used to eliminate the need to manage credentials using code, and they can be created using different methods. Let's use the Azure Cloud Shell to create our managed identity. Open the Azure portal and request a Cloud shell.

Customize the following PowerShell code to your environment:

```
New-AzUserAssignedIdentity -ResourceGroupName <RESOURCEGROUP> -Name
<USER ASSIGNED IDENTITY NAME> -Location <LOCATION>
```

The following screenshot tells us that the managed identity was created successfully.

> **Tip**
>
> Make sure that you select the correct subscription if you want to deploy AVD in a dedicated subscription.

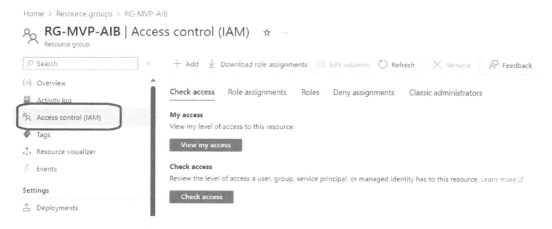

```
PowerShell ∨   ⏻  ?  ⚙  🗔  🖳  { }  🗔

MOTD: SqlServer has been updated to Version 22!

VERBOSE: Authenticating to Azure ...
VERBOSE: Building your Azure drive ...
PS /home/dominiek> New-AzUserAssignedIdentity -ResourceGroupName RG-MVP-AIB -Name MI-AIB -Location westeurope

Name    Location    ResourceGroupName
----    --------    -----------------
MI-AIB  westeurope  RG-MVP-AIB

PS /home/dominiek> []
```

Figure 6.35 – The managed identity was created

Step 4 – create a custom role

In this step, we will create a custom role at the resource group level. Open the resource group that was created in a previous step, **Access control (IAM)**.

Home > Resource groups > RG-MVP-AIB

RG-MVP-AIB | Access control (IAM) ☆ ⋯
Resource group

🔍 Search		＋ Add ↓ Download role assignments ☰ Edit columns ↻ Refresh ✕ Remove 🗨 Feedback
[≡] Overview		Check access Role assignments Roles Deny assignments Classic administrators
Activity log		
Access control (IAM)		**My access**
Tags		View my level of access to this resource.
Resource visualizer		**View my access**
Events		**Check access**
Settings		Review the level of access a user, group, service principal, or managed identity has to this resource. Learn more ⧉
Deployments		**Check access**

Figure 6.36 – Access control at the resource group level

Click + **Add** and select **Add custom role**. Enter a name for the custom role and optionally a description. IT admins can choose to clone an existing role, start from scratch, which would involve some search and configuration work, or start from JSON. Let's use a JSON file and prepare the file with the following code. Make sure to change the subscription ID and customize the code to your needs:

```json
{
    "properties": {
        "roleName": "Custom - AzureImageBuilder",
        "description": "Permissions for Azure Image Builder",
        "assignableScopes": [
            "/subscriptions/00000000-0000-0000-0000-000000000000/
resourceGroups/RG-MVP-AIB"
        ],
        "permissions": [
            {
                "actions": [
                    "Microsoft.Compute/galleries/read",
                    "Microsoft.Compute/galleries/images/read",
                    "Microsoft.Compute/galleries/images/versions/
read",
                    "Microsoft.Compute/galleries/images/versions/
write",
                    "Microsoft.Compute/images/read",
                    "Microsoft.Compute/images/write",


"Microsoft.Network/VirtualNetworks/read",


"Microsoft.Network/virtualNetworks/subnets/join/action"
                ],
                "notActions": [],
                "dataActions": [],
                "notDataActions": []
            }
        ]
    }
}
```

Make sure to review the permissions for the new custom role.

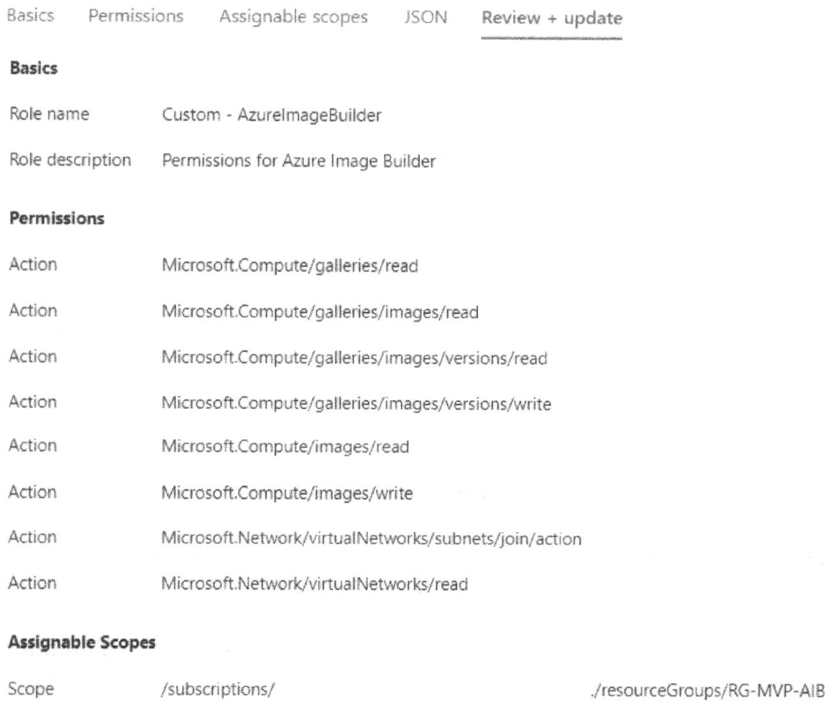

Basics   Permissions   Assignable scopes   JSON   Review + update

Basics

Role name   Custom - AzureImageBuilder

Role description   Permissions for Azure Image Builder

Permissions

Action   Microsoft.Compute/galleries/read

Action   Microsoft.Compute/galleries/images/read

Action   Microsoft.Compute/galleries/images/versions/read

Action   Microsoft.Compute/galleries/images/versions/write

Action   Microsoft.Compute/images/read

Action   Microsoft.Compute/images/write

Action   Microsoft.Network/virtualNetworks/subnets/join/action

Action   Microsoft.Network/virtualNetworks/read

Assignable Scopes

Scope   /subscriptions/   ./resourceGroups/RG-MVP-AIB

Figure 6.37 – Creating the required custom role

Step 5 – add a role assignment

We have arrived at the last mandatory step to get Azure Image Builder all set up and ready to go. In this step, we assign the custom role to the managed identity we created earlier. From the **Access control (IAM)** blade, select + **Add**, followed by **Add role assignment**. Complete the following steps:

1. In the **Role** tab, search for the custom role and select it.

2. In the **Members** tab, select **Managed identity** and add the managed identity that was created in the previous steps.

3.   Review the configuration and create the role assignment.

Add role assignment   ...

Role	Members	Review + assign

Role	Custom - AzureImageBuilder		
Scope	/subscriptions/abe87a40-1ea5-4025-b64c-f74bd67b4e5c/resourceGroups/RG-MVP-AIB		
Members	Name	Object ID	Type
	MI-AIB	7dcdf723-9db3-4208-8118-506036c3422c	Managed Identity ⓘ
Description	No description		

Figure 6.38 – An example of the role assignment

That concludes the mandatory steps to get Azure Image Builder up and running. Remember that there are two optional steps you have to take in the following scenarios:

- The image needs to be distributed across an Azure Compute Gallery. As an IT admin, you can decide how to store the custom image, and you have two options:

  - **Managed image**: This is a generalized image and is stored only once in the Azure region

  - **Azure Compute Gallery**: Store images in an Azure Compute Gallery if the images need to be shared with others or replicated to other Azure regions

- The image needs access to an existing network when the image is being built. In this case, the managed identity needs access to the virtual network.

Creating a custom image template

Now that all the prerequisites have been met, it's high time to create a custom image template. To do so, sign into the Azure portal and search for **Azure Virtual Desktop**. Go to **Manage > Custom image templates**.

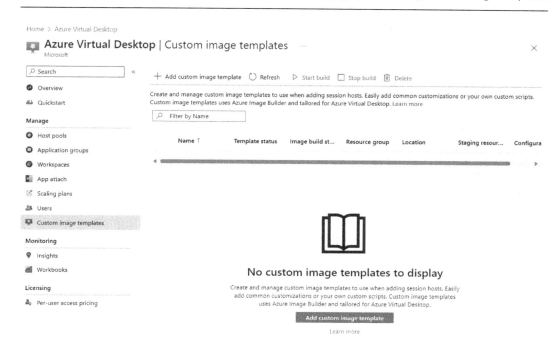

Figure 6.39 – An overview of custom image templates

Click the **Add custom image template** button to start the process of creating a custom image template. Provide a name for the template and select the Azure subscription and resource group, along with the location and managed identity:

Create custom image template ...

① **Basics**   ② Source image   ③ Distribution targets   ④ Build properties   ⑤ Customizations   ⑥ Tags   ⑦ Review and create

Create an Azure Image Builder template that will be used to generate a custom image. Pre-defined customizations that are most popular amongst Azure Virtual Desktop customers are provided, along with the ability to add your own customizations. Learn more

Template name * ⓘ
> Techlab-CI-Dec23

Import from existing template * ⓘ
> Yes
> Browse image templates
> ⦿ No

Subscription * ⓘ
> Visual Studio Enterprise-abonnement ⌄

Resource group * ⓘ
> RG-MVP-AIB ⌄

Location * ⓘ
> West Europe ⌄

Managed identity * ⓘ
> mi-azureimagebuilder ⌄

Figure 6.40 – An example of the basic configuration

In the second step, we can select the source type of the image, and there are three options:

- **Platform image (marketplace)**: This allows the IT admin to select an image from the Azure Marketplace. These images have been prepared by Microsoft.

- **A managed image**: This allows the IT admin to start from an existing managed image.

- **Azure Compute Gallery**: This allows the IT admin to start from an existing image that was uploaded to the Azure Compute Gallery.

Create custom image template ···

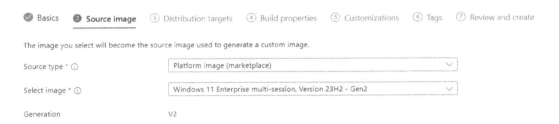

Figure 6.41 – An example of how to select the source image

The third step allows the IT admin to define where the newly created image will be stored. Check the box for the desired location, and enter the required details for the selected step:

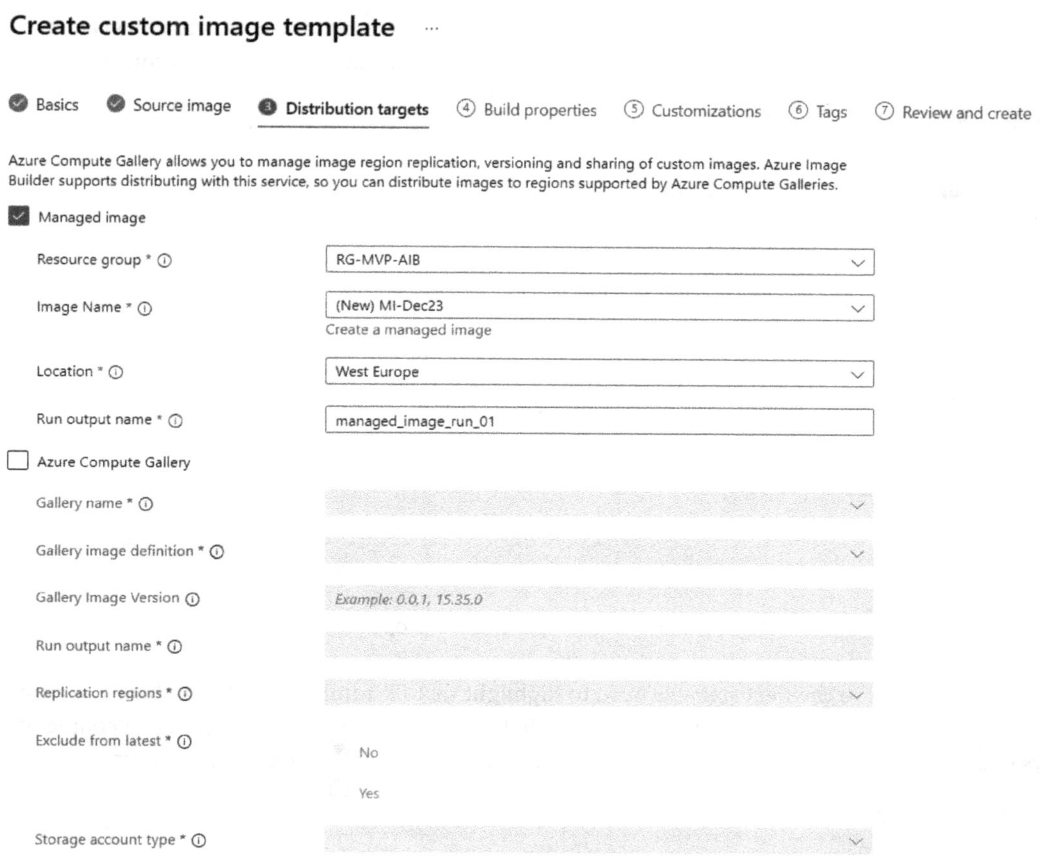

Create custom image template   ...

Basics   Source image   ❸ **Distribution targets**   ④ Build properties   ⑤ Customizations   ⑥ Tags   ⑦ Review and create

Azure Compute Gallery allows you to manage image region replication, versioning and sharing of custom images. Azure Image Builder supports distributing with this service, so you can distribute images to regions supported by Azure Compute Galleries.

☑ Managed image

Resource group * ⓘ	RG-MVP-AIB ⌄
Image Name * ⓘ	(New) MI-Dec23 ⌄
	Create a managed image
Location * ⓘ	West Europe ⌄
Run output name * ⓘ	managed_image_run_01

☐ Azure Compute Gallery

Gallery name * ⓘ	⌄
Gallery image definition * ⓘ	⌄
Gallery Image Version ⓘ	Example: 0.0.1, 15.35.0
Run output name * ⓘ	
Replication regions * ⓘ	⌄
Exclude from latest * ⓘ	No
	Yes
Storage account type * ⓘ	⌄

Figure 6.42 – An example of storing the template as a managed image

The fourth step is all about defining various build properties such as build timeout (in minutes) and the VM size that should be used for this build, along with the OS disk size and virtual network configuration.

Create custom image template   ...

✓ Basics ✓ Source image ✓ Distribution targets ④ **Build properties** ⑤ Customizations ⑥ Tags ⑦ Review and create

The Vm used to create a custom image will use these properties.

Build timeout (minutes) ⓘ	240
Build VM size * ⓘ	Standard_D2s_v4 - Recommended for Gen 2 ⌄
	See all sizes
OS disk size (GB) ⓘ	127
Staging group ⓘ	

Virtual network configuration

VNet ⓘ	vnet01 ⌄
Subnet ⓘ	default ⌄

Figure 6.43 – An example of build properties

Before we continue to the next step, we need to highlight that IT admins need to disable the Azure Private Link service on the subnet that is selected in the previous screenshot. There are a couple of ways to perform this action; we will use the default Powershell code provided by Microsoft:

```
$subnet = 'default'
$net = @{
    Name = 'myVNet'
    ResourceGroupName = 'myResourceGroup'
}
$vnet = Get-AzVirtualNetwork @net
($vnet >Select -ExpandProperty subnets >Where-Object {$_.Name -eq
$subnet}).privateLinkServiceNetworkPolicies = "Disabled"
$vnet >Set-AzVirtualNetwork
```

Make sure to change the values of the variables to match your environment.

The fifth step involves customizations, and this is where a lot of the custom magic happens! We highly recommend becoming familiar with the built-in scripts and the option to upload custom scripts that will be run when a new image is built.

IT admins can add the built-in scripts and even customize them to their needs by clicking on the + **Add built-in script** button. These built-in scripts are grouped together in the following categories:

- OS-specific scripts

- Azure Virtual Desktop scripts
- MSIX app attach scripts
- Other scripts

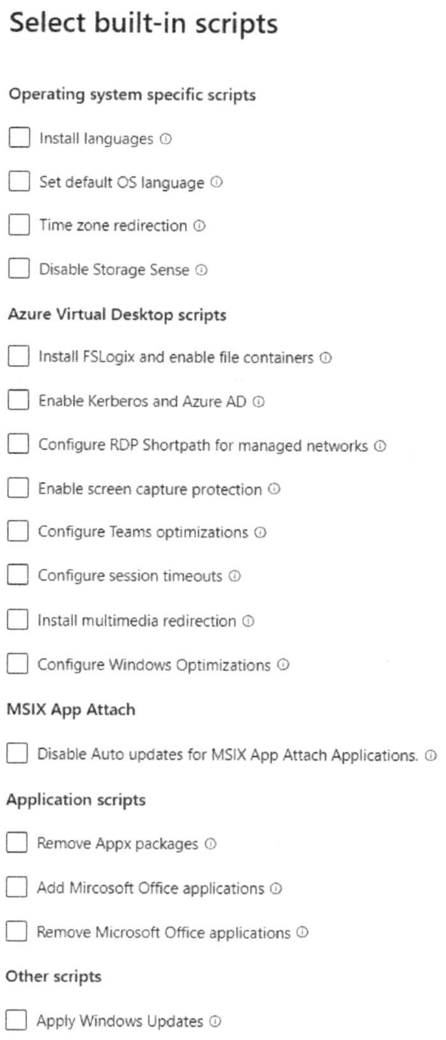

Select built-in scripts

Operating system specific scripts

☐ Install languages ⓘ

☐ Set default OS language ⓘ

☐ Time zone redirection ⓘ

☐ Disable Storage Sense ⓘ

Azure Virtual Desktop scripts

☐ Install FSLogix and enable file containers ⓘ

☐ Enable Kerberos and Azure AD ⓘ

☐ Configure RDP Shortpath for managed networks ⓘ

☐ Enable screen capture protection ⓘ

☐ Configure Teams optimizations ⓘ

☐ Configure session timeouts ⓘ

☐ Install multimedia redirection ⓘ

☐ Configure Windows Optimizations ⓘ

MSIX App Attach

☐ Disable Auto updates for MSIX App Attach Applications. ⓘ

Application scripts

☐ Remove Appx packages ⓘ

☐ Add Mircosoft Office applications ⓘ

☐ Remove Microsoft Office applications ⓘ

Other scripts

☐ Apply Windows Updates ⓘ

Figure 6.44 – An overview of the built-in scripts

Since we are focusing on applying updates, we can simply check the **Apply Windows Updates** box and save the customization.

The customization appears in the script overview.

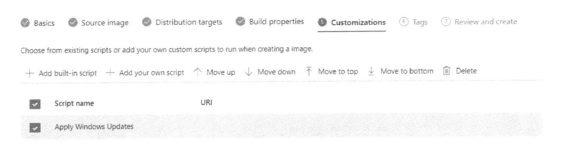

Figure 6.45 – This customization will install any outstanding updates

The last steps consist of adding tags and reviewing the configuration. It can take a bit of time before the newly created custom image template appears in the overview.

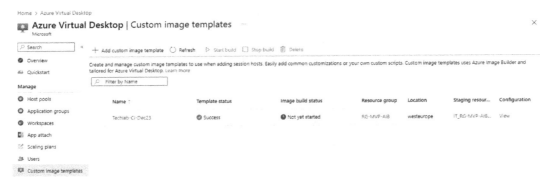

Figure 6.46 – The template has been created successfully

The custom image template has been created successfully. Click the template and then the **Start build** button in the ribbon to submit the template to Azure Image Builder.

Figure 6.47 – Azure Image Builder will start to create the image

The custom image will be saved once the process is completed.

Using custom image templates as part of the update strategy

The template remains available once it's created or submitted to Azure Image Builder. This template can be reused to create another custom image template that contains all the settings of the original template. To start this process, click the + **Add custom image template** button in the ribbon. Give the new template a name and select **Yes** to import from the existing template. Click **Browse image templates** and select the desired template. Most other required settings will automatically be duplicated from the template.

Home > Azure Virtual Desktop | Custom image templates >

Create custom image template   ···

① **Basics**   ② Source image   ③ Distribution targets   ④ Build properties   ⑤ Customizations   ⑥ Tags   ⑦ Review and create

Create an Azure Image Builder template that will be used to generate a custom image. Pre-defined customizations that are most popular amongst Azure Virtual Desktop customers are provided, along with the ability to add your own customizations. Learn more

Template name * ⓘ	Techlab-CI-Jan24
Import from existing template * ⓘ	◉ Yes
	Browse image templates
	○ No
Subscription * ⓘ	Visual Studio Enterprise-abonnement
Resource group * ⓘ	RG-MVP-AIB
Location * ⓘ	West Europe
Managed identity * ⓘ	mi-azureimagebuilder

Figure 6.48 – Duplicating an existing template

These settings need to be addressed manually:

- Provide a new image name in *step 3*.

- Select the vNet and subnet in *step 4*.

- Optionally, IT admins can change other customizations to provide further updates to the image

Save the new template once the settings have been configured, and wait a couple of minutes before the newly created template shows up in the overview:

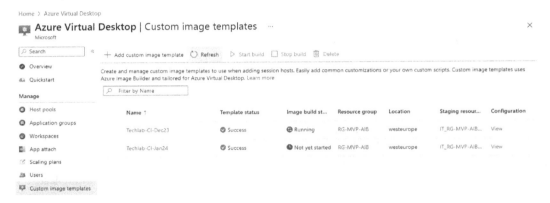

Figure 6.49 – The duplicated template becomes available

Submitting this template to Azure Image Builder will result in an updated image that can be used in Azure Virtual Desktop.

It is a pretty easy and fast process to create an updated image for Azure Virtual Desktop once the requirements for Azure Image Builder have been configured. Being able to duplicate makes this solution a perfect candidate to use to update images for Azure Virtual Desktop. Another way to create an updated image for your environment is to create the custom image yourself. That's what we will cover in the next topic!

Manually creating custom images

We discussed custom image templates, why it's a great solution to create custom images for Azure Virtual Desktop environments, and how easy it is to update these images. However, this solution cannot be used for Windows 365. In this topic, we will cover how to create a custom image tailored to the needs of a company for both Windows 365 and Azure Virtual Desktop manually, with the main goal of creating an image with all the available updates. We will talk about the various images and locations where they are stored. Let's take a look at the relevant technical terms:

- **Gallery images**: These images are created by Microsoft and can be used for Windows 365 Enterprise and Frontline Cloud PCs. There is a gallery image for Windows 10 and Windows

11 that has OS optimizations and a version of Windows 10/11 that has the Microsoft 365 Apps installed. This version has several optimizations configured to create the best user experience possible. Here is an overview of the optimizations:

- The image is replicated to every Azure region for a quick provisioning experience.

- The image is updated each month with the latest security updates.

- The image is optimized with OS optimizations for best performance in virtualized environments, such as Windows 365, by optimizing Windows services for virtual environments, removing unnecessary **Universal Windows Platform** (**UWP**) packages, and disabling actions in the task scheduler.

- The version that has the Microsoft 365 Apps installed has all the previously mentioned optimizations along with the following optimizations:

  - The Microsoft 365 apps are already installed

  - The Microsoft Teams app is already installed

  - Teams is already optimized to run on a virtual environment by configuring the **IsWVDEnvironment** registry key

  - C++ runtime is installed

  - The WebRTC Redirector service is installed to provide a better user experience in virtual environments for Microsoft Teams

  - Microsoft Edge settings are optimized to run on virtualized environments by configuring sleeping tabs, a startup boost, first-time optimizations, and the synchronization of browser components

  - Microsoft Outlook first-time run settings are configured so that Outlook will automatically sign on using the Microsoft Entra ID credentials and support for other profiles

- **Custom images**: A custom image is created by the IT admin. It's based on a Windows 10 or Windows 11 image and customized to meet the demands of the company. The optimizations could be anything from installing the latest updates to installing applications or configuring settings using PowerShell scripts. Custom images are supported for Windows 365 Enterprise and Frontline as well as Azure Virtual Desktop.

- **Marketplace images**: These images are populated by Microsoft and made available for download on the Azure marketplace via the Azure portal. These images are perfect as a baseline to create a custom image or a vanilla installation of the OS in an Azure VM.

The prerequisites to creating a custom image

The first step is to make sure that the image meets the requirements. Currently, the requirements are as follows:

- Only Enterprise images are supported. Business is not supported.
- For Windows 10, build 21H2 or later
- For Windows 11, build 21H2 or later
- Only generation 2 virtual machine images are supported.
- Images need to be generalized.
- Multi-session is only supported for Azure Virtual Desktop. Multi-session is not supported for Windows 365.
- Recovery partitions are not supported and need to be deleted if present.
- For Windows 365, use a 64 GB OS disk. The size of the OS disk will be resized automatically once the image is deployed to a Cloud PC. The disk will be resized to the size of the Windows 365 license.
- Images for Azure Virtual Desktop can be stored as a managed image or in an Azure Compute Gallery. Images for Windows 365 can only be stored as a managed image as the Azure Compute Gallery is not supported.
- IT admins need to be a member of the Global Administrator, Windows 365 Administrator, or Intune Administrator role to have the correct permissions to upload and manage the custom image.
- Make sure that the FSLogix agent is installed for Azure Virtual Desktop environments.

Creating a custom image for Windows 365

Sign in to the Azure portal and search for `Marketplace`. The IT admin has two options at this point:

- **Search for Windows 11**: This provides a vanilla installation of Windows 11, which means that all customizations and optimizations have to be performed by the IT admin.
- **Search for a Cloud PC**: This provides access to an optimized gallery image provided by Microsoft. This means that the aforementioned optimizations are already in place.

The following screenshot shows the Cloud PC template and its variations in the Azure Marketplace:

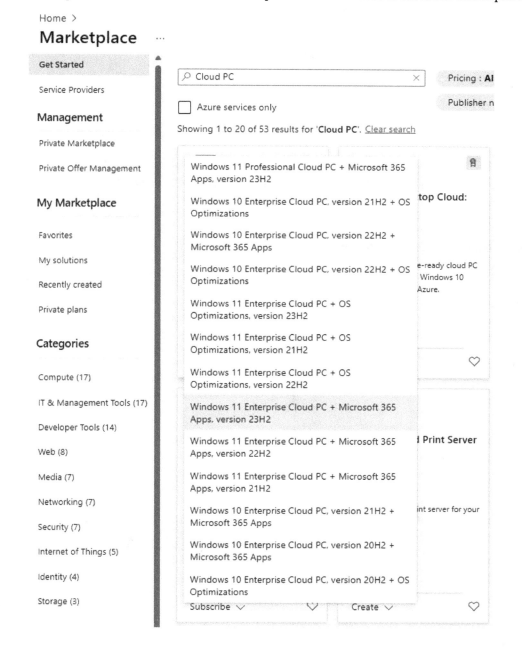

Figure 6.50 – An overview of Cloud PC images in the Azure Marketplace

We will use a Windows 11 Enterprise image, as this image can be used for Windows 365 and Azure Virtual Desktop. The process to create a custom image is as follows:

Figure 6.51 – The steps to create a custom image for Windows 365

Creating a VM

Sign in to the **Azure portal** >**Marketplace**. Search for Windows 11.

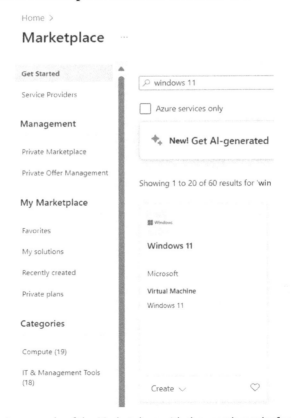

Figure 6.52 – An example of the Marketplace with the search results for Windows 11

Select the desired version in the drop-down box and click the **Create** button.

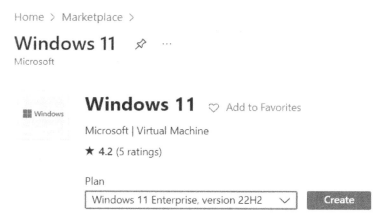

Figure 6.53 – Selecting Windows 11 Enterprise, version 22H2

This action continues with creating a VM:

1. Make sure to fill in the required information. Take special notice of the following:

    - **Availability options**: No infrastructure redundancy required
    - **Security type**: Standard

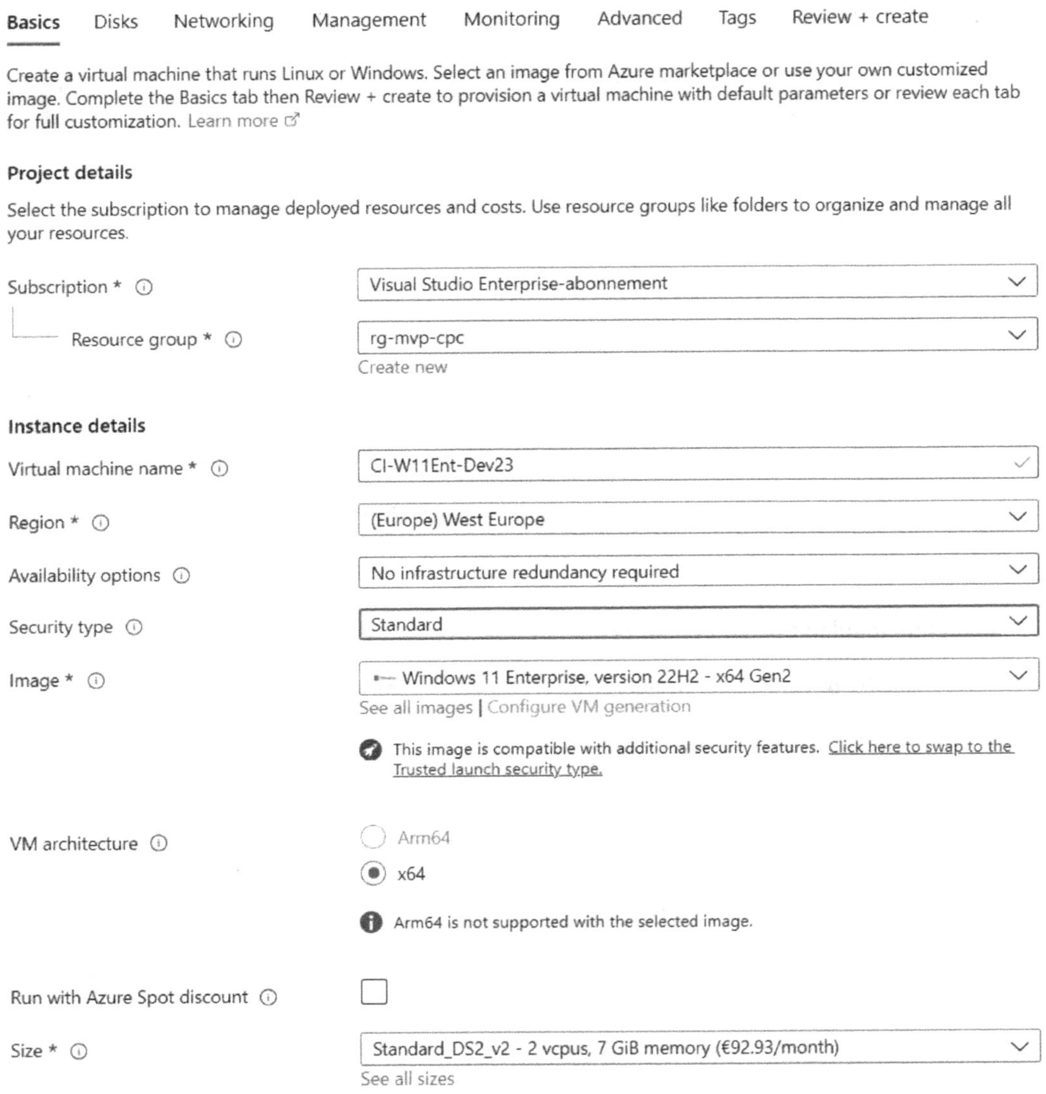

Basics   Disks   Networking   Management   Monitoring   Advanced   Tags   Review + create

Create a virtual machine that runs Linux or Windows. Select an image from Azure marketplace or use your own customized image. Complete the Basics tab then Review + create to provision a virtual machine with default parameters or review each tab for full customization. Learn more ☁

Project details

Select the subscription to manage deployed resources and costs. Use resource groups like folders to organize and manage all your resources.

Subscription * ⓘ	Visual Studio Enterprise-abonnement ⌄
└── Resource group * ⓘ	rg-mvp-cpc ⌄
	Create new

Instance details

Virtual machine name * ⓘ	CI-W11Ent-Dev23 ✓
Region * ⓘ	(Europe) West Europe ⌄
Availability options ⓘ	No infrastructure redundancy required ⌄
Security type ⓘ	Standard ⌄
Image * ⓘ	•— Windows 11 Enterprise, version 22H2 - x64 Gen2 ⌄
	See all images	Configure VM generation
	⦿ This image is compatible with additional security features. Click here to swap to the Trusted launch security type.
VM architecture ⓘ	◯ Arm64
	⦿ x64
	ⓘ Arm64 is not supported with the selected image.
Run with Azure Spot discount ⓘ	☐
Size * ⓘ	Standard_DS2_v2 - 2 vcpus, 7 GiB memory (€92.93/month) ⌄
	See all sizes

Figure 6.54 – The basic information to create a VM

2.   Selecting the correct disk type and options. IT admins can keep the default options or change **Premium SSD** to **Standard SSD** to save on costs:

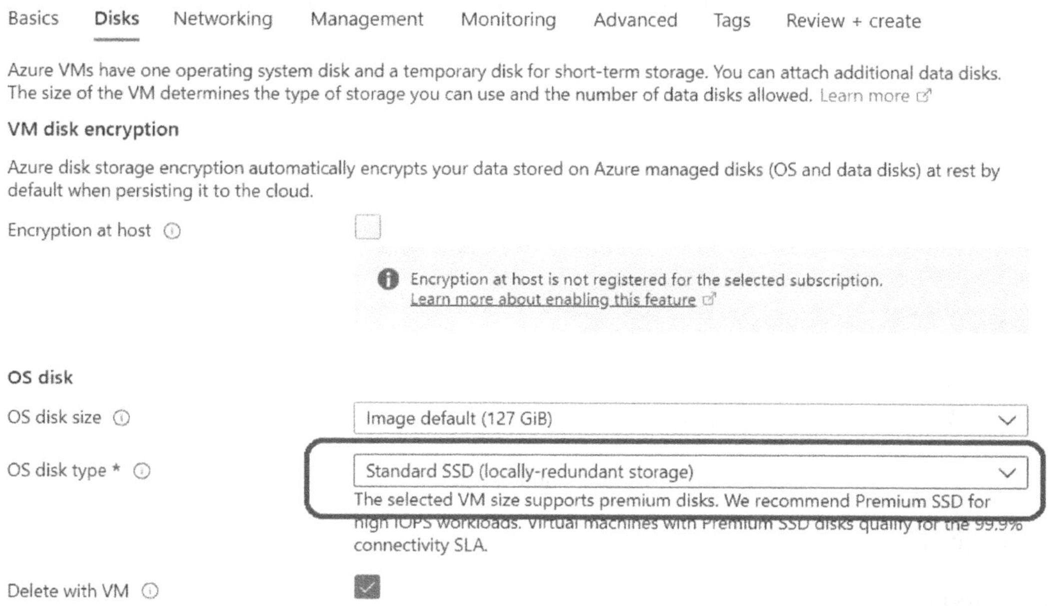

Basics   **Disks**   Networking   Management   Monitoring   Advanced   Tags   Review + create

Azure VMs have one operating system disk and a temporary disk for short-term storage. You can attach additional data disks. The size of the VM determines the type of storage you can use and the number of data disks allowed. Learn more ⊏⟩

VM disk encryption

Azure disk storage encryption automatically encrypts your data stored on Azure managed disks (OS and data disks) at rest by default when persisting it to the cloud.

Encryption at host ⓘ

☐

ⓘ Encryption at host is not registered for the selected subscription. Learn more about enabling this feature ⊏⟩

OS disk

OS disk size ⓘ | Image default (127 GiB)   ⌄ |

OS disk type * ⓘ | Standard SSD (locally-redundant storage)   ⌄ |
                         The selected VM size supports premium disks. We recommend Premium SSD for
                         high IOPS workloads. Virtual machines with Premium SSD disks qualify for the 99.9%
                         connectivity SLA.

Delete with VM ⓘ   ☑

Figure 6.55 – Configuring the disk

The following steps can be left to default, so let's summarize them.

3.   **Networking**: Determine how IT admins will connect to the VM. The easiest but least secure way is to connect via the internet. The more secure method is by connecting to its private IP, but keep in mind that this requires a desktop in the same private subnet.

4.   **Management**: You can use the default settings.

5.   **Monitoring**: You can use the default settings.

6.   **Advanced**: You can use the default settings.

7.   **Tags**: You can add tags if you want.

8.   **Review and create**: This step provides an overview of all the selected settings.

It takes a couple of moments before the new VM is created. You know the process is complete once you see a screen like this:

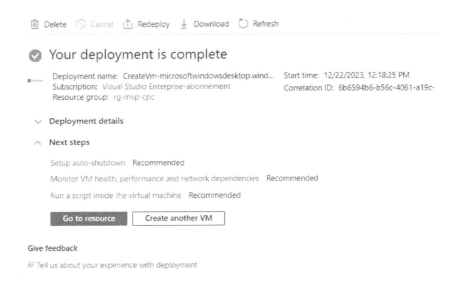

Figure 6.56 – The deployment of the VM is complete

The VM will power on automatically, so we can continue to customize the VM.

Customizing the VM

IT admins have to perform all of the necessary customizations to the image. These customizations could be anything, including installing applications in the image, running a required PowerShell Script, and, of course, installing Microsoft updates. To do so, sign into the newly created VM via the public or private IP, depending on the choice that was made in the previous step.

Installing the updates is done via running Windows Update:

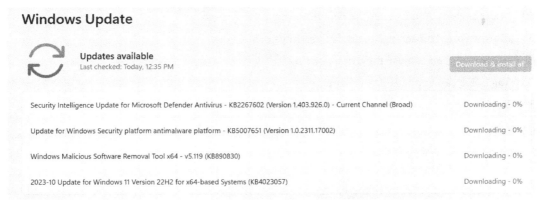

Figure 6.57: Installing all available updates in the VM

We recommend restarting the VM before starting the capture process to make sure that all delayed write operations are committed.

If the image is stored as a managed image, to be used with Windows 365 or Azure Virtual Desktop, remember to generalize it. This operation will remove any computer-specific information such as Windows drivers or the **security identifier** (**SID**).

Run the following command in an elevated prompt to generalize the image:

```
C:\Windows\System32\Sysprep\sysprep.exe /generalize /shutdown /oobe
```

The process is complete once the VM shuts down.

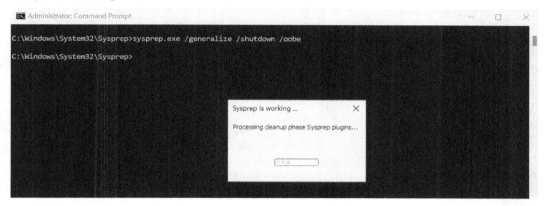

Figure 6.58 – The image is prepared for capturing

Capturing the updated image

Now that all of the customizations have been applied and the VM is sysprepped and shut down, we can continue with the capture process. Sign in to the **Azure portal** > **Virtual machines** and select the VM that was prepared in the previous steps.

Make sure that the VM is stopped, and click the **Capture** button.

Figure 6.59 – Start the capture process

In the **Basics** tab, IT admins have to select a valid Azure subscription and the resource group. Make sure to do the following:

- Select **No, capture only a managed image**, since storing the image in an Azure Compute Gallery is not supported for Windows 365.

- Check the **Automatically delete this virtual machine after creating the image** box. Remember that the VM is generalized, which means no further actions are allowed on it.

Finish this process by adding tags if required, and review the configuration in the overview at the end. Make sure that the validation steps are passed, as shown in the following screenshot.

Figure 6.60 – The capture process is about to start

Keep in mind that the capture process takes up a bit of time.

Adding the custom image to Microsoft Intune

IT admins have to make Microsoft Intune aware that there's a custom image available before the image can be deployed to Cloud PCs. Sign in to the **Microsoft Intune admin center** >**Devices** >**Provisioning** >**Windows 365** and select the **Custom images** tab.

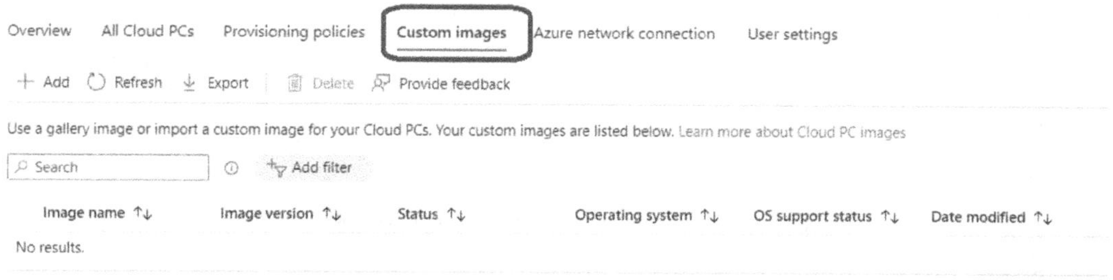

Overview   All Cloud PCs   Provisioning policies   Custom images   Azure network connection   User settings

+ Add   ○ Refresh   ↓ Export   🗑 Delete   ⌻ Provide feedback

Use a gallery image or import a custom image for your Cloud PCs. Your custom images are listed below. Learn more about Cloud PC images

🔍 Search   ○   ⌄ Add filter

Image name ↑↓	Image version ↑↓	Status ↑↓	Operating system ↑↓	OS support status ↑↓	Date modified ↑↓
No results.					

Figure 6.61 – An overview of the custom images for Windows 365

Click the + **Add** button in the ribbon to add the newly created image.

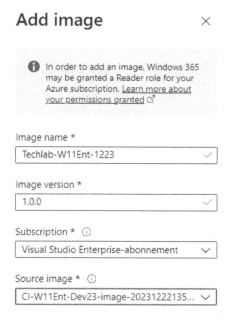

Figure 6.62 – Adding the custom image to Windows 365

The custom image will appear in the overview once it's uploaded. Microsoft Intune will detect which OS is used and whether it is currently supported.

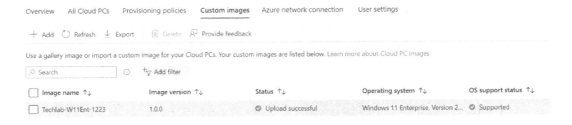

Figure 6.63 – The image upload was successful

The only thing left to do is to assign the custom image to a provisioning policy or update an existing one.

Creating a custom image for Azure Virtual Desktop

In this section, we will walk you through the steps that are needed to create a custom image to use with Azure Virtual Desktop, with the main goal of deploying an updated image with the newest Microsoft updates.

To create a custom image, we need a new VM. In the **Azure portal**, go to **Virtual Machines >Create >Azure virtual machine**.

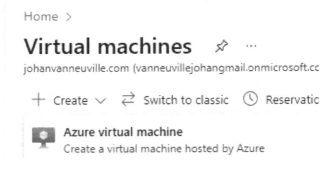

Figure 6.64 – Create an Azure VM

Fill in the required details and select the desired image. In this example, the IT admin takes the latest Windows 11 with the Microsoft 365 apps installed. FSLogix is also already pre-installed. Don't forget to block the public inbound ports and enter the local administrator account and password.

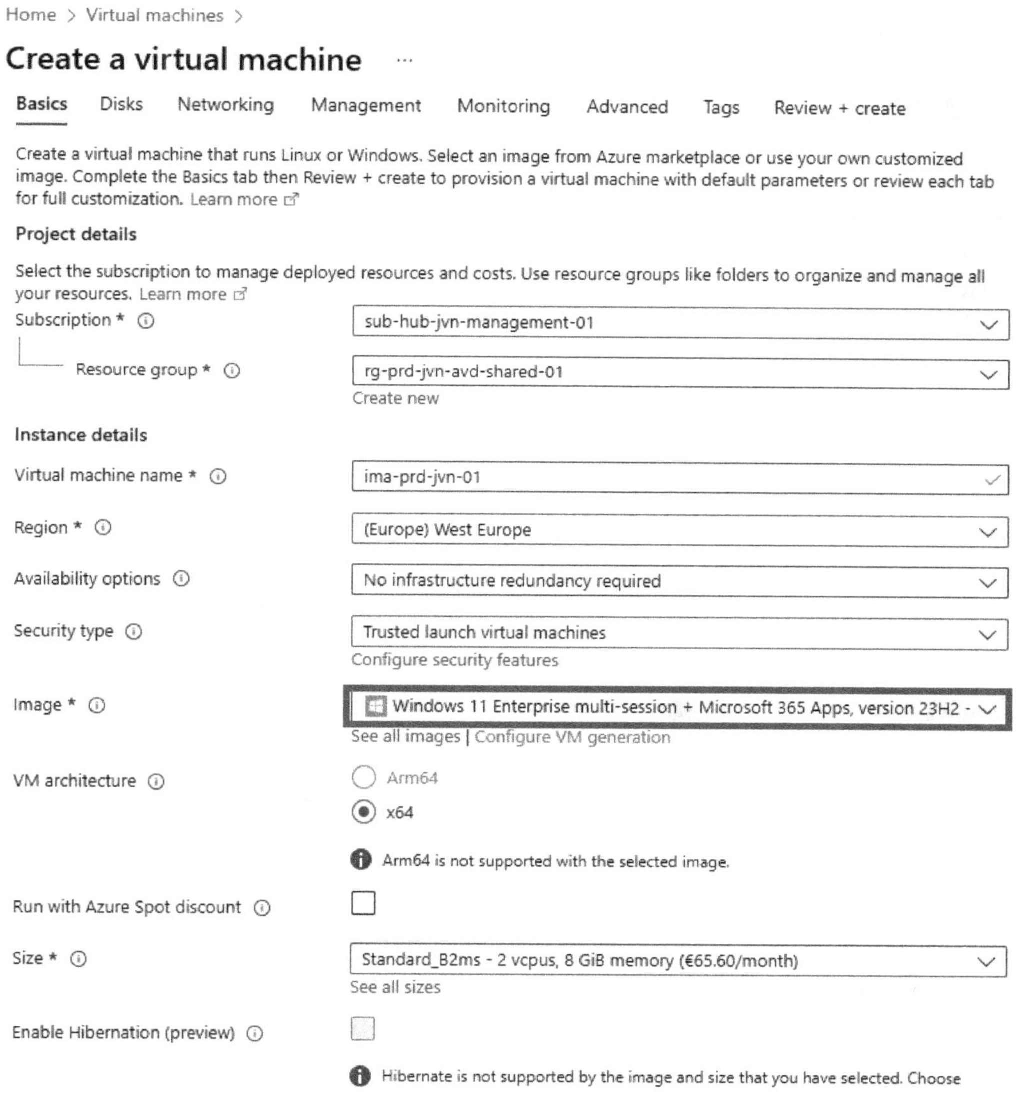

Home > Virtual machines >

Create a virtual machine   ...

Basics   Disks   Networking   Management   Monitoring   Advanced   Tags   Review + create

Create a virtual machine that runs Linux or Windows. Select an image from Azure marketplace or use your own customized image. Complete the Basics tab then Review + create to provision a virtual machine with default parameters or review each tab for full customization. Learn more ☐

Project details

Select the subscription to manage deployed resources and costs. Use resource groups like folders to organize and manage all your resources. Learn more ☐

Subscription * ⓘ

> sub-hub-jvn-management-01 ⌄

⌐
└──── Resource group * ⓘ

> rg-prd-jvn-avd-shared-01 ⌄
>
> Create new

Instance details

Virtual machine name * ⓘ

> ima-prd-jvn-01 ✓

Region * ⓘ

> (Europe) West Europe ⌄

Availability options ⓘ

> No infrastructure redundancy required ⌄

Security type ⓘ

> Trusted launch virtual machines ⌄
>
> Configure security features

Image * ⓘ

> ⊞ Windows 11 Enterprise multi-session + Microsoft 365 Apps, version 23H2 - ⌄
>
> See all images | Configure VM generation

VM architecture ⓘ

> ◯ Arm64
>
> ⦿ x64

> ⓘ Arm64 is not supported with the selected image.

Run with Azure Spot discount ⓘ

> ☐

Size * ⓘ

> Standard_B2ms - 2 vcpus, 8 GiB memory (€65.60/month) ⌄
>
> See all sizes

Enable Hibernation (preview) ⓘ

> ☐

> ⓘ Hibernate is not supported by the image and size that you have selected. Choose

Figure 6.65 – Create a VM

Under the next tab, **Disks**, the IT admin can choose to limit the cost by selecting **Standard SSD**. Also, it is important to select **Delete with VM**. This way, the disk will also be deleted when the VM is deleted during the capture process.

Basics   **Disks**   Networking   Management   Monitoring   Advanced   Tags   Review + create

⚠ The desired performance might not be reached due to the maximum virtual machine disk performance cap. The current virtual machine size supports up to 24 MBps. The total for disks attached to 'ima-prd-jvn-01' is 100 MBps. <u>Learn more</u> ⃞

Azure VMs have one operating system disk and a temporary disk for short-term storage. You can attach additional data disks. The size of the VM determines the type of storage you can use and the number of data disks allowed. Learn more ⃞

VM disk encryption

Azure disk storage encryption automatically encrypts your data stored on Azure managed disks (OS and data disks) at rest by default when persisting it to the cloud.

Encryption at host ⓘ

ℹ Encryption at host is not registered for the selected subscription.
<u>Learn more about enabling this feature</u> ⃞

OS disk

OS disk size ⓘ
| Image default (127 GiB)   ⌄ |

OS disk type * ⓘ
| Standard SSD (locally-redundant storage)   ⌄ |
The selected VM size supports premium disks. We recommend Premium SSD for high IOPS workloads. Virtual machines with Premium SSD disks qualify for the 99.9% connectivity SLA.

Delete with VM ⓘ   ✓

Key management ⓘ
| Platform-managed key   ⌄ |

Figure 6.66 – Image disk selection

Let's summarize the rest of the tabs before hitting the **Create** button:

- **Networking**: Select the correct virtual network and subnet, and set the public IP to **None for security**. Also, select **Delete NIC when VM is deleted** and set the **Load Balancing** options to **None**.

- **Management**: When selecting **Login with Azure AD**, don't forget to delete the VM extension before running Sysprep.

- **Monitoring**: If preferred, the IT admin can choose to use a custom storage account for the boot diagnostics or use the managed option.

- **Advanced**: Can be left as default.

- **Tags**: Add the necessary tags if needed.

- **Review + create**: Review all the details and click **Create**.

The deployment will take a couple of minutes.

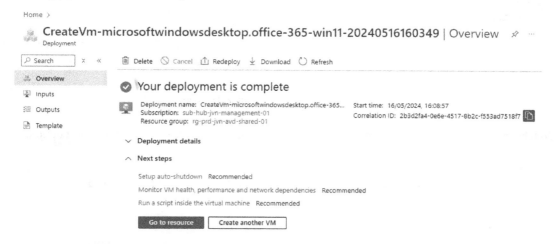

Figure 6.67 – The finished VM deployment

Customizing the VM

When the VM is successfully deployed, the IT admin can make the necessary modifications to the image. These can be installing an application, changing Windows settings, running Windows updates, and so on. To connect to this image, the IT admin can use Azure Bastion, which is covered in *Chapter 8, Configuring Access Control*.

It's recommended that the IT admin takes a snapshot of the disk before running sysprep in case something goes wrong during this step. Make sure that the VM is in a **Stopped (deallocated)** state.

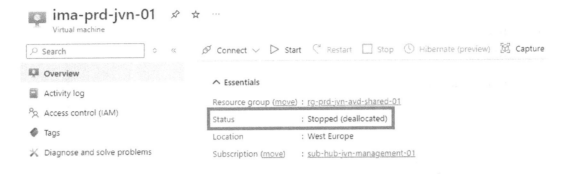

Figure 6.68 – The image in a deallocated state

To take the snapshot, the IT admin needs to go to the VM disk and choose the **Create snapshot** option.

Figure 6.69 – Create snapshot

Fill in the required details, such as the name of the snapshot and in what resource group the snapshot needs to be created, and then click **Review + create**.

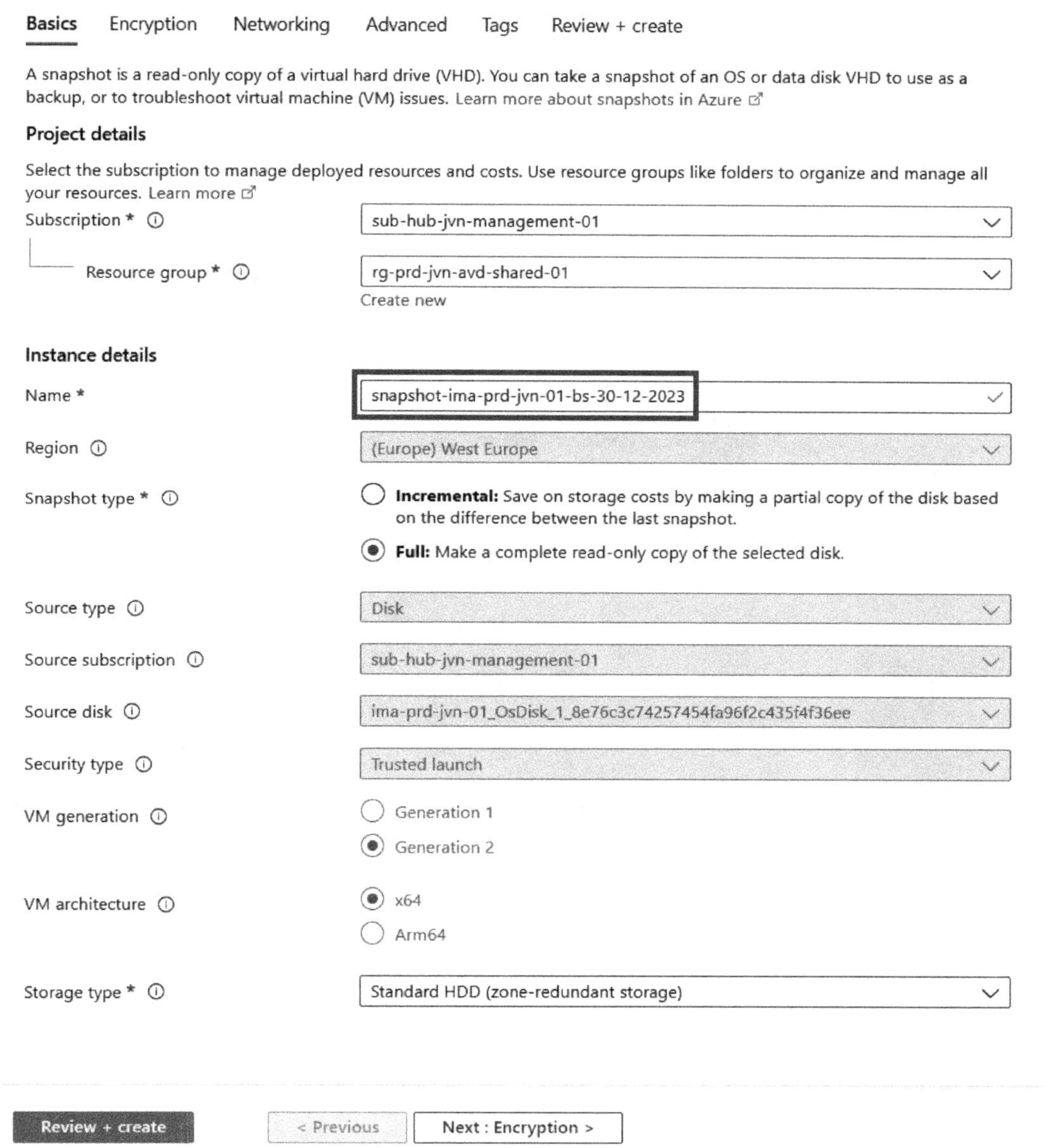

Basics Encryption Networking Advanced Tags Review + create

A snapshot is a read-only copy of a virtual hard drive (VHD). You can take a snapshot of an OS or data disk VHD to use as a backup, or to troubleshoot virtual machine (VM) issues. Learn more about snapshots in Azure ⟋

Project details

Select the subscription to manage deployed resources and costs. Use resource groups like folders to organize and manage all your resources. Learn more ⟋

Subscription * ⓘ	sub-hub-jvn-management-01 ⌄
└─ Resource group * ⓘ	rg-prd-jvn-avd-shared-01 ⌄
	Create new

Instance details

Name *	snapshot-ima-prd-jvn-01-bs-30-12-2023 ✓
Region ⓘ	(Europe) West Europe ⌄

Snapshot type * ⓘ
- ◯ **Incremental:** Save on storage costs by making a partial copy of the disk based on the difference between the last snapshot.
- ◉ **Full:** Make a complete read-only copy of the selected disk.

Source type ⓘ	Disk ⌄
Source subscription ⓘ	sub-hub-jvn-management-01 ⌄
Source disk ⓘ	ima-prd-jvn-01_OsDisk_1_8e76c3c74257454fa96f2c435f4f36ee ⌄
Security type ⓘ	Trusted launch ⌄

VM generation ⓘ
- ◯ Generation 1
- ◉ Generation 2

VM architecture ⓘ
- ◉ x64
- ◯ Arm64

Storage type * ⓘ	Standard HDD (zone-redundant storage) ⌄

[Review + create]   [< Previous] [Next : Encryption >]

Figure 6.70 – Snapshot creation

The other tabs can be customized to the IT admin's liking. Now, the IT admin can restart the image and start the sysprep process. (Use the command we mentioned earlier or go to `C:\Windows\System32\Sysprep` and run `Sysprep.exe`.)

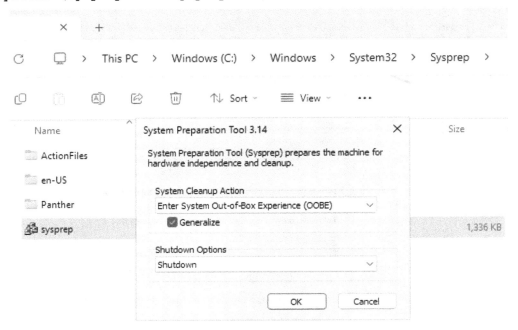

Figure 6.71 – Sysprep

Creating an image version

Now, it's time to capture the prepared VM and create an image. Open the **Azure portal**, go to **Virtual Machines**, and select **Capture** in the ribbon on the **Overview** tab.

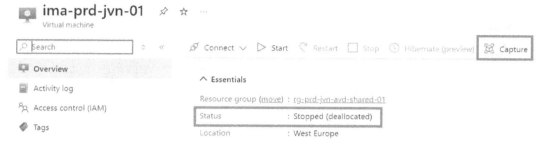

Figure 6.72 – The Capture button

Azure Compute Gallery

During the next process, the IT admin will create a new image version and store this in an Azure Compute Gallery. This is an Azure resource where the images can be stored. The gallery also provides the option to replicate the images in a secondary region if this is required. The first thing that the IT admin needs is an image definition. This is a resource that contains info about the image such as the following:

- The OS type
- The security type
- Publisher info

The following screenshot is an example of the basic settings to create an image:

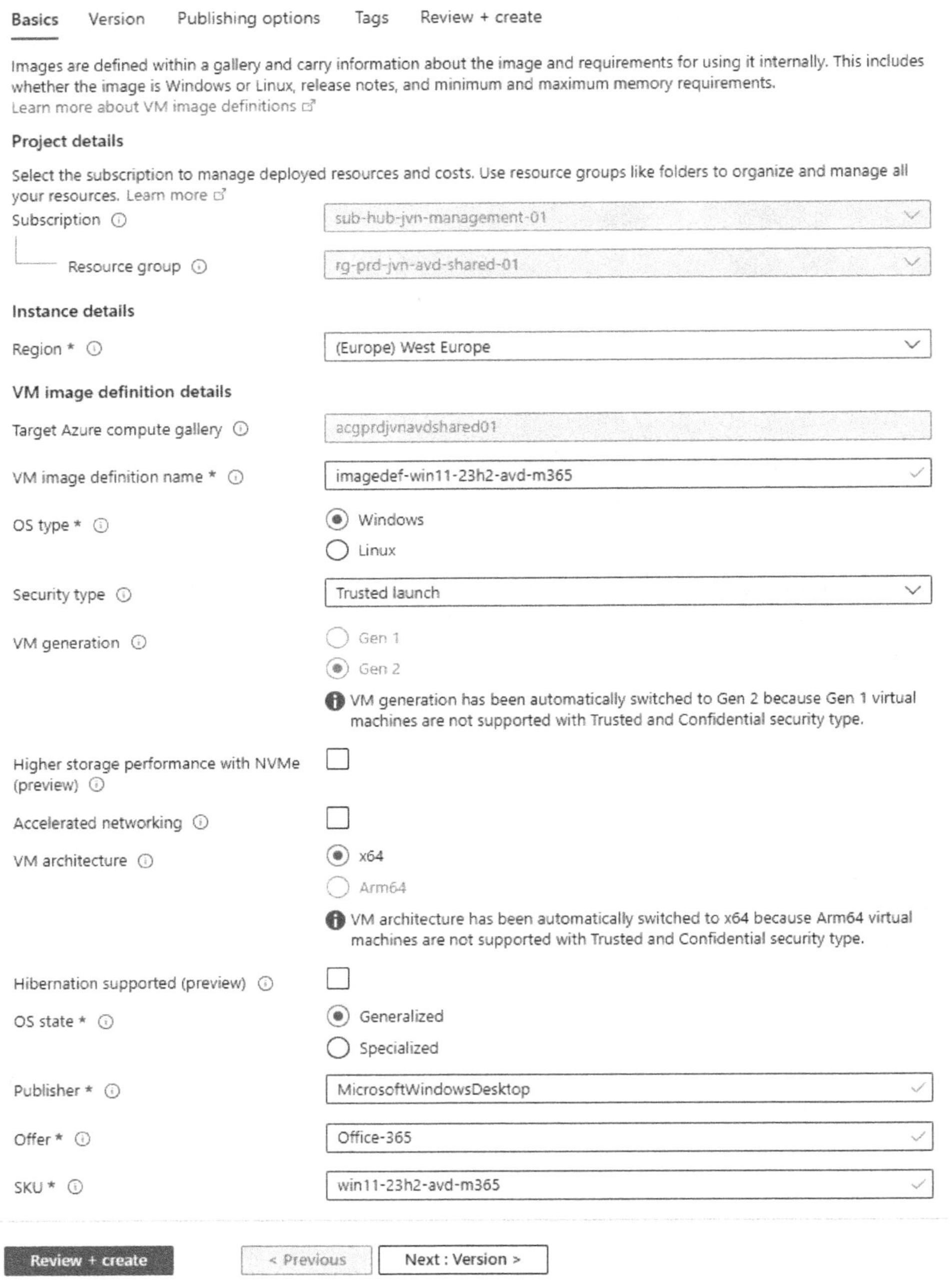

Basics   Version   Publishing options   Tags   Review + create

Images are defined within a gallery and carry information about the image and requirements for using it internally. This includes whether the image is Windows or Linux, release notes, and minimum and maximum memory requirements.
Learn more about VM image definitions ⬡

Project details

Select the subscription to manage deployed resources and costs. Use resource groups like folders to organize and manage all your resources. Learn more ⬡

Subscription ⓘ   sub-hub-jvn-management-01   ⌄

└──── Resource group ⓘ   rg-prd-jvn-avd-shared-01   ⌄

Instance details

Region * ⓘ   (Europe) West Europe   ⌄

VM image definition details

Target Azure compute gallery ⓘ acgprdjvnavdshared01

VM image definition name * ⓘ   imagedef-win11-23h2-avd-m365   ✓

OS type * ⓘ   ⦿ Windows
                                ◯ Linux

Security type ⓘ   Trusted launch   ⌄

VM generation ⓘ   ◯ Gen 1
                                ⦿ Gen 2

                                ⓘ VM generation has been automatically switched to Gen 2 because Gen 1 virtual machines are not supported with Trusted and Confidential security type.

Higher storage performance with NVMe (preview) ⓘ   ☐

Accelerated networking ⓘ   ☐

VM architecture ⓘ   ⦿ x64
                                ◯ Arm64

                                ⓘ VM architecture has been automatically switched to x64 because Arm64 virtual machines are not supported with Trusted and Confidential security type.

Hibernation supported (preview) ⓘ   ☐

OS state * ⓘ   ⦿ Generalized
                                ◯ Specialized

Publisher * ⓘ   MicrosoftWindowsDesktop   ✓

Offer * ⓘ   Office-365   ✓

SKU * ⓘ   win11-23h2-avd-m365   ✓

[Review + create]   [< Previous]   [Next : Version >]

Figure 6.73 – Create an image definition

The version step here is not needed because the version will be created during the capturing phase. The next step is to review and create the definition.

Create a VM image definition ...

✓ Validation passed

Basics   Version   Publishing options   Tags   **Review + create**

Basics

Subscription	sub-hub-jvn-management-01
Resource group	rg-prd-jvn-avd-shared-01
Region	West Europe
Target Azure compute gallery	acgprdjvnavdshared01
VM image definition name	imagedef-win11-23h2-avd-m365
OS type	Windows
Security type	Trusted launch
VM generation	V2
Higher storage performance with NVMe (preview)	SCSI
Accelerated networking	Disabled
VM architecture	x64
Hibernation supported (preview)	No
OS state	Generalized
Publisher	MicrosoftWindowsDesktop
Offer	Office-365
SKU	win11-23h2-avd-m365

Figure 6.74 – Image definition creation

Now that both the Azure compute Gallery and the image definition are created, it's time for the IT admin to start the capturing process. In this step, the IT admin needs to add the version number, and it's also possible to add more target regions and replica counts.

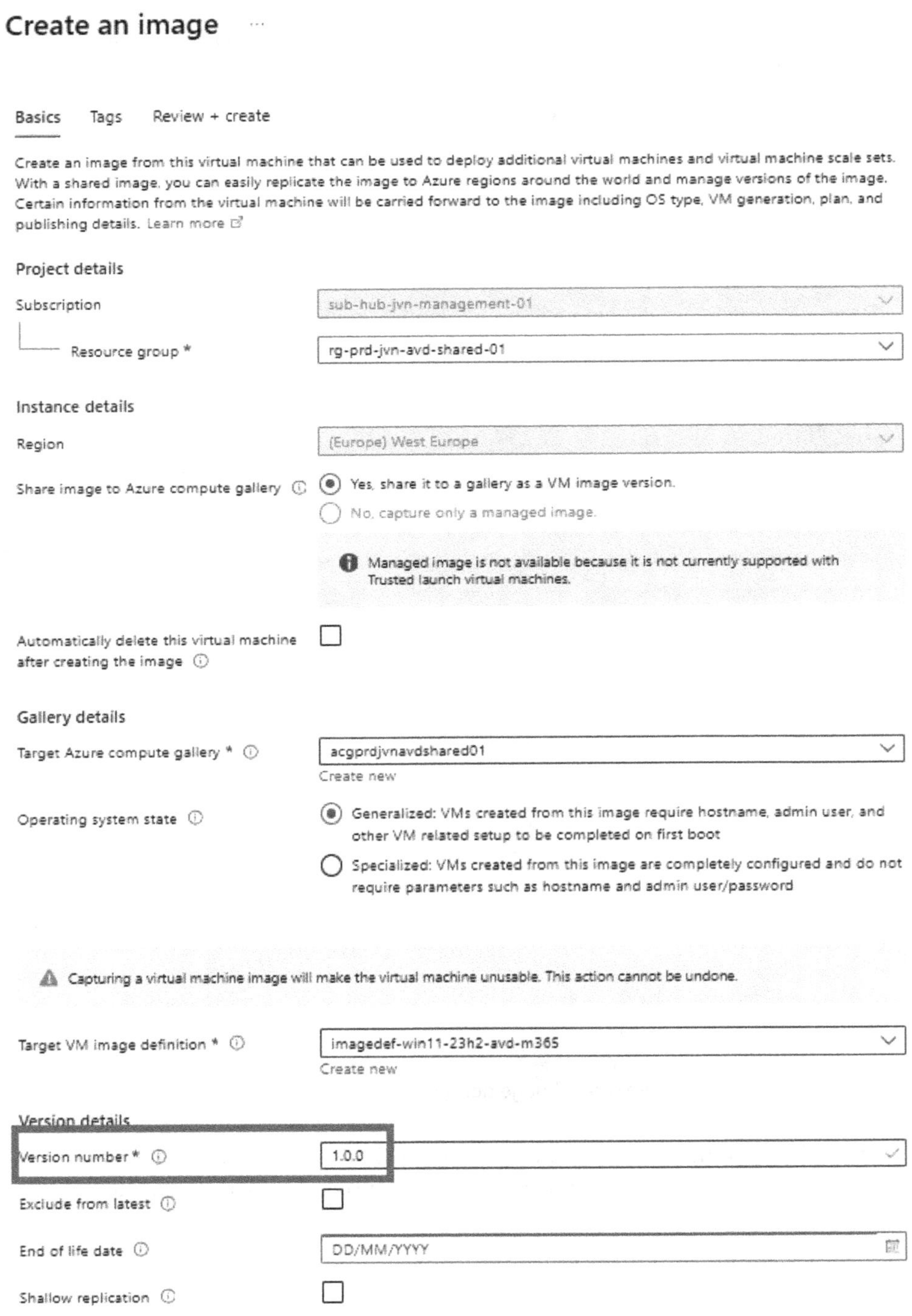

Create an image ...

Basics   Tags   Review + create

Create an image from this virtual machine that can be used to deploy additional virtual machines and virtual machine scale sets. With a shared image, you can easily replicate the image to Azure regions around the world and manage versions of the image. Certain information from the virtual machine will be carried forward to the image including OS type, VM generation, plan, and publishing details. Learn more ⬀

Project details

Subscription

> sub-hub-jvn-management-01

Resource group *

> rg-prd-jvn-avd-shared-01

Instance details

Region

> (Europe) West Europe

Share image to Azure compute gallery ⓘ   ⦿ Yes, share it to a gallery as a VM image version.

◯ No, capture only a managed image.

ⓘ Managed image is not available because it is not currently supported with Trusted launch virtual machines.

Automatically delete this virtual machine after creating the image ⓘ   ☐

Gallery details

Target Azure compute gallery * ⓘ

> acgprdjvnavdshared01

Create new

Operating system state ⓘ   ⦿ Generalized: VMs created from this image require hostname, admin user, and other VM related setup to be completed on first boot

◯ Specialized: VMs created from this image are completely configured and do not require parameters such as hostname and admin user/password

⚠ Capturing a virtual machine image will make the virtual machine unusable. This action cannot be undone.

Target VM image definition * ⓘ

> imagedef-win11-23h2-avd-m365

Create new

Version details

Version number * ⓘ   1.0.0

Exclude from latest ⓘ   ☐

End of life date ⓘ   DD/MM/YYYY

Shallow replication ⓘ   ☐

Figure 6.75 – Azure Virtual Desktop image capture

Add some tags to identify the resource, and then click **Review + create**.

Basics   Tags   Review + create

Tags are name/value pairs that enable you to categorize resources and view consolidated billing by applying the same tag to multiple resources and resource groups. Learn more about tags ◻'

Note that if you create tags and then change resource settings on other tabs, your tags will be automatically updated.

Name ⓘ	Value ⓘ	
Environment	: AVD PRD	🗑
Purpose	: ImageVersion	🗑
	:	

Figure 6.76 – The image version tags

The capturing process will take a while, but when it's completed, the IT admin can start deploying session hosts.

✓ Validation passed

Basics   Tags   Review + create

Basics

Subscription	sub-hub-jvn-management-01
Resource group	rg-prd-jvn-avd-shared-01
Region	West Europe
Share image to Azure compute gallery	Yes
Automatically delete this virtual machine after creating the image	No
Azure compute gallery	acgprdjvnavdshared01
Operating system state	Generalized
Target VM image definition	imagedef-win11-23h2-avd-m365
Version number	1.0.0
Source virtual machine	ima-prd-jvn-01
Exclude from latest	No
End of life date	None
Shallow replication	No

Replication

Default replica count	1
Replication	West Europe: 1

Tags

Environment	AVD PRD
Purpose	ImageVersion

Figure 6.77 – Capturing and Review + create

This concludes this chapter; let's summarize what we have learned.

Summary

In this chapter, you learned how to determine which cloud-based update management solution from Microsoft best fits the needs of your company and how to implement and use these solutions. You also learned how to create your own custom images and how they can be used to install the newest updates.

In the next chapter, we will continue our journey as we take a look at threat detection and prevention. We will discuss topics such as Microsoft Defender for Endpoint, how to use tamper protection, and how disk encryption works for Windows 365 and Azure Virtual Desktop. Did you know that it actually works differently for each solution?

7

Threat Detection and Prevention

In this chapter, we will continue our journey by exploring the security controls that IT admins can use to secure the desktops of their organizations. We will start by introducing Microsoft Defender for Endpoint and how to enroll Cloud PCs and desktops that live in Azure Virtual Desktop. We will explore tamper protection and how this feature helps to protect the desktop of the user. And last but not least, we will cover the various ways of encrypting data on the virtual desktop.

In this chapter, we're going to cover the following main topics:

- Microsoft Defender for Endpoint
- Tamper protection
- Encrypting data on the virtual desktop

Microsoft Defender for Endpoint

An important step to keep your desktop safe is to make sure that it is protected against malware. **Microsoft Defender for Endpoint** (**MDE**) is a great solution to make sure that threats are detected and mitigated. As an enterprise endpoint security platform, Microsoft Defender for Endpoint can detect, prevent, investigate, and respond to advanced attacks.

> **Note**
> Did you know that MDE not only keeps your desktops safe? It can also keep other endpoints safe, including smartphones, tablets, servers, and even network endpoints such as access points, routers, and firewalls.

Requirements for Microsoft Defender for Endpoint

The following are the more common requirements for desktops:

- A Defender for Endpoint license. This could be a Plan 1 or Plan 2 license.
- Microsoft Defender for Business (if the company is a small business).
- An up-to-date browser as management is done via a web page. Microsoft Edge and Google Chrome are supported.
- A supported operating system:

  - Windows 11 Enterprise
  - Windows 11 Enterprise IoT
  - Windows 11 Education
  - Windows 11 Pro
  - Windows 11 Pro Education
  - Windows 10 Enterprise
  - Windows 10 Enterprise LTSC 2016 or later
  - Windows 10 Enterprise IoT including LTSC
  - Windows 10 Education
  - Windows 10 Pro
  - Windows 10 Pro Education

- Windows 365 is supported. The Cloud PC should run one of the supported operating systems mentioned previously.
- Azure Virtual Desktop is supported.
- Hardware requirements:

  - CPU: Minimum of 2 cores, 4 cores preferred
  - Memory: 1 GB minimum, 4 preferred

Enrolling Windows 365 Cloud PCs into Microsoft Defender for Endpoint

It's a two-step process to enroll Cloud PCs into Microsoft Defender for Endpoint:

1. Enable the Microsoft Intune connection.

   Let's connect Microsoft Defender for Endpoint to Microsoft Intune. To do so, sign in to the Microsoft Defender portal at https://security.microsoft.com > **Settings** > **Endpoints** > **Advanced features** > **Microsoft Intune connection** and toggle the switch to **On**.

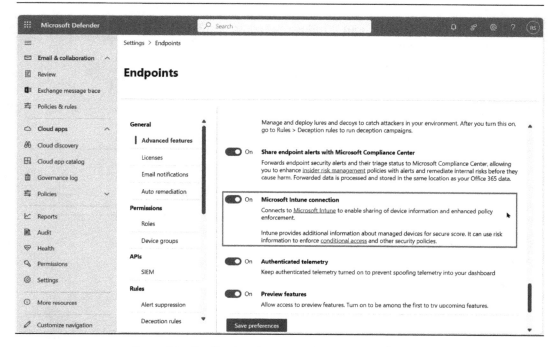

Figure 7.1 – Configuring the connection to Microsoft Intune

2. Use an Endpoint Detection and Response policy to target desktops.

    Next, we have to make sure that the desired desktops are targeted. Sign in to **Microsoft Intune admin center** > **Endpoint Security**, go to **Manage** > **Endpoint detection and response**, and create a device configuration profile.

IT admins can create multiple device configuration profiles and use it to target different groups of devices. Click **+ Create** button to create a new profile.

Select the desired platform:

- **Windows 10, Windows 11, and Windows Server**

- **Linux**: There is a long list of supported Linux distributions. Make sure to verify that your distribution is supported before targeting Linux desktops.

- **macOS**: The following versions of macOS are supported:

    - 14 (Sonoma)

    - 13 (Ventura)

    - 12 (Monterey)

- **Windows 10, Windows 11, and Windows Server (ConfigMgr)**: Select this option if your desktops are hybrid managed.

The following is a screenshot of the available platforms:

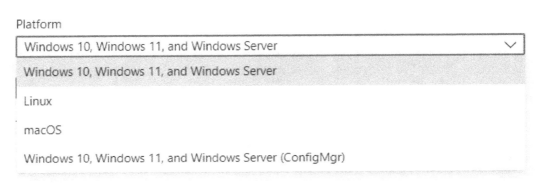

Figure 7.2 – Select the desired platform

Give the EDR policy a name and a description (optionally).

Figure 7.3 – Filling in the basics of the EDR policy

There are three configuration settings for Microsoft Defender for Endpoint:

- **Microsoft Defender for Endpoint client configuration package type:** Select **Auto from connector**. This will ensure that the onboarding package from the Defender for Endpoint deployment is used.

  There are cases where it's not possible to create a connection between MDE and Intune. For those cases, IT admins can select **Onboard** to configure the custom blob.

- **Sample Sharing:** Enabling this feature will make sure that MDE shares a file with Microsoft for deep analysis. It's recommended to turn this feature on to make full use of MDE capabilities, but make sure to turn this feature off for desktops that access sensitive company data.

- **Telemetry Reporting Frequency:** This feature is deprecated and no longer has an impact on desktops.

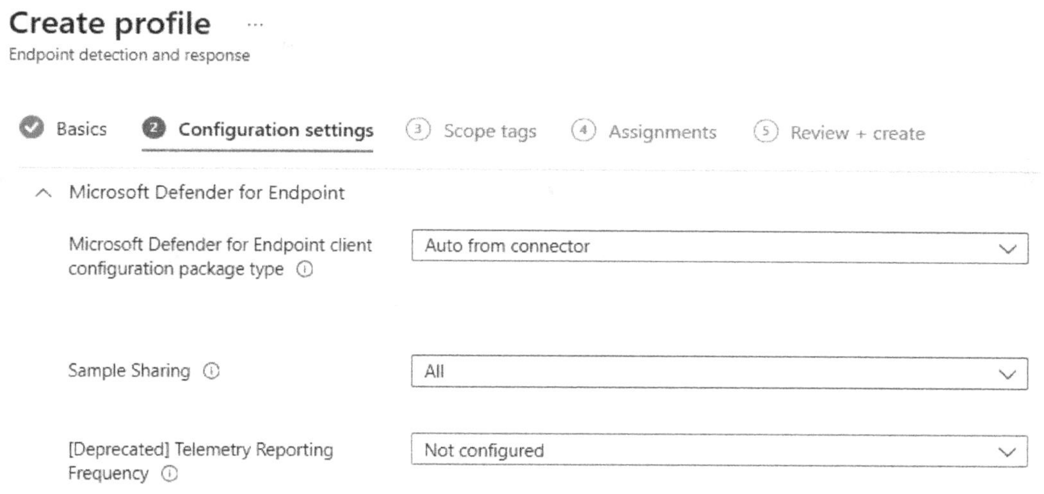

Create profile ⋯
Endpoint detection and response

☑ Basics　❷ Configuration settings　③ Scope tags　④ Assignments　⑤ Review + create

⌄ Microsoft Defender for Endpoint

Microsoft Defender for Endpoint client configuration package type ⓘ

| Auto from connector ⌄ |

Sample Sharing ⓘ

| All ⌄ |

[Deprecated] Telemetry Reporting Frequency ⓘ

| Not configured ⌄ |

Figure 7.4 – Configuration settings for the EDR policy

In the next step, IT admins can add **scope tags** if applicable and continue to the **assignments** step. Click the **+ All devices** button to target all the devices. Other options are to select a group containing specific devices or use the built-in devices group and apply a filter. An example would be to filter for Windows 365 Cloud PCs.

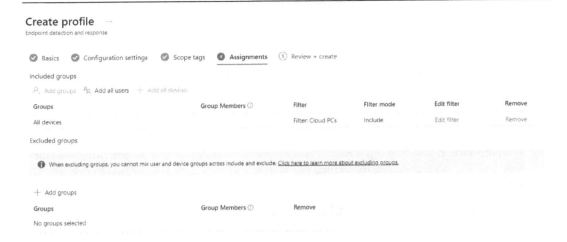

Figure 7.5 – Example of assigning the EDR policy to Cloud PCs

After a while, the EDR policy will be applied to the targeted desktops:

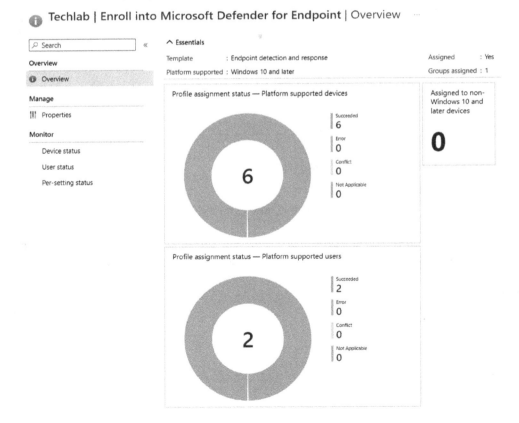

Figure 7.6 – Example of a successfully assigned and applied EDR policy

The device will appear in the **Microsoft Defender portal** > **Assets** > **Devices**.

Figure 7.7 – Devices in the Microsoft Defender portal

In the next section, we will cover how to use a security baseline as a starting point.

Using a security baseline as a starting point

Enrolling the desktops into Microsoft Defender for Endpoint is the first step. IT admins have to make sure that these newly enrolled desktops are configured safely and securely. Did you know that Microsoft has **security baselines**? These baselines contain settings for a specific solution and the good news is that there is a security baseline for Microsoft Defender for Endpoint as well:

1. Sign in to **Microsoft Intune admin center** and go to **Endpoint Security** > **Security Baselines**.

2. Let's deploy the Microsoft Defender for Endpoint security baseline. Click on **Microsoft Defender for Endpoint Baseline**.

Figure 7.8 – Available security baselines in Microsoft Intune

3. Click the + **Create profile** button.

Figure 7.9 – The first step to deploy the security baseline

4. Give the MDE baseline profile a name and optionally a description.

Figure 7.10 – Example of the basics

All of the settings have been preconfigured in the **Configuration settings** step. These settings are categorized into the following groups:

- **Attack Surface Reduction Rules**

- **BitLocker**

- **Device Guard**

- **Device Installation**

- **DMA Guard**

- **Firewall**

- **Microsoft Defender**

- **Smart Screen**

5. We recommend reviewing each of these settings before deploying this security baseline. By reviewing these settings IT admins make sure that there will be no unwanted side effects after deploying the baseline. For example, Windows 365 Cloud PCs do not support BitLocker and this baseline will configure BitLocker by default. To solve this issue, switch the slider shown in *Figure 7.11* to **Not configured**:

Figure 7.11 – By default, BitLocker will be configured

6. Continue to the scope tags once all of the settings have been properly reviewed. Add scope tags if required and assign the same desktops that are enrolled into Microsoft Defender for Endpoint. Note that filters cannot be used in this step:

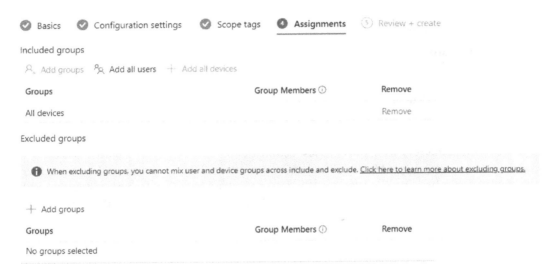

Figure 7.12 – Example of assigning the security baseline to the built-in all devices group

7. Review the settings and assignments in the last step and create the policy:

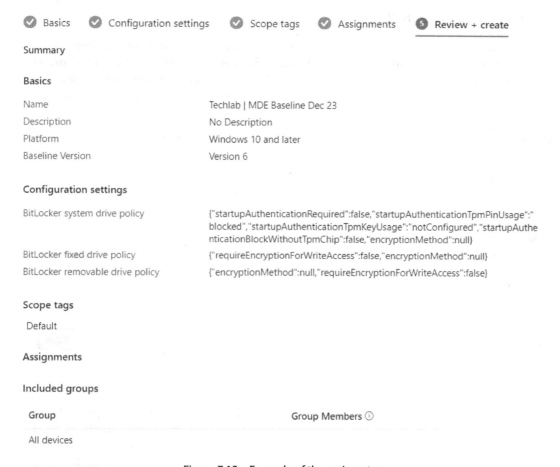

Figure 7.13 – Example of the review step

Enrolling an Azure Virtual Desktop session host into Microsoft Defender for Endpoint

Now that the reader knows how to enroll Cloud PCs, let's continue and do the same for Azure Virtual Desktop session hosts. To achieve this, we can use two methods:

- Using Defender for Cloud
- Using an onboarding script

Defender for Cloud enrollment

Let's start with the first step and enable the Server plan in Defender for Cloud for the subscription. Go to the **Azure portal** > **Microsoft Defender for Cloud** > **Environment Settings** > **Select the correct subscription containing the AVD deployment** > **Defender Plans and turn on Servers plan**. Using Plan 1 is enough for the basic functionality. If you want to be able to use all options, then Plan 2 is required.

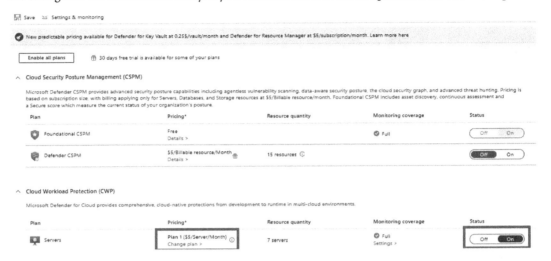

Figure 7.14 – Activate the Defender Server plan

After enabling the plan the session hosts will start appearing in the Microsoft security portal. Go to `https://security.microsoft.com` and go to the **Devices** menu. The IT admin can filter the results by entering, for example, the first characters of the session hosts.

Figure 7.15 – Onboarded session in the security portal

After enabling the Server plan, an extension will be added to each session host. This can be viewed when going to the **Azure portal** > **Virtual Machines** > **example virtual machine** > **Extensions + Applications** as shown in the following figure.

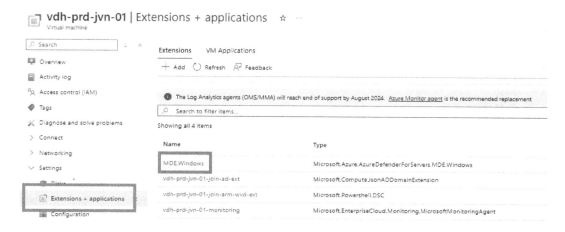

Figure 7.16 – Defender extension on session host

Onboarding package method

There is also another option to onboard the session hosts. The IT admin can also use an onboarding package that can be downloaded from the Defender portal. This script can then be used in a **Group Policy Object** (**GPO**). There are different ways of using the onboarding package, but the following method is recommended for Azure Virtual Desktop.

The first step for this method is to download the onboarding package. Go to **https://security.microsoft.com** > **Settings** > **Endpoints** > **Device Management** > **Onboarding** and download the script for non-persistent devices as shown in *Figure 7.17*.

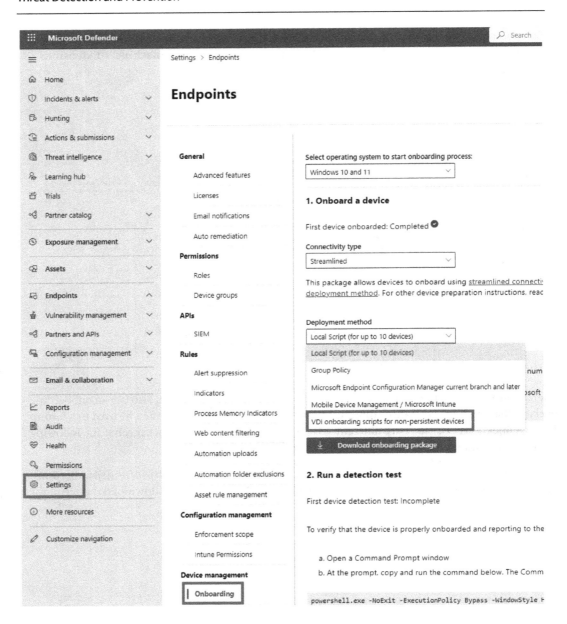

Figure 7.17 – Downloading the onboarding package

After downloading the package, the IT admin needs to unzip it to see what is inside.

Name	Status	Date modified	Type	Size
Onboard-NonPersistentMachine	⊘	12/01/2024 15:54	Windows PowerS...	21 KB
WindowsDefenderATPOnboardingScript	⊘	12/01/2024 15:54	Windows Comma...	17 KB

Figure 7.18 – Files in the onboarding package

There are two main options for using these files:

- **Multiple entries for each device – one for each session**: For this option, copy the `WindowsDefenderATPOnboardingScript.cmd` file

- **Single entries for each device**: For this option, copy both files

For each option, the file(s) need to be placed in `C:\WINDOWS\System32\GroupPolicy\Machine\Scripts\Startup`. If the IT admin doesn't see this folder, it might be hidden or it's possible that it needs to be created. An easy way to get this script on the session host is by using an image. The process of creating this image is explained in *Chapter 6, Update Management Strategies*.

Now that the files are ready, the IT admin needs to create a GPO to trigger the script. The setting that needs to be modified is **Computer configuration** > **Windows Settings** > **Scripts** > **Startup**.

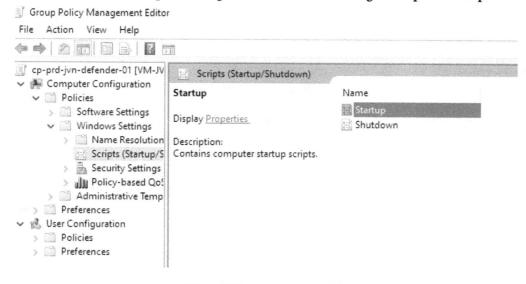

Figure 7.19 – Startup script GPO

Upon opening the startup scripts, select the **PowerShell Scripts** tab and press the **Add** button.

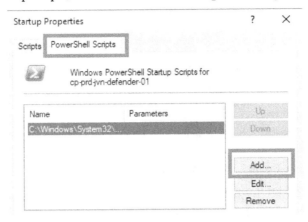

Figure 7.20 – PowerShell tab

In the next window, press **Browse** and select the PowerShell file.

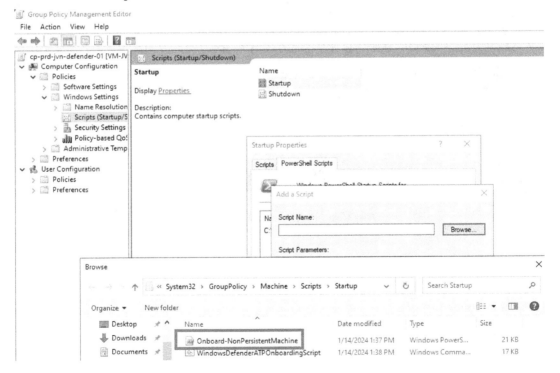

Figure 7.21 – Selecting the script

Now press **OK** and **Apply** to finalize the configuration.

Figure 7.22 – Script selected

This is the final step to configure the Defender enrollment using GPO. The next time that a session host starts, the PowerShell script will be triggered and the hosts will be enrolled in Defender in Endpoint.

At this point, we covered how to enroll desktops into Microsoft Defender for Endpoint and how to use the MDE security baseline as a starting point. This will ensure that Microsoft Defender for Endpoint will keep your organization's desktops safe. But how do IT admins make sure that MDE will run as planned and not be turned off by accident by a user? Or even worse, by malware? That's where a feature named **tamper protection** comes in.

Introducing tamper protection

In the previous chapter, we discussed how to configure Microsoft Defender for Endpoint and how to enroll desktops to make sure that they are protected against threats. But how do IT admins know that the required components for MDE are running, and their desktops are safe? That is where tamper protection comes in. Once enabled, alerts are raised in the Microsoft Defender portal in case tampering has been detected.

Enabling tamper protection

IT admins can use one of four ways to enable tamper protection depending on the design of their IT infrastructure:

- **Using the Microsoft Defender portal**: Use this method to enable or disable tamper protection for the entire tenant

- **Microsoft Intune admin center or Configuration Manager**: Use this method to enable or disable tamper protection for the entire tenant, or for a group of desktops or users

- **Configuration Manager with tenant attach**: Use this method to enable or disable tamper protection for the entire tenant, or for a group of desktops or users

- **Windows Security app**: Use this method to enable or disable tamper protection on a single desktop

Let's enable tamper protection using the Microsoft Intune admin center:

1. Sign in to the Microsoft Intune admin center and go to **Endpoint Security** > **Antivirus**, then click the **+ Create policy** button under the **AV Policies** tab.

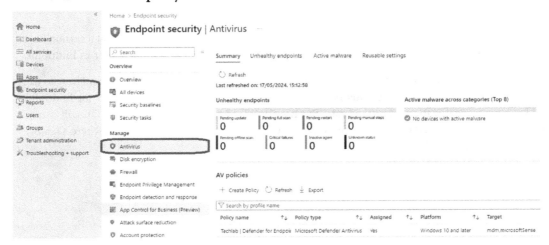

Figure 7.23 – Create a policy to enable tamper protection using Microsoft Intune

2. Select **Windows 10, Windows 11, and Windows Server** as the platform and **Windows Security Experience** as the profile type:

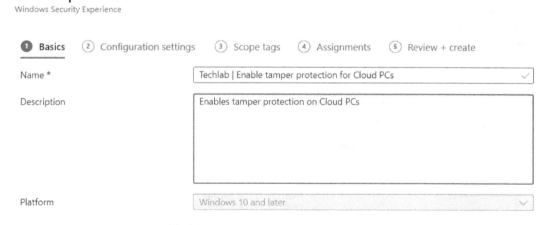

Create a profile   ✕

Platform

| Windows 10, Windows 11, and Windows Server | ⌄ |

Profile

| Windows Security Experience | ⌄ |

Windows Security Experience

The Windows Security app is used by a number of Windows security features to provide notifications about the health and security of the machine. These include notifications about firewalls, antivirus products, Windows Defender SmartScreen, and others.

Figure 7.24 – Select the platform and profile type

3. Give the profile a name and a description:

Create profile   ⋯
Windows Security Experience

① Basics   ② Configuration settings   ③ Scope tags   ④ Assignments   ⑤ Review + create

Name * | Techlab | Enable tamper protection for Cloud PCs | ✓ |

Description | Enables tamper protection on Cloud PCs |

Platform | Windows 10 and later | ⌄ |

Figure 7.25 – The basics tab of creating a profile

4. In the **Defender** tab, set **TamperProtection (Device)** to **On**.

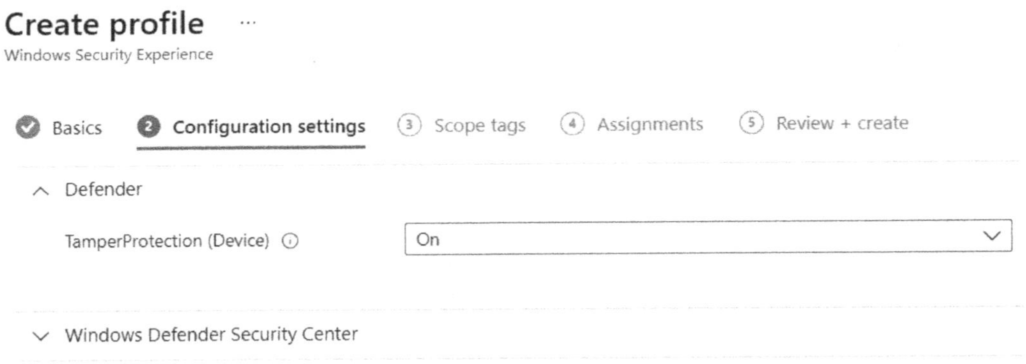

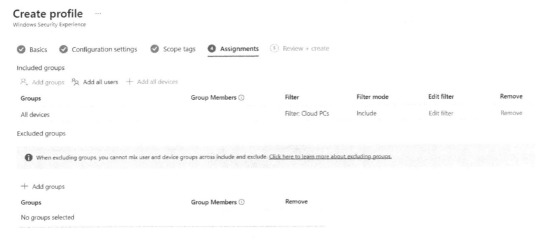

Figure 7.26 – Enable tamper protection in the configuration settings tab

5. Add scope tags if required and continue to the **Assignments** tab. Assign this profile to all devices or a group of devices. IT admins can make use of filters to assign this profile to only Cloud PCs, for example.

Figure 7.27 – Assigning the profile

6. Finish up by reviewing the configuration and create the profile. The newly created profile will appear in the AV policies overview:

AV policies

+ Create Policy   ○ Refresh   ↓ Export

🔍 Search by profile name

Policy name		Policy type		Assigned		Platform
Techlab | Defender for Endpoint	↑↓	Microsoft Defender Antivirus	↑↓	Yes	↑↓	Windows 10 and later
Techlab | Enable tamper protection for Cloud PCs		Windows Security Experience		Yes		Windows 10 and later

Figure 7.28 – Overview of the AV policies

Let's find out how to verify that tamper protection is enabled in the next section.

Verifying the tamper protection status

IT admins can verify that tamper protection is enabled on a desktop by running the following PowerShell command. It might take a bit of time to search for the properties since it will show a long list:

```
Get-MpComputerStatus
```

Search for the **IsTamperProtected** and **RealTimeProtectionEnabled** properties:

```
PS C:\Users\DominiekVerham> Get-MpComputerStatus


AMEngineVersion                   : 1.1.23110.2
AMProductVersion                  : 4.18.23110.3
AMRunningMode                     : Normal
AMServiceEnabled                  : True
AMServiceVersion                  : 4.18.23110.3
AntispywareEnabled                : True
AntispywareSignatureAge           : 0
AntispywareSignatureLastUpdated   : 1/1/2024 9:59:57 PM
AntispywareSignatureVersion       : 1.403.1501.0
AntivirusEnabled                  : True
AntivirusSignatureAge             : 0
AntivirusSignatureLastUpdated     : 1/1/2024 9:59:56 PM
AntivirusSignatureVersion         : 1.403.1501.0
BehaviorMonitorEnabled            : True
ComputerID                        : 27FC3296-194D-4910-B283-9A4F90F76FE2
ComputerState                     : 0
DefenderSignaturesOutOfDate       : False
DeviceControlDefaultEnforcement   :
DeviceControlPoliciesLastUpdated  : 11/30/2023 1:35:54 PM
DeviceControlState                : Disabled
FullScanAge                       : 4294967295
FullScanEndTime                   :
FullScanOverdue                   : False
FullScanRequired                  : False
FullScanSignatureVersion          :
FullScanStartTime                 :
InitializationProgress            : ServiceStartedSuccessfully
IoavProtectionEnabled             : True
IsTamperProtected                 : True
IsVirtualMachine                  : True
```

Figure 7.29 – Overview of all the properties

Perhaps it is better to run the PowerShell command and filter for these properties:

```
Get-MpComputerStatus | select
IsTamperProtected,RealTImeProtectionEnabled
```

The result is shown in the following screenshot:

```
PS C:\Users\DominiekVerham> Get-MpComputerStatus | select IsTamperProtected,RealTImeProtectionEnabled

IsTamperProtected RealTImeProtectionEnabled
----------------- -------------------------
             True                      True
```

Figure 7.30 – Filtered result to check if the desktop is using tamper protection

Tamper-protected settings

We discussed what tamper protection is and how to set it up. Now let's take a look at the settings that tamper protection protects:

- **Virus and threat protection remains enabled**: Virus and threat protection scans your desktop for known threats. IT admins can use this feature to run a quick or full scan.

- **Real-time protection remains turned on**: Real-time protection means that Defender will scan your endpoint for threats during regular use.

- **Behavior monitoring remains turned on**: Behavior monitoring keeps an eye on how a process behaves once it's being executed. Behavior monitoring can stop a threat even when it's already running.

- **Antivirus protection, including IOfficeAntivirus remains enabled**: These components are required to keep Microsoft Defender for Endpoint up and running.

- **Cloud protection remains enabled**: Cloud protection enhances the standard real-time protection by adding rapid identification of new threats.

- **Security intelligence updates occur**: Security intelligence is used by Microsoft in their anti-malware products. Updates are acquired using Windows Update.

- **Automatic actions are taken on detected threats**: Microsoft Defender for Endpoint remediates a threat once it's detected.

- **Notifications are visible in the Windows Security app on Windows desktops**: Notifications are displayed in the Windows Security app.

- **Archived files are scanned**: Microsoft Defender for Endpoint scans archive files for threats, such as .zip files.

In the next section, we will cover encryption on virtual desktops.

Encrypting data on the virtual desktop

Encrypting data on a physical Windows desktop is usually done by leveraging BitLocker Drive Encryption (BitLocker for short). BitLocker can be configured individually on a desktop or managed centrally via a GPO or a policy in Microsoft Intune.

BitLocker uses AES encryption and stores the encryption keys in the **Trusted Platform Module** (**TPM**) chip on the motherboard of the desktop. Nowadays, modern desktops are equipped with a compatible TPM chip but it's also possible to store the encryption keys on removable storage if the desktop does not have a TPM chip. For centrally managed desktops it's possible to store the BitLocker recovery key in Active Directory or Entra ID. But what about Cloud PCs?

Encryption for Windows 365 Cloud PCs

BitLocker is not supported for Windows 365 Cloud PCs. Instead, Windows 365 uses the following two techniques to keep data safe:

- Encryption of data at rest
- Encryption of data in transit

Encryption of data at rest means that when data is stored in Azure, it will automatically be encrypted. This is part of Azure Storage server-side encryption (or SSE for short). Components of the Cloud PC that are included are disks, snapshots, and images. By default, Azure will use platform-managed keys. It's also possible to use customer-managed keys if a company uses Microsoft Purview in case IT admins want to use their own key.

In addition to SSE, Windows 365 Cloud PCs are now protected using a technique that is called **host-based encryption**. With host-based encryption, the data is encrypted on the host, which means that it is already encrypted once it is sent over the network.

Host-based encryption does not have any performance impact on the Cloud PC, it's free to use, and it does not need any configuration from IT admins! Host-based encryption does not replace encryption of data in transit, instead, it adds another layer of data security.

Encryption of data in transit means that communication sent over the internet, or between the various AVD components internally in Azure, is encrypted with TLS 1.2. This encryption aims to keep data safe while traveling over the network.

Encryption for Azure Virtual Desktop session hosts

Unlike Windows 365 Cloud PCs, the OS disk of an Azure Virtual Desktop session host can be encrypted using Azure Disk Encryption. This can be done in multiple ways. The Azure portal can be used or the IT admin can use PowerShell, Terraform, Cloud Shell, or Bicep. A complete overview of the encryption methods supported for AVD can be found at `https://learn.microsoft.com/en-us/azure/virtual-machines/disk-encryption-overview`.

Azure Disk Encryption uses Azure Key Vault to store the encryption key. Make sure that Key Vault is enabled for Azure Disk Encryption. This can be enabled after the creation of the key vault. Go to the **Key Vault > Settings > Access configuration** and enable **Azure Disk Encryption for volume encryption**.

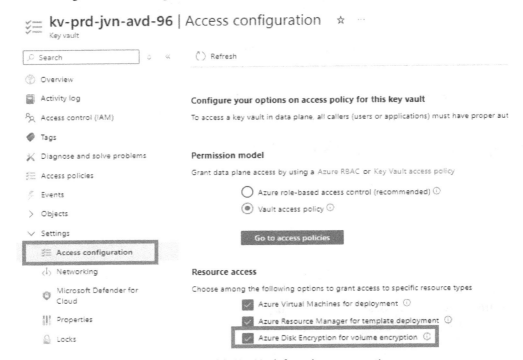

Figure 7.31 – Enable Key Vault for volume encryption

Let's have a look at how the IT admin can use the Azure portal to set up encryption.

First of all, go to the disk of a **session host** and select the **Disk** blade, then select **Additional settings**.

Figure 7.32 – Disk blade session host

Here the IT admin needs to choose what disk needs to be encrypted. Let's take the OS disk in this example because a session host won't have a data disk attached to it.

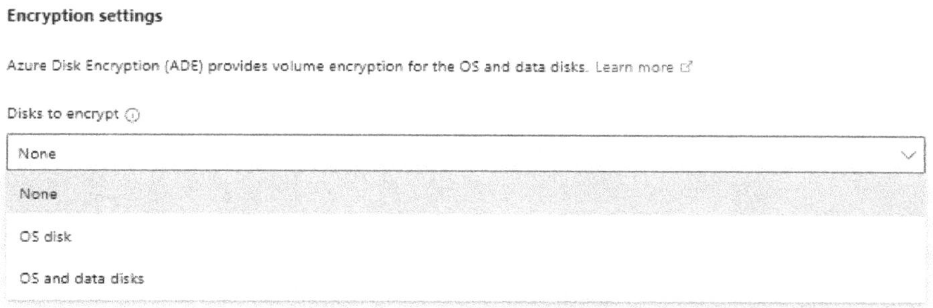

Encryption settings

Azure Disk Encryption (ADE) provides volume encryption for the OS and data disks. Learn more ☐

Disks to encrypt ⓘ

None	⌄
None	
OS disk	
OS and data disks	

Figure 7.33 – Disk selection for disk encryption

When selecting the OS disk, the IT admin gets the option to choose a key vault. When done, select **Save** so that the encryption process can begin.

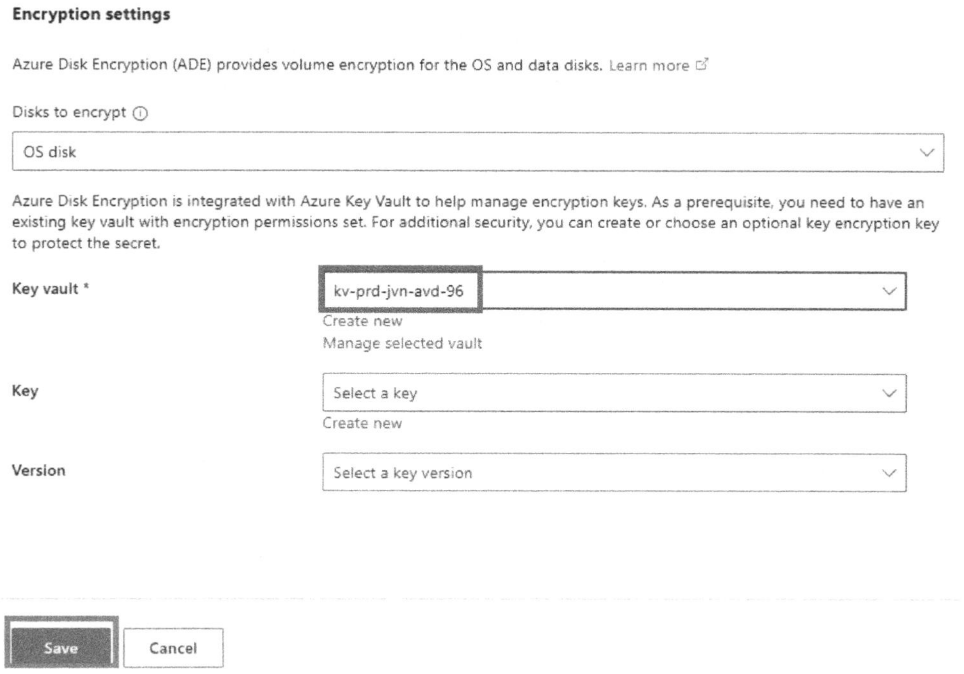

Encryption settings

Azure Disk Encryption (ADE) provides volume encryption for the OS and data disks. Learn more ☐

Disks to encrypt ⓘ

OS disk	⌄

Azure Disk Encryption is integrated with Azure Key Vault to help manage encryption keys. As a prerequisite, you need to have an existing key vault with encryption permissions set. For additional security, you can create or choose an optional key encryption key to protect the secret.

Key vault * | kv-prd-jvn-avd-96 | ⌄ |
Create new
Manage selected vault

Key | Select a key | ⌄ |
Create new

Version | Select a key version | ⌄ |

| Save | Cancel |

Figure 7.34 – Selecting a key vault

There is an option to use a Key Encryption Key but this is optional.

Azure Disk Encryption is done by installing an extension on the session host. During the deployment, the status can be viewed in the **Extensions + applications** menu of the virtual machine. This process will take a couple of minutes.

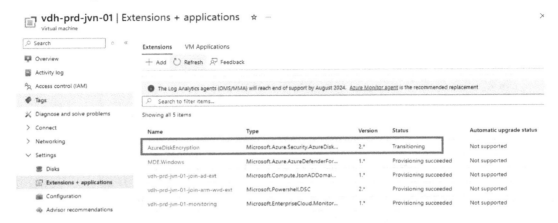

Figure 7.35 – Azure Disk Encryption transitioning

When the deployment is successful, the IT admin can view the status of the disk in the overview of the session host. It can also be viewed in the **Disks** blade of the virtual machine.

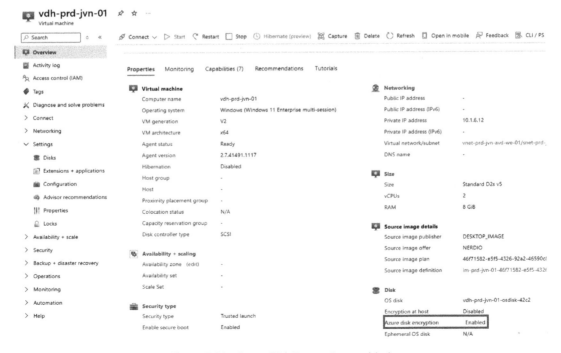

Figure 7.36 – Azure Disk Encryption enabled

The second option that the IT admin has is to enable Azure Disk Encryption using **Infrastructure as Code (IaC)**. Let's have a look at the PowerShell method for this example.

Open the PowerShell ISE and enter the following variables that need to be changed to fit the organization:

```
$KVRGname = 'rg-prd-jvn-avd-management-01';
$VMRGName = 'rg-prd-jvn-avd-shared-sessionhosts-01'
$vmName = 'vdh-prd-jvn-03'
$KeyVaultName = 'kv-prd-jvn-avd-96'
$KeyVault = Get-AzKeyVault -VaultName $KeyVaultName -ResourceGroupName
$KVRGname
$diskEncryptionKeyVaultUrl = $KeyVault.VaultUri
$KeyVaultResourceId = $KeyVault.ResourceId
```

Now let's run the PowerShell command to activate encryption. Make sure to select the correct subscription first with the `Set-AzContext -SubscriptionId "subscriptionid"` command:

```
Set-AzVMDiskEncryptionExtension -ResourceGroupName $VMRGname
-VMName $vmName -DiskEncryptionKeyVaultUrl $diskEncryptionKeyVaultUrl
-DiskEncryptionKeyVaultId $KeyVaultResourceId;
```

After running the code, the following output will be visible:

Figure 7.37 – Output of the PowerShell command

Let's now have a look at what we have learned in this chapter.

Summary

In this chapter, you've learned how to use Microsoft Defender for Endpoint to detect and prevent threats on the desktop. You also learned how tampering, performed either manually or via malware, can be prevented and monitored. You learned how to encrypt AVD session hosts with Azure Disk Encryption, and lastly, you learned why the most common way of encrypting data is not supported or even necessary on a Cloud PC. Instead, Windows 365 relies on encryption at rest together with encryption of data in transit to keep your data safe!

We hope that you enjoyed this chapter and that you join us in the next chapter as we take a look at various topics related to access control. We will discuss everything from role-based access control and Azure Bastion to solutions such as Windows LAPS, Microsoft Entra PIM, and JIT for admins.

8

Configuring Access Control

In this chapter, the journey of securing virtual desktops continues, with topics such as how to control access to virtual desktops with **Role-Based Access Control** (**RBAC**). You will learn how to connect to session hosts in a secure way with Azure Bastion. You will also learn how to use **Just in Time** (**JIT**) access in combination with Azure Bastion so that IT admins can connect in a secure way. Furthermore, we will talk about how to secure access control with the use of Azure **Privileged Identity Management** (**PIM**). We will finish the chapter with a look at how Windows **Local Administrator Password Solution** (**LAPS**) can help you manage local admin passwords for your devices. We will explain why it's so important that the zero-trust principle is applied. All the security features covered in this chapter will further strengthen the security of your environment.

These topics are generally very broad but will be limited in scope for the purpose of this book. Most topics will also reference each other because these technologies can be configured independently, but when combined, they provide much more security.

This chapter will cover the following topics:

- RBAC
- Using Azure Bastion for admins
- Configuring JIT for admins
- Microsoft Entra PIM
- Windows LAPS

Configuring Role-Based Access Control (RBAC)

A critical function for any organization is to control who can access what resources. It's always very easy to grant access to resources on a per-user basis. However, this will make it very difficult to manage the security of an environment. By using RBAC, the IT admin can follow the **zero-trust** principle and make sure that no admin has too many privileges. This method can also prevent any unauthorized access to systems if an IT admin account is compromised.

There are three standard built-in roles in Azure that an IT admin can have:

- **Owner:** This can be a user of a group with full control over the Azure subscription(s), including privileges for adding roles to users or groups

- **Contributor:** This role grants full access to manage Azure resources, but this role doesn't allow to manage role assignments in Azure

- **Reader:** This role makes it possible to view all resources but does not allow you to make any changes

RBAC for AVD

The following built-in roles are available to manage Azure Virtual Desktop. These can be found in the **Roles** section of the IAM blade of the AVD subscription, and they can also be found in any other subscription by using the search term `Desktop`.

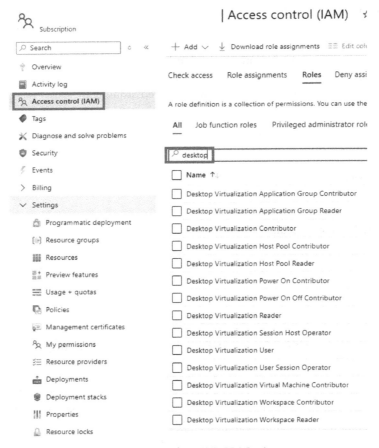

Figure 8.1 – Built-in AVD RBAC roles

It's possible to create security groups for all these separate roles. This way, it becomes easier to manage these permissions.

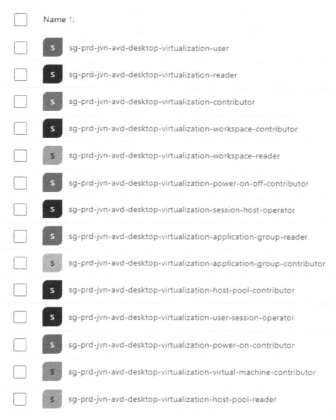

Figure 8.2 – Security groups for built-in roles in AVD

Another method to manage the permissions is to assign them based on the following three levels.

- **Management group**: `sg-mg-jvn-avd-reader`
- **Subscription**: `sg-sub-jvn-avd-reader`
- **Resource group**: `sg-rg-prd-jvn-avd-backplane-reader`

To assign the permissions on each of those levels, the IT admin can create dedicated security groups for the different built-in standard roles, **Reader**, **Contributor**, and **Owner**. This can be done in the **Access control (IAM)** blade of either the management, subscription, or resource group.

It's very important when creating security groups for RBAC permissions that they are enabled for Entra ID roles. Entra ID roles give people who are assigned role-specific permissions on the management-, subscription-, or resource-group level. To make a security group, go to `https://entra.microsoft.com` > **Groups** > **New Group**. Enter all the details about the group and don't forget to put the slider to **Yes**.

It is also possible to use an Active Directory security group that is synced to Entra ID and nest that in the Entra ID group.

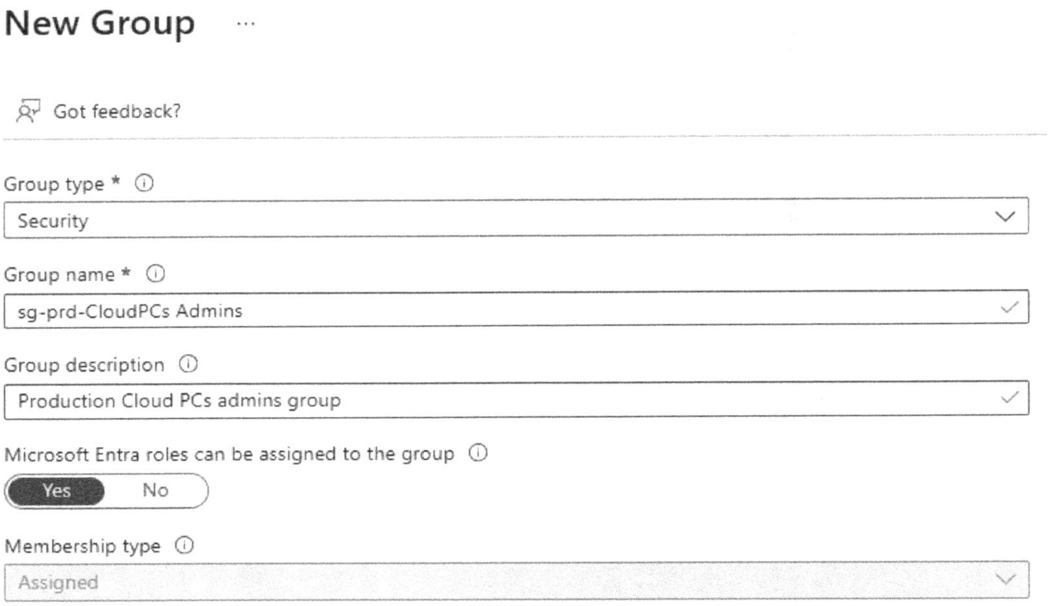

New Group ...

 Got feedback?

Group type * ⓘ

| Security | ⌄ |

Group name * ⓘ

| sg-prd-CloudPCs Admins | ✓ |

Group description ⓘ

| Production Cloud PCs admins group | ✓ |

Microsoft Entra roles can be assigned to the group ⓘ

(**Yes**   No)

Membership type ⓘ

| Assigned | ⌄ |

Figure 8.3 – Creating an Entra ID role

Management group RBAC assignment

The highest level that an IT admin can use to assign permission is at the management group level. This is a recommended practice from Microsoft that is well explained in the Cloud Adoption Framework for Azure: `https://learn.microsoft.com/en-us/azure/cloud-adoption-framework/ready/landing-zone/design-area/resource-org-management-groups`.

When starting out in Azure, it's recommended that you create a management group structure. This helps with the overall governance of the environment. The following example is of an enterprise-scale management group structure that also has a management group for Azure Virtual Desktop with a subscription in it. Assigning permissions to the AVD management group means less overhead when the organization has multiple AVD subscriptions.

Figure 8.4 – Enterprise-scale management group structure

Using the **Access control (IAM)** blade of the management group, an IT admin can give the necessary role to the security group.

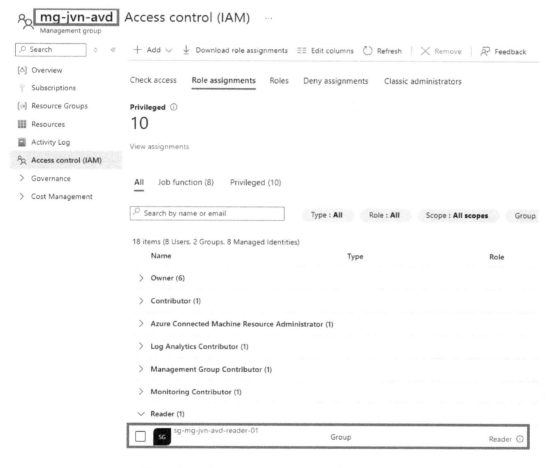

Figure 8.5 – Management group IAM role assignment

The next level that an Entra ID role can be assigned at is the subscription level.

Subscription RBAC assignment

The second level where IT admins can assign permissions is the *subscription level*. Ideally, AVD should be deployed in a separate subscription. This makes it easy for the IT admin to assign permissions.

Separate Entra ID security groups can be created for the three different built-in roles of **Reader**, **Contributor**, and **Owner**.

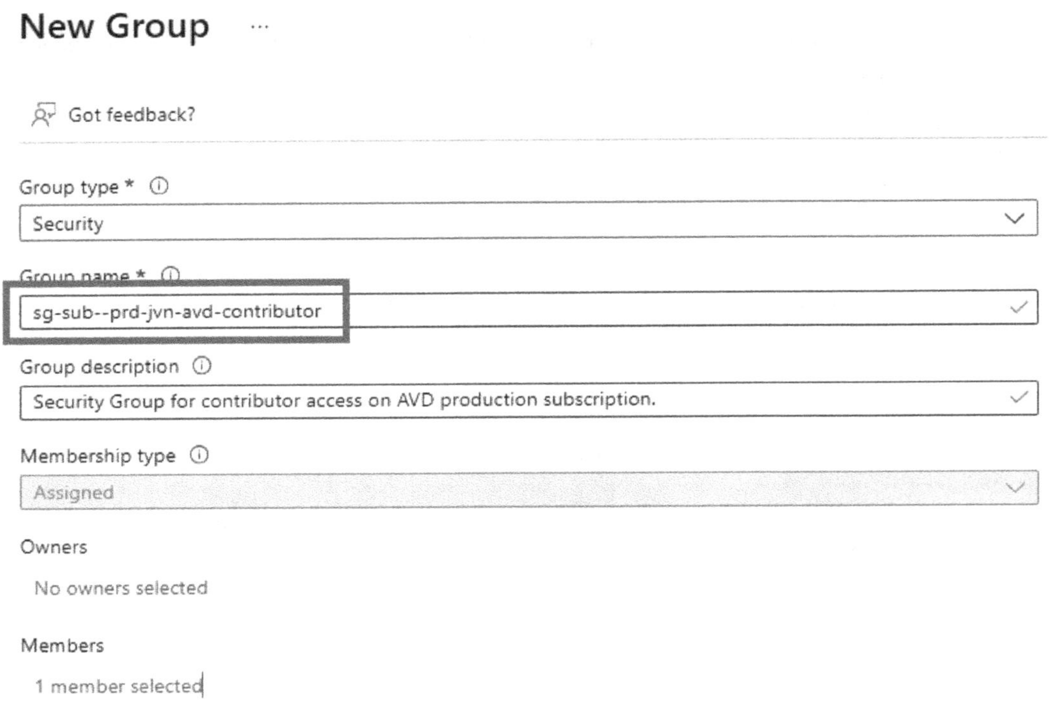

New Group   ...

Got feedback?

Group type * ⓘ

Security   ⌄

Group name * ⓘ

sg-sub--prd-jvn-avd-contributor   ✓

Group description ⓘ

Security Group for contributor access on AVD production subscription.   ✓

Membership type ⓘ

Assigned   ⌄

Owners

No owners selected

Members

1 member selected

Figure 8.6 – Contributor security group for an AVD production subscription

This security group can then be assigned to the subscription. This is done in the **Access control (IAM)** blade of the subscription. Another option is to automate this with the help of Terraform, Azure PowerShell, Bicep.

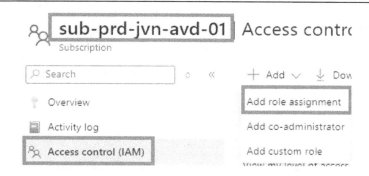

Figure 8.7 – Adding a role assignment AVD subscription

Now that you have learned how to assign permissions at the management group and subscription levels, it's time to learn about the resource group level.

Resource group RBAC assignment

The last option when assigning RBAC permissions for AVD is to go for the resource group level, using the same procedure as seen before. The following group can be created:

New Group   ⋯

Got feedback?

Group type * ⓘ

Security	⌄

Group name * ⓘ

sg-rg-prd-jvn-avd-storage-contributor	✓

Group description ⓘ

Security group for production AVD storage contributor	✓

Membership type ⓘ

Assigned	⌄

Owners

No owners selected

Members

1 member selected

Figure 8.8 – AVD storage resource group security group

RBAC for Windows 365

Of course, Microsoft also provides built-in roles to manage Windows 365. When searching for these roles, the following can be found in Entra ID roles and Administrators:

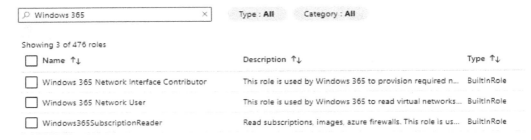

Figure 8.9 – Windows 365 built-in roles

To manage these roles, an IT admin can make dedicated security groups.

New Group   ...

🙋 Got feedback?

Group type * ⓘ

| Security | ⌄ |

Group name * ⓘ

| sg-prd-Windows365-admin | ✓ |

Group description ⓘ

| Production Windows365 Admin security group | ✓ |

Microsoft Entra roles can be assigned to the group ⓘ

(**Yes**   No)

Membership type ⓘ

| Assigned | ⌄ |

Figure 8.10 – Windows 365 built-in role security group

There are also other roles available, but for the IT admin to find them, they have to go to the Intune admin center. These roles will only become visible after preparing the tenant for cloud PCs. More info can be found using the following URL: `https://learn.microsoft.com/en-us/windows-365/enterprise/deployment-overview`.

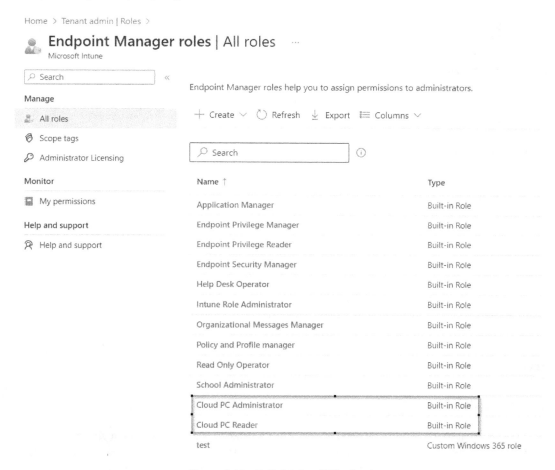

Figure 8.11 – Built-in cloud PC roles

It's recommended that, as with Azure Virtual Desktop, the IT admin creates dedicated security groups that have these roles assigned to them.

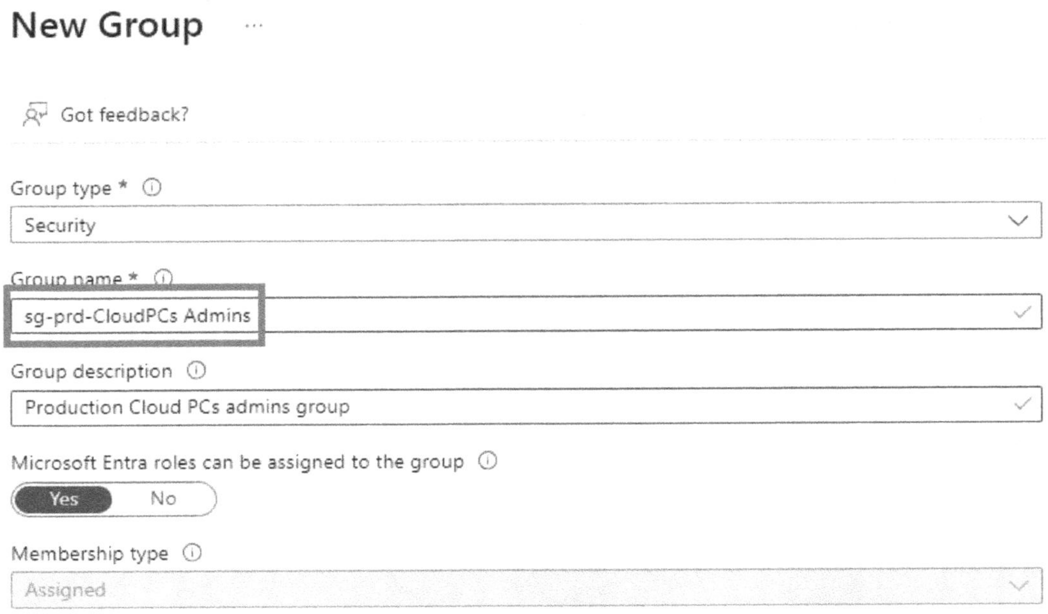

New Group   ...

🗨 Got feedback?

Group type * ⓘ

Security   ∨

Group name * ⓘ

sg-prd-CloudPCs Admins   ✓

Group description ⓘ

Production Cloud PCs admins group   ✓

Microsoft Entra roles can be assigned to the group ⓘ

(**Yes**   No)

Membership type ⓘ

Assigned   ∨

Figure 8.12 – Cloud PC admin security group creation

This concludes our coverage of how to configure RBAC for both Windows 365 and AVD. Let's now see how Azure Bastion can help IT admins manage AVD session hosts.

Azure Bastion

It can happen that an IT admin will need to perform some administrative tasks on a virtual desktop. Connecting in a secure way can be done by using **Azure Bastion**. This is a fully managed PaaS service, meaning that Microsoft manages the solution completely. This allows the IT admin to connect to the Azure virtual machine using a private IP address directly from the browser. This eliminates the need for a public IP address on the session host and adds more security to the virtual desktop.

Azure Bastion is available in three versions – Developer, Basic, and Standard – with each offering its own benefits. More information about the different versions can be found here: `https://learn.microsoft.com/en-us/azure/bastion/bastion-overview`.

In a typical hub-spoke network topology, the Bastion host is placed in the hub virtual network that is connected via virtual network peering to an AVD virtual network, as shown in *Figure 8.13*. The exception is the Developer SKU.

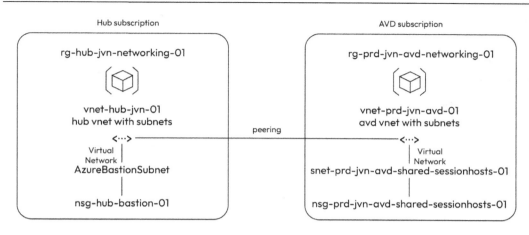

Figure 8.13 – Bastion in a hub-spoke network topology

For IT admins to use Azure Bastion, they need some permissions:

- Reader role on the Bastion host
- Reader role on the virtual machine network interface or NIC
- Reader role on the target virtual machine
- Reader role on the virtual network if the virtual machine is on a peered virtual network

To ensure that IT admins have the correct permissions for all the session hosts, a custom role can be created and assigned to a security group on the AVD management group as explained in the previous section of this chapter.

Azure Bastion custom role

To create an Azure Bastion custom role, go to the **Azure portal** > **Microsoft Entra ID** > **Roles and administrators** and select **New custom role**.

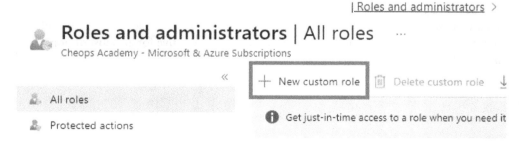

Figure 8.14 – New custom role

1. The first thing that is needed is to give this role a name. As already mentioned in this book, follow your organization's naming convention, if one exists.

Create a custom role ...

Figure 8.15 – Bastion custom role name

2. The next step is to add permissions to the role, in this case, the specific permissions for Azure Bastion.

Permission		Description		Permission type
Microsoft.Network/bastionHosts/read		Gets a Bastion Host		Action
Microsoft.Network/networkInterfaces/read		Gets a network interface definition.		Action
Microsoft.Compute/virtualMachines/read		Get the properties of a virtual machine		Action
Microsoft.Network/virtualNetworks/read		Get the virtual network definition		Action

Figure 8.16 – Adding permissions to the custom role

3. The next step is a very important step. It is to assign the role to the correct scope. In this case, we are assigning the custom role to the Azure Virtual Desktop management group. This way, if more subscriptions are added, the role is automatically active for all subscriptions in the management group.

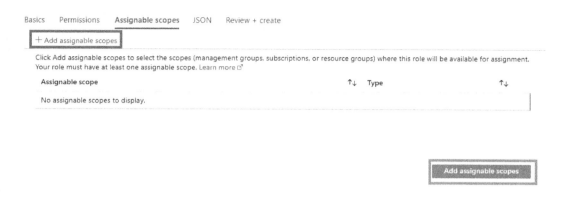

Figure 8.17 – Adding the scope

4.   Search for the correct management group and select it.

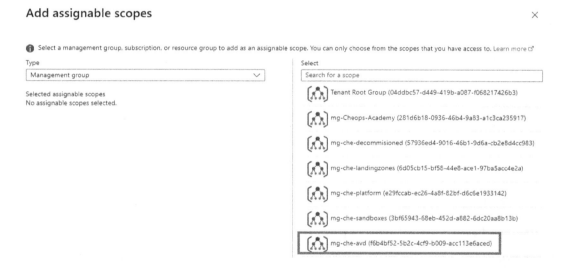

Figure 8.18 – Selecting a management group

5. The last step is to review and create the role.

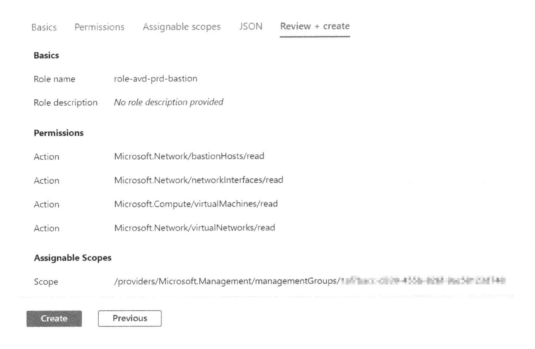

Figure 8.19 – Review and create the custom role

Using Azure Bastion

Let's see how to use Azure Bastion now that our custom role is created.

To use Azure Bastion, an IT admin has to go to the session host and select **Bastion** in the left blade. If the user has all the required permissions, a login screen will appear. On this screen, you can choose which authentication type you want to use. As you can see in the following figure, an IT admin can choose between a regular VM password and a password from Azure Key Vault.

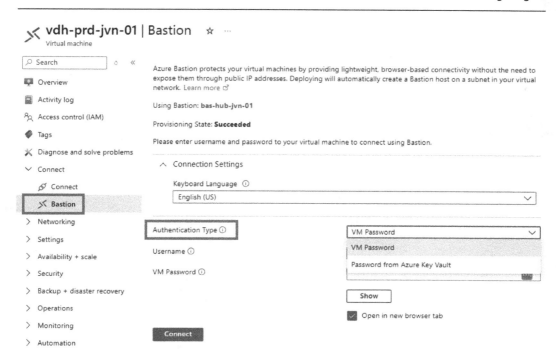

Figure 8.20 – Connecting to a session host with Azure Bastion

Now that you know how Azure Bastion can help IT admins perform tasks on session hosts, let's see how this feature can be made even more secure when it's combined with JIT access.

Configuring JIT

By default, IT admins can connect to a session host through RDP on port 3389. Even with Microsoft Entra PIM in place, making sure that IT admins don't have permissions active the entire time, the RDP port is still reachable.

This is where JIT comes in. This setting needs to be activated in Defender for Cloud and is included in **Defender for Servers plan 2**. This adds extra security controls to the session hosts. In the Azure portal, search for Microsoft Defender for Cloud and then select **Environment Settings**, as seen in the following figure.

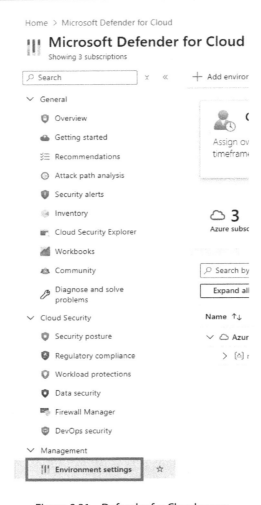

Figure 8.21 – Defender for Cloud menu

In the **Environment settings** blade, an entire overview of the management group structure is displayed. An IT admin can continue by selecting the subscription where they want to activate session hosts for JIT access.

Figure 8.22 – Selecting a subscription

Defender for Servers has two different plans, but for JIT to work, the IT admin needs to enable plan 2 and hit **Save**.

Figure 8.23 – Enabling Defender for Servers

After enabling **Defender for Servers**, it's time to enable the session hosts for JIT. This is done in the **Workload protections** blade from Defender for Cloud.

Figure 8.24 – Workload protections

JIT has three different states that session hosts can be in:

- **Configured**: This means the session host is configured and will show all data from JIT requests and connection details.

- **Not Configured**: This is for session hosts that don't have JIT enabled but support the feature.

- **Unsupported**: This is for session hosts that don't support JIT. This can be caused because there is no **Network Security Group (NSG)** or firewall configured, or both.

In the following figure, you can see that the session hosts are in the **Not Configured** state.

Figure 8.25 – JIT Not Configured session hosts

Let's configure them:

1. Start by selecting the checkboxes and selecting **Enable JIT on 2 VMs.**

Figure 8.26 – Activating JIT

2. Here the IT admin has the option to configure the source and protocol that they can use to connect.

Figure 8.27 – Selecting ports for JIT

3. Since the session hosts have the Windows operating system, there is no need for port 22. Let's configure this so that only **TCP port 3389** is available from the Azure Bastion subnet in the HUB virtual network. The maximum request time can be configured as anything up to 24 hours.

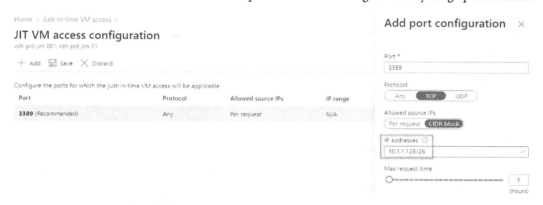

Figure 8.28 – Configuring the JIT access ports

4. When ready, click on **Save**.

Figure 8.29 – Saving the JIT access ports

After configuring the JIT access ports, the two session hosts will now be visible in the **Configured** tab of the **Just-in-Time access** blade. Here, the IT admin can see who connected to the session hosts and when they did so.

Now that JIT access has been configured, an extra deny rule has been added for each of the session hosts to the network security group that is connected to the subnet where the session hosts are.

Figure 8.30 – JIT network security group rules

With this configuration in place, an IT admin can request access to the session hosts when they need it. This can be done in the **Just-in-Time access** blade by selecting a session host in the **Configured** tab and selecting **Request access**.

Figure 8.31 – Request access in the Just-in-Time blade

On the request access screen, the IT admin switches **Toggle** to **On** and sets the slider for **Allowed source IP** on **IP Range**. This will automatically fill in the Azure Bastion subnet as configured. Access is requested by clicking **Open ports**.

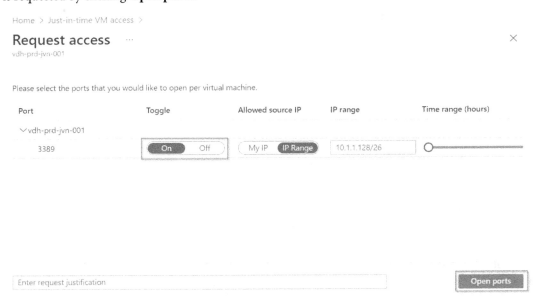

Figure 8.32 – JIT request access

The IT admin can also request access from the session host itself. Go to the virtual machine window and go to **Settings** > **Connect** > **Request access**.

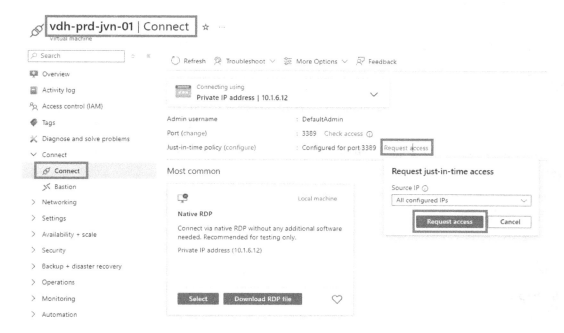

Figure 8.33 – Request JIT session host

When access is given, Defender will add an extra allow rule to the Network Security Group to allow the traffic. The IT admin is now able to connect to the session host using Azure Bastion.

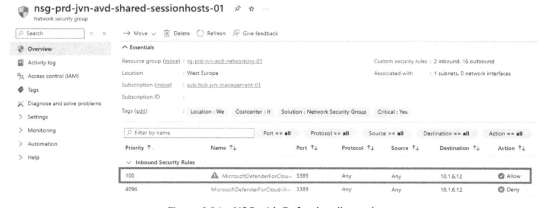

Figure 8.34 – NSG with Defender allow rule

So far, we have learned how to connect to Azure Virtual Desktop session hosts using Azure Bastion and how to secure a Bastion connection with JIT access. The last step in securing an RDP connection is to use Microsoft Entra PIM.

Microsoft Privileged Identity Management

When an organization wants to protect its admins and privileged roles, **Microsoft Entra Privileged Identity Management** or **Microsoft Entra PIM** is the go-to service in Azure. By using this service, IT admins can make sure that no admin has access to their permissions all the time. The advantage of using PIM is also that there is an audit trail tracking when an admin activates their role.

To use Microsoft Entra PIM, an organization needs to have the correct license. One of the following is required before Microsoft Entra PIM can be used:

- Microsoft Entra ID Governance
- Microsoft Entra ID P2
- Microsoft 365 E5

The next steps require PIM to be configured in your environment.

In the previous section of this chapter, we configured Azure Bastion. In this section, let's combine the custom roles that were created earlier in this chapter:

1. In the Azure portal, go to **Microsoft Entra PIM** > **Azure resources** and put the scope on **Azure Virtual Desktop Management Group**:

Privileged Identity Management | Azure resources ...
Privileged Identity Management

↑ Activate role

«

Quick start

Tasks

🔡 My roles

🔲 My requests

🔲 Approve requests

🔲 Review access

Manage

◈ Microsoft Entra roles

🔳 Groups

🔲 Azure resources

Activity

🔳 My audit history

Troubleshooting + Support

✖ Troubleshoot

🔳 New support request

ℹ️ Switch back to the legacy Azure resource experience.

Scope defines a set of resources. Select a scope below to manage an Azure resource.
Learn more

ℹ️ You can only view and manage resources to which you have permissions. Check your access.
Learn more

☐ Search by management group id or subscription id ⓘ

[⟨∴⟩] Management groups ⓘ

| mg-   avd | ∨ |

⚷ Subscriptions ⓘ

| Select the subscription | ∨ |

[⬛] Resource groups ⓘ

| Select the resource group | ∨ |

◼ Resources ⓘ

| Select the resource | ∨ |

Current selection

Name   [⟨∴⟩] mg-   -avd

Resource Id   📋 /providers/Microsoft.Management/manage
                        mentGroups/f6b4bf52-5b2c-4cf9-b009-
                        acc113e6aced

Type   Management group

Location   -

Manage resource   **Clear all selections**

Figure 8.35 – Azure resource selection management group

2. Click the **Add assignments** button to start the process.

Figure 8.36 – PIM add assignment

3. Here the IT admin needs to select the custom Entra ID role that was created for Bastion.

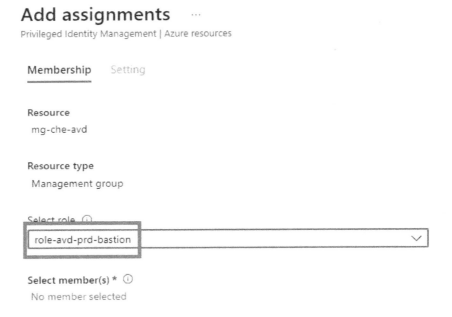

Figure 8.37 – Role selection in Bastion

4. The next step here is to select members. Here the IT admin chooses the security group that has been created.

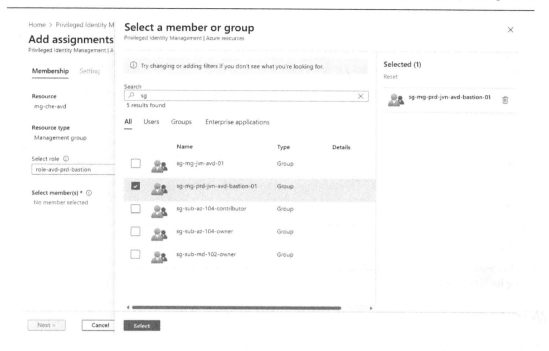

Figure 8.38 – Security group selection for PIM assignment

5.   The last step in PIM assignment is to decide whether the assignment type will be eligible or active. For security reasons, it's better to go with **Eligible**. The amount of time that the group is eligible for can also be chosen here, with the maximum being one year. When done, click on **Assign**.

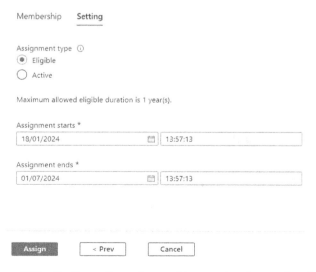

Figure 8.39 – Configure the assignment type and assignment period

After configuring this custom role assignment, everybody in the security group will see the role in PIM when navigating to **Microsoft Entra PIM** > **My roles** > **Azure resources**. Here the role can be activated, and the IT admin can use Azure Bastion on the session hosts after a JIT request.

Of course, Microsoft Entra PIM also works for the built-in roles of Azure Virtual Desktop and Cloud PCs.

Figure 8.40 – Azure Bastion role in Microsoft Entra PIM

Now that you have learned about Microsoft Entra PIM, let's have a look at the last section of this chapter and see how Windows LAPS can help IT admins manage the local administrator passwords of devices.

Windows Local Administrator Password Solution (LAPS)

By default, every Windows device has a local administrator account that has a password associated with it. To ensure the safety of that password, Microsoft has a feature called **Windows LAPS**. This feature automatically manages and takes a backup of this administrator account on both Entra ID-joined and Active Directory-joined devices.

Windows LAPS is available for the following OS platforms:

- Windows 11 22H2, with the April 11, 2023 update
- Windows 11 21H2, with the April 11, 2023 update
- Windows 10, with the April 11, 2023 update
- Windows Server 2022, with the April 11, 2023 update
- Windows Server 2019, with the April 11, 2023 update

As already mentioned, the configuration of this feature depends on the type of device. Let's take a look at the configuration for Active Directory-joined devices first.

Windows LAPS Azure Virtual Desktop

As mentioned in the introduction, Windows LAPS works with hybrid joined devices. These devices can back up their passwords to both Microsoft Entra ID and Windows Server Active Directory. However, the feature can't be configured to back up passwords to both at the same time.

The first step that needs to be done is to enable this feature in the Azure portal: `https://portal.azure.com` > **Microsoft Entra ID** > **Devices** > **Device Settings** > **Local administrator settings**.

To enable this feature, set the slider to **Yes** and click **Save** as shown in *Figure 8.41*.

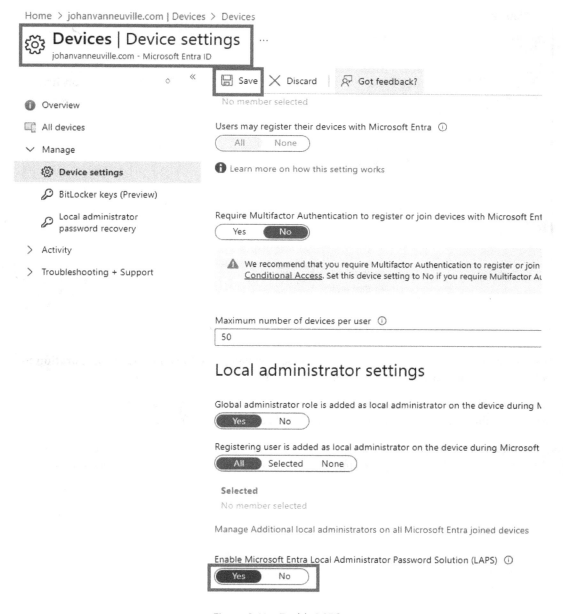

Figure 8.41 – Enable LAPS

To make this feature work on hybrid joined devices, the IT admin needs to create a **Group Policy Object (GPO)**.

On a domain controller, go to **Group Policy Management** and start creating a GPO.

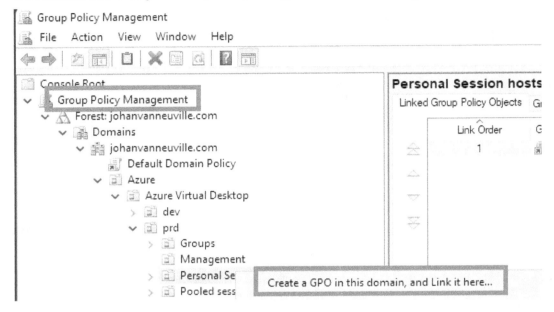

Figure 8.42 – Create a LAPS GPO

Give the policy a name and start editing the policy by navigating to **Computer Configuration > Policies > Administrative Templates > System > LAPS**.

The settings that the IT admin can configure here are the same for both cases, so let's have a look at the options that need to be configured for Entra ID because they are fewer:

1. **Password Settings:** With these settings, the IT admin can configure password complexity, length, and age. Since the backup directory will be Entra ID, the minimum amount of days must be 7.

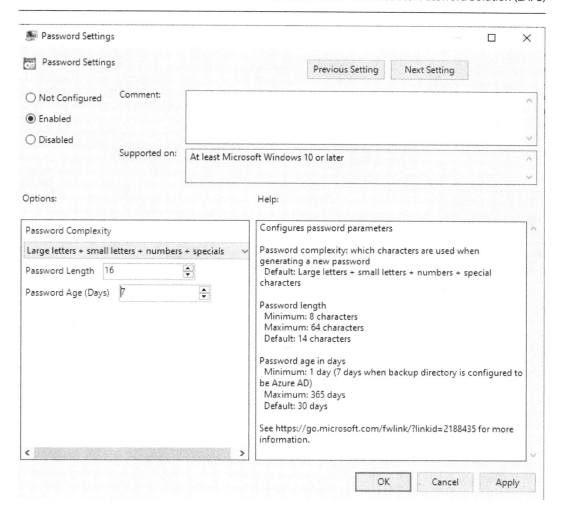

Figure 8.43 – LAPS password settings

2. **Post-authentication actions**: With these actions, the IT admin can configure what happens when the password has been used. If the grace period is set to 0, these settings will be disabled, and the password will be reset immediately. In this example, the grace period is 1 hour.

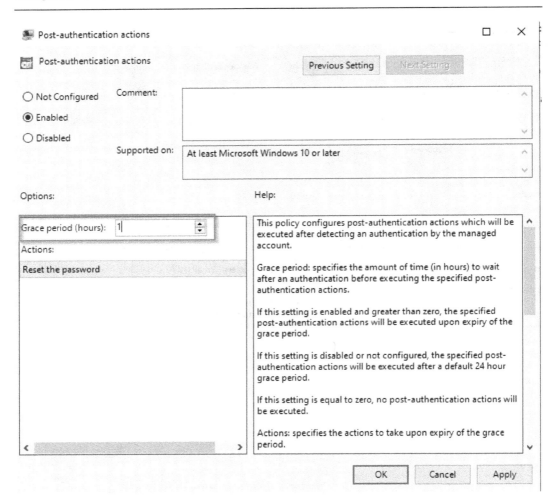

Figure 8.44 – Post-authentication actions

3. **Configure password backup directory:** Here, the IT admin can specify where the password will be stored. It is very important to note that only one location can be active. Let's take Entra ID because, for Active Directory, another step is needed. The extra step is shown in Figure 8.46, if you want to use Active Directory.

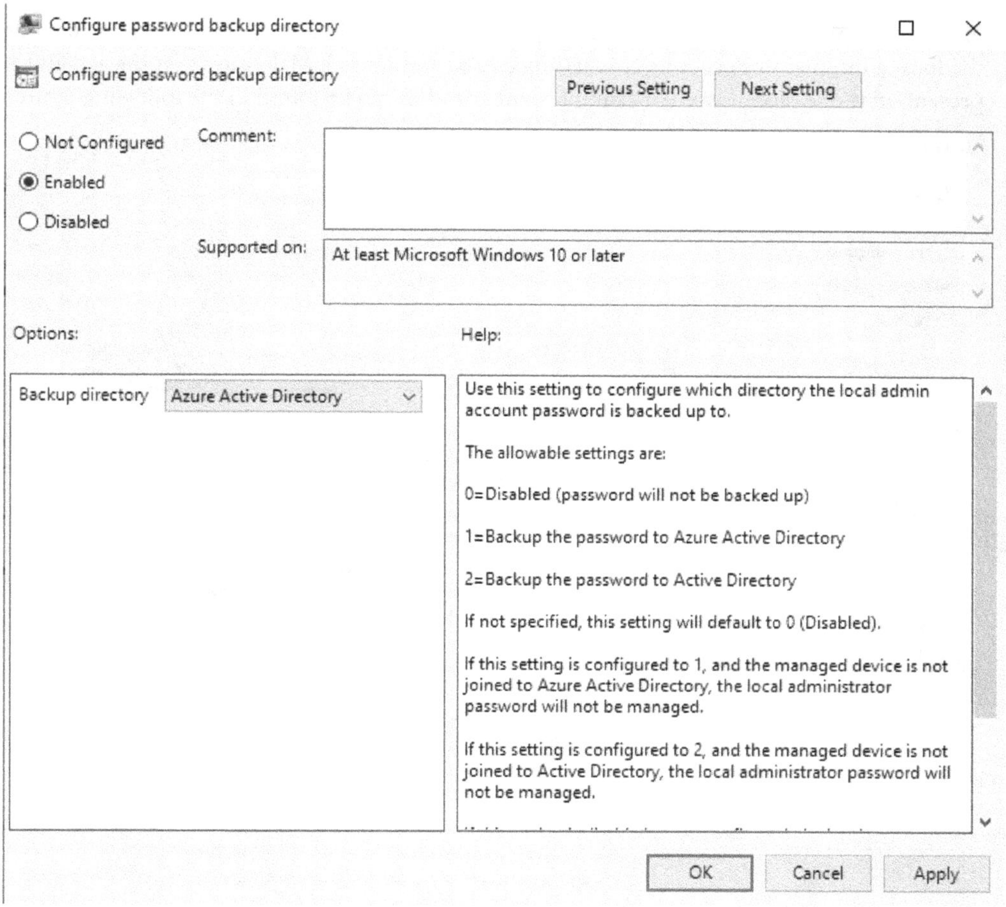

Figure 8.45 – Backup directory for LAPS

The following PowerShell command needs to be run as administrator if the IT admin wants to use Active Directory as the backup directory.

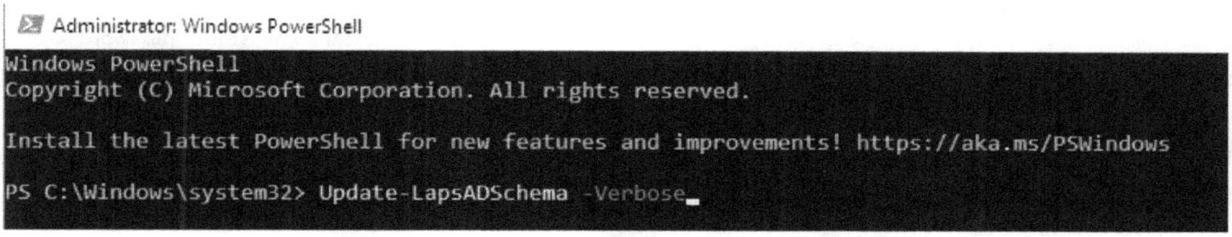

Figure 8.46 – The Update-LapsADSchema PowerShell command

4. **Name of administrator account to manage**: If the organization has a policy for how to name the local administrator account, this setting can be configured. Make sure that the account is present on the session hosts. An example configuration can be found in the following figure.

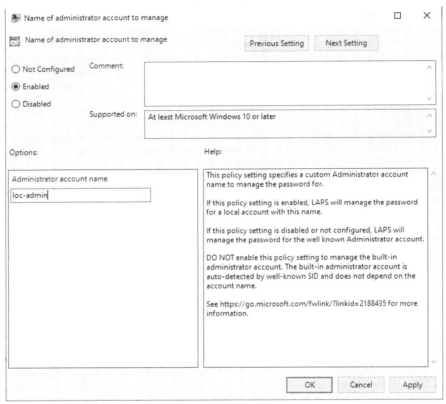

Figure 8.47 – Local administrator account name

After configuring all these settings, go to `https://entra.microsoft.com` > **Devices** > **All devices**, select a device with an active policy, and view the local administrator password:

Figure 8.48 – Show the local administrator account and password

If **Active Directory** was chosen as a backup directory, the IT admin needs to open the properties of the session host and click on the **LAPS** tab.

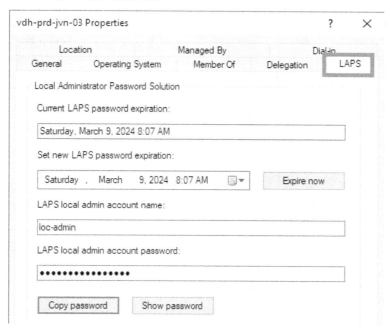

Figure 8.49 – The LAPS tab

Let's continue with Windows LAPS, but this time, we will configure it using Intune for Cloud PCs.

Windows LAPS for Cloud PCs

Using Windows Local Administrator Password Solution is also supported for Windows 365 Cloud PCs. Enabling Windows LAPS for Cloud PCs is a three-step process:

1. Enable Windows LAPS in Microsoft Entra ID.
2. Enable the local administrator account.
3. Configure Windows LAPS.

Make sure that the account that is used to enable Windows LAPS is a member of the following roles:

- Global Admin
- Cloud Device Admin
- Intune Service Admin

Enabling Windows LAPS in Microsoft Entra ID

IT admins with the correct roles can enable Windows LAPS in Microsoft Entra ID. This is the same setting as was configured in the previous step. Here is a quick recap: sign in to the **Microsoft Entra** portal and go to **Devices** > **All Devices** > **Devices settings**. Switch the slider to **Yes** for **Enable Microsoft Entra Local Administrator Password Solution** and click the **Save** button in the ribbon at the top.

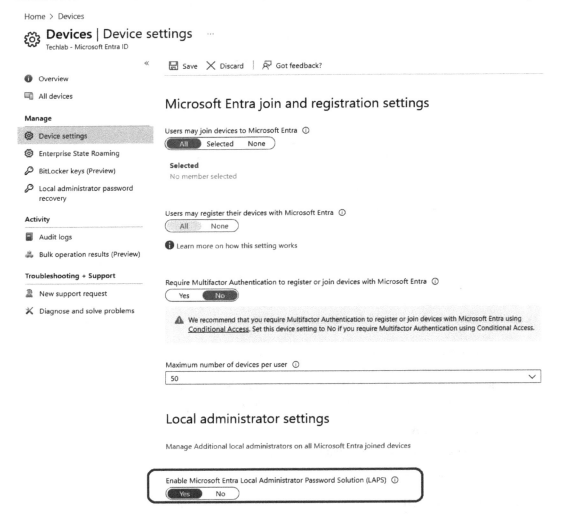

Figure 8.50 – Enabling Windows LAPS in the Microsoft Entra portal

Enabling the local administrator account

The following steps need to be taken to enable the local administrator account:

1. Sign in to the Microsoft Intune admin center and go to **Devices** > **Policy** > **Configuration profiles**. Select + **Create** > + **New Policy**. Select the following:

    -   **Platform**: Windows 10 and later

    -   **Profile type**: Settings catalog

    Give the profile a name and optionally a description:

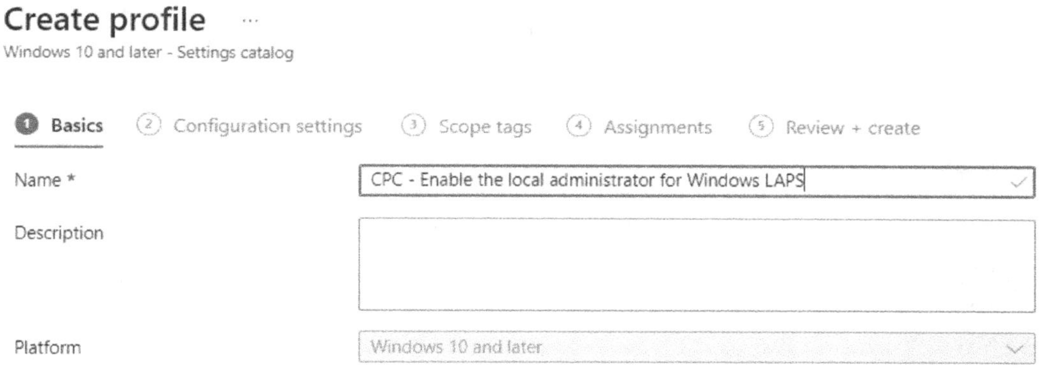

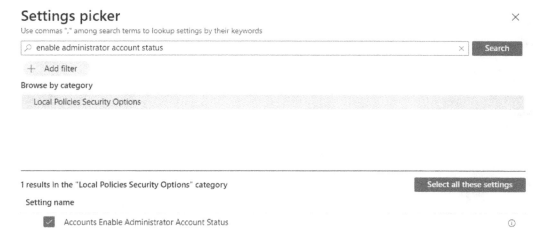

Figure 8.51 – Give the profile a name and optionally a description

2. Use the settings picker tool to add the required settings. Search for **enable administrator account status**.

Settings picker

Use commas "," among search terms to lookup settings by their keywords

enable administrator account status

+ Add filter

Browse by category

Local Policies Security Options

1 results in the "Local Policies Security Options" category — Select all these settings

Setting name

☑ Accounts Enable Administrator Account Status

Figure 8.52 – Adding the required settings to the policy

3.   For the **Accounts Enable Administrator Account Status** setting, switch the slider to **Enable**.

Home > Devices | Configuration profiles >

Create profile   ...
Windows 10 and later - Settings catalog

✅ Basics   ② **Configuration settings**   ③ Scope tags   ④ Assignments   ⑤ Review + create

+ Add settings ⓘ

∧   Local Policies Security Options   Remove category

ℹ 49 of 50 settings in this category are not configured

Accounts Enable Administrator Account   🔘 Enable   ⊖
Status ⓘ

Figure 8.53 – Enable the administrator account

4.   Add scope tags if they are required and continue to the **Assignments** tab.

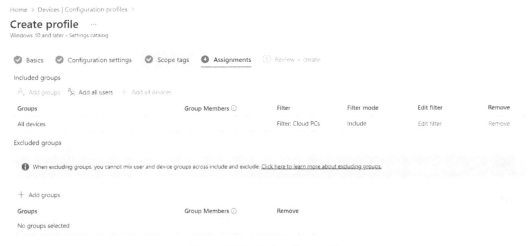

Figure 8.54 – Assign the profile

5. Finish up by reviewing and creating the profile:

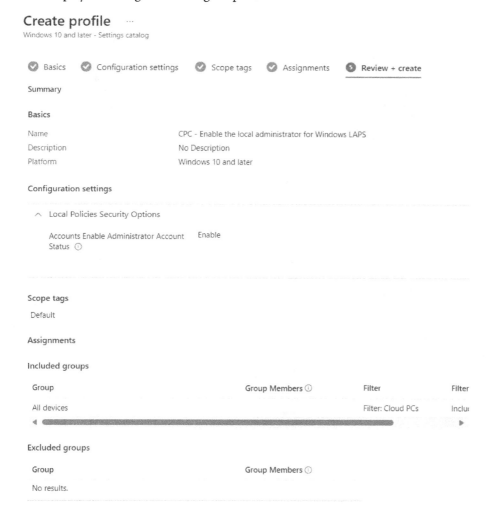

Figure 8.55 – Review the profile

Now that the local administrator account is enabled, we can configure LAPS for Windows 365.

Configuring Windows LAPS

The last step is to configure Windows LAPS. Observe the following steps:

1. Navigate to **Endpoint security** > **Manage** > **Account Protection**. Click the **+ Create** button and select the following:

   - **Platform**: Windows 10 and later

- **Profile**: Local admin password solution (Windows LAPS)

Create a profile   ✕

Platform

| Windows 10 and later | ⌄ |

Profile

| Local admin password solution (Windows LAPS) | ⌄ |

Local admin password solution (Windows LAPS)

Windows Local Administrator Password Solution(Windows LAPS) is a Windows feature that automatically manages and backs up the password of a local administrator account on your Azure Active Directory - joined or Windows Server Active Directory - joined devices.

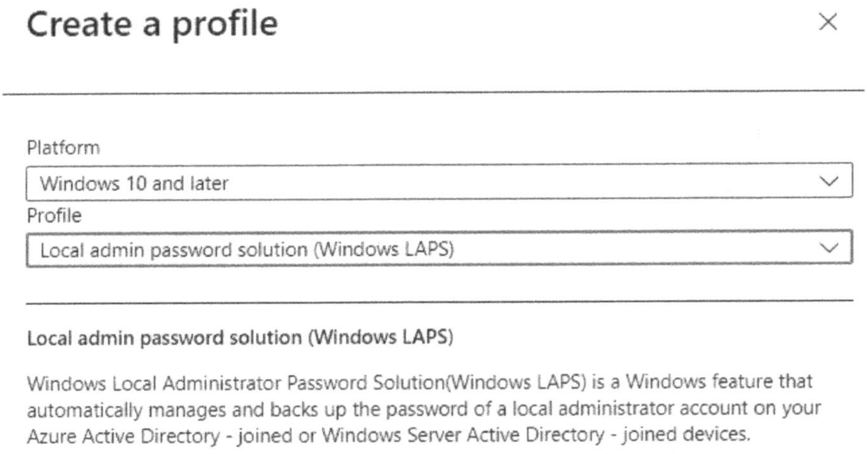

Figure 8.56 – Creating an account protection policy for Windows LAPS

2.   Give the profile a name and optionally a description:

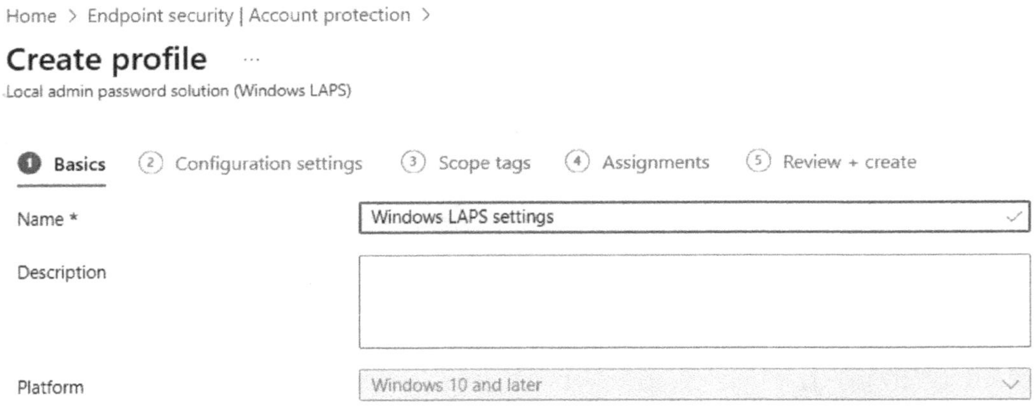

Home > Endpoint security | Account protection >

Create profile   ⋯
Local admin password solution (Windows LAPS)

| **①** **Basics** | ② Configuration settings | ③ Scope tags | ④ Assignments | ⑤ Review + create |

| Name * | Windows LAPS settings | ✓ |

Description

Platform

| Windows 10 and later | ⌄ |

Figure 8.57 – The basics of creating a profile

The following settings can be configured for Windows LAPS:

- **Backup Directory**: Where should the passwords be backed up? Valid options are **Disabled** (password will not be backed up), **Backup the password to Azure AD only**, **Backup the password to Active Directory only**, or not configured.

- **Password Age Days**: By default, this age is set to 30 days if not specified. It determines how long the password should be kept before it is replaced.

- **Administrator Account Name**: Enter the name of the local admin account that already exists. At the time of writing, Microsoft has just announced that LAPS will create the account automatically if it does not exist, but currently, it does not.

- **Password Complexity**: How complex should the password be? The valid options are as follows: **Large letters, Large letters + small letters, Large letters + small letters + numbers, Large letters + small letters + numbers + special characters**, or not configured.

- **Password Length**: How long should the password be? If not specified, the default is 14 characters.

- **Post Authentication Actions**: What action should be performed once the grace period expires? The valid options are **Reset password**, **Reset the password and logoff the managed account**, **Reset the password**, and **Reboot**.

- **Post Authentication Reset Delay**: How many hours should pass after authentication before the post-authentication actions are executed? If not specified, the default will be set to 24 hours.

The following is an example of configuring LAPS:

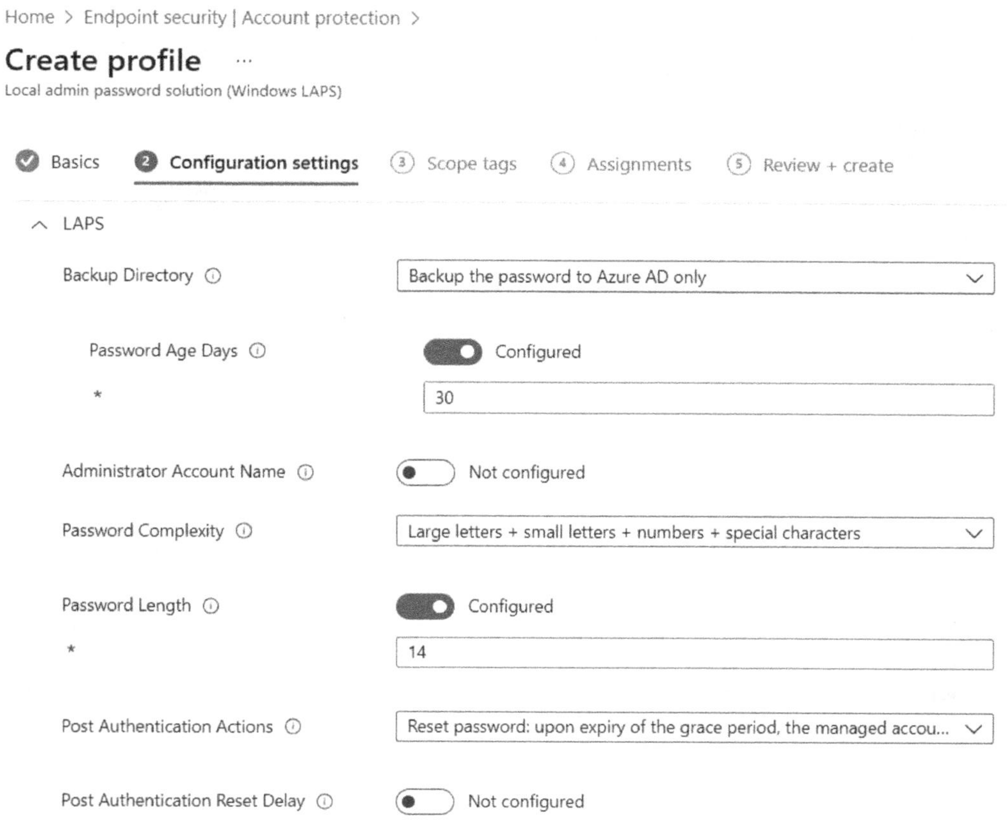

Home > Endpoint security | Account protection >

Create profile   ⋯
Local admin password solution (Windows LAPS)

   ✅ Basics   **2 Configuration settings**   ③ Scope tags   ④ Assignments   ⑤ Review + create

∧ LAPS

Backup Directory ⓘ	Backup the password to Azure AD only ⌄
Password Age Days ⓘ	🔘 Configured
*	30
Administrator Account Name ⓘ	⚫ Not configured
Password Complexity ⓘ	Large letters + small letters + numbers + special characters ⌄
Password Length ⓘ	🔘 Configured
*	14
Post Authentication Actions ⓘ	Reset password: upon expiry of the grace period, the managed accou... ⌄
Post Authentication Reset Delay ⓘ	⚫ Not configured

Figure 8.58 – Configuring the Windows LAPS settings

3.   Add scope tags if applicable and assign the profile:

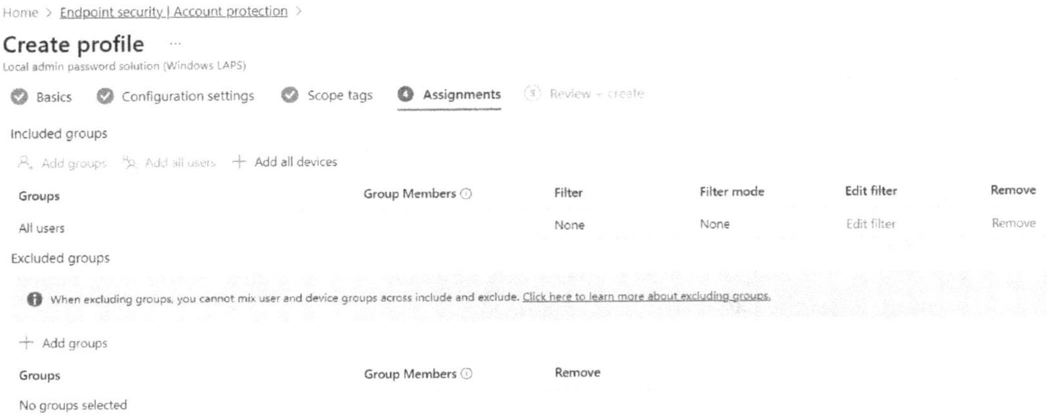

Home > Endpoint security | Account protection >

Create profile ...
Local admin password solution (Windows LAPS)

✅ Basics   ✅ Configuration settings   ✅ Scope tags   ④ Assignments   ⑤ Review - create

Included groups

👤 Add groups   👥 Add all users   + Add all devices

Groups	Group Members ⓘ	Filter	Filter mode	Edit filter	Remove
All users		None	None	Edit filter	Remove

Excluded groups

ⓘ When excluding groups, you cannot mix user and device groups across include and exclude. Click here to learn more about excluding groups.

+ Add groups

Groups	Group Members ⓘ	Remove
No groups selected		

Figure 8.59 – Assign the profile to the devices

4.   The last step is to review and create the profile.

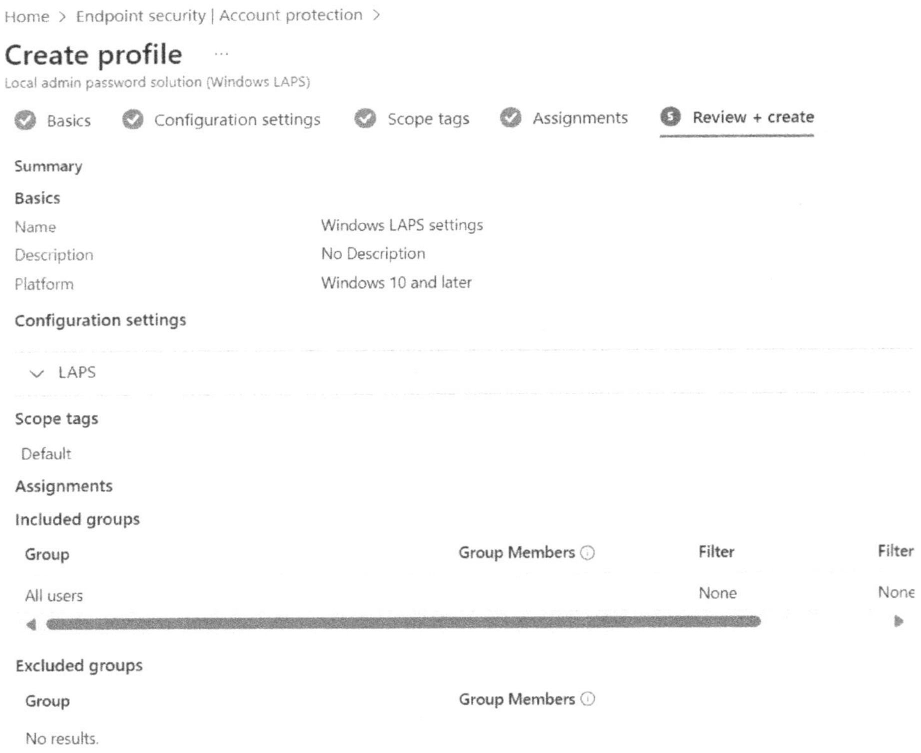

Home > Endpoint security | Account protection >

Create profile ...
Local admin password solution (Windows LAPS)

✅ Basics   ✅ Configuration settings   ✅ Scope tags   ✅ Assignments   ⑤ Review + create

Summary

Basics

Name	Windows LAPS settings
Description	No Description
Platform	Windows 10 and later

Configuration settings

∨ LAPS

Scope tags

Default

Assignments

Included groups

Group	Group Members ⓘ	Filter	Filter
All users		None	None

Excluded groups

Group	Group Members ⓘ
No results.	

Figure 8.60 – Review the configuration

5. The profile will become visible in the **Account protection** overview:

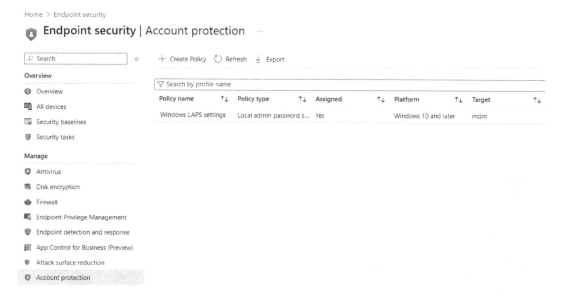

Figure 8.61 – Overview of the Account protection profiles

Now that the profile is configured and assigned to the devices, we can retrieve the LAPS password in the next part of this chapter.

Retrieving the password

Passwords can be retrieved by accessing the Microsoft Intune admin center, going to **Devices > Windows 365 > All Cloud PCs** , selecting the desired Cloud PC, and clicking **Local admin password**:

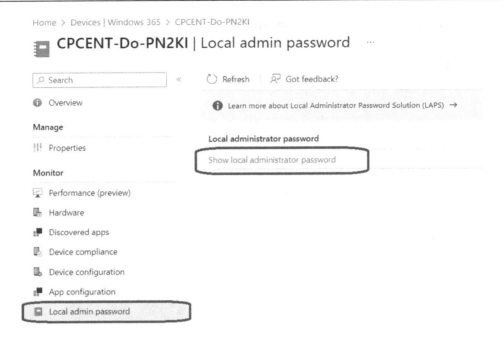

Figure 8.62 – Example of a local administrator password for a Cloud PC in Intune

Select **Show local administrator password** to get access to the password:

Figure 8.63 – Revealing the password

Did you know that it's possible to manually rotate the password using a device action?

Manually rotating the password

Navigate to the Cloud PC in the Microsoft Intune admin center. Select **Rotate local admin password** in the ribbon:

Figure 8.64 – The Rotate local admin password device action

Microsoft Intune will show the following popup to make sure that you want to continue:

Rotate local admin password - CPCENT-Do-PN2KI

If you rotate the local admin password on this device, you'll lose the old password used on the device. A single password will be generated to your identity provider (Microsoft Entra ID or Active Directory) after you restart the device. Password will expire automatically within the period specified in the policy. Rotate password anyway?

Yes   No

Figure 8.65 – Manually changing the password

After a bit of time, the password will be changed:

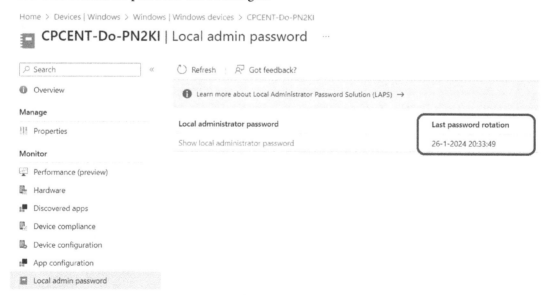

Figure 8.66 – The password has changed

This concludes this chapter, where you have learned why RBAC is so important to configure. In the next chapter, we'll continue this security journey and have a look at how IT admins can start securing Windows 365.

Summary

In this chapter, we have learned how to configure RBAC for Windows 365 and AVD. Furthermore, we also learned how to secure IT admin access by combining JIT, Azure Bastion, and Microsoft Entra PIM. To conclude this chapter, you learned how LAPS can help secure virtual desktops.

In the next chapter, we will explore various ways of securing Windows 365 Cloud PCs.

Part 4: Additional Security Controls per Solution

The fourth part of the book discusses security controls for either Windows 365, Azure Virtual Desktop, or Azure infrastructure. It covers Windows 365-specific security controls such as the security guidelines, Endpoint Privilege Management to allow elevated tasks to be executed by a regular user, and how to create and export a cloud PC restore point. This part covers how to create backups of the session hosts and FSLogix profiles, how to secure access to AVD using private endpoints, and how to implement security for your AD DS environment. It concludes with securing the Azure infrastructure by configuring security at the storage level, configuring network security using Azure Firewall or NSGs, and deploying AVD on dedicated hosts. By the end of this chapter, you will have a deeper understanding of how to improve security for either Windows 365, Azure Virtual Desktop, or Azure infrastructure.

This part contains the following chapters:

- *Chapter 9, Securing Windows 365*
- *Chapter 10, Securing Azure Virtual Desktop*
- *Chapter 11, Securing Azure Infrastructure*

Securing Windows 365

In the previous chapters, we covered the shared controls that can be used to secure both Windows 365 Cloud PCs and Azure Virtual Desktop. In this chapter, we will continue our journey by covering the various security controls that are available for Windows 365 only. Don't worry, though – we will guide you through the various Azure Virtual Desktop and Azure infrastructure security controls in *Chapter 10, Securing Azure Virtual Desktop*, and in *Chapter 11, Securing Azure Infrastructure*.

In this chapter, we're going to cover the following main topics:

- Introducing the Windows 365 advanced deployment guide
- Security guidelines for Windows 365
- Local admin rights
- Endpoint Privilege Management
- Creating and exporting Cloud PC restore points
- Placing a Cloud PC under review
- Tips and tricks from the field

Introducing the Windows 365 advanced deployment guide

Let's say a company wants to move to Windows 365 Cloud PCs or use Cloud PCs for a group of users. Where would an IT admin start to implement the service correctly? Did you know that Microsoft released the Windows 365 advanced deployment guide to help IT admins do just that? Think of it as a checklist that assists IT admins in preparing and planning to use Windows 365 Cloud PCs in the tenant. It does not actually deploy Windows 365.

The Windows 365 advanced deployment guide can be found in the Microsoft 365 admin center (https://admin.microsoft.com) by clicking on **Setup** > **Advanced deployment guides & assistance** > **All guides** > **Device management** and searching for **Windows 365 Enterprise deployment checklist**.

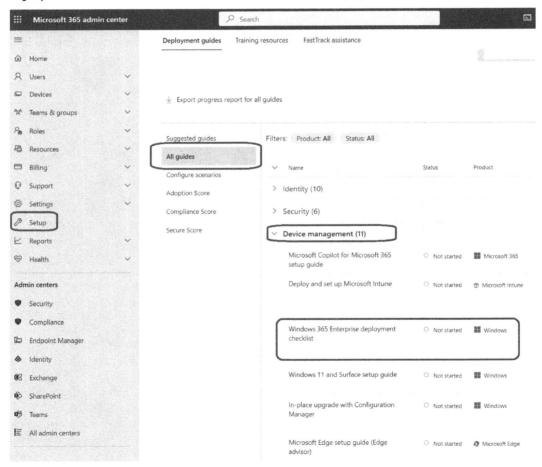

Figure 9.1 – Location of the Windows 365 Enterprise deployment checklist

Simply click on **Windows 365 Enterprise deployment checklist** to open the checklist:

Home > Advanced deployment guides & assistance > Windows 365 Enterprise deployment checklist

● Overview

○ Deployment options

○ Pre-deployment

○ Review

○ Finish

Overview for Windows 365 Enterprise

Windows 365 Enterprise is a cloud-based service that provisions and hosts Cloud PCs. Administrators can deploy, manage, and scale Windows 365 Cloud PCs to fit their needs. Individual users can more securely access and stream their personalized Windows experience. This includes updating apps, data, content, and settings from the Microsoft Cloud to any device, any time, with their Windows 365 Cloud PCs.

What to expect

This guide will help you prepare your organization for the following Windows 365 Cloud PC tasks:

- **Provision Cloud PCs.** Creating and managing Cloud PCs for Windows 365 is performed within the Intune administration portal. To get started, assign a Windows 365 license to a user and then create a provisioning policy in the Intune portal. The provisioning profile will ask you a few questions about how the PCs should be configured.

- **Choose your network for Cloud PCs.**

  ○ Deploy Cloud PCs that are Microsoft Entra ID joined to either an existing Microsoft Entra virtual network (Microsoft Entra ID subscription required) or a provided Microsoft-hosted network.

  ○ If an existing Microsoft Entra ID network is chosen, you must create one or more Microsoft Entra Network Connections (ANCs) to connect Windows 365 with your Microsoft Entra subscription. This virtual network requires networking access to Active Directory domain controller.

  ○ Health checks are performed on an ANC to verify that the Microsoft Entra subscription and virtual networks are properly configured. An Microsoft Entra network supports both Microsoft Entra ID joined or Hybrid Microsoft Entra joined configurations.

- **Choose images.** Microsoft provides a variety of pre-configured Gallery images that are updated, maintained, and cloud optimized to use with Windows 365. You can select either Windows 10 or Windows 11, both include Microsoft 365 apps. Localization customizations can be specified in the provisioning profile and during provisioning. Windows 365 will orchestrate the installation of locale for Windows and Microsoft 365 Apps. Customers can choose to bring their own image (not preferred) if desired.

- **Connect to your Cloud PCs.** After your Cloud PCs are provisioned, users can connect to their cloud from a variety of clients that include browser clients (best on Microsoft Edge, and also supports Chrome and Safari), fully featured desktop clients for Windows and Mac, and mobile clients for iOS, iPadOS, and Android OS.

Figure 9.2 – Overview of the Windows 365 Enterprise deployment checklist

The checklist will guide IT admins through several deployment tasks. These tasks are explained next.

Deployment options

The **Deployment options** step is used to determine which configuration of Windows 365 will be used. You can choose from the following options to deploy Windows 365 Enterprise:

- **Microsoft Entra ID join with Microsoft-hosted network**: Cloud PCs will be joined to Entra ID only.

- **Microsoft Entra ID join with Azure Network Connection**: In this deployment, Cloud PCs will be joined to Microsoft Entra ID only and they can be connected to an existing on-premises network using an Azure network connection.

- **Microsoft Entra hybrid join with Azure Network Connection**: Cloud PCs will be joined to a local Active Directory domain and synchronized to Microsoft Entra ID. They will be able to connect to an existing corporate network using the Azure network connection.

Pre-deployment options

The **Pre-deployment** options section guides IT admins through the following design choices:

- **Identity**:

  - Has a user with the necessary Microsoft Entra role been identified for setting up Windows 365?

- **Networking**:

  - Do the users' physical devices have access to the Remote Desktop client URLs?

  - Will the latency from users' location to their Cloud PC be acceptable?

  - Do you plan to leverage **Remote Desktop Protocol (RDP)** Shortpath for public works?

- **Licensing**:

  - Have you acquired the correct license and subscription types?

  - Do you plan to use the resize feature?

- **Management**:

  - Has Intune been configured to use the default **Mobile Device Management (MDM)** URLs?

  - Is there an Intune enrollment restriction policy to block Windows devices from Intune enrollment?

  - Has co-management been set up in Configuration Manager and any workloads moved to Intune?

  - Do you plan to deploy Windows Update to Cloud PCs?

  - Do you plan to use Windows Autopatch to manage updates on Cloud PCs?

  - Are there any packages (like apps or configurations) deployed to all devices or users that can impact Cloud PCs?

  - Has the device configuration policy for Endpoint analytics enrollment been configured to include Cloud PCs?

  - Has a dynamic group that includes all Cloud PCs been created?

- **Security**:

  - Is there a requirement to use Conditional Access when connecting to the Windows 365 service?

  - Will Cloud PCs be onboarded into Microsoft Defender for Endpoint or with a non-Microsoft endpoint protection solution?

  - Have existing Windows, Microsoft Defender, and Microsoft Edge baselines been targeted to all devices?

  - Do you plan to deploy the Windows 365 security baseline in Intune?

  - Do you need to block RDP device redirections (like with the clipboard or drives)?

- **Applications**:

  - Does a custom image need to be built for localization or unique application purposes?

  - Do you plan to deploy Teams media optimizations instead of using Windows 365 gallery image?

  - Have the limitations with Teams in virtual desktop environments been reviewed?

  - Do you need apps or configurations installed before users sign in to their Cloud PCs?

- **User experience**:

  - Has the correct Cloud PC subscription been identified for app workloads to be run on Cloud PCs?

  - If redirection of devices is required, should the table showing Remote Desktop client support for redirection be reviewed?

  - Is there a plan to deploy the Windows 365 app for Windows 11/10 devices or a supported Remote Desktop client to users' devices?

  - Has the environment been set up to use email addresses to subscribe to a workspace in the Remote Desktop client?

Each task can be opened to get detailed information about it. IT admins can assign each task to themselves or another IT admin and even configure on the following statuses:

- **Not started** (default)
- **In progress**
- **Completed**
- **Backlog**
- **Not applicable**

Most of these tasks have a URL where IT admins can find more information about the task. The following example provides an overview of the **Do you need to block RDP device redirection (like with the clipboard or drives)?** task, as found in the **Security** part of the checklist:

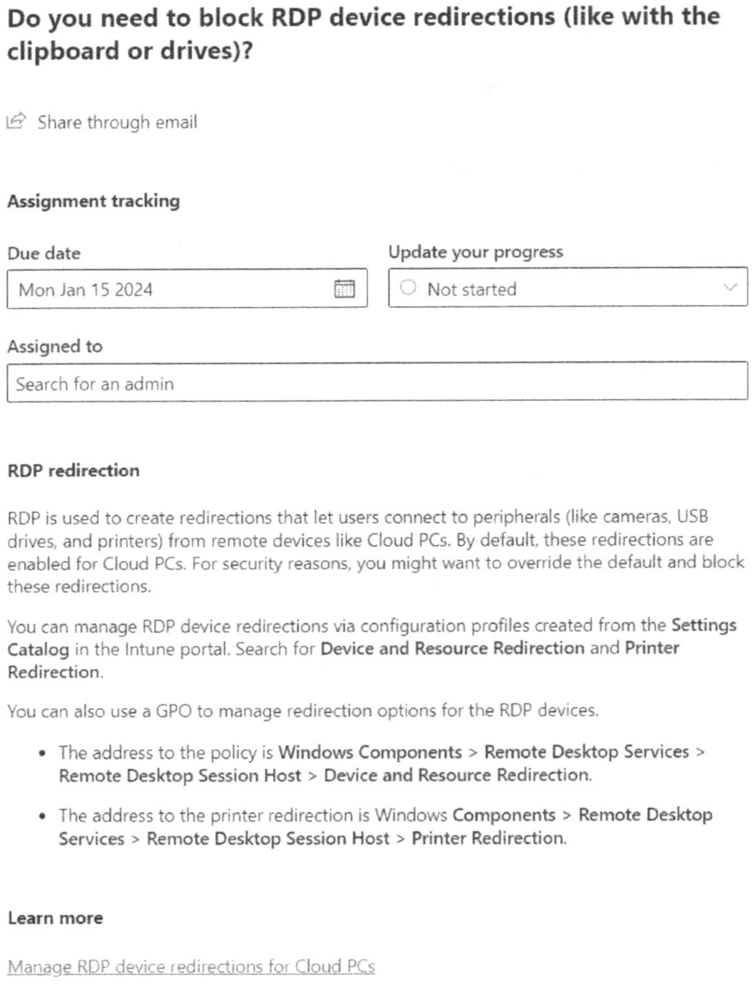

Do you need to block RDP device redirections (like with the clipboard or drives)?

↪ Share through email

Assignment tracking

Due date

| Mon Jan 15 2024 | 🗓 |

Update your progress

| ○ Not started | ⌄ |

Assigned to

| Search for an admin |

RDP redirection

RDP is used to create redirections that let users connect to peripherals (like cameras, USB drives, and printers) from remote devices like Cloud PCs. By default, these redirections are enabled for Cloud PCs. For security reasons, you might want to override the default and block these redirections.

You can manage RDP device redirections via configuration profiles created from the **Settings Catalog** in the Intune portal. Search for **Device and Resource Redirection** and **Printer Redirection**.

You can also use a GPO to manage redirection options for the RDP devices.

- The address to the policy is **Windows Components** > **Remote Desktop Services** > **Remote Desktop Session Host** > **Device and Resource Redirection**.

- The address to the printer redirection is Windows **Components** > **Remote Desktop Services** > **Remote Desktop Session Host** > **Printer Redirection**.

Learn more

Manage RDP device redirections for Cloud PCs

Figure 9.3 – Detailed view of a task in the Windows 365 Enterprise checklist

Since each task can be configured individually, IT admins can use this checklist to document the preparation for Windows 365 (Enterprise) Cloud PCs. Once the checklist is done, it will use a **Completed** status.

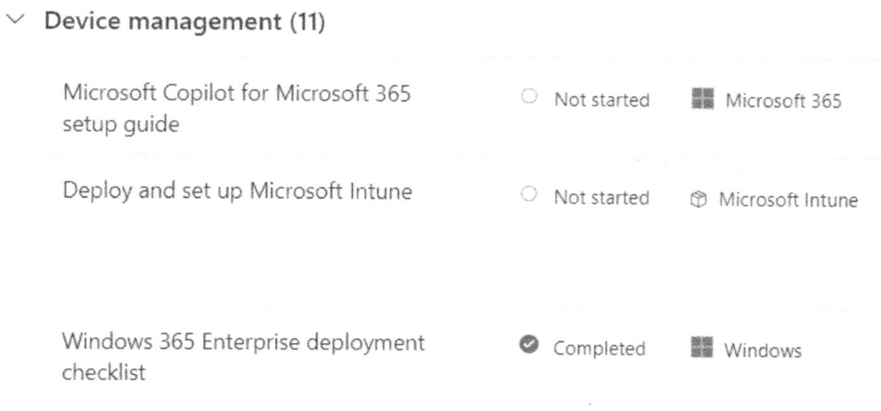

Figure 9.4 – The checklist has been completed

Another great way to prepare for Windows 365 Cloud PCs is by reviewing Microsoft's security guidelines for Windows 365. That's what we will cover next!

Security guidelines for Windows 365

While the Windows 365 advanced deployment guide is meant to assist IT admins with presenting design questions, the security guidelines should be interpreted as best practices for companies who are implementing Windows 365. Currently, there are six guidelines to improve security for Windows 365:

- Apply Conditional Access policies:

  - Conditional access policies are used to control access to devices and apps by requiring MFA, for example.

- Use Microsoft Defender for Endpoint:

  - Microsoft Defender for Endpoint is an enterprise-class solution to detect and prevent malware, for example. By enrolling in Microsoft Defender for Endpoint, IT admins make sure that Cloud PCs are safe while in use by end users.

- Use compliance policies with Conditional Access policies in Microsoft Intune:

  - Compliance policies are a collection of settings requirements that a Cloud PC needs to meet. If a Cloud PC fails to meet these requirements, it will be considered non-compliant. In turn, Conditional Access policies can add security by preventing access to Cloud PCs or apps from non-compliant devices.

- Keep Windows 11/10 up to date:

  - Use a supported update strategy to keep your operating system up to date to protect against attacks or exploits.

- Cloud PC users should not be members of the local administrators' group:

  - Users with local administrative rights can perform administrative tasks, such as installing applications or running scripts. While this is very useful in some cases, it makes much more sense that users are not members of the local administrators' group.

- Subscribe Cloud PCs to Microsoft Defender for Endpoint:

  - Subscribed Cloud PCs will share security information with Microsoft Defender for Endpoint. This way, IT admins can use the Microsoft Defender portal to view unhealthy Cloud PCs, and the Cloud PCs can respond to remediation measures.

  - Security data is sent to Microsoft 365 Secure Score, which, in turn, gives IT admins an impression of the security posture.

We already touched on the subject of local administrator rights. Did you know that these are configured using something called a **user settings object?**

Local admin rights

Microsoft recommends assigning standard user rights to the users of Cloud PCs. However, there might come a time when IT admins need to change the rights of the user. Let's take a look at how these user rights are configured on a Cloud PC.

IT admins can easily configure the rights of the user on a Cloud PC by creating user settings objects in Microsoft Intune. In fact, the following three settings can be configured in a user settings object:

- **Enable Local admin**

- **Enable users to reset their Cloud PCs**

- **Allow user to initiate restore service** and set a frequency of restore points

These user settings objects are accessible at **Microsoft Intune admin center > Devices > Windows 365 > User settings**.

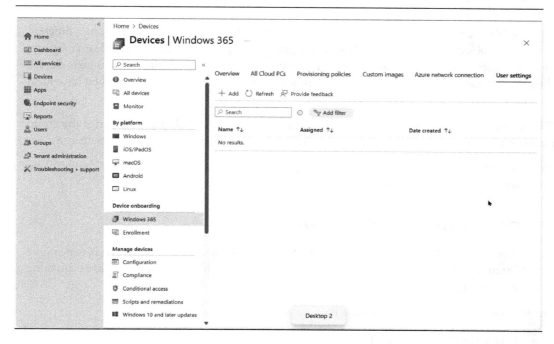

Figure 9.5 – An example of user settings objects in Microsoft Intune

IT admins can create a new user settings object by clicking on the + **Add** button in the ribbon. The following screenshot is an example of the settings that can be configured:

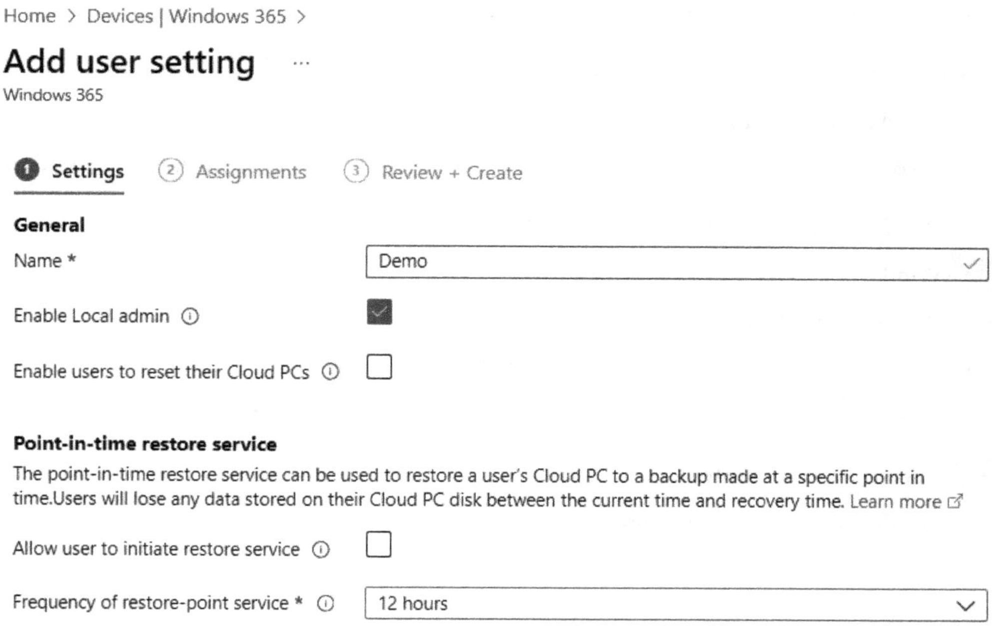

Home > Devices | Windows 365 >

Add user setting   ...
Windows 365

① **Settings**   ② Assignments   ③ Review + Create

General

Name *   Demo   ✓

Enable Local admin ①   ✓

Enable users to reset their Cloud PCs ①   ☐

Point-in-time restore service

The point-in-time restore service can be used to restore a user's Cloud PC to a backup made at a specific point in time.Users will lose any data stored on their Cloud PC disk between the current time and recovery time. Learn more ⟋

Allow user to initiate restore service ①   ☐

Frequency of restore-point service * ①   12 hours   ⌄

Figure 9.6 – Example of the user settings

It is possible to change the user rights of the user on a Cloud PC by temporarily assigning a different user settings object to a specific user. As seen in *Figure 9.5*, it's possible to create multiple user settings objects. If user settings objects are assigned to separate groups, all an IT admin has to do is change the group membership of a user. The user will need to sign in again and they will then have local admin rights.

The same is true for removing local admin rights. The IT admin would have to change the group membership of the user and the user will then have standard user rights once they sign in again.

There is another way to temporarily grant administrative rights to a standard user, which is by using Endpoint Privilege Management.

Endpoint Privilege Management

The idea of **Endpoint Privilege Management** (**EPM**) is to allow standard users to run tasks that require administrative rights, without assigning local administrative rights. These tasks could be anything from installing applications on the desktop to updating drivers.

The following are the requirements for EPM:

- One of the following licenses:

  - Microsoft Intune plan 1

  - A standalone license for EPM

  - License for the Microsoft Intune suite

- Microsoft Entra joined or Microsoft Entra Hybrid joined

- Enrolled in Microsoft Intune or co-managed

- Make sure that the operating system is supported for EPM with one of the following versions:

  - Windows 11 v22H2 or later, with KB5022913

  - Windows 11 v21H2 or later, with KB5023774

  - Windows 10 v22H2 or later, with KB5023774

  - Windows 10 v21H2 or later, with KB5023774

  - Windows 10 v20H2 or later, with KB5023774

- Windows 365 is supported

- Azure Virtual Desktop is not supported

EPM is configured via **Microsoft Intune Admin Center** > **Endpoint security** > **Manage** > **Endpoint Privilege Management**.

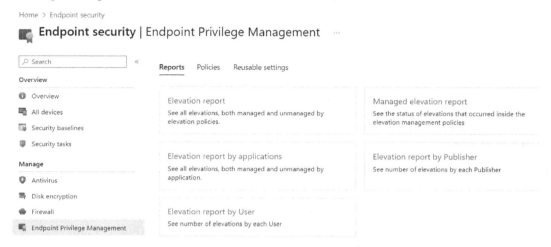

Figure 9.7 – Endpoint Privilege Management in Microsoft Intune

EPM is divided into three tabs in Microsoft Intune. These tabs are as follows:

- **Reports**: *Figure 9.7* shows the different reports and their purposes

- **Policies**: Use this tab to create and manage policies

- **Reusable settings**: Use this tab to manage certificates that validate files that are managed by EPM elevation rules

Let's take a look at the policies. From the **Policies** tab, IT admins can click the **+ Create policy** button. A blade will appear in Intune on the right-hand side where IT admins can choose between the following:

- **Elevation rules policy**: Use this policy type to determine what actions should be made available for standard users

- **Elevation settings policy**: Use this policy type to enable EPM on clients

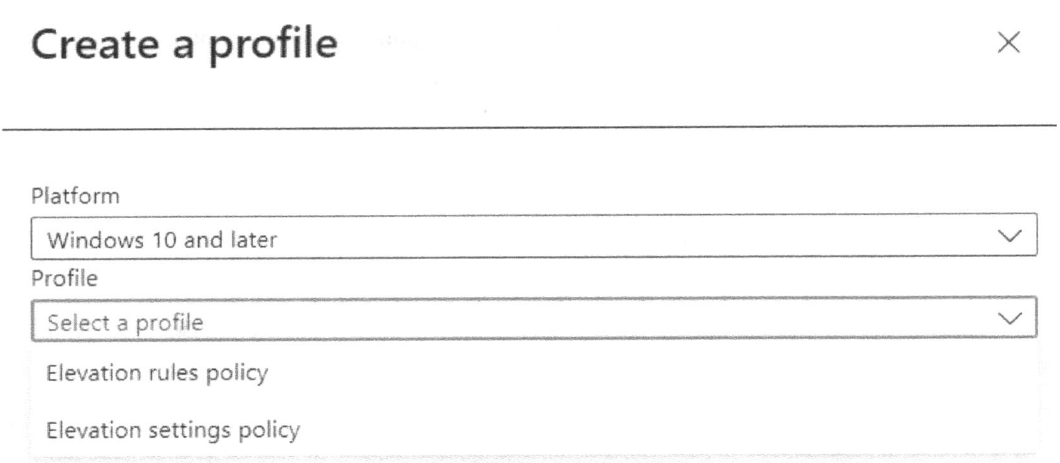

Create a profile   ✕

Platform

Windows 10 and later   ⌄

Profile

Select a profile   ⌄

Elevation rules policy

Elevation settings policy

Figure 9.8 – Elevation policy types

Let's take a look at how to create these policies.

Creating an elevation settings policy

An elevation settings policy instructs a client to enable EPM. Creating an EPM works as follows:

1. Give the policy a name and optionally a description.

2. Enable EPM and select options for the following settings:

    *   **Send elevation data for reporting**: This can be set to **Yes** or **No**. If set to **Yes**, the device will send diagnostic data to Microsoft. This data is used to make sure that the EPM components on the device are healthy. If set to **No**, the device will not send this data to Microsoft.

    *   **Reporting scope**: This can be set to either **Diagnostic data and managed elevations only**, **Diagnostic data and all endpoint elevations**, or **Diagnostic data only**.

    *   **Default elevation response**: Use this option to determine the default response for an elevation request of any file that is not managed by an elevation rule policy. This can be set to one of the following:

        *   **Deny all requests**: Users cannot perform an elevate request action for files that are not specifically specified in the Windows elevation rule policy.

        *   **Require user permissions**: This setting makes sure that the user has the same validation options as specified in the Windows elevation rule policy.

        *   **Not configured**: This setting is not configured by default. The behavior will follow the **Deny all requests** setting.

The following is an example of the setting to enable EPM:

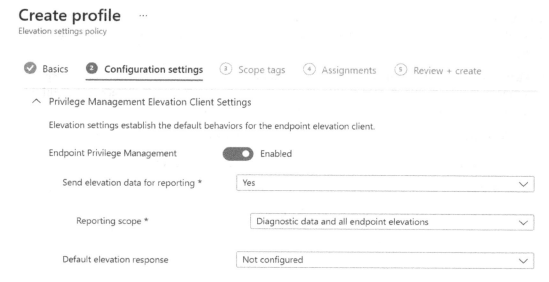

Figure 9.9 – Enabling Endpoint Privilege Management

Finalize the policy by adding scope tags if they apply and assign the policy to a group of devices. The policy will appear in the **Policies** tab once it's been created.

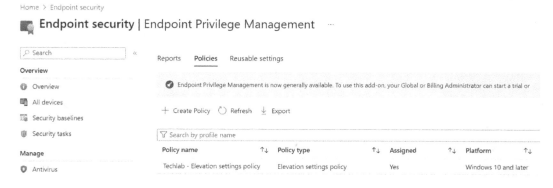

Figure 9.10 – Overview of the available EPM policies

Now, it's time to define what actions users can perform that require administrative rights.

Creating an elevation rules policy

IT admins can create an elevation rules policy in the same location in the Microsoft Intune admin center. Before we dive head first into creating a rules policy, we would like to discuss how an elevation rules policy works.

An **elevation rules policy** is used to define tasks that require elevated rights. Each policy requires one or more rule properties, or in simpler terms, actions that users can perform. Let's explain this by using an example, allowing users to run **Registry Editor**.

Each rule property has the following options that can be configured:

- **Rule name**: This allows users to start the Registry Editor application
- **Description**: This allows users to run Registry Editor

Make sure to select **Elevation rules policy** in the first step (shown in *Figure 9.8*):

Figure 9.11 – Creating an elevation rules policy

Provide the policy with a name and, optionally, a description, as shown here:

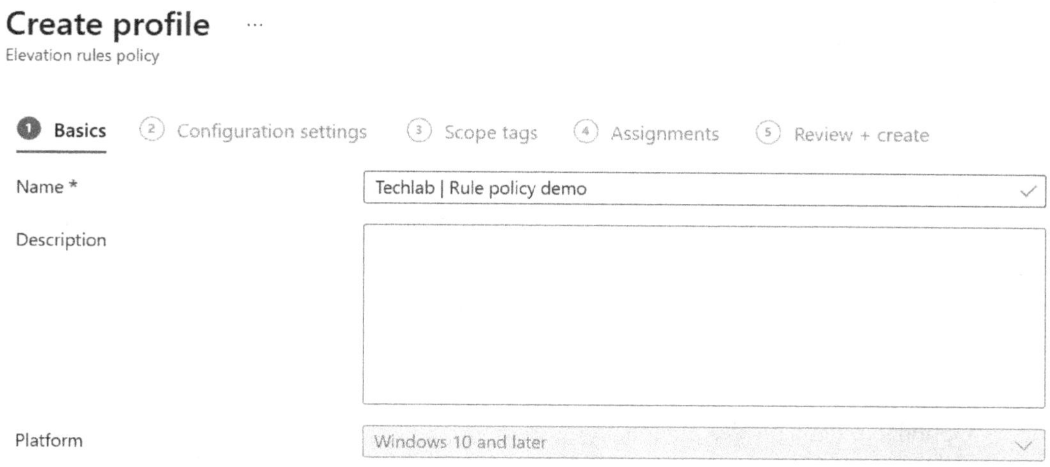

Create profile ···
Elevation rules policy

① **Basics**   ② Configuration settings   ③ Scope tags   ④ Assignments   ⑤ Review + create

Name *   Techlab | Rule policy demo   ✓

Description

Platform   Windows 10 and later   ⌄

Figure 9.12 – Filling in the Basics section of the rules policy

Let's continue to the **Configuration settings** step to configure one or more rule properties:

- **Elevation type**: IT admins have the option to specify whether elevation requests are allowed automatically or whether users need to provide a business justification:

  - **User confirmed**: The user will have to provide a business justification or authenticate to Windows before the elevation action can be completed:

    - **Business justification**: The user will have to provide a justification to perform the elevation action. Once provided, the action that is defined as the default elevation response will be used.

    - **Windows authentication**: The user will have to authenticate to perform the elevation action. Once provided, the action that is defined as the default elevation response will be used.

  - **Automatic**: Selecting **Automatic** as the elevation type will result in an automatic elevation. There is no interaction with the user.

- **Child process behavior**: Some applications have dependencies. By starting the main application, a child application is started automatically to make sure that the application runs as it should. This option allows IT admins to decide what happens to these child processes. Do you want to run them in an elevated context as well? Valid choices are as follows:

  - **Allow child processes to run elevated**

  - **Require rule to elevate**

  - **Deny all**

  - **Not configured**

- **File information**:

  - Provide the filename

  - **File path**: Enter the path where the file lives

  - **Signature source**: IT admins have the option to include a certificate that is used to validate the integrity of the file. This can be done by adding a separate certificate for each file or using a single certificate for multiple files by using a certificate in **Reusable settings**.

  - **File hash**: A file hash is a requirement for **Automatic** elevations. For **User confirmed** elevations, IT admins can choose between providing a file hash or using a certificate.

  - Optional: Provide a minimum version.

  - Optional: Enter a file description.

  - Optional: Provide a product name.

  - Optional: Provide an internal name.

- Once completed, the configuration settings will look like this:

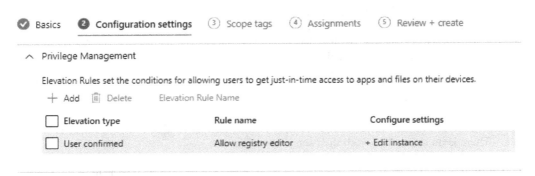

Figure 9.13 – Example of allowing Registry Editor in an elevation rules settings policy

Finish the policy by adding scope tags, if they are applicable. Assign the policy to a group or multiple groups. Review the settings in the final step and create the profile. Once created, the **Policies** tab will look like this:

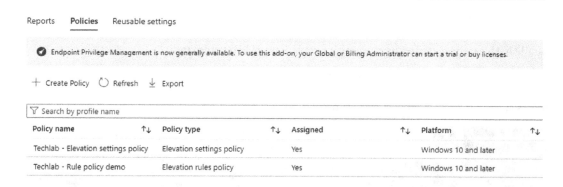

Figure 9.14 – Overview of the Policies tab

Once the policies have been applied, users can start to use the application. They have to right-click on the file and select the **Run with elevated access** option. As configured in the elevation rule policy, users will have to provide a business justification:

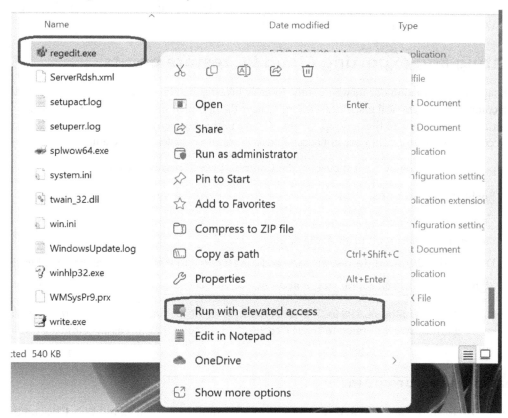

Figure 9.15 – Running the application using the Run with elevated access option

Acquiring the file hash

The file hash can be acquired by running a simple PowerShell command:

```
Get-FileHash -Path "path\file"
```

Here is an example of the PowerShell command:

Figure 9.16 – Example of the PowerShell command

This concludes the section about EPM. In the next section, we will discuss the ability to log in to a Cloud PC locally.

Creating and exporting Cloud PC restore points

What happens if a situation occurs where some forensic investigation has to take place on a Cloud PC? When companies use physical machines, IT admins have the option to sign in with their administrative credentials to gain access to the desktop. Cloud PCs live in the data center at Microsoft, and they are only accessible to the user. They are not accessible to IT admins – at least, by default.

To support the scenario that we just described, IT admins have to perform five steps:

1. Enable Windows LAPS.
2. Create a restore point.
3. Export the restore point to an Azure Storage account.
4. Download and convert the restore point and use Hyper-V to start the virtual machine locally.
5. Sign in using the local administrator account.

We already covered Windows LAPS in *Chapter 8*, *Configuring Access Control*. In this section, we will cover how IT admins have the option to create a custom restore point that, just as an automatic restore point, can be exported for later use.

Creating a restore point

Sign in to **Microsoft Intune admin center** > **Devices** > **Windows 365** > **All Cloud PCs**. Click on the desired Cloud PC. Select **Restore points** in the menu.

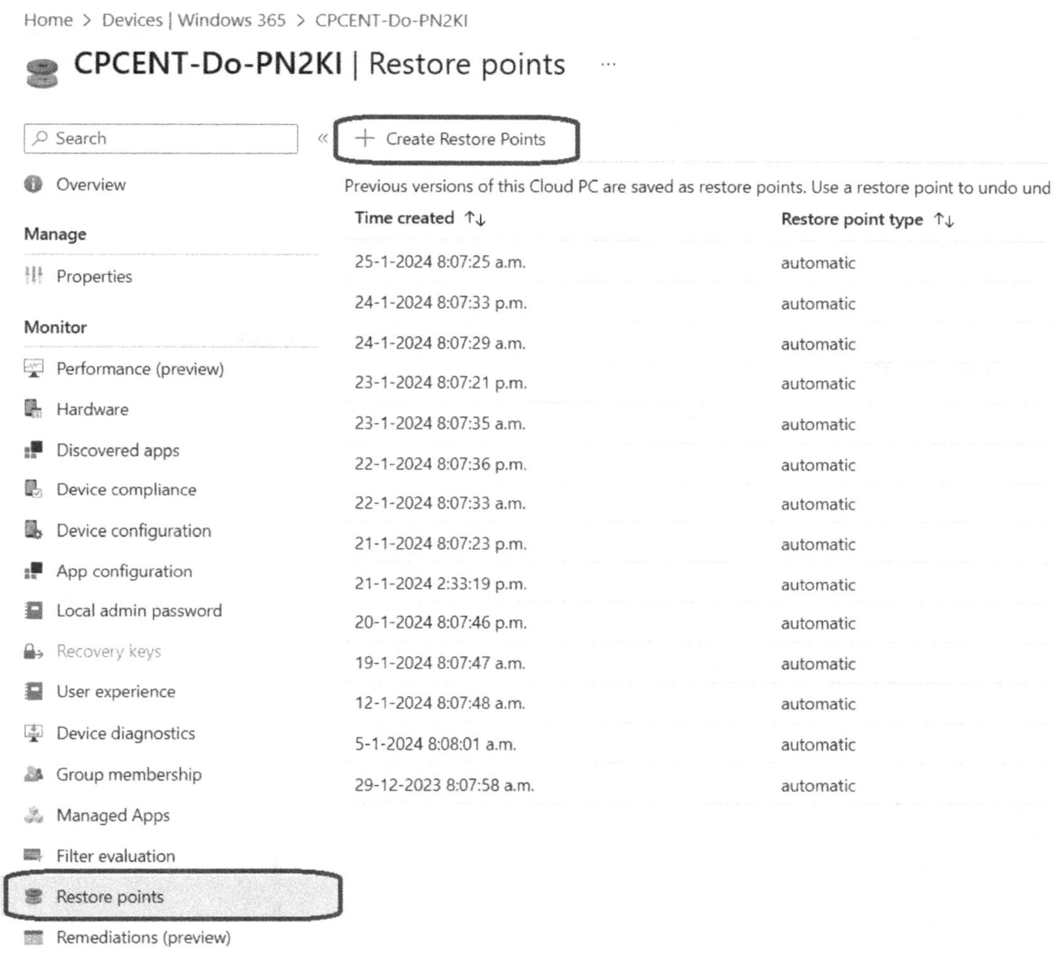
Home > Devices | Windows 365 > CPCENT-Do-PN2KI
CPCENT-Do-PN2KI | Restore points
Search
Create Restore Points
Overview
Manage
Properties
Monitor
Performance (preview)
Hardware
Discovered apps
Device compliance
Device configuration
App configuration
Local admin password
Recovery keys
User experience
Device diagnostics
Group membership
Managed Apps
Filter evaluation
Restore points
Remediations (preview)
Previous versions of this Cloud PC are saved as restore points. Use a restore point to undo und
Time created
Restore point type
25-1-2024 8:07:25 a.m. automatic
24-1-2024 8:07:33 p.m. automatic
24-1-2024 8:07:29 a.m. automatic
23-1-2024 8:07:21 p.m. automatic
23-1-2024 8:07:35 a.m. automatic
22-1-2024 8:07:36 p.m. automatic
22-1-2024 8:07:33 a.m. automatic
21-1-2024 8:07:23 p.m. automatic
21-1-2024 2:33:19 p.m. automatic
20-1-2024 8:07:46 p.m. automatic
19-1-2024 8:07:47 a.m. automatic
12-1-2024 8:07:48 a.m. automatic
5-1-2024 8:08:01 a.m. automatic
29-12-2023 8:07:58 a.m. automatic

Figure 9.17 – Restore points overview of a Cloud PC

This will trigger a notification telling the IT admin that creating a custom restore point can take an hour or longer.

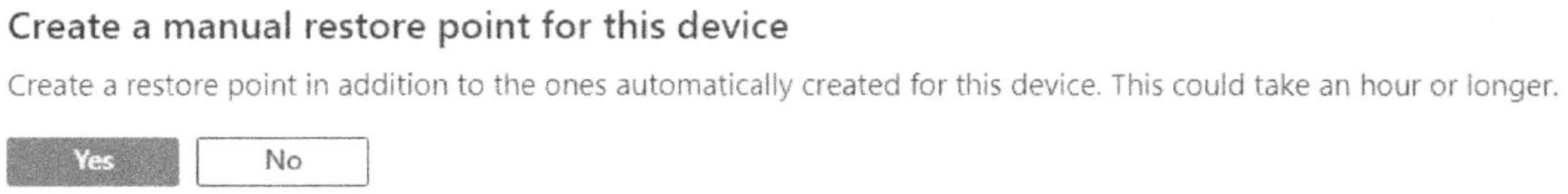
Create a manual restore point for this device
Create a restore point in addition to the ones automatically created for this device. This could take an hour or longer.
Yes
No

Figure 9.18 – Notification when creating a custom restore point

The restore point will show up in the **Restore points** overview and it will show the status of **Manual**.

Now that we have discussed manual restore points, I want to take a moment to talk about automatic restore points. You can see the **automatic** status in *Figure 9.17*. These restore points, as you might have guessed, are created automatically as determined in the user settings policy. Or are they?

These are the types of restore points;

- **Short-term**: These are the restore points that IT admins configure in the user settings policy. They can have an interval of 4, 6, 12, 16, or 24 hours.

- **Long-term**: There are a total of four long-term restore points, which are automatically created after 7 days.

- **On-demand**: These are the manual restore points that we are discussing in this section.

Let's find out how to export a restore point now that we know how to create a manual restore point.

Exporting a restore point

The next step is to export a restore point, which can be performed from the **Restore points** menu from a Cloud PC. Click the three dots on the right-hand side (**…**) and select **Share**.

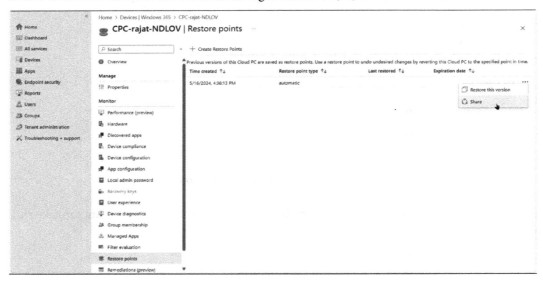

Figure 9.19 – Sharing a restore point to an Azure Storage account

Select the subscription and the Azure Storage account and share the restore point:

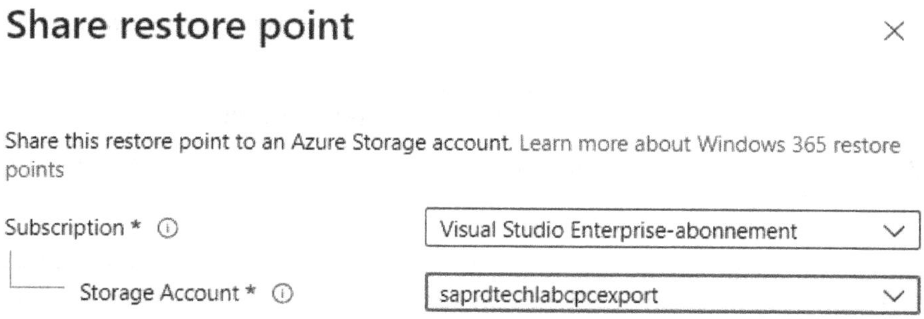

Share restore point   ✕

Share this restore point to an Azure Storage account. Learn more about Windows 365 restore points

Subscription * ⓘ | Visual Studio Enterprise-abonnement   ⌄ |

       └──── Storage Account * ⓘ | saprdtechlabcpcexport   ⌄ |

Figure 9.20 – Selecting the subscription and the Azure Storage account

> **Tip**
> Did you know that IT admins can export restore points in bulk?

To do so, go to the **Devices** blade in the Microsoft Intune admin center and select the **Share Cloud PC restore point to storage** device action.

IT admins can either download the restore point using the Azure portal or use an app such as **Azure Storage Explorer**, which significantly improves the download speed.

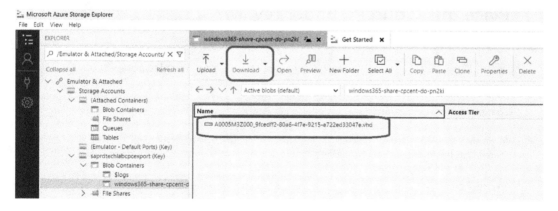

Figure 9.21 – Downloading the restore point using the Azure Storage Explorer app

This concludes how to manually create and share a restore point to an Azure Storage account.

Placing a Cloud PC under review

Windows 365 Cloud PCs have the option to be placed under review. In this case, one of two things happen:

- The Windows 365 service will create and share a restore point to an Azure Storage account. IT admins can share this restore point with internal or external investigators.

- IT admins have the option to prevent the user from signing in to the Cloud PC for as long as the Cloud PC is under review. This is an optional step; it is not mandatory.

Placing a Cloud PC under review is done on the Cloud PC. Sign in to **Microsoft Intune admin center** > **Devices** > **Windows 365** > **All Cloud PCs**. Select the desired Cloud PC. The **Place the Cloud PC under review** device action is hidden under the three dots (…).

Figure 9.22 – The Place Cloud PC under review device action

Select the subscription where the Azure Storage account lives and select the appropriate Azure Storage account. Decide whether the user should be able to access the Cloud PC during the review process:

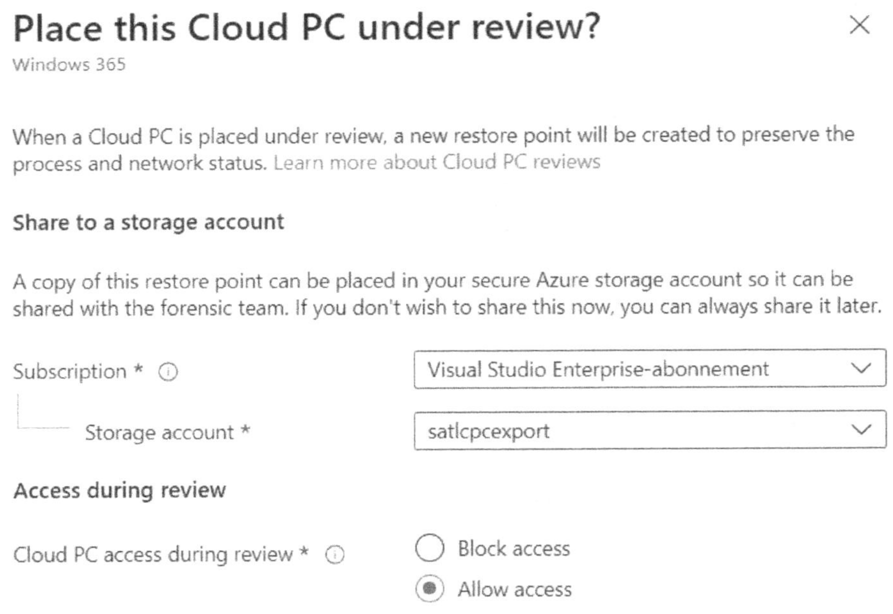

Place this Cloud PC under review?   ✕
Windows 365

When a Cloud PC is placed under review, a new restore point will be created to preserve the process and network status. Learn more about Cloud PC reviews

Share to a storage account

A copy of this restore point can be placed in your secure Azure storage account so it can be shared with the forensic team. If you don't wish to share this now, you can always share it later.

Subscription * ⓘ	Visual Studio Enterprise-abonnement ∨
⌐ Storage account *	satlcpcexport ∨

Access during review

Cloud PC access during review * ⓘ   ◯ Block access
                                       ◉ Allow access

Figure 9.23 – Placing a Cloud PC under review

Intune will remind the IT admin which choice has been made:

Figure 9.24 – Access to the Cloud PC is allowed during the review process

It's interesting to mention that the name of the restore point shows that it was created by placing a Cloud PC under review:

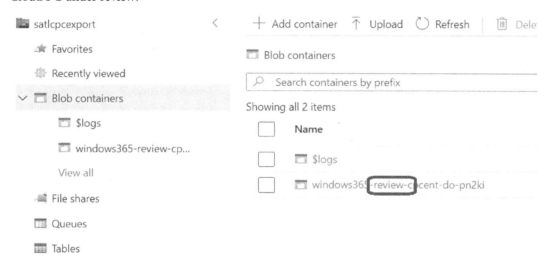

Figure 9.25 – The name of the restore point includes the word review

Ending the review of a Cloud PC

IT admins can end the review of a Cloud PC once the investigation is complete. To do so, select the **This device is being reviewed** banner, select the **Remove from review** option, and confirm by clicking the **Remove** button:

Figure 9.26 – Ending the review of a Cloud PC

That concludes the options to use restore points for forensic investigation.

Tips and tricks

In this section, we would like to share some tips and tricks that might help you. These tips and tricks are specifically for Windows 365. We hope you enjoy these tips and that they will help you in the field.

Tip 1 – Use Windows 365 Boot with multiple Cloud PCs

Using Windows 365 Boot will convert a desktop into a secure kiosk. Users will sign directly into their Cloud PC, providing a seamless experience. But what happens when a user has multiple Cloud PCs? Which Cloud PC is used to sign in?

Users have the option to select the Cloud PC that will be used when a user signs in to a Windows 365 Boot endpoint. The option is named **Boot into this Cloud PC** and is found in the Windows 365 web client (`https://windows365.microsoft.com`). It also works in the new Windows app web client (`https://windows365.microsoft.com/ent#/`).

Navigate to the Cloud PC and open the Cloud PC options (**…**). Select **Settings**.

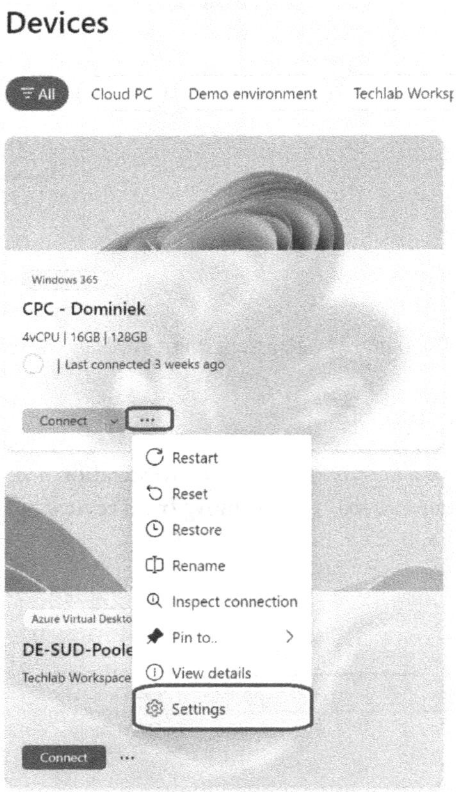

Figure 9.27 – Settings of a Cloud PC

From **Integrated experiences** > **Boot to this Cloud PC**, select the checkbox next to **Connect while signed in to device**.

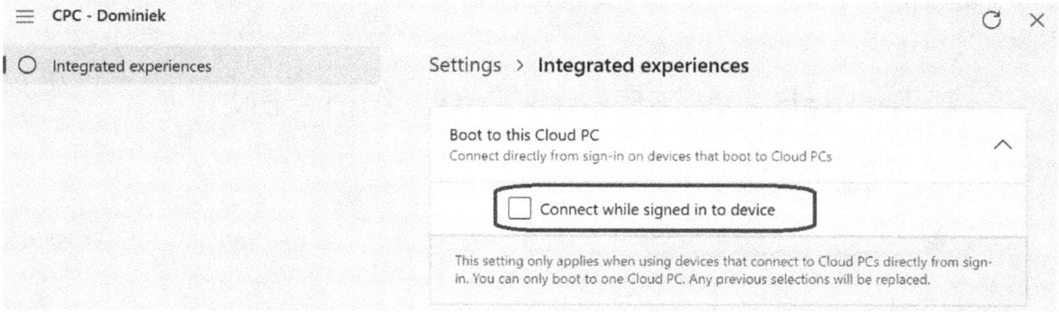

Figure 9.28 – Connect while signed in to device

Tip 2 – Make sure that users always have to sign in to the Cloud PC

In some scenarios, it makes sense to make sure that users always have to sign in to their Cloud PC. Of course, users will have to sign in to the Windows app and they can connect to their Cloud PC from there. If the user disconnects or signs out of the Cloud PC, the app will still be signed in. All the user has to do is to click the **Connect** button again and the connection to the Cloud PC will be made. The same is true for the web client.

This tip is meant to save IT admins a lot of time checking out Conditional Access. The solution for this scenario is to simply disable **single sign-on** (**SSO**) in the provisioning policy. By disabling SSO, the user will have to authenticate each time a connection is made to the Cloud PC.

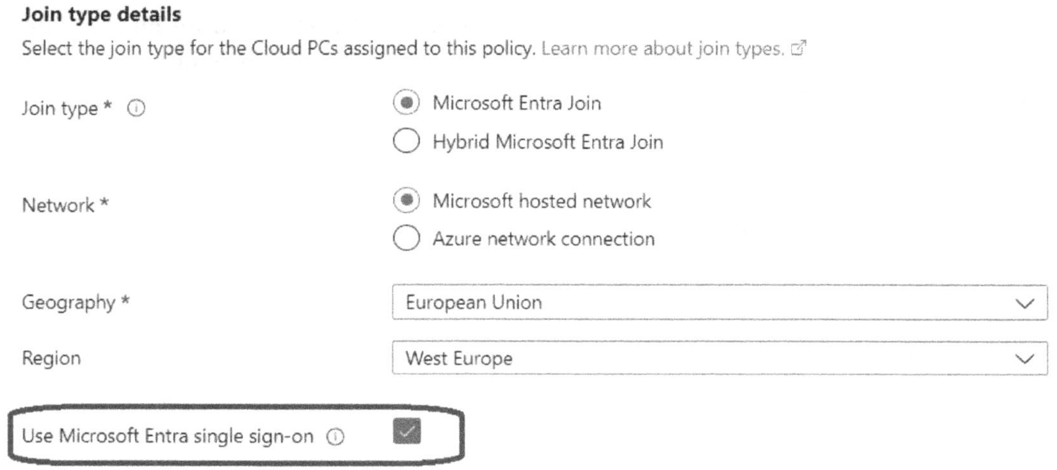

Figure 9.29 – SSO is part of a provisioning policy for Windows 365

Make sure to save the configuration. Did you know that you can ensure that the changes take place on existing Cloud PCs? To do so, open the provisioning policy and click the **Apply current configuration** button at the top:

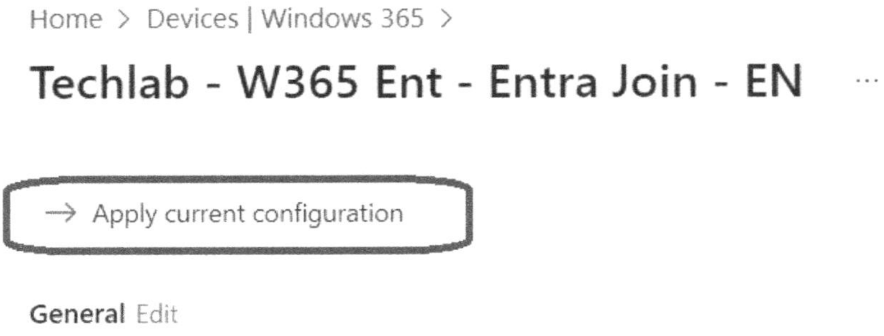

Home > Devices | Windows 365 >

Techlab - W365 Ent - Entra Join - EN   ...

→ Apply current configuration

General Edit

Figure 9.30 – The Apply current configuration button in a provisioning policy

This concludes the tips and tricks. We hope you enjoyed this dedicated Windows 365 chapter.

Summary

In this chapter, you learned how to plan for a Windows 365 deployment by using the Windows 365 advanced deployment guide and how to use the security guidelines to provide a secure environment for users to work in. You learned how local administrative rights are configured and used for Windows 365 and how EPM assists users in performing tasks that require elevated rights without assigning local administrator permission. Lastly, you learned how local IT admins or internal/external investigators can perform forensic investigations using Cloud PC restore points, either created manually or by placing a Cloud PC under review.

We will shift the focus from Windows 365 to **Azure Virtual Desktop** (**AVD**) and Azure infrastructure in the next two chapters. In these chapters, we will guide you on how to securely configure AVD and the Azure infrastructure components.

10

Securing Azure Virtual Desktop

In the previous chapter, we learned how Windows 365 can be secured. Now, it's time to look at **Azure Virtual Desktop** (**AVD**) and some of the different ways of securing it. We will start by learning how to configure backups for the session hosts and the FSLogix profiles. Then, we will move on to the configuration of private endpoints for the AVD host pool and workspaces. We will continue with confidential computing and configuring AppLocker. Next, we will discuss the importance of securing OneDrive, and we will end the chapter by looking at the structure of Active Directory.

This chapter covers the following topics:

- Configuring backups
- Securing AVD with private endpoints
- AVD and confidential computing
- Configuring AppLocker
- Securing OneDrive
- Active Directory structure and security

Configuring backups

In this section, we will look at why backups are needed, how to configure them, and how to restore a session host or FSLogix profile. Let's kick off with the backup and restore process for the session hosts.

It's important, especially with users who have a personal session host, that this host is protected. These users are typically developers who need to be able to install specific programs and tools on the session host for which they are given local administrator permissions. To make sure that these kinds of machines can be recovered quickly, the IT admin can configure a **virtual machine** backup in the Azure portal.

Creating a Recovery Services vault

The first resource that the IT admin needs to create before they can start doing backups is the vault. This is done by going to **Backup center** in Azure, selecting **Vaults**, and selecting **+Vault**. They then need to select the vault that has support for Azure Virtual Machines, which is **Recovery Services vault**, and press **Continue**.

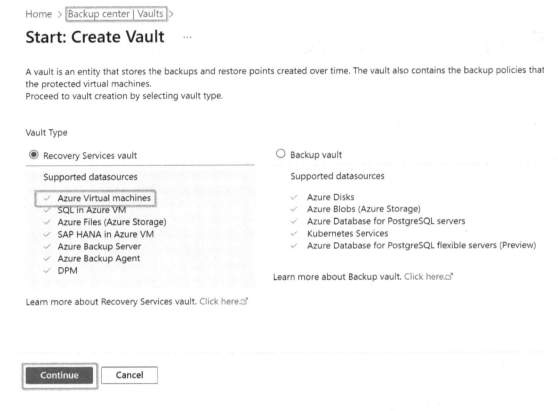

Figure 10.1 – Choosing Recovery Services vault

Let's look at all the steps that are needed to create this vault:

1. Choose the correct subscription, resource group, and location, and give the vault a name that follows the organization's naming convention.

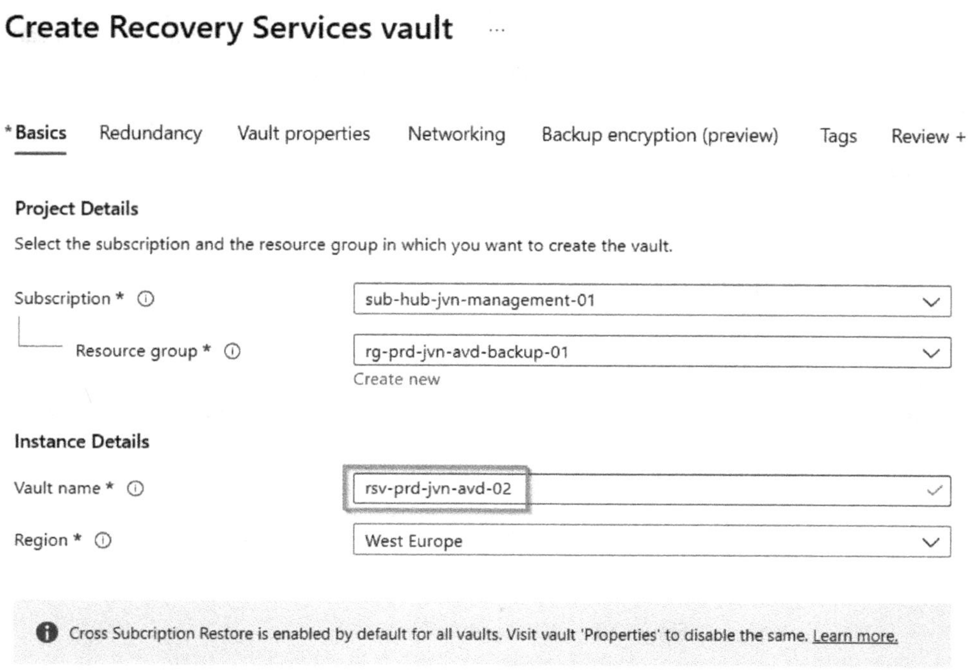

Create Recovery Services vault   ...

* **Basics**   Redundancy   Vault properties   Networking   Backup encryption (preview)   Tags   Review + create

Project Details

Select the subscription and the resource group in which you want to create the vault.

Subscription * ⓘ

> Resource group * ⓘ

sub-hub-jvn-management-01   ⌄

rg-prd-jvn-avd-backup-01   ⌄
Create new

Instance Details

Vault name * ⓘ

rsv-prd-jvn-avd-02   ✓

Region * ⓘ

West Europe   ⌄

ⓘ Cross Subcription Restore is enabled by default for all vaults. Visit vault 'Properties' to disable the same. Learn more.

Figure 10.2 – Vault basic details

2. The next step is configuring **Redundancy**, but be aware that this option can no longer be changed after protecting items. Which option the IT admin chooses depends on the needs of the organization and how crucial the protected items are.

Home > Backup center | Vaults > Start: Create Vault >

Create Recovery Services vault   ...

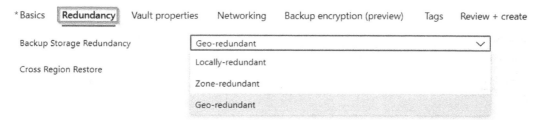

* Basics   **Redundancy**   Vault properties   Networking   Backup encryption (preview)   Tags   Review + create

Backup Storage Redundancy

Cross Region Restore

Geo-redundant   ⌄
Locally-redundant
Zone-redundant
Geo-redundant

Figure 10.3 – Selecting the redundancy

3. The next step is called **Vault properties** and it is used to enable immutable storage. You can either use this type of storage or configure a private endpoint in the **Networking** tab to secure the vault after creation. For this demo, we will leave it at public access.

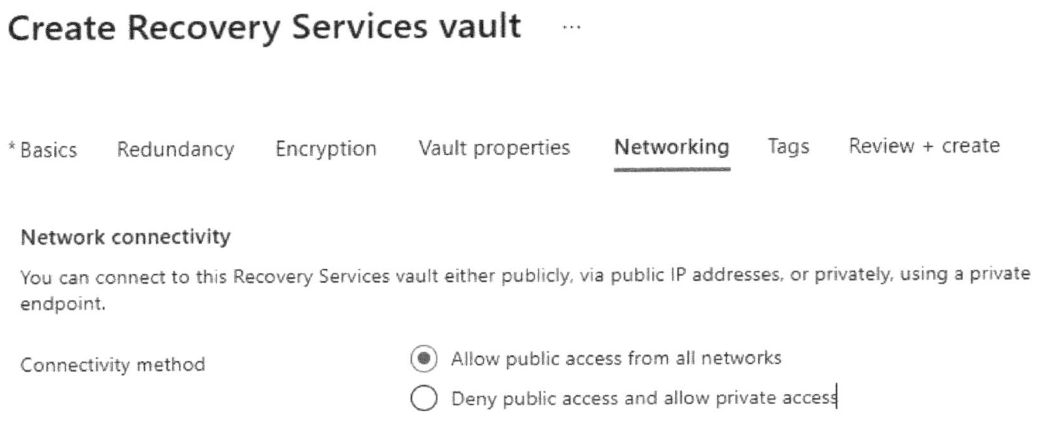

Create Recovery Services vault   ⋯

* Basics   Redundancy   Encryption   Vault properties   **Networking**   Tags   Review + create

Network connectivity

You can connect to this Recovery Services vault either publicly, via public IP addresses, or privately, using a private endpoint.

Connectivity method   ● Allow public access from all networks
                                       ○ Deny public access and allow private access

Figure 10.4 – Vault networking

4. The next step to create the vault is to assign the necessary tags to the vault and click **Review + create**.

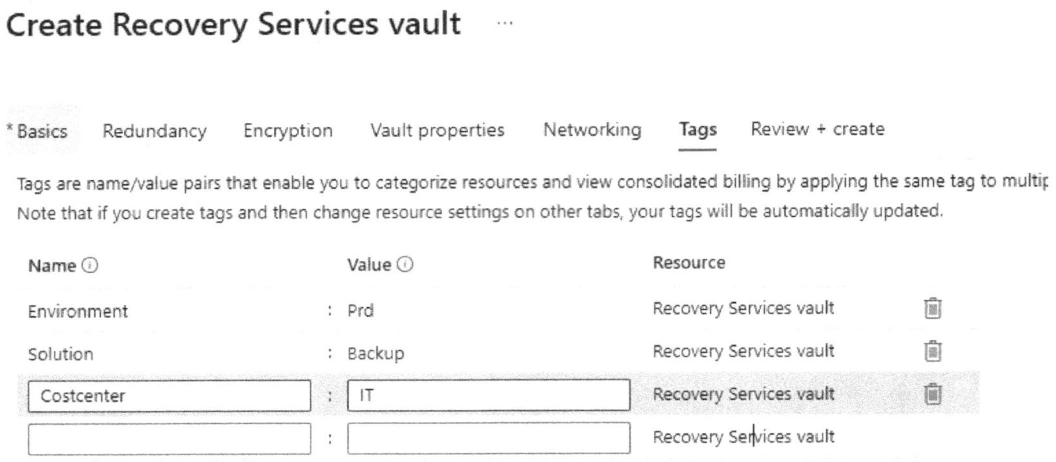

Create Recovery Services vault   ⋯

* Basics   Redundancy   Encryption   Vault properties   Networking   **Tags**   Review + create

Tags are name/value pairs that enable you to categorize resources and view consolidated billing by applying the same tag to multip
Note that if you create tags and then change resource settings on other tabs, your tags will be automatically updated.

Name ⓘ		Value ⓘ	Resource	
Environment	:	Prd	Recovery Services vault	🗑
Solution	:	Backup	Recovery Services vault	🗑
Costcenter	:	IT	Recovery Services vault	🗑
	:		Recovery Services vault	

Figure 10.5 – Assigning tags to the vault

5.   Make sure that all settings are correct and click **Create**.

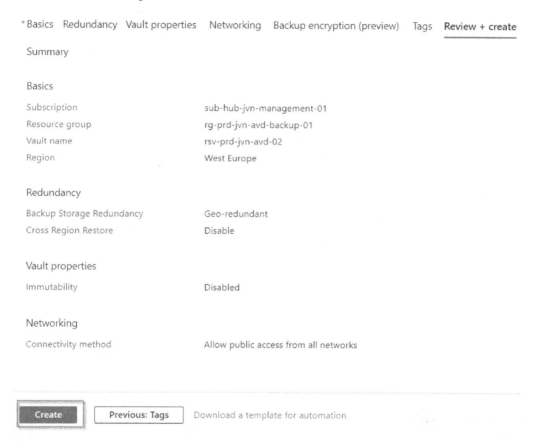

Create Recovery Services vault   ...

* Basics   Redundancy   Vault properties   Networking   Backup encryption (preview)   Tags   **Review + create**

Summary

Basics

Subscription	sub-hub-jvn-management-01
Resource group	rg-prd-jvn-avd-backup-01
Vault name	rsv-prd-jvn-avd-02
Region	West Europe

Redundancy

Backup Storage Redundancy	Geo-redundant
Cross Region Restore	Disable

Vault properties

Immutability	Disabled

Networking

Connectivity method	Allow public access from all networks

| Create | | Previous: Tags | Download a template for automation |

Figure 10.6 – Review and create the vault

Now that the Recovery Services vault has been created, it's time to create the backup policy.

Backup policy session hosts

Before the IT admin can do a backup, they will first need to create a backup policy. This policy will define when a backup takes place and for how long the backup will be retained. Let's go through the steps to create one:

1.   Go to the **Azure portal** > **Backup center** > **Backup policies** and select **+ Add**.

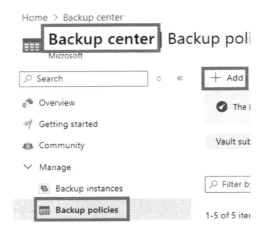

Figure 10.7 – Adding a backup policy

2. Click on **Select vault**, choose the correct vault, and click **Next**.

Figure 10.8 – Choosing the correct backup vault

3. The first thing that is needed is to choose the policy type; this can be **Standard** or **Enhanced**. In this example, the IT admin chooses **Enhanced** because this has support for trusted launch virtual machines.

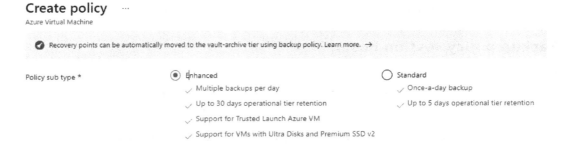

Figure 10.9 – Policy types

4. Let's fill in the details such as the name, schedule, and the number of days that the instant restore point will be retained. To make it easier to manage the policies, the IT admin can put the retention details in the name, as shown in the following figure.

Figure 10.10 – Naming the policy

5. The final step of creating this policy is to define the retention periods. The following is an example.

Figure 10.11 – Configuring the retention periods

6. Microsoft has a default naming convention for the instant recovery points resource group. However, the IT admin has the option to use a custom resource group so that they can follow the organization's naming convention.

Azure Backup Resource Group (Optional) ⓘ

| rg-prd-jvn-avd-backup ✓ | n | 01   ✓ |

Figure 10.12 – Instant recovery points resource group configuration

7. When created, the policy will be visible in the Backup center, as shown next.

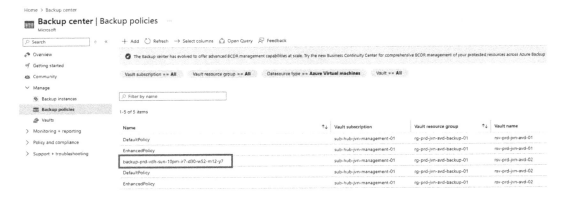

Figure 10.13 – Newly created custom backup policy

Now that the vault and the policy are created, the IT admin needs an easy way to configure the backup for the session hosts. This can be done per host or in the Backup center. The IT admin needs to make sure that when new session hosts are created, the backup is configured automatically. To ensure this, they can use a built-in policy.

To configure this built-in policy, they need to go to **Policy** in the Azure portal, select **Definitions**, search for `configure backup`, and select the correct definition, as shown in the following figure. This can also be done in **Backup center**.

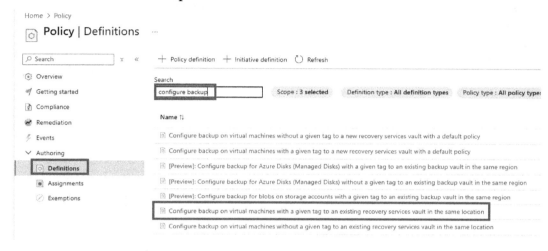

Figure 10.14 – Searching for the correct policy

Before the policy is active, the IT admin needs to assign it by going through the configuration steps. Note that it's also possible to create an initiative first and then continue with the next steps.

Figure 10.15 – Assigning the policy

Let's go through the steps to assign the policy:

1. The first step is determining the scope of the policy. The IT admin can choose the entire AVD subscription but, in this case, chooses only the resource group where the personal session hosts are.

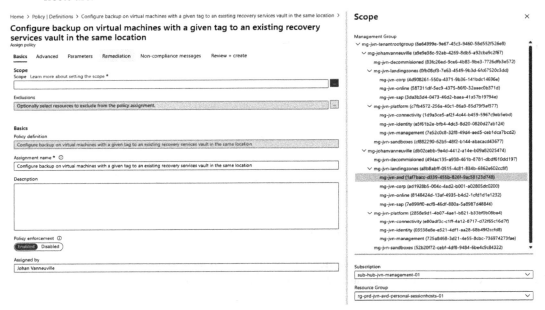

Figure 10.16 – Policy scope configuration

2. The **Advanced** tab can be skipped so let's look at the parameters that need to be configured. Here, the IT admin specifies the tag name and value and the backup policy that will be used in the policy.

Figure 10.17 – Policy parameters

3. The next tab is to configure the remediation. Here, the option is to create a remediation task that will configure all existing session hosts in scope with the selected existing managed identity. This identity is specifically for this backup policy. Make sure that this managed identity is assigned to the session hosts, or the backup policy won't work. There is a built-in policy to assign the managed identity to the session hosts. However, at the time of writing this book, this is still in preview: **[Preview]: Assign Built-In User-Assigned Managed Identity to Virtual Machines**.

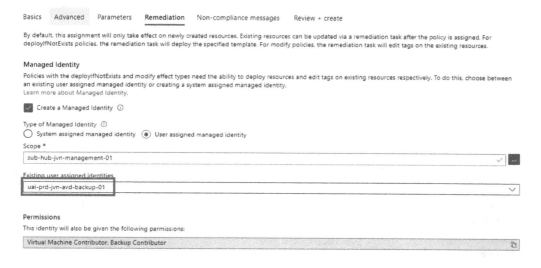

Figure 10.18 – Backup policy remediation

4. The last step is to review and create the policy.

The IT admin can check the status of the backup in **Backup center** > **Backup instances**.

Figure 10.19 – Backup instances

Restoring session hosts

Now that the IT admin has configured the recovery services vault, configured the backup, and a backup has been done, it's time to recover a session host. This might be needed when, for example, the OS is corrupt or if the host has been compromised with ransomware. Let's look at the steps:

1. To restore a session host, go to **Backup center** > **Backup instances** and select **Restore**.

Figure 10.20 – Backup center Restore option

2. To start the restore, click **Select backup instance**, choose the virtual machine that needs to be restored, and click **Select**.

Figure 10.21 – Choosing the virtual machine instance

3. On the next screen, the IT admin can review the vault and session host.

Home > Backup center | Backup instances >

Start: Restore   ...

Datasource type	Azure Virtual machines
Vault type	Recovery Services vault
Backup instance *	vdh-prd-jvn-04 Select backup instance
Vault	rsv-prd-jvn-avd-02

ⓘ The selected vault is not enabled with Cross Region Restore (CRR) hence restore in secondary region is not

Restore Region   ● Primary Region
                  ○ Secondary Region

Continue   Cancel

Figure 10.22 – Selecting the backup instance

4. Now, the IT admin needs to select the restore point that they want to use and click **OK**.

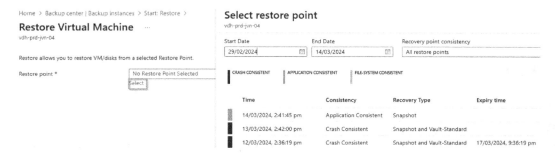

Figure 10.23 – Selecting the restore point

5. The last step is to choose whether the current machine needs to be replaced or to create a new session host. When choosing to replace it, the IT admin needs to select the storage account and select **Restore**.

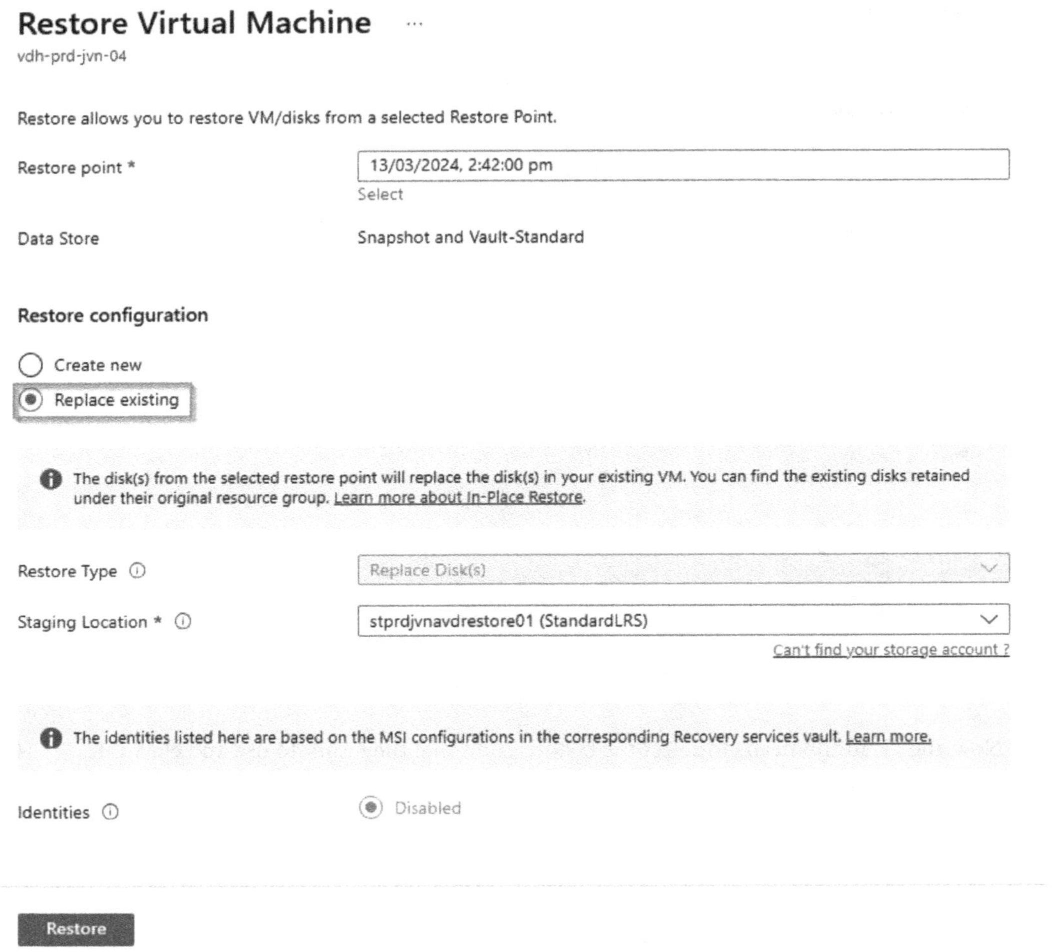

Restore Virtual Machine   ...
vdh-prd-jvn-04

Restore allows you to restore VM/disks from a selected Restore Point.

Restore point *	13/03/2024, 2:42:00 pm
	Select
Data Store	Snapshot and Vault-Standard

Restore configuration

○ Create new
◉ Replace existing

ℹ The disk(s) from the selected restore point will replace the disk(s) in your existing VM. You can find the existing disks retained under their original resource group. Learn more about In-Place Restore.

Restore Type ⓘ	Replace Disk(s) ⌄
Staging Location * ⓘ	stprdjvnavdrestore01 (StandardLRS) ⌄
	Can't find your storage account ?

ℹ The identities listed here are based on the MSI configurations in the corresponding Recovery services vault. Learn more.

Identities ⓘ	◉ Disabled

Restore

Figure 10.24 – Selecting the restore options

6. Make sure the session host is deallocated when trying to perform a restore. If the session host is running, an error will be displayed.

Figure 10.25 – Restore error message

7. When successfully triggered, the restore will be visible in **Backup center** > **Backup jobs**.

Figure 10.26 – Backup jobs status

Now that you know how to configure the backup and perform a restore for the personal AVD session host, let's move on to securing FSLogix by creating a backup for the Azure file share.

Backup policy for FSLogix

Besides protecting the session hosts, IT admins can also protect the file share where the FSLogix user profiles are located. These can be located on Azure NetApp Files and Azure Files. In this example, we will take a look at Azure Files. This could be useful in case the profile gets corrupt and the users have done many customizations to their profile. To start configuring the backup, the IT admin needs to create a separate backup policy in the Backup center. Let's go through the steps:

1. The first step is to choose the data source (which, in this case, is **Azure Files**) and the vault and click **Continue**.

Home > Backup center | Backup policies >

Start: Create Policy ···

Datasource type	Azure Files (Azure Storage) ⌄
Vault type	Recovery Services vault
Vault *	rsv-prd-jvn-avd-02 Select vault

Figure 10.27 – Choosing the data source type Files storage

2. Let's give the policy a name according to the organization's naming convention and configure the amount of backup and retention. The settings in the following figure are an example.

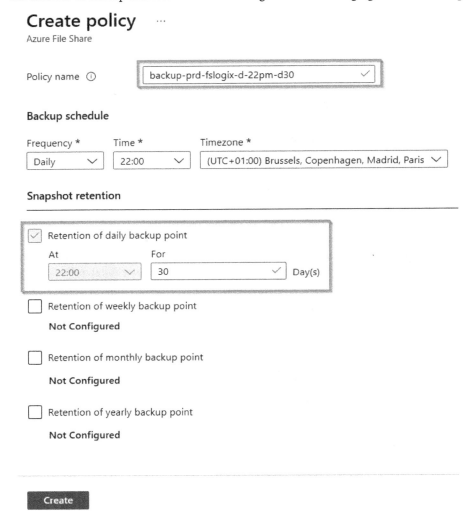

Create policy ...
Azure File Share

Policy name ⓘ

backup-prd-fslogix-d-22pm-d30 ✓

Backup schedule

Frequency *   Time *   Timezone *

Daily ∨   22:00 ∨   (UTC+01:00) Brussels, Copenhagen, Madrid, Paris ∨

Snapshot retention

☑ Retention of daily backup point

At   For

22:00 ∨   30 ✓ | Day(s)

☐ Retention of weekly backup point

Not Configured

☐ Retention of monthly backup point

Not Configured

☐ Retention of yearly backup point

Not Configured

Create

Figure 10.28 – Creating the FSLogix backup schedule

3. The next step after creating the backup policy is to configure the backup of the file share in **Backup center**. The first step is to configure the backup and choose the **Datasource type** and **Vault** options.

Start: Configure Backup ⋯

Datasource type

Select the datasource type for which you want to configure backup. To understand capabilities and limitations of supported datasource types refer here.

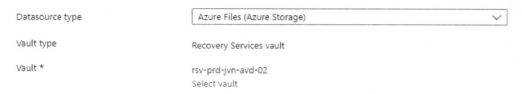

Datasource type   Azure Files (Azure Storage)   ⌄

Vault type   Recovery Services vault

Vault *   rsv-prd-jvn-avd-02
                                        Select vault

Figure 10.29 – Configuring the backup

4. Select the storage account, file share, and backup policy, and select **Enable backup**, as shown in the following figure. It will register to the Recovery Services vault.

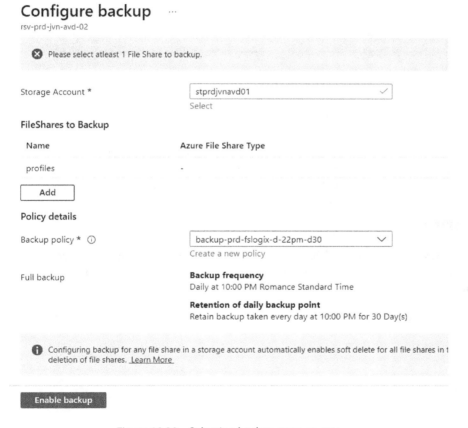

Configure backup ⋯
rsv-prd-jvn-avd-02

> ⊗ Please select atleast 1 File Share to backup.

Storage Account *   stprdjvnavd01   ✓
                             Select

FileShares to Backup

Name	Azure File Share Type
profiles	-

[Add]

Policy details

Backup policy * ⓘ   backup-prd-fslogix-d-22pm-d30   ⌄
                            Create a new policy

Full backup   **Backup frequency**
                          Daily at 10:00 PM Romance Standard Time

                          Retention of daily backup point
                          Retain backup taken every day at 10:00 PM for 30 Day(s)

> ⓘ Configuring backup for any file share in a storage account automatically enables soft delete for all file shares in t deletion of file shares. Learn More

[Enable backup]

Figure 10.30 – Selecting backup components

After enabling the backup, the IT admin can view the status of the Azure Files backup in the Backup center.

Figure 10.31 – Backup center backup status configured

The IT admin can also check the status of the backup to see whether there are any issues with it. In this example, we see that the backup is completed. To view this, you need to set **Datasource type** to **Azure Files**.

Figure 10.32 – Backup center backup status completed

Now that the FSLogix backup is configured, let's see how to restore an FSLogix profile.

Restoring an FSLogix profile

In the previous section, you have learned how to configure the backup for the storage account where the FSLogix profiles are located. In case of an issue, the backup can be restored to either the full file share or from an individual profile. Let's see how to do this:

1. Go to **Backup center** > **Backup instances** > **Select storage account and file share** > **File Recovery**.

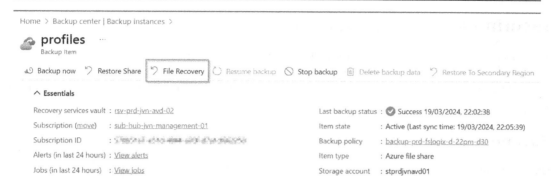

Figure 10.33 – Restoring FSLogix

2. Now, the IT admin needs to select the restore point and whether to restore at the original location or an alternate location. Using the **Add File** button, the IT admin can select the FSLogix profile and the . vhd file from the impacted user. When done, they need to press **Select** and **Restore**.

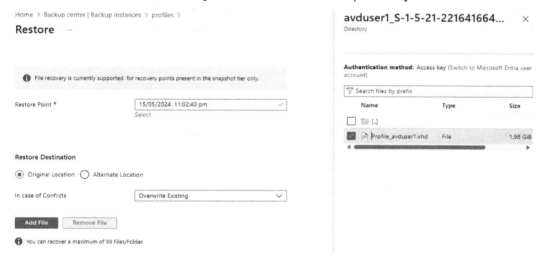

Figure 10.34 – Selecting the restore point for .vhd file

This concludes the section about securing AVD with the help of Azure Backup. We will now learn how private endpoints help to secure an AVD environment.

Securing AVD with private endpoints

In this section, we will learn how to further secure the AVD environment. By default, AVD components such as host pools and workspaces are deployed with public access. With the help of private endpoints, it's possible to restrict public access, but it works differently for both components. Let's first look at host pools and their options.

Host pool private endpoints

The IT admin can choose how to make the host pool(s) private. The options are as follows:

- **Enable public access from all networks**
- **Enable public access for end users, use private access for session hosts**
- **Disable public access and use private access**

Go to the Azure portal and the AVD portal and select the host pool to configure for private access. On the **Networking** tab, the IT admin can select the preferred option. Note that these private endpoints can also be configured from Private Link Center. Private Link Center is where you can manage all private endpoints and links.

Figure 10.35 – Host pool Networking

The first way to make the host pool private is to allow end users to connect publicly but to use private access for the session host, as you can see in the preceding figure. This means that the session hosts won't use the public internet to contact the AVD infrastructure such as gateway or broker but will use the private connection instead. When choosing this option, the IT admin needs to create a private endpoint.

Let's look at the steps that are needed to enable private access for the session hosts:

1. The first step is to select the resource group, name of the private endpoint, network interface name, and region. In this example, we have used a resource group dedicated to these private endpoints.

Create a private endpoint   ···

1 Basics   ② Resource   ③ Virtual Network   ④ DNS   ⑤ Tags   ⑥ Review + create

Use private endpoints to privately connect to a service or resource. Your private endpoint must be in the same region as your virtual network, but can be in a different region from the private link resource that you are connecting to. Learn more ☐

Project details

Subscription * ①	sub-hub-jvn-management-01 ⌄
Resource group * ①	rg-prd-jvn-avd-privatelink-01 ⌄
	Create new

Instance details

Name *	pe-01-vdpool-prd-jvn-avd-01 ✓
Network Interface Name *	nic-01-pe-01-vdpool-prd-jvn-avd-01 ✓
Region *	West Europe ⌄

Figure 10.36 – Private endpoint name details

2. In the **Resource** tab, the IT admin needs to select an option for **Target sub-resource**. For a host pool, there is one: the **connection** sub-resource.

Create a private endpoint   ···

✓ Basics   **2 Resource**   ③ Virtual Network   ④ DNS   ⑤ Tags   ⑥ Review + create

Private Link offers options to create private endpoints for different Azure resources, like your private link service, a SQL server, or an Azure storage account. Select which resource you would like to connect to using this private endpoint. Learn more ☐

Subscription	sub-hub-jvn-management-01 (578b51a7-e51d-4844-a70f-d7a1cf662250)
Resource type	Microsoft.DesktopVirtualization/hostpools
Resource	vdpool-prd-jvn-avd-01
Target sub-resource * ①	connection ⌄

Figure 10.37 – Private endpoint sub-resource

3. The **Virtual Network** tab is important because, here, the IT admin decides in which subnet the private endpoint will be. It's recommended to create a separate subnet for these private endpoints because some resources require more than one. This way, you can group all these resources and the IT admin doesn't lose any space in the session hosts subnet. For this private endpoint, four IPs are required, as can be seen in the following figure. To continue, select **Dynamically allocate IP address** and let Azure work its magic.

✓ Basics   ✓ Resource   ❸ **Virtual Network**   ④ DNS   ⑤ Tags   ⑥ Review + create

Networking

To deploy the private endpoint, select a virtual network subnet. Learn more ☐
Virtual network ⓘ | vnet-prd-jvn-avd-we-01 (rg-prd-jvn-avd-networking-01)   ⌄ |

Subnet * ⓘ | snet-prd-jvn-avd-privatelink-01   ⌄ |

Network policy for private endpoints   Disabled (edit)

Private IP configuration

○ Dynamically allocate IP address
◉ Statically allocate IP address

Member Name	Name	Private IP
broker		
diagnostics		
gateway-ring-map		
web		

Application security group

Configure network security as a natural extension of an application's structure. ASG allows you to group virtual machines and define network security policies based on those groups. You can specify an application security group as the source or destination in an NSG security rule Learn more ☐

+ Create

Application security group

| ⌄ |

Figure 10.38 – Private endpoint subnet

4. Before adding the necessary tags, the IT admin needs to configure the DNS integration. This can be done in two ways:

    •   Create a DNS zone on the domain controller and create a conditional forwarder to Azure DNS 168.63.129.16

    •   Create a private DNS zone in Azure

In this example, the IT admin creates a private DNS zone in the hub resource group for DNS.

✓ Basics   ✓ Resource   ✓ Virtual Network   **④ DNS**   ⑤ Tags   ⑥ Review + create

Private DNS integration

To connect privately with your private endpoint, you need a DNS record. We recommend that you integrate your private endpoint with a private DNS zone. You can also utilize your own DNS servers or create DNS records using the host files on your virtual machines. Learn more ☐
Integrate with private DNS zone   ● Yes ○ No

Configuration name	Subscription	Resource group	Private DNS zone
privatelink-wvd-microsoft...	sub-hub-jvn-manage... ⌄	rg-hub-jvn-dns-01 ⌄	privatelink.wvd.microsoft....

Figure 10.39 – DNS settings

5. The final step is to add the tags, review the settings, and click on **Create**.

✓ Basics   ✓ Resource   ✓ Virtual Network   ✓ DNS   **⑤ Tags**   ⑥ Review + create

Tags are name/value pairs that enable you to categorize resources and view consolidated billing by applying the same tag to multiple resources and resource groups. Learn more about tags ☐

Note that if you create tags and then change resource settings on other tabs, your tags will be automatically updated.

Name ⓘ	Value ⓘ	Resource	
Costcenter	: IT	All resources	🗑
Critical	: Yes	All resources	🗑
Solution	: PrivateEndpoint	All resources	🗑
Environment	: Prd	2 selected ⌄	🗑
	:	2 selected ⌄	

Figure 10.40 – Private endpoint tags

6. A really important step when a **Network Security Group** (**NSG**) or firewall is in use is to block the public traffic to the **WindowsVirtualDesktop** service tag. If the IT admin configured a rule to allow the traffic, they now need to deny that traffic, as shown in the following figure. This way, the IT admin makes sure that the traffic to that service tag doesn't go through the internet but through the private endpoint.

1000	Allow_443_WindowsVirtualDesktop_Outbound	443	TCP	VirtualNetwork	WindowsVirtualDesktop	⊗ Deny

Figure 10.41 – NSG deny rule AVD

After configuring the private endpoint for the host pool, it's time to do the same for the workspace.

Workspace private endpoints

The second option to use private endpoints for AVD is to make the access for users private. For this, we need to change the **Networking** settings of the workspace and set it as **Disable public access and use private access**, and save it.

Figure 10.42 – Workspace networking

The private endpoints can also be created in **Private Link Center**.

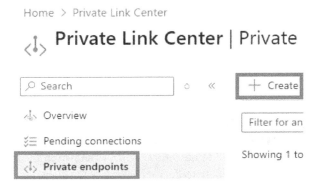

Figure 10.43 – Creating private endpoints in Private Link Center

Let's have a look at the steps that are needed to create the private endpoint in **Private Link Center**:

1. The first step is the same as with the host pool, so choose a name, network interface name, resource group, and region.

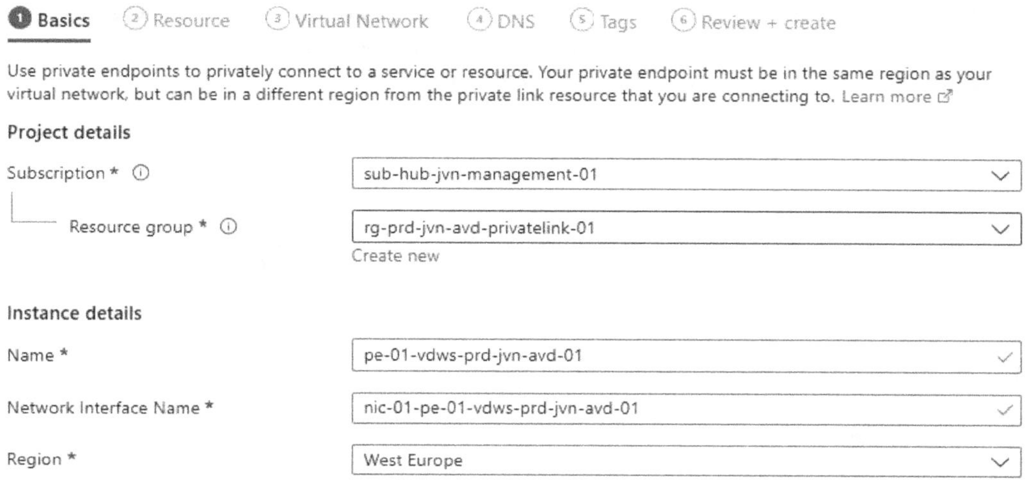

1 Basics   ② Resource   ③ Virtual Network   ④ DNS   ⑤ Tags   ⑥ Review + create

Use private endpoints to privately connect to a service or resource. Your private endpoint must be in the same region as your virtual network, but can be in a different region from the private link resource that you are connecting to. Learn more ☐

Project details

Subscription * ⓘ

```
sub-hub-jvn-management-01                                          ∨
```

Resource group * ⓘ

```
rg-prd-jvn-avd-privatelink-01                                     ∨
```
Create new

Instance details

Name *

```
pe-01-vdws-prd-jvn-avd-01                                         ✓
```

Network Interface Name *

```
nic-01-pe-01-vdws-prd-jvn-avd-01                                  ✓
```

Region *

```
West Europe                                                       ∨
```

Figure 10.44 – Choosing a private endpoint workspace name

2. The second part of the creation is to choose the correct workspace and the sub-resource. For the workspace sub-resource, the IT admin can choose either **feed** or **global**. Let's choose **feed** for this one and look at **global** later.

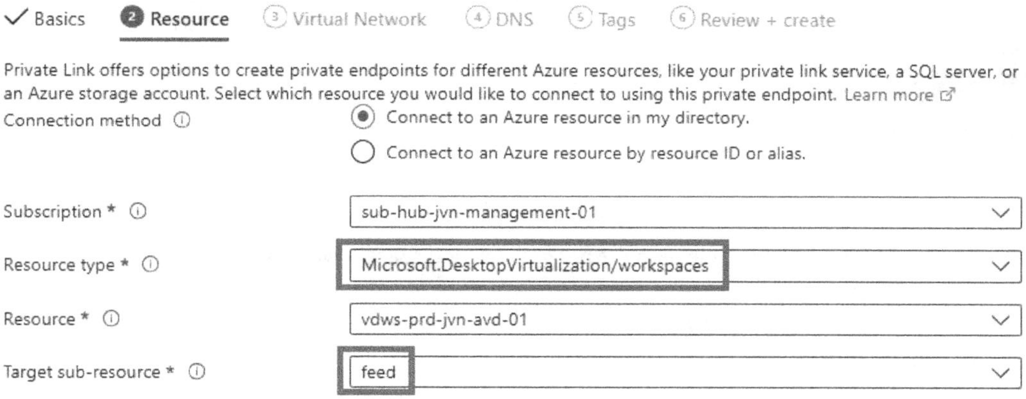

✓ Basics   **2 Resource**   ③ Virtual Network   ④ DNS   ⑤ Tags   ⑥ Review + create

Private Link offers options to create private endpoints for different Azure resources, like your private link service, a SQL server, or an Azure storage account. Select which resource you would like to connect to using this private endpoint. Learn more ☐

Connection method ⓘ   ⦿ Connect to an Azure resource in my directory.

                             ◯ Connect to an Azure resource by resource ID or alias.

Subscription * ⓘ

```
sub-hub-jvn-management-01                                          ∨
```

Resource type * ⓘ

```
Microsoft.DesktopVirtualization/workspaces                        ∨
```

Resource * ⓘ

```
vdws-prd-jvn-avd-01                                                ∨
```

Target sub-resource * ⓘ

```
feed                                                              ∨
```

Figure 10.45 – Selecting the workspace

3. In the **Virtual Network** tab, the IT admin chooses the separate dedicated subnet for private endpoints. When selecting *static*, you will see that two more IPs will be used for this private endpoint. It is recommended to use the *dynamic* option.

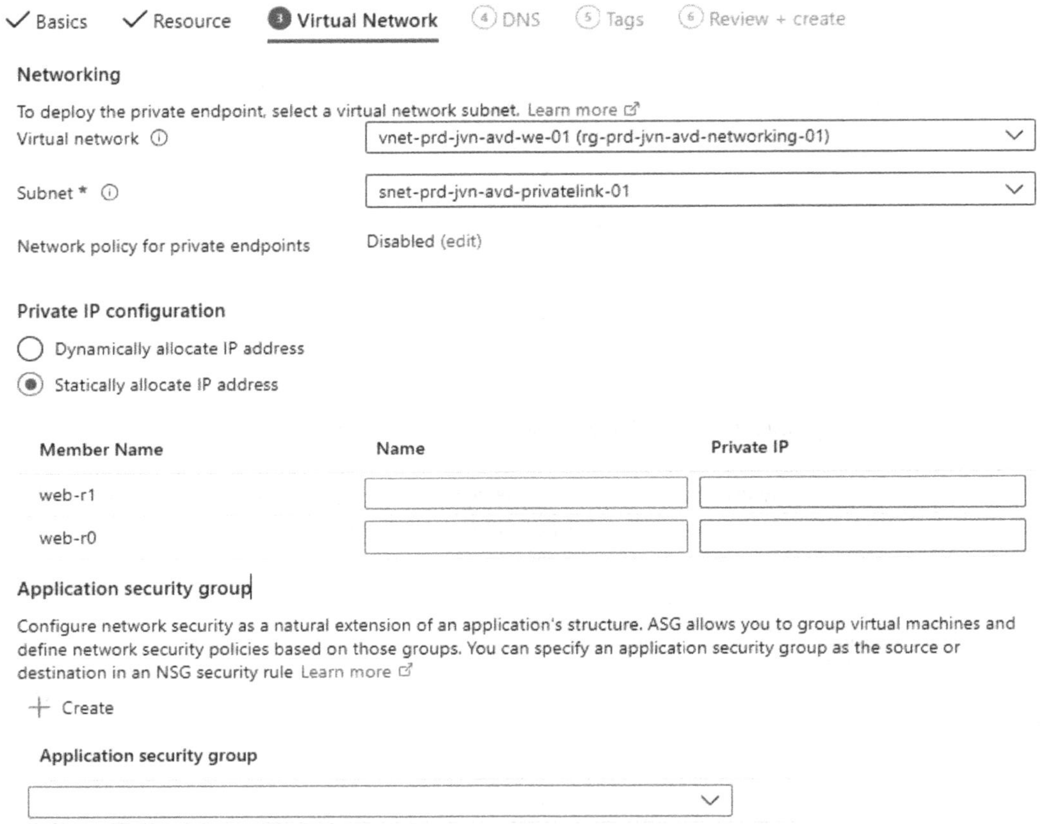

Figure 10.46 – Selecting the network for workspace private endpoint

4. The final important step is to choose the DNS integration. The IT admin chooses the DNS zone in the hub.

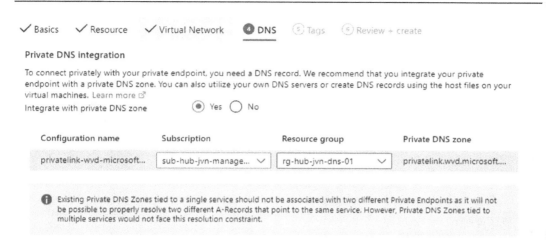

Figure 10.47 – Selecting the DNS zone

5. Let's add the necessary tag and then click on **Review + create**.

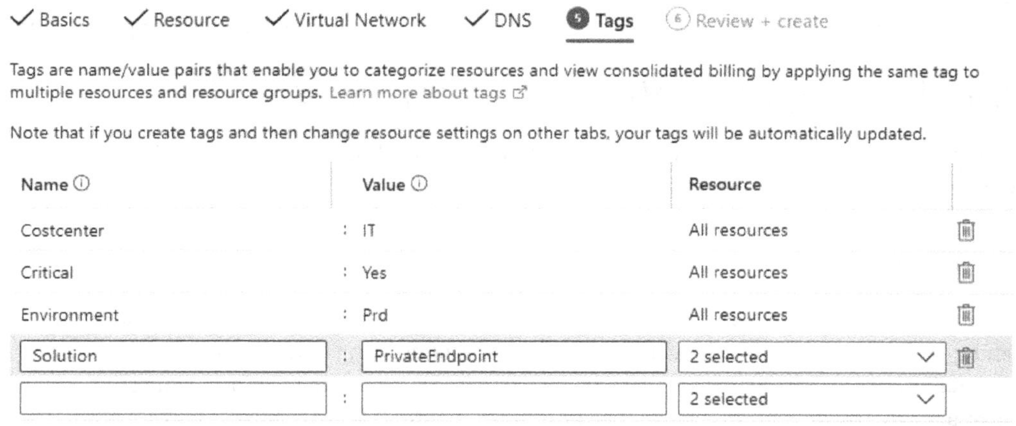

Figure 10.48 – Workspace private endpoint tag

As already mentioned, there is a second sub-resource for the workspace private endpoint. It's recommended to create a separate workspace for the **global** workspace sub-resource. Be aware that when doing this, all workspace discoveries will be made private.

It is really important that after making the workspace private, you need to change the network settings from the host pool to **Disable public access and use private access**.

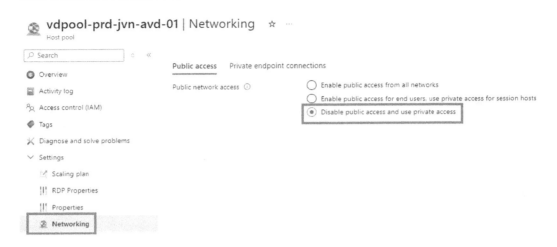

Figure 10.49 – Host pool private access

It is also very important to know that when the IT admin disables public access, the end users must be connected to the private network. This can be done with an S2S VPN, ExpressRoute, or with the use of a P2S VPN tunnel. Next to this, the IT admin has to make sure that DNS is working correctly.

Trusted launch and confidential computing

As well as securing the software, network, and OS layer, the IT admin also needs to think about the hardware layer. Luckily, Microsoft provides several options to achieve this.

Trusted launch

Trusted launch is offered on Gen 2 Azure virtual machines. It offers several security enhancements that can be enabled separately. When starting the process of creating a new Azure virtual machine in the portal, the trusted launch is automatically selected. However, the IT admin can select which options to activate. By default, **Enable secure boot** and **Enable vTPM** are selected, as shown in the following figure.

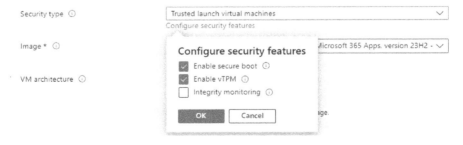

Figure 10.50 – Configuring trusted launch

Let's discuss what each option does:

- **Enable secure boot**: This feature will protect the virtual machine from rootkits that overwrite the firmware, boot kits that replace the OS bootloader, kernel rootkits that replace a piece of the OS kernel, and driver rootkits that replace drivers on the OS.

- **Enable vTPM**: vTPM is available and is a virtualized version of a hardware-trusted platform module. This vTPM is also compliant with the TPM2.0 spec.

- **Integrity monitoring**: When this last option is enabled, an extension is installed on the virtual machine. With this extension installed, Defender for Cloud can remotely validate whether your virtual machine has booted in a healthy way. There will be a low severity recommendation visible in Defender for Cloud when this extension is not installed.

Home > Microsoft Defender for Cloud | Recommendations > Guest Attestation extension should be installed on supported Windows virtual machines >

Guest Attestation extension should be installed on supported Windows virtual machines ...

⊘ Exempt   ⊙ Enforce   ☑ View policy definition   ⚡ Open query

Severity | Freshness interval
| Low | 🕐 **30 Min**

∧ Description

Install Guest Attestation extension on supported virtual machines to allow Microsoft Defender for Cloud to proactively attest and monitor the boot integrity. Once installed, boot integrity

∧ Related recommendations (3)

Recommendation ↑↓	Dependency type ↑↓	Affected resources ↑↓
☲ Secure Boot should be enabled on supported Windows virtual machines	Prerequisite	1 of 7
☲ vTPM should be enabled on supported virtual machines	Prerequisite	1 of 7
☲ Virtual machines guest attestation status should be healthy	Dependent	None

∨ Remediation steps

∧ Affected resources

Unhealthy resources (3)   Healthy resources (0)   Not applicable resources (0)

▽ Search virtual machines

	Name ↑↓	Subscription	Owner ↑↓	Due date	Status ↑↓	Last change date
☐	🖥 vm-prd-mgmt-01	sub-hub-jvn-management-01				05/01/2024, 14:11:05
☐	🖥 vdh-prd-jvn-01	sub-hub-jvn-management-01				22/03/2024, 18:20:42
☐	🖥 ima-prd-jvn-01	sub-hub-jvn-management-01				16/05/2024, 17:02:00

Figure 10.51 – Defender for Cloud recommendation

The IT admin can make sure that this is enabled on all session hosts by assigning a built-in policy to the AVD subscription. At the time of writing this book, the policy is in preview.

Figure 10.52 – Guest attestation extension policy

It is important to know that the security type can be changed from **Standard** to **Trusted launch virtual machines** for existing machines when the machine is stopped and deallocated. Be aware that the virtual machine needs to be a Gen 2 machine for this.

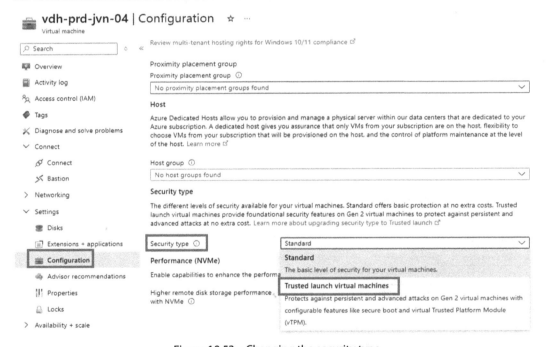

Figure 10.53 – Changing the security type

When choosing **Trusted launch virtual machines**, the IT admin can choose which options to turn on.

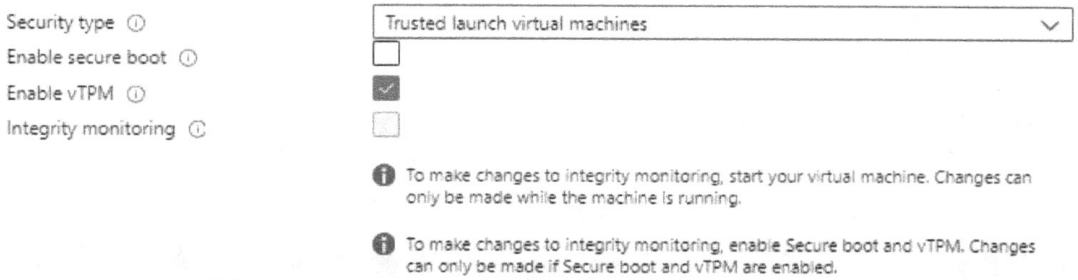

Figure 10.54 – Trusted launch options

It's important to know that when the IT admin deploys a session host based on a golden image, this golden image is also created with the trusted launch security type.

Now that you know the benefits of using trusted launch and how to activate it, it's time to look at confidential virtual machines.

Confidential computing

In Azure, the storage and traffic can be encrypted. When using confidential computing, the data that is in use can also be encrypted. The Azure *Dcasv5* and *Ecasv5* virtual machines series have a **Trusted Execution Environment** (**TEE**) that features SEV-SNP security capabilities from AMD. This TEE denies the hypervisor from accessing the virtual machine's memory and state. Besides AMD, the IT admin can also use Intel-powered virtual machines. The DCesv5 and ECesv5 series utilize the **Intel Trust Domain Extensions** (**Intel TDX**).

Since July 2023, the IT admin can create AVD session hosts on confidential computing hardware. This can be done in the Azure portal or with Infrastructure as Code.

There are two options to deploy confidential session hosts for the OS disk encryption:

- OS disk encryption using a **Platform-Managed Key** (**PMK**)
- OS disk encryption using a **Customer-Managed Key** (**CMK**)

If the organization has a requirement to use its own key, then there are a few more resources to create before deploying the session hosts:

- Azure Key Vault with Premium SKU and purge protection enabled
- Azure Key Vault key with the CVM confidential operation policy
- Disk encryption set with Key Vault key associated
- Access policy for the disk encryption set on the Key Vault
- Optionally, an Azure Key Vault-managed HSM

Before the IT admin can deploy confidential session hosts, they first need to give the confidential VM service principal access to the tenant. This is done using the following command in Cloud Shell or with Azure PowerShell:

```
Connect-AzureAD -Tenant "your tenant ID"
New-AzureADServicePrincipal -AppId bf7b6499-ff71-4aa2-97a4-
f372087be7f0 -DisplayName "Confidential VM Orchestrator"
```

When the command is run, the IT admin will see the outcome of the command.

Figure 10.55 – Confidential VM orchestrator command

To deploy, in the Azure portal, go to **Azure Virtual Desktop** > **Host pool** > **Session hosts** and click on **+ Add**. It's required to have a valid registration key before you can add a session host to a host pool. If there is no registration key, then the IT admin will see an error telling them to generate one.

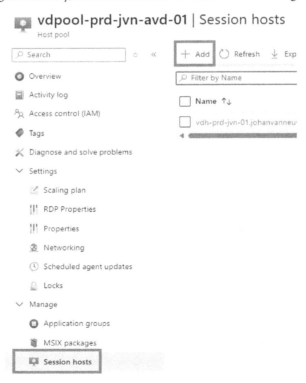

Figure 10.56 – Adding a confidential session host

When selecting **Confidential virtual machines** as the security type, **Virtual machine size** will change automatically to **Standard DC2ads v5**, as shown in the following figure. However, it's still possible to choose another SKU if needed. The **Enable vTPM** option is grayed out because this is enabled by default.

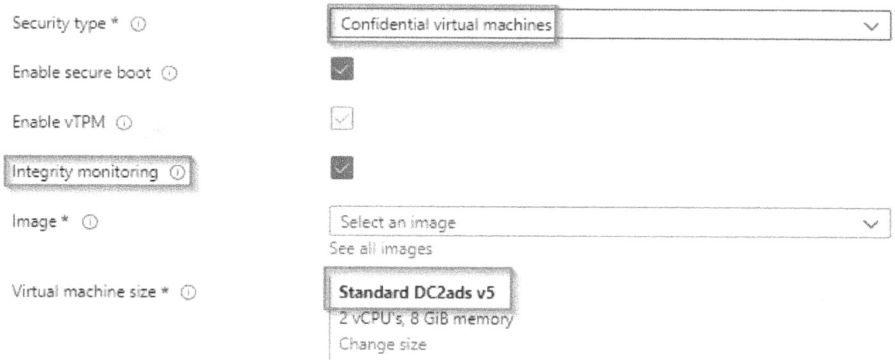

Figure 10.57 – Choosing the security type

It is important to know that the following OS types are supported for confidential computing with AVD:

- Windows 11 Enterprise 22H2
- Windows 11 Enterprise Multi-session 22h2
- Windows Server 2019 and 2022

When the session host is built, the security type is visible in the portal.

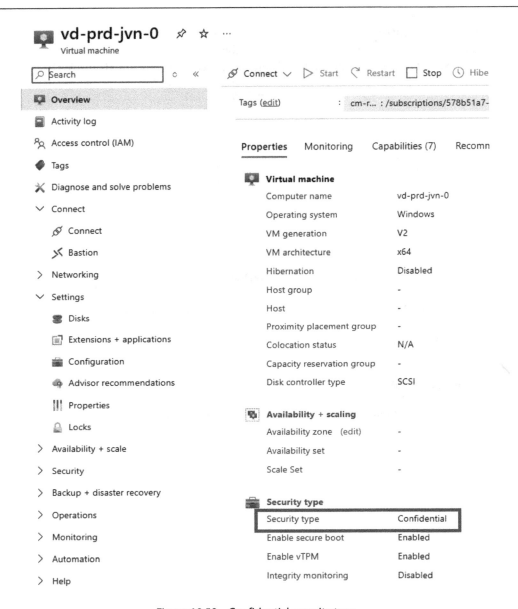

Figure 10.58 – Confidential security type

To ensure that the host pools don't mix the different security types, it's recommended to create separate host pools for each security type.

Let's continue this chapter and find out how the IT admin can prevent end users from installing applications in an AVD environment.

Configuring AppLocker

A very important aspect to secure is the applications that are running on the session hosts. It can happen that an end user needs a different kind of application than the one that is installed, so they will download and install it. When working in a pooled environment, the end user doesn't know on which session hosts they are working, so the IT admin doesn't want them to be able to install applications. To ensure that nobody can install applications on the session hosts, the IT admin can deny the end users the possibility to install applications. This is where **AppLocker** can help. With AppLocker, the IT admin can configure rules to deny end users from installing applications. Let's go to **Group Policy Management** and see how to configure this:

1. Create a new GPO and go to **Computer Configuration** > **Windows Settings** > **Security Settings** > **Application Control Policies** > **AppLocker**.

2. The first thing the IT admin does is configure the rule enforcement and turn it on for the Windows Installer rules.

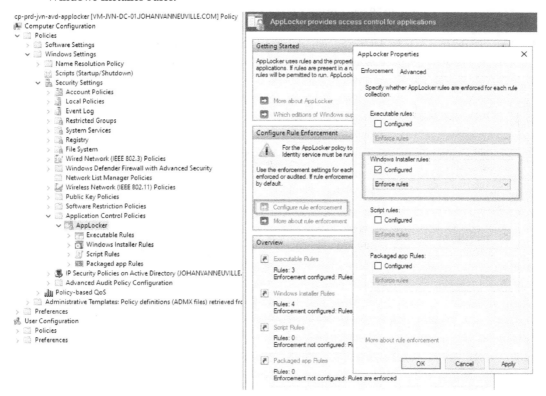

Figure 10.59 – Configuring AppLocker

3. To ensure that no end users can install any applications, the IT admin creates a new Windows Installer rule.

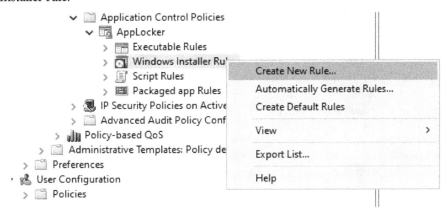

Figure 10.60 – Creating a new Windows Installer rule

4. The IT admin needs to determine whether the policy will allow or deny permission; in this case, it will deny the user in the security group from running any executable file.

Figure 10.61 – Assigning the group AppLocker policy

5. The next option is to choose how to block the end users from installing applications. Here, the IT admin chooses **Path**. This can be different in your organization. It's also possible to create a rule that blocks an application from a certain publisher or by using a file hash.

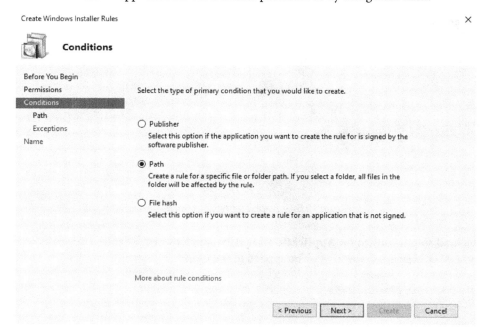

Figure 10.62 – AppLocker policy conditions

6. To make sure that the end users can't install applications on the session host, we need to block all locations where the installers might be on the session host. The IT admin can do this with **Path** configured as * . *.

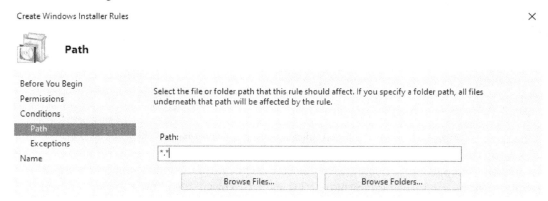

Figure 10.63 – AppLocker policy path

7. The **Exceptions** step can be skipped, and in the last step, a name needs to given for this rule.

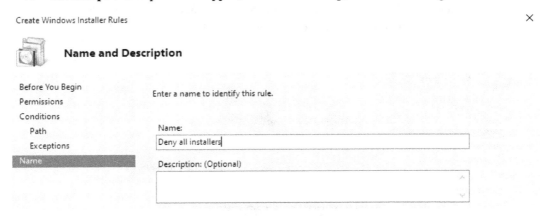

Figure 10.64 – AppLocker policy name

8. The final step is to turn on **Application Identity Services** in the **System Services** security options. Otherwise, the rule won't be applied to the users.

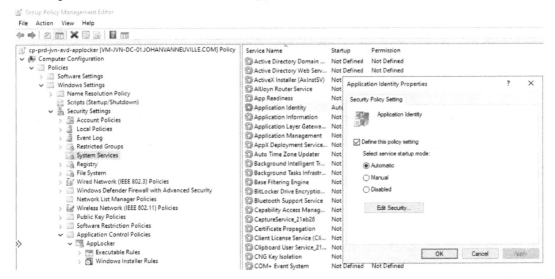

Figure 10.65 – Application Identity Properties

Now that all these settings are configured, the end user can test the policy and try to install an application. In this example, they download VLC and try to install it but it is blocked, as shown in the following figure.

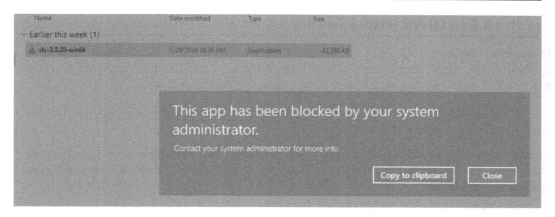

Figure 10.66 – AppLocker blocked message

With the power of AppLocker, IT admins can make sure that end users can't install software on a pooled AVD environment.

Let's continue securing AVD and have a look at how the IT admin can secure the use of OneDrive.

Securing OneDrive

One of the big advantages of using OneDrive is that end users can have access to their files from anywhere and on any device. This is no different on AVD, but to ensure that OneDrive is being used securely, the IT admin can enforce some settings. This section will cover some general settings that will increase security. Of course, it depends on the organization, and which settings they will enforce:

- **Use OneDrive Files On-Demand**
- **Silently move Windows known folders to OneDrive**
- **Prevent users from syncing personal OneDrive accounts**
- **Prevent users from syncing from other organizations**

The configuration for OneDrive can be done in two ways: with a GPO or via Intune. Both are possible for Cloud PCs and AVD session hosts.

Securing OneDrive with a GPO

To create the OneDrive GPO, the IT admin needs the correct `.admx` and `.adml` files for OneDrive. To obtain these, the IT admin needs to install OneDrive on a machine from `https://www.microsoft.com/nl-be/microsoft-365/onedrive/download`.

The `.admx` file needs to be put in the domain's central store and the `.adml` file needs to go into the appropriate language folder, such as `en-us`.

As always with a GPO, the IT admin needs to go to the **Group Policy Management** console and create a new policy. The settings that they need are in **Computer Configuration** > **Policies** > **Administrative Templates** > **OneDrive**.

Figure 10.67 – OneDrive GPO settings

Securing OneDrive with Intune

To configure these settings in Intune, the IT admin needs to create a configuration profile and use **Settings picker** to get the OneDrive settings.

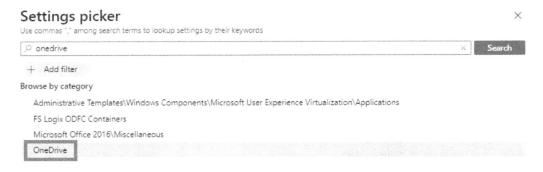

Figure 10.68 – OneDrive Settings picker

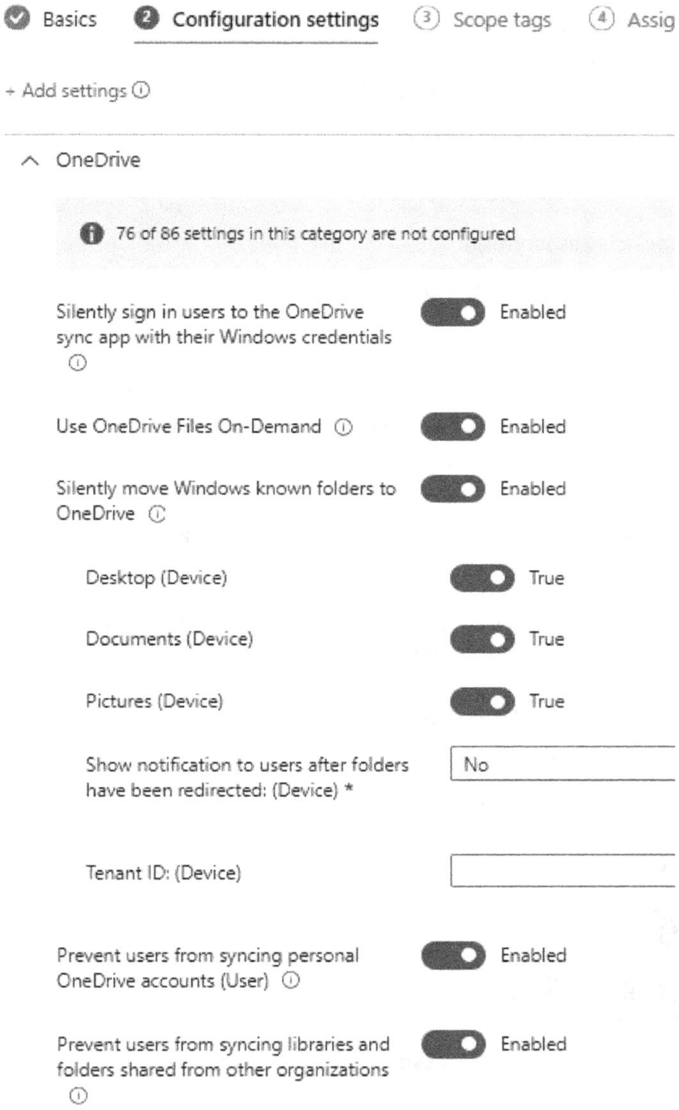

Basics   2 Configuration settings   3 Scope tags   4 Assig

+ Add settings ⓘ

∧ OneDrive

ℹ 76 of 86 settings in this category are not configured

Silently sign in users to the OneDrive   ⬤ Enabled
sync app with their Windows credentials
ⓘ

Use OneDrive Files On-Demand ⓘ   ⬤ Enabled

Silently move Windows known folders to   ⬤ Enabled
OneDrive ⓘ

Desktop (Device)   ⬤ True

Documents (Device)   ⬤ True

Pictures (Device)   ⬤ True

Show notification to users after folders   No
have been redirected: (Device) *

Tenant ID: (Device)

Prevent users from syncing personal   ⬤ Enabled
OneDrive accounts (User) ⓘ

Prevent users from syncing libraries and   ⬤ Enabled
folders shared from other organizations
ⓘ

Figure 10.69 – OneDrive settings in Intune

Currently, OneDrive is being used on a full desktop, but in 2023, Microsoft announced a public preview of OneDrive as a remote app. This will enable companies that don't want to use a full desktop to still use OneDrive. This feature is not yet production-ready because there are some prerequisites:

- Windows 11 Enterprise Multi-session version 22h2, build 25905 or later through the Insider channel
- Install OneDrive per machine on the session hosts
- Configure OneDrive as a remote app
- Host pool running in a validation environment
- The latest version of FSLogix

With the configuration of OneDrive, the IT admin has made sure that AVD and Cloud PCs are more secure, and that data loss can be minimized. Also, by using OneDrive, the end users will always have their files with them, especially in a pooled AVD environment.

Active Directory structure and security

When the IT admin creates a new session host, they have the option to connect to **Active Directory (AD)**. It is recommended that not everyone has access to these objects, so it's a good idea to have a good structure in place. This structure includes the following:

- Separated **Organizational Unit (OU)**
- Separated GPO for each environment
- Dedicated service account to domain join

Let's discuss these next.

Separated OU

It's important to limit the access to the session hosts AD objects to apply zero trust on these objects. Because of this, the IT admin can create separate OUs for each environment. This way, somebody with access to the development (`dev`) hosts doesn't have access to the production (`prd`) hosts.

In the following example, the IT admin has created a structure to organize `prd` and `dev`:

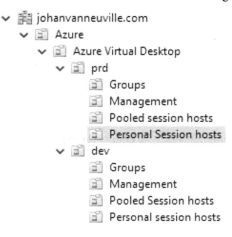

Figure 10.70 – AD structure

Separated GPO for each environment

Next to the AD structure is the active directory; it's also important to have a good structure in place for applying the settings to the session hosts. The following figure is an example of the GPO structure.

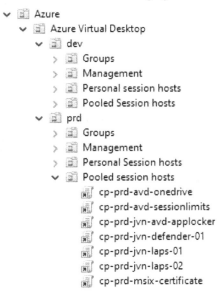

Figure 10.71 – AVD group policies

Dedicated service account to domain join

One of the most important steps during the deployment of an AD or hybrid joined device is the domain join step.

It's recommended that a separate service account be used to perform this action. This account also doesn't have other permissions in AD besides the domain join permissions. This account can also be used to configure the storage account that will be used for FSLogix or MSIX app attach. There will be more on this in *Chapter 11, Securing Azure Infrastructure*.

The following figure shows two different service accounts for the `prd` and `dev` environments.

Name	Type	Description
svc-prd-avd-01	User	AVD prd service account
svc-dev-avd-01	User	AVD dev service account

Figure 10.72 – AVD service accounts for prd and dev

To make sure that they have the minimal required permissions, the IT admin needs to delegate control in AD. The following steps need to be followed:

1. Right-click on the correct OU and select **Delegate Control…**.

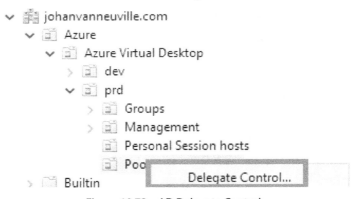

Figure 10.73 – AD Delegate Control…

2. Press **Next** on the first screen and select the correct account on the next screen.

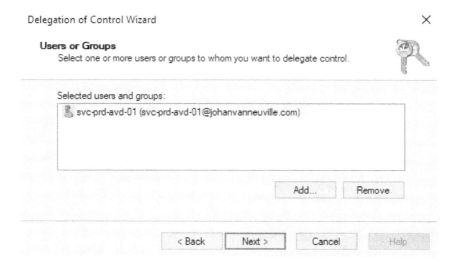

Figure 10.74 – Selecting the service account

3. Select **Create a custom task to delegate** and press **Next**.

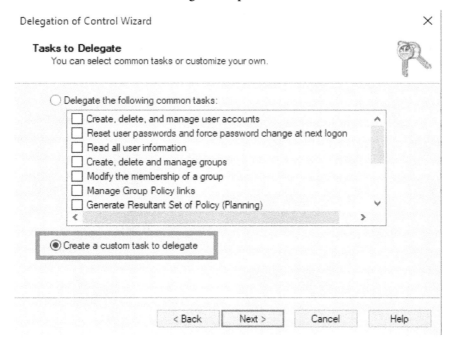

Figure 10.75 – Creating a custom task

4. In the next step, select **Computer objects**, select the two checkboxes underneath, and click **Next**.

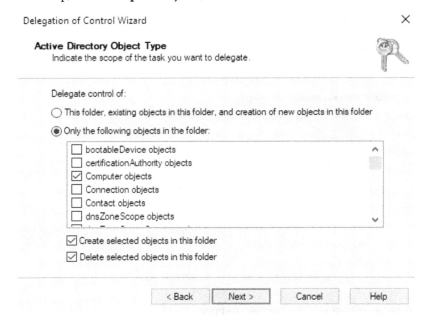

Figure 10.76 – Selecting the object type for permissions

5. In the **Permissions** section, select the required permissions to create and delete child objects. Click **Next** and finish.

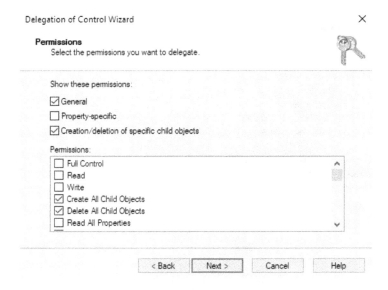

Figure 10.77 – Selecting permissions

After following these steps, the service account is ready to be used by the IT admin to domain join the session hosts. It's recommended to use separate accounts for `prd` and `dev`. This way, the environments are totally split, which adds more security.

Summary

This concludes our chapter on securing AVD where you learned different methods that can be used to secure an AVD environment, such as denying public access to the AVD service, making sure that there is a backup in place. and denying end users from installing applications on a pooled environment.

In the next chapter, we will learn how to secure the Azure platform with technologies such as firewalls, NSG, using a dedicated host, and Defender for Cloud.

11
Securing Azure Infrastructure

After securing AVD in the previous chapter, we will now learn how to configure the security of the storage for AVD with RBAC but also look at using **network security groups** (**NSGs**). Further in the chapter, we will see how to configure NSGs and firewalls to make sure that all AVD communications work, as well as see how dedicated hosts can help IT admins isolate session hosts.

This chapter covers the following topics:

- Configuring storage security
- Configuring network security with Azure Firewall
- Configuring network security with NSGs
- Deploying AVD on dedicated hosts
- Configuring Defender for Cloud for an AVD subscription
- Protection using Azure VPN gateway

Configure storage security

When working with AVD, and especially with pooled host pools, the IT admin needs to configure the storage account for FSLogix and make it secure so that only the session host can access it. This is done with the help of the following:

- RBAC roles on the storage account
- Applying the correct NTFS permissions on the file share
- Configuring private access using a private endpoint
- Configuring NSGs

Let's explore them one by one.

RBAC roles on the storage account

The first thing that needs to be configured on the storage account is the Azure permissions for the IT admins and the end users. This is done by assigning specific built-in roles on the storage account and file share. Of course, to assign these permissions, the IT admin has to create a storage account and file share first.

Be aware that in order to configure these permissions, an identity source such as Active Directory Domain Services (ADDS), Entra Domain Services, or Entra Kerberos needs to be configured.

The following permissions need to be configured for both the end users and IT admins:

- **End user permissions**: These permissions are needed on the file share where the FSLogix profiles are located. The IT admin needs to assign the **Storage File Data SMB Share Contributor** built-in role to the end users. Ideally, this is done by assigning the permission to a security group. This is done by going to the **Azure portal** > **Storage account** > **File share** > **Access Control**.

Figure 11.1 – The FSLogix user's RBAC role

- **Admin permissions**: The IT admin who needs to be able to change the permissions will get the **Storage File Data SMD Share Elevated** permission. This permission is needed to change the NTFS permissions on the file share. The permissions are assigned in the same way as the end user permissions.

Figure 11.2 – The FSLogix admin's RBAC role

Applying the correct NTFS permissions

To make FSLogix work, the IT admin also needs to assign the correct NTFS permissions to the end users. Without these permissions, no vhd(x) will be created for an end user. The vhd(x) is the virtual hard drive that contains the user profile. There are a couple of steps that need to be done first:

1. Before the IT admin can assign permission, they need to connect to the file share. This is done using a drive mapping. The **drive mapping** can easily be done using the script that is available in the Azure portal > **Storage account** > **File share** > **Connect** > **Show Script**, which you need to copy. It's recommended to use a management server for these kinds of activities.

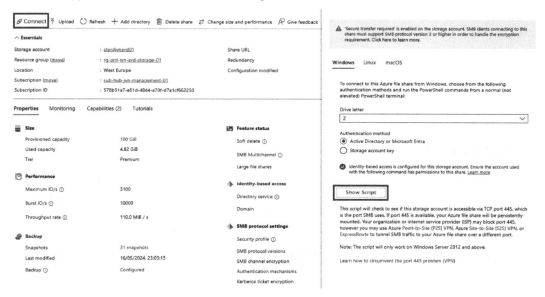

Figure 11.3 – The drive mapping script

2. When the drive mapping is done, the NFTS permissions can be set using the following script. The IT admin needs to change the mounted drive letter, the DOMAIN name, and the group name to suit the organization:

```
icacls <mounted-drive-letter>: /grant "<DOMAIN\GroupName>:(M)"
icacls <mounted-drive-letter>: /grant "Creator Owner:(OI)(CI)
(IO)(M)"
icacls <mounted-drive-letter>: /remove "Authenticated Users"
icacls <mounted-drive-letter>: /remove "Builtin\Users"
```

When both the RBAC roles and NTFS permissions are set, the users will get an FSLogix profile when logging on as an AVD session host.

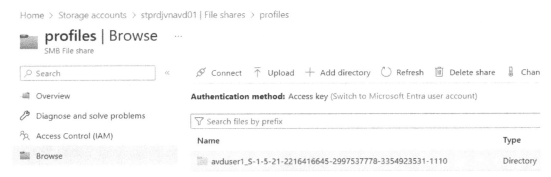

Figure 11.4 – A FSLogix profile on the file share

Let's continue the process of securing the storage account with the help of private endpoints.

Configuring private access using a private endpoint

In the past, when creating a storage account, it would be publicly accessible. Obviously, this is not OK from a security perspective. Nowadays, when you create a storage account, there is an option to create a private endpoint and connect it to the storage account. The benefit of this is that, in this case, the only resources that will have access to the storage account are the session hosts.

Let's have a look at the steps to create the private endpoint. This does require some resources to be created upfront:

- A storage account and file share for FSLogix profiles

- A dedicated subnet for private endpoints in the AVD spoke virtual network

To configure the private endpoint, the IT admin can use the Private Link Center or the **Networking** menu in the storage account. In this example, the configuration is done using the storage account **Networking** blade.

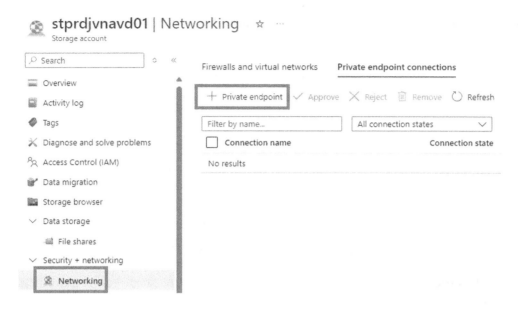

Figure 11.5 – The storage account Networking blade

Follow these steps to configure the private endpoint:

1. In the **Basics** tab, the IT admin select the correct resource group. The recommended practice is to put the resources in a dedicated resource group. The instance details are important if an organization has a strict naming convention to follow. The following figure shows an example.

Create a private endpoint   ...

① **Basics**	② Resource	③ Virtual Network	④ DNS	⑤ Tags	⑥ Review + create

Use private endpoints to privately connect to a service or resource. Your private endpoint must be in the same region as your virtual network, but can be in a different region from the private link resource that you are connecting to. Learn more

Project details

Subscription * ⓘ

> sub-hub-jvn-management-01

Resource group * ⓘ

> rg-prd-jvn-avd-privatelink-01

Create new

Instance details

Name *

> pe-01-stprdjvnavd01

Network Interface Name *

> nic-01-pe-01-stprdjvnavd01

Region *

> West Europe

Figure 11.6 – The private endpoint basics

2. The **Resource** tab is automatically filled, since the creation is done from the **Storage account** blade.

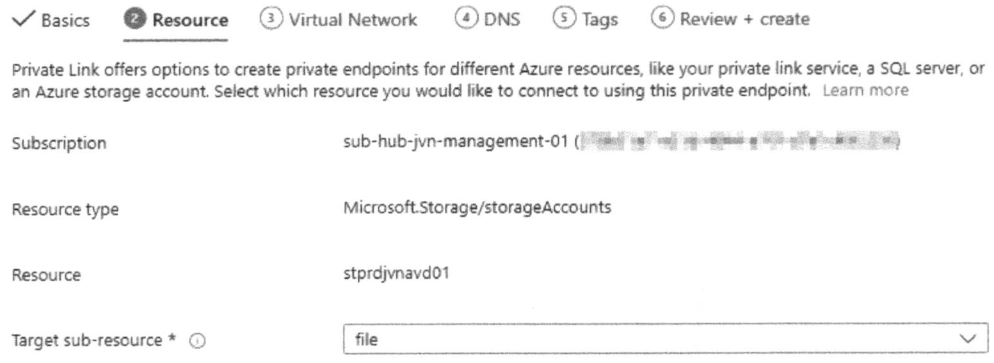

✓ Basics   ② **Resource**   ③ Virtual Network   ④ DNS   ⑤ Tags   ⑥ Review + create

Private Link offers options to create private endpoints for different Azure resources, like your private link service, a SQL server, or an Azure storage account. Select which resource you would like to connect to using this private endpoint. Learn more

Subscription	sub-hub-jvn-management-01 (▓▓▓▓▓▓▓▓▓▓▓▓▓)
Resource type	Microsoft.Storage/storageAccounts
Resource	stprdjvnavd01
Target sub-resource * ⓘ	file ⌄

Figure 11.7 – The private endpoint target resource

3. In the **Virtual Network** tab, the IT admin select the AVD virtual network and the dedicated private link subnet.

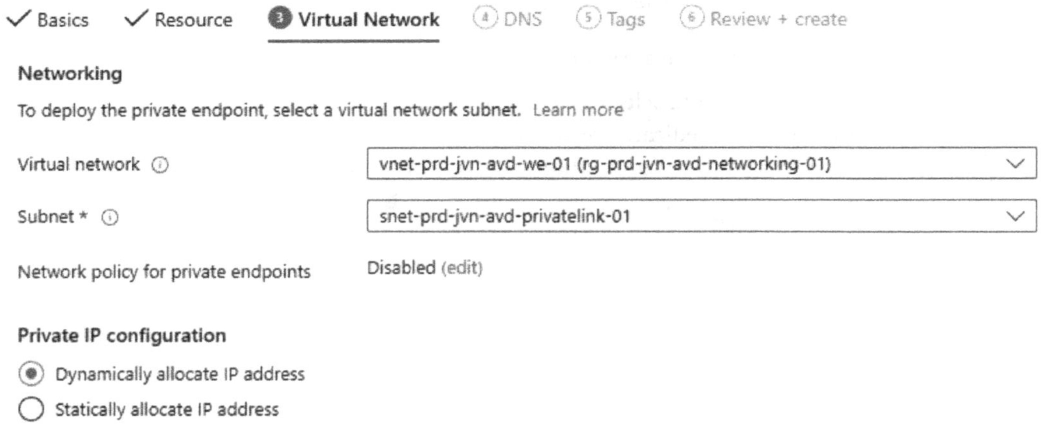

✓ Basics   ✓ Resource   ③ **Virtual Network**   ④ DNS   ⑤ Tags   ⑥ Review + create

Networking

To deploy the private endpoint, select a virtual network subnet. Learn more

Virtual network ⓘ	vnet-prd-jvn-avd-we-01 (rg-prd-jvn-avd-networking-01) ⌄
Subnet * ⓘ	snet-prd-jvn-avd-privatelink-01 ⌄
Network policy for private endpoints	Disabled (edit)

Private IP configuration

◉ Dynamically allocate IP address
○ Statically allocate IP address

Figure 11.8 – The private endpoint subnet

4. For private endpoints to work, they need to be resolvable on a network. For this, a DNS zone is required. In this example, the IT admin uses a private DNS zone in the hub DNS resource group. The private DNS zone from Microsoft has a specific naming convention and can't be changed. For Azure files, the Private DNS zone is called `privatelink.file.core.windows.net`.

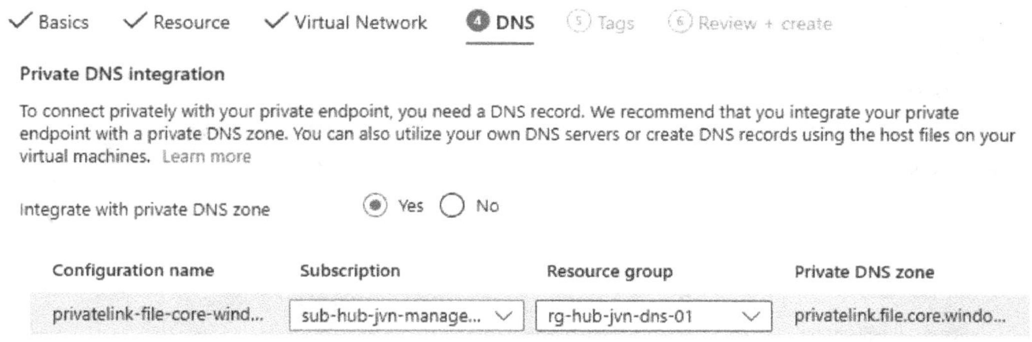

✓ Basics ✓ Resource ✓ Virtual Network ④ **DNS** ⑤ Tags ⑥ Review + create

Private DNS integration

To connect privately with your private endpoint, you need a DNS record. We recommend that you integrate your private endpoint with a private DNS zone. You can also utilize your own DNS servers or create DNS records using the host files on your virtual machines. Learn more

Integrate with private DNS zone ⦿ Yes ○ No

Configuration name	Subscription	Resource group	Private DNS zone
privatelink-file-core-wind...	sub-hub-jvn-manage... ⌄	rg-hub-jvn-dns-01 ⌄	privatelink.file.core.windo...

Figure 11.9 – A private DNS

5. Let's add some tags and review everything, and then let Azure do its magic.

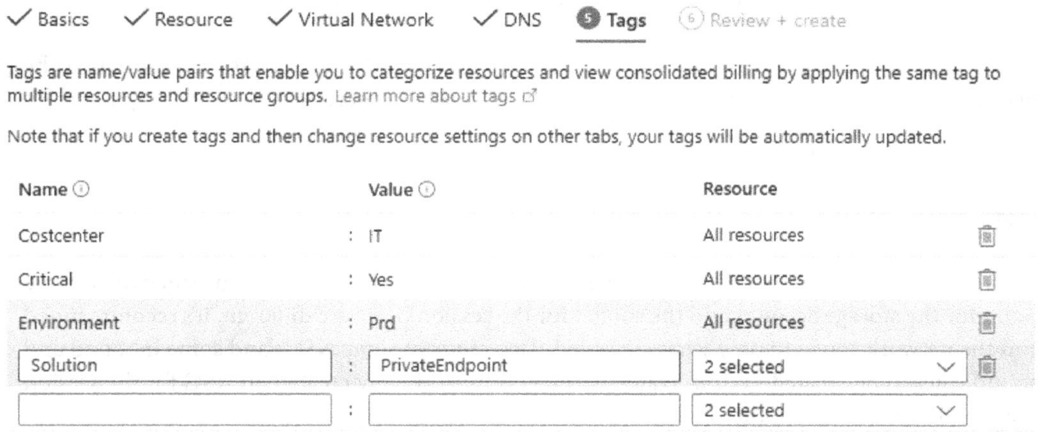

✓ Basics ✓ Resource ✓ Virtual Network ✓ DNS ⑤ **Tags** ⑥ Review + create

Tags are name/value pairs that enable you to categorize resources and view consolidated billing by applying the same tag to multiple resources and resource groups. Learn more about tags ⌕

Note that if you create tags and then change resource settings on other tabs, your tags will be automatically updated.

Name ⓘ		Value ⓘ	Resource	
Costcenter	:	IT	All resources	🗑
Critical	:	Yes	All resources	🗑
Environment	:	Prd	All resources	🗑
Solution	:	PrivateEndpoint	2 selected ⌄	🗑
	:		2 selected ⌄	

Figure 11.10 – The private endpoint tags

6. After the deployment is finished, the IT admin need to disable public access to the storage account.

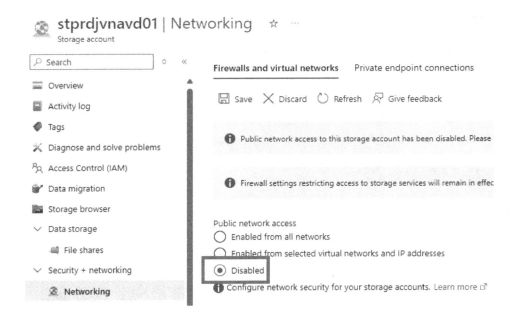

Figure 11.11 – The storage account's public access disabled

By disabling public access and enabling the private endpoint, the IT admin has made sure that the storage account is more secure and only accessible from inside the network.

Let's now see how NSGs can help add security.

Configuring NSGs

By default, communication between subnets in the same virtual network is open. Since the private endpoint for the storage account and the subnet for the session hosts are different, it's recommended to limit the network traffic to only what is needed. This requires some NSGs and some inbound and outbound rules to be created. In this example, the IT admin already created an NSG for the session hosts and will now create another for the private link subnet:

1. In the Azure portal, go to **Network security groups** and click on **Create**.

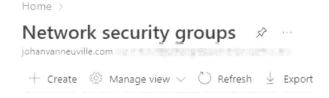

Figure 11.12 – Creating an NSG

2. The first details that need to be filled in are the resource group, the name of the NSG, and the location.

Create network security group   ···

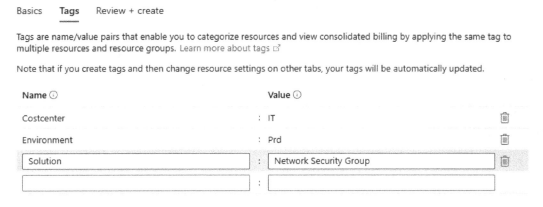

Figure 11.13 – The NSG basics

3. The last step is, again, the required tags, and then click on **Review + create**.

Create network security group   ···

Basics   **Tags**   Review + create

Tags are name/value pairs that enable you to categorize resources and view consolidated billing by applying the same tag to multiple resources and resource groups. Learn more about tags ⌕

Note that if you create tags and then change resource settings on other tabs, your tags will be automatically updated.

Name ⓘ		Value ⓘ	
Costcenter	:	IT	🗑
Environment	:	Prd	🗑
Solution	:	Network Security Group	🗑
	:		

Figure 11.14 – The NSG tags

Now that both NSGs are in place, it's time to configure the inbound and outbound security rules. To allow the traffic from the session hosts to the private endpoint, the IT admin need to allow ports 443 and 445 over the TCP protocol.

In this case, there is an outbound rule in the NSG for the session hosts to the subnet where the private endpoint is located.

Figure 11.15 – NSG rules for the FSLogix session hosts

Because the traffic is going to the private link subnet, the private link NSG also needs to have an inbound security rule for the same ports and protocol. It's also important to block all other traffic with a deny rule.

With these rules in place, only the session hosts will be able to reach the private endpoint.

Figure 11.16 – The NSG rules for the private endpoint

This concludes this section about configuring security for the storage account that is needed for AVD. We will now learn how to create and configure an Azure firewall to protect an AVD environment.

Configure network security with Azure Firewall

In this section, we will learn why it's a good idea to protect an AVD environment with the use of an Azure firewall or any other network virtual appliance, such as Checkpoint or Fortinet.

Typically, in a hub-spoke network topology, the firewall or NVA is located in the hub network. With the help of a **User Defined Route** (**UDR**), all the traffic from the AVD virtual network will be redirected to the firewall.

The first resource that the IT admin needs to create is the Azure firewall. This can be done using the Azure portal or with infrastructure as code. In this example, the firewall is deployed using PowerShell.

Before we begin, we need to make sure there are a few resources already deployed, such as the following:

- A resource group
- A hub virtual network
- `AzureFirewallSubnet` with a /26 subnet size
- `AzureFirewallManagementSubnet` with a /26 subnet size

The following figure shows a virtual network with both the firewall subnets.

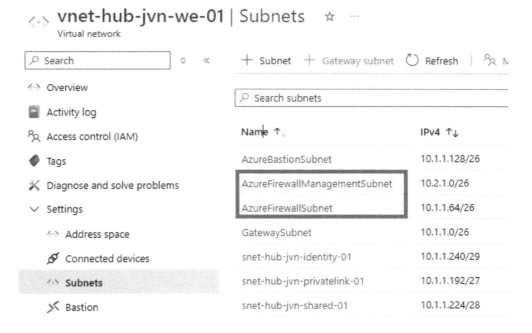

Figure 11.17 – Azure firewall subnets

Using IP groups in firewall policies

Let's say an IT admin who works in a large enterprise environment wants to make sure that it's easy to manage the different policies. It's not easy to keep track of all the separate subnets that are in use.

To alleviate this, IP groups can be used. This is an Azure resource that combines multiple IP ranges in one resource.

The following PowerShell script will deploy an IP group that contains two different AVD subnets:

```
#IPGroup
$rgnamevnetavd = "rg-prd-jvn-avd-networking-01"
$prefix = "jvn"
$region = "west europe"
$subnets = @("10.1.6.0","10.1.6.96")
$tags = @{"Environment"="Prd";"Solution"="IPGroup";"Costcenter"="IT"}
New-AzIpGroup -Name "ipg-prd-jvn-avd-01" -ResourceGroupName
$rgnamevnetavd -Location $region -IpAddress $subnets -Tag $tags
```

The following screenshot shows the outcome of running the script.

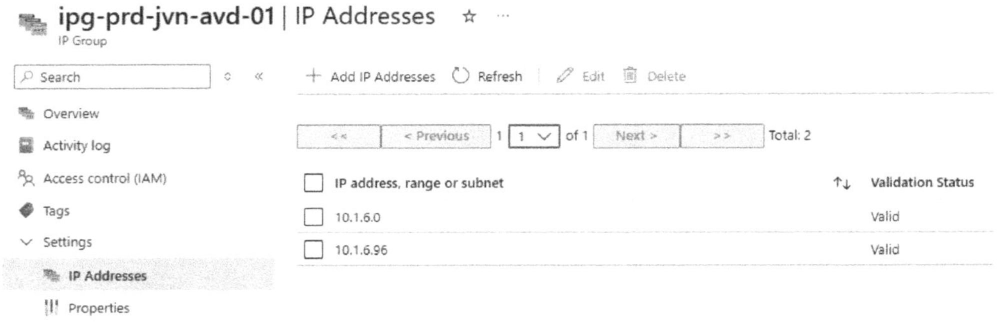

Figure 11.18 – The IP group

The next resource that needs to be created is the firewall. In Azure, there are three different SKUs available. You can find out which SKU best fits the organization at https://learn.microsoft.com/en-us/azure/firewall/choose-firewall-sku:

- Azure Firewall Basic
- Azure Firewall Standard
- Azure Firewall Premium

In this example, the IT admin will deploy the standard SKU:

```
$region = "west europe"
$rgname = "rg-hub-jvn-networking-01"
$tagspip = @
{"Environment"="Hub";"Solution"="PublicIP";"Costcenter"="IT"}

# Get a Public IP's for the firewall
```

```
$FWpip = New-AzPublicIpAddress -Name "pip-01 -hub-jvn-fw-01"
-ResourceGroupName $rgname `
  -Location $region  -AllocationMethod Static -Sku Standard
 # Get a Public IP for the firewall Management
$FWmgtpip = New-AzPublicIpAddress -Name "pip-02-hub-jvn-fw-01"
-ResourceGroupName $rgname `
  -Location $region  -AllocationMethod Static -Sku Standard -Tag
$tagspip


  # Create the firewall
$region = "west europe"
$rgname = "rg-hub-jvn-networking-01"
$tagsfw = @
{"Environment"="Hub";"Solution"="Firewall";"Costcenter"="IT"}


$Azfw = New-AzFirewall -Name "fw-hub-jvn-01" -ResourceGroupName
$rgname -Location $region -VirtualNetwork $vnet -PublicIpAddress
$FWpip -ManagementPublicIpAddress $FWmgtpip
```

After running the code, the IT admin can view the firewall in the Azure portal.

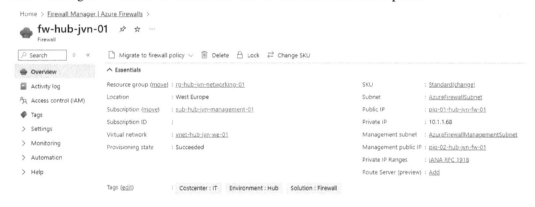

Figure 11.19 – An Azure firewall overview

Now that the firewall is in place, the IT admin needs to find a way to redirect all the AVD traffic to the firewall. This can be accomplished by using a UDR. This route will override the route that the Azure traffic normally uses. To create this UDR, the IT admin can use the following PowerShell script. It's important to change the variable to match your environment:

```
$region = "west europe"
$rgnamevnetavd = "rg-prd-jvn-avd-networking-01"
$vnetavd = "vnet-prd-jvn-avd-01"
$routetable = New-AzRouteTable -Name "udr-prd-jvn-avd-01"
-resourcegroupname $rgnamevnetavd -Location $region
```

```
$subnets = "0.0.0.0/0"
Get-AzRouteTable `
  -ResourceGroupName $rgnamevnetavd `
  -Name "udr-prd-jvn-avd-01" `
  | Add-AzRouteConfig `
  -Name "route-avd" `
  -AddressPrefix $subnets `
  -NextHopType "VirtualAppliance" `
  -NextHopIpAddress $AzfwPrivateIP `
  | Set-AzRouteTable
```

The last thing that the IT admin needs to do is to assign the UDR with the AVD subnets containing the session hosts:

```
vnetavd = Get-AzVirtualNetwork -Name "vnet-prd-jvn-avd-we-01"
-ResourceGroupName "rg-prd-jvn-avd-networking-01"
Set-AzVirtualNetworkSubnetConfig -VirtualNetwork $vnetavd
-AddressPrefix $subnets -Name "snet-prd-jvn-avd-shared-
sessionhosts-01" -RouteTable $routetable | Set-AzVirtualNetwork
```

After running both pieces of code, the UDR can be viewed in the Azure portal.

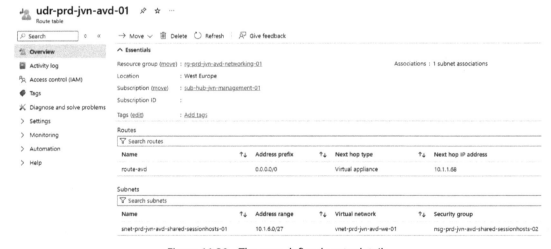

Figure 11.20 – The user-defined route details

Now that the firewall and UDR are created, the IT admin needs to create the rules to allow the AVD traffic through. If this is not done, the session hosts won't be able to communicate with the AVD backend services.

Before the IT admin can create the necessary AVD rules, they need to create a firewall policy. The following PowerShell code will deploy the policy:

```
# Firewall policy
$fwpol = New-AzFirewallPolicy -Name "policy-fw-hub-jvn-01"
-ResourceGroupName $rgname -Location $region $tagsfwp
```

The IT admin can view the policy in the Azure portal after running the code.

Figure 11.21 – An Azure firewall policy

Now, it's time to start creating the rules for the AVD traffic. Go to **Firewall Policy** > **Rule collections**, and add a rule collection group.

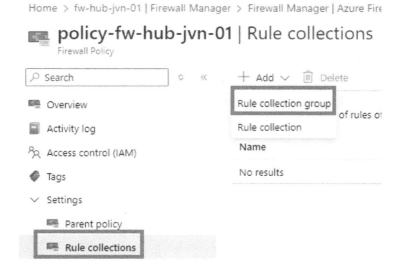

Figure 11.22 – An Azure firewall rule collection group

Choose a name for the rule collection group, give it a priority, and hit **Save**:

Add a rule collection group

Rule collection groups can include rule collections of various types. Rule collection group priority affects the order in which rules are executed.

Name *

> rules-prd-jvn-avd-01   ✓

Priority *

> 100   ✓

Figure 11.23 – Creating a rule collection group

The next resource that the IT admin needs to create is the rule collection.

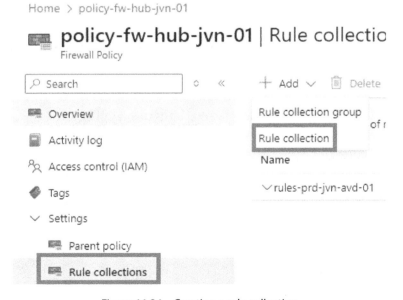

Figure 11.24 – Creating a rule collection

The AVD admin needs to create the rules so that the AVD session hosts can communicate with the backend services from AVD. If this is not done, the hosts will have an unavailable status, and users won't be able to connect. To make creating the rules easier, the IT admin will target the source type to the IP Group that was created earlier.

All the rules that need to be created can be viewed here:

```
https://learn.microsoft.com/en-gb/azure/firewall/protect-azure-
virtual-desktop?tabs=azure&WT.mc_id=EM-MVP-5003320#host-pool-outbound-
access-to-azure-virtual-desktop
```

The name can be chosen, but it's recommended to use the purpose of the rule as the name. This makes it easier to troubleshoot if there are any issues.

Add a rule collection   ✕

Name *	rules-avd-prd	⌄
Rule collection type *	Application	⌄
Priority *	100	⌄
Rule collection action	Allow	⌄
Rule collection group *	DefaultApplicationRuleCollectionGroup	⌄

Rules

Name *	Source type	Source	Protocol *	TLS inspection	Destination Type *	Destination *	
Allow_443_Window...	IP Group	1 selected	Https:443	☐ TLS inspection	FQDN Tag	WindowsVirtualDes...	🗑 ••
Allow_443_AzureM...	IP Group	1 selected	Https:443	☐ TLS inspection	FQDN	*.prod.warm.ingest....	🗑 ••
Allow_1688_Azure_...	IP Group	1 selected	Https:1688	☐ TLS inspection	FQDN	kms.core.windows.n...	🗑 ••
Allow_443_AzureCl...	IP Group	1 selected	Https:443	☐ TLS inspection	FQDN	wvdportalstoragebl...	🗑 ••
Allow_80_AzureMet...	IP Group	1 selected	Http:80	☐ TLS inspection	FQDN	169.254.169.254	🗑 ••
Allow_AVD_Health	IP Group	1 selected	Http:80	☐ TLS inspection	FQDN	168.63.129.16	🗑 ••

Figure 11.25 – Adding AVD rules

To ease this process, Microsoft has published a template you can use that contains all the required rules:

```
https://github.com/Azure/RDS-Templates/tree/master/
AzureFirewallPolicyForAVD
```

When saved, the rule collection will be visible as well as the amount of rules that it contains.

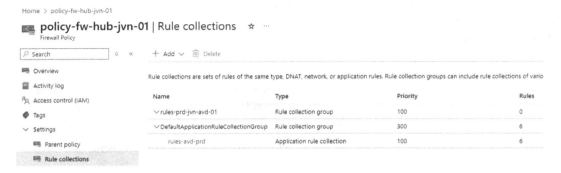

Figure 11.26 – A rule collection overview

To check whether all the rules work, go to the **Azure Virtual Desktop** blade in the Azure portal and then **Host pools** > **Session hosts**, and select one active session host to check that the health check for the AVD service is all green.

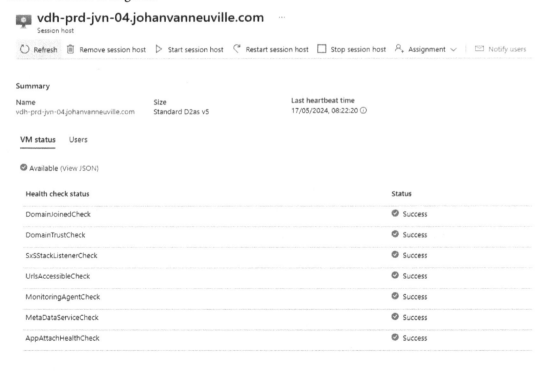

Figure 11.27 – A session host health check

Now that you know how to add more security using an Azure firewall, let's continue securing Azure with the help of NSGs.

Configure network security with NSGs

In the previous part of this chapter, you learned how Azure Firewall can be used to protect the AVD environment. However, not all organizations use a firewall in Azure. To stay secure, these companies might use an NSG to keep their network secure. An NSG uses inbound and outbound rules to control the traffic.

Let's have a look at creating an NSG with the following Azure PowerShell script. The first part is the variables. Replace these variables to match your organization:

```
$avdvnet = Get-AzVirtualNetwork -Name vnet-prd-jvn-avd-we-01
-ResourceGroupName rg-prd-jvn-avd-networking-01
$sharedsessionhostssubnet = Get-AzVirtualNetworkSubnetConfig
-VirtualNetwork $avdvnet -Name "snet-prd-jvn-avd-shared-
sessionhosts-01"
$tagsnsgavd = @
{"Environment"="Prd";"Solution"="NSG";"Costcenter"="IT"}

New-AzNetworkSecurityGroup -Name "nsg-prd-jvn-avd-shared-
sessionhosts-02" -ResourceGroupName "rg-prd-jvn-avd-networking-01"
-Location 'West Europe' -Tag $tagsnsgavd
```

After running the code, the NSG is visible in the portal with the default rules.

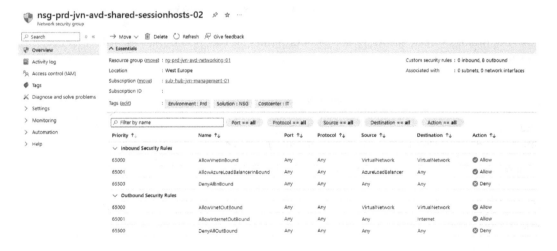

Figure 11.28 – An NSG with default rules

Currently, the NSG is not yet linked to the subnet. In order to connect them both, the IT admin runs the following line of code:

```
Set-AzVirtualNetworkSubnetConfig -Name $sharedsessionhostssubnet.
Name -VirtualNetwork $avdvnet -NetworkSecurityGroupId $nsg.Id
-AddressPrefix $sharedsessionhostssubnet.AddressPrefix -ResourceId
$sharedsessionhostssubnet.id
Set-AzVirtualNetwork -VirtualNetwork $avdvnet
```

The following screenshot shows the NSG with the associated subnet.

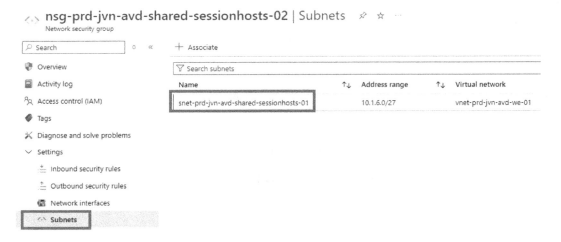

Figure 11.29 – The NSG with its associated subnet

It's also important to create the necessary outbound rules for the AVD traffic. The rules that need to be created can be viewed at `https://learn.microsoft.com/en-us/azure/virtual-desktop/required-fqdn-endpoint?tabs=azure`.

The rules can be created using the following PowerShell code:

```
#Rule1
$nsg | Add-AzNetworkSecurityRuleConfig -Name "Allow_443_
WindowsVirtualDesktop_Outbound" -Description "Allow_443_
WindowsVirtualDesktop_Outbound" -Access Allow `
    -Protocol TCP -Direction Outbound -Priority 1000
-SourceAddressPrefix "VirtualNetwork" -SourcePortRange * `
    -DestinationAddressPrefix WindowsVirtualDesktop
-DestinationPortRange 443


#Rule2
$nsg | Add-AzNetworkSecurityRuleConfig -Name "Allow_1688_AzureKMS_
Outbound" -Description "Allow_1688_AzureKMS_Outbound" -Access Allow `
```

```
    -Protocol TCP -Direction Outbound -Priority 1001
-SourceAddressPrefix "VirtualNetwork" -SourcePortRange * `
    -DestinationAddressPrefix Internet -DestinationPortRange 1688

#Rule3
$nsg | Add-AzNetworkSecurityRuleConfig -Name "Allow_443_AzureCloud_
Outbound" -Description "Allow_443_AzureCloud_Outbound" -Access Allow `
    -Protocol TCP -Direction Outbound -Priority 1002
-SourceAddressPrefix "VirtualNetwork" -SourcePortRange * `
    -DestinationAddressPrefix AzureCloud -DestinationPortRange 443

#Rule4
$nsg | Add-AzNetworkSecurityRuleConfig -Name "Allow_443_
AzureFrontDoor.Frontend_Outbound" -Description "Allow_443_
AzureFrontDoor.Frontend_Outbound" -Access Allow `
    -Protocol TCP -Direction Outbound -Priority 1003
-SourceAddressPrefix "VirtualNetwork" -SourcePortRange * `
    -DestinationAddressPrefix AzureFrontDoor.Frontend
-DestinationPortRange 443

#Rule5
$nsg | Add-AzNetworkSecurityRuleConfig -Name "Allow_AVD_Metadata_
Outbound" -Description "Allow_AVD_Metadata_Outbound" -Access Allow `
    -Protocol TCP -Direction Outbound -Priority 1004
-SourceAddressPrefix "VirtualNetwork" -SourcePortRange * `
    -DestinationAddress 169.254.169.254    -DestinationPortRange 80

#Rule6
$nsg | Add-AzNetworkSecurityRuleConfig -Name "Allow_AVD_Health"
-Description "Allow_AVD_Health" -Access Allow `
    -Protocol TCP -Direction Outbound -Priority 1005
-SourceAddressPrefix "VirtualNetwork" -SourcePortRange * `
    -DestinationAddress 168.63.129.16    -DestinationPortRange 80

#Rule7
$nsg | Add-AzNetworkSecurityRuleConfig -Name "Allow_443_AzureMonitor_
Outbound" -Description "Allow_443_AzureMonitor_Outbound" -Access Allow
`
    -Protocol TCP -Direction Outbound -Priority 1006
-SourceAddressPrefix "VirtualNetwork" -SourcePortRange * `
    -DestinationAddressPrefix AzureMonitor -DestinationPortRange 443

# Update the NSG.
$nsg | Set-AzNetworkSecurityGroup
```

After running the code, the rules will be visible in the NSG.

+ Add   Hide default rules   Refresh   Delete   Give feedback

Network security group security rules are evaluated by priority using the combination of source, source port, destination, destination port, and protocol to allow or deny the traffic. A security rule can't have the same priority and dire
security rules, but you can override them with rules that have a higher priority. Learn more

Priority ↑.	Name ↑↓	Port ↑↓	Protocol ↑↓	Source ↑↓	Destination ↑↓	Action ↑↓
1000	Allow_443_WindowsVirtualDesktop_--	443	TCP	VirtualNetwork	WindowsVirtualDesktop	✔ Allow
1001	Allow_1688_AzureKMS_Outbound	1688	TCP	VirtualNetwork	Internet	✔ Allow
1002	Allow_443_AzureCloud_Outbound	443	TCP	VirtualNetwork	AzureCloud	✔ Allow
1003	Allow_443_AzureFrontDoor.Fronten--	443	TCP	VirtualNetwork	AzureFrontDoor.Frontend	✔ Allow
1004	Allow_AVD_Metadata_Outbound	80	TCP	VirtualNetwork	169.254.169.254	✔ Allow
1005	Allow_AVD_Health	80	TCP	VirtualNetwork	168.63.129.16	✔ Allow
1006	Allow_443_AzureMonitor_Outbound	443	TCP	VirtualNetwork	AzureMonitor	✔ Allow
4096	Deny_All_Outbound	Any	Any	Any	Any	✖ Deny
65000	AllowVnetOutBound	Any	Any	VirtualNetwork	VirtualNetwork	✔ Allow
65001	AllowInternetOutBound	Any	Any	Any	Internet	✔ Allow
65500	DenyAllOutBound	Any	Any	Any	Any	✖ Deny

Figure 11.30 – NSG AVD outbound rules

To make sure that no other traffic is allowed out, the IT admin can create a deny rule with a lower priority than the allow rules.

| 4096 | Deny_All_Outbound | Any | Any | Any | Any | ✖ Deny |

Figure 11.31 – An NSG AVD deny rule

After configuring the NSG rules, the networking traffic is configured for the session hosts. Let's continue and focus on how to use an Azure dedicated host to secure AVD.

Deploying AVD on dedicated hosts

After learning about securing AVD using a firewall and NSGs, it's time for the final part of this chapter. Another method of adding security to AVD is to make sure that no other organization can influence your session hosts. Normally, session hosts are deployed on shared hardware. To increase security, the IT admin can deploy a dedicated host. This is a physical server that the organization can use to host AVD session hosts. Using these dedicated hosts, the IT admin can make sure that the organization doesn't have to share hardware with other organizations.

Because a dedicated host requires a certain amount of vCPU, the IT admin will have to make a quota request for the specific virtual machine size that the organization wants to use. Using the following link, the IT admin can find the required virtual machine size: `https://learn.microsoft.com/en-us/azure/virtual-machines/dedicated-host-general-purpose-skus`.

A quota request can be made for the subscription by going to **Subscription** > **Usage + quotas**. When the request has been implemented, the IT admin will be notified by Microsoft support.

Figure 11.32 – Quota request

When the quota request has been approved and implemented, the IT admin can deploy the necessary resources. Before a dedicated host can be deployed, a **host group** must be deployed. This host group can then contain one or more dedicated hosts. The following Azure PowerShell script can be used to deploy the host group after changing the variables to fit the organization:

```
$rgName = "rg-prd-$prefix-avd-backplane-01"
$location = "west europe"
$prefix = "jvn"
$spoke = "prd"
$solution = "avd"
$tagsdhg = @{"Environment"="Prd";"Solution"="DedicatedHostGroup";
"Costcenter"="IT"}
$hostGroup = New-AzHostGroup `
    -Name "dhg-$spoke-$prefix-$solution-01" `
    -ResourceGroupName $rgName `
    -Location $location `
    -Zone 1 `
    -EnableUltraSSD `
    -PlatformFaultDomain 2 `
    -Tag $tagsdhg `
```

The following screenshot shows a dedicated host overview.

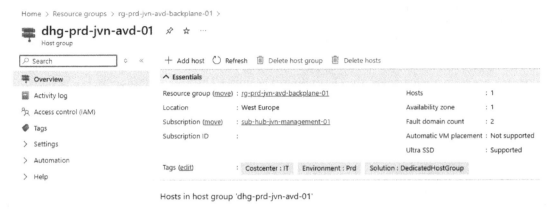

Hosts in host group 'dhg-prd-jvn-avd-01'

Figure 11.33 – A dedicated host group

The next step is to deploy the first dedicated host. This can be done using the following PowerShell script. Again, change the variables to your own:

```
    ##dedicated host
  $tagsdh = @
{"Environment"="Prd";"Solution"="DedicatedHost";"Costcenter"="IT"}
  $dHost = New-AzHost `
   -HostGroupName $hostGroup.Name `
   -Location $location -Name dh-prd-jvn-avd-01 `
   -ResourceGroupName $rgName `
   -Sku DDSv4-Type2 `
   -PlatformFaultDomain 1 `
   -Tag $tagsdh
```

After deploying the dedicated host, the IT admin can see in the overview what virtual machine sizes are available and how many can be deployed on the host.

Figure 11.34 – The dedicated host

Now, the IT admin needs to move the session hosts onto the dedicated host. To do this, the session host must be deallocated and be in the same availability zone as the dedicated host. Also, the virtual machine size must be available on the host.

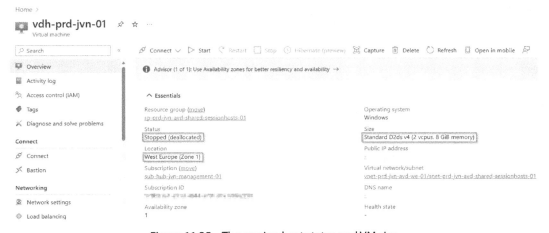

Figure 11.35 – The session host status and VM size

The IT admin can change the dedicated host configuration, as seen in the following screenshot.

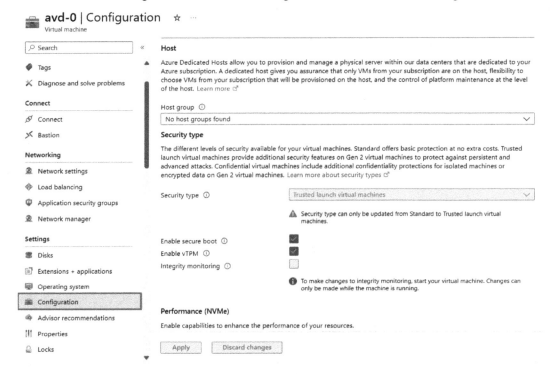

Figure 11.36 – The session host settings for the dedicated host

After changing these settings, the session host will be moved to the dedicated host. It's important to know that it's not possible to deploy a session host on a host group at this stage in the portal. To achieve this, the IT admin can use automation.

Next, let's look at Defender for Cloud and how it can help to secure an AVD environment.

Configuring Defender for Cloud

We mentioned **Microsoft Defender for Cloud** previously in *Chapter 7, Threat Detection and Prevention*, and let's focus on it now. This service is a **cloud-native application protection platform** (**CNAPP**) that helps the IT admin keep the Azure environment safe from various cyber threats and vulnerabilities.

Defender for Cloud can be activated per subscription, and the IT admin can choose what resources they would like to activate for protection. It's recommended that an AVD environment is deployed on a dedicated subscription.

To activate Defender for Cloud, the IT admin needs to go to the Azure portal > **Microsoft Defender for Cloud** > **Environment** settings and choose the correct subscription.

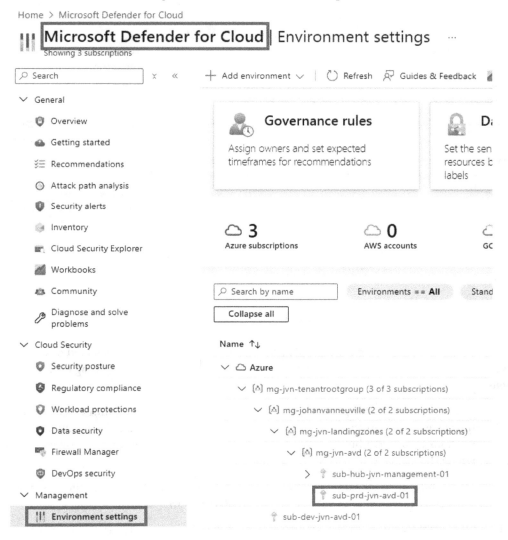

Figure 11.37 – Choosing a subscription for Defender for Cloud

On the **Settings** screen, the IT admin needs to enable the plans that need to be activated by toggling the sliders to **On** and pressing **Save**.

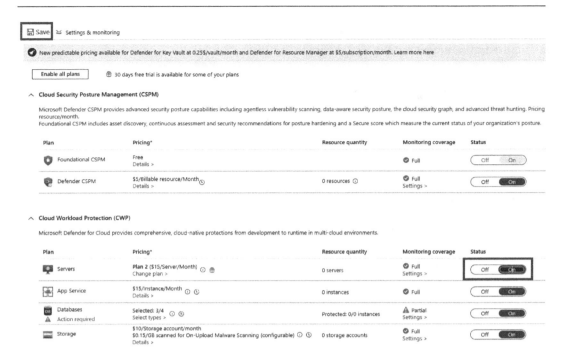

Figure 11.38 – Enabling Defender for Cloud plans

Most of these defender plans have multiple pricing and options that can be enabled or disabled. However, it depends on a company's preference whether they will enable everything or not for the various resources.

Besides enabling the Defender plans for the AVD subscription, the IT admin can also enable the **Continuous export** feature. This feature can be used to export detailed security alerts and recommendations to an event hub, Log Analytics workspace, or **Security Information and Event Management (SIEM)** system such as Microsoft Sentinel.

To enable this feature, go to the same menu as shown in *Figure 11.39* and select **Continuous export**. Then, select whether to export to **Event hub** or **Log Analytics Workspace**.

The IT admin has the choice of what data types to configure for export. The following screenshot gives an example.

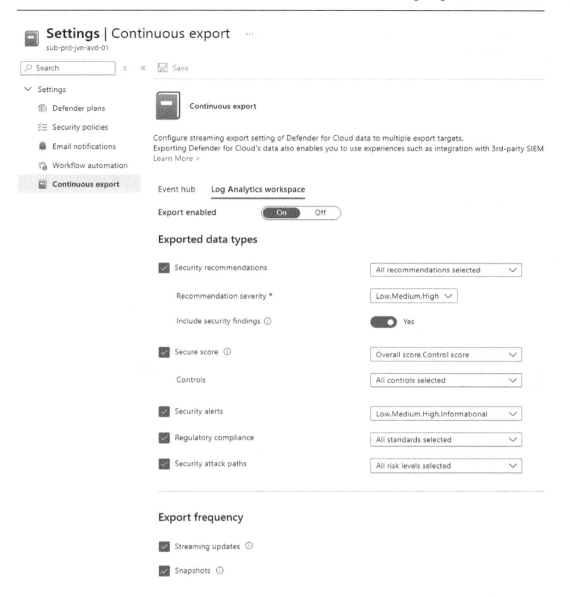

Figure 11.39 – Selecting the data types for export

The last step is to select the export configuration and target. In this example, it is for the central Log Analytics workspace, as shown in the following screenshot.

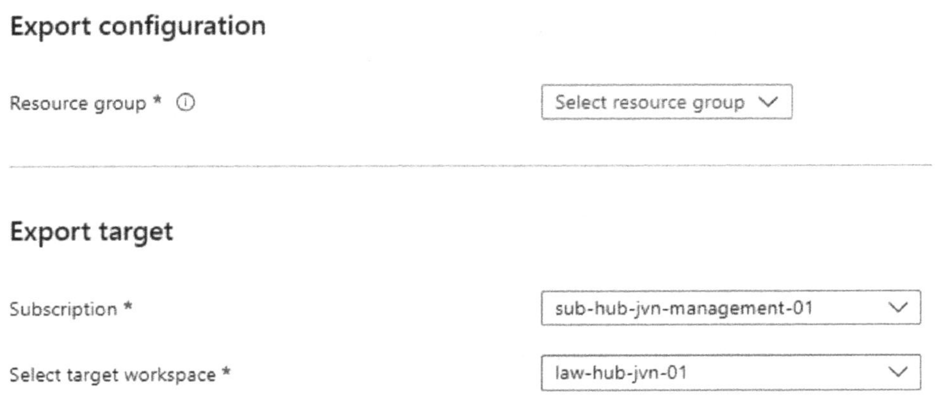

Export configuration

Resource group * ⓘ | Select resource group ⌄ |

Export target

Subscription * | sub-hub-jvn-management-01   ⌄ |

Select target workspace * | law-hub-jvn-01   ⌄ |

Figure 11.40 – The export configuration and target

After adding more security by enabling Defender for Cloud and continuous export, let's take a look at the final topic of this chapter and see how to deploy an Azure VPN gateway to connect to a secure AVD environment.

Deploying an Azure VPN gateway

In this section, we will learn how to protect an AVD environment with a VPN gateway. When the AVD environment is configured with private access, the user needs a method to make a private connection to the Azure environment. This can be accomplished by using a VPN connection. The IT admin can provision an Azure VPN gateway to ensure that the users can connect over a private network. There are two different kinds of VPN tunnels that can be created:

- A **site-to-site (S2S)** VPN connection
- A **point-to-site (P2S)** VPN connection

Before creating the VPN gateway, the IT admin needs to create a subnet that will be used by the gateway. This subnet needs to have the name GatewaySubnet and a subnet mask of /27 or larger.

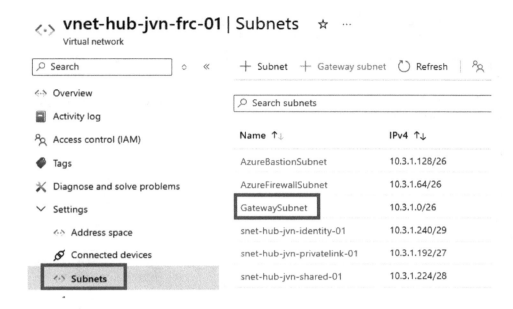

Figure 11.41 – GatewaySubnet

To deploy the VPN gateway, the IT admin can use the following PowerShell script. The variables need to be changed to fit the organization:

```
$vnet = Get-AzVirtualNetwork -Name "vnet-hub-jvn-frc-01"
-ResourceGroupName rg-hub-jvn-networking-02
$region = "west europe"
$rgname = "rg-hub-jvn-networking-02"
$tagsvgw = @{"Environment"="Hub";"Solution"="VPN
Gateway";"Costcenter"="IT"}
$gatewaysubnet = Get-AzVirtualNetworkSubnetConfig -VirtualNetwork
$vnet -Name "GatewaySubnet"


$ngwpip = New-AzPublicIpAddress -Name "pip-hub-jvn-vpng-01"
-ResourceGroupName "rg-hub-jvn-networking-02" -Location "France
Central" -AllocationMethod Dynamic
$vnet = Get-AzVirtualNetwork -Name "vnet-hub-jvn-frc-01"
-ResourceGroupName "rg-hub-jvn-networking-02"
#$vnet = New-AzVirtualNetwork -AddressPrefix "10.254.0.0/27" -Location
"UK West" -Name vnet-gateway -ResourceGroupName "vnet-gateway" -Subnet
$subnet
$subnet = Get-AzVirtualNetworkSubnetConfig -name 'gatewaysubnet'
-VirtualNetwork $vnet
$ngwipconfig = New-AzVirtualNetworkGatewayIpConfig -Name ngwipconfig
-SubnetId $subnet.Id -PublicIpAddressId $ngwpip.Id
```

```
New-AzVirtualNetworkGateway -Name "vpng-hub-jvn-01" -ResourceGroupName
"rg-hub-jvn-networking-02" -Location "France Central"
-IpConfigurations $ngwIpConfig  -GatewayType "Vpn" -VpnType
"RouteBased" -GatewaySku "Basic" -CustomRoute 192.168.0.0/24 -Tag
$tagsvgw
```

After running the code, which can take a while, the IT admin will see an overview of the VPN gateway, as shown in the following figure.

Figure 11.42 – The VPN gateway

The next step for the IT admin is to create a P2S connection so that the end users can connect from their physical devices.

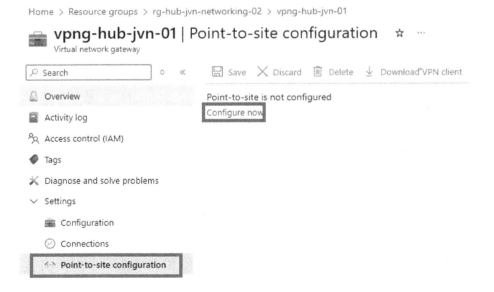

Figure 11.43 – Configuring P2S

In this example, the IT admin configures the Azure Active Directory or Entra ID authentication method using the following parameters. More information about all these options can be found here: `https://learn.microsoft.com/en-us/azure/vpn-gateway/openvpn-azure-ad-tenant`.

The **Additional routes** to the advertise field, in this example, should be filled with the subnet for the AVD session hosts. When done, click **Save** at the top.

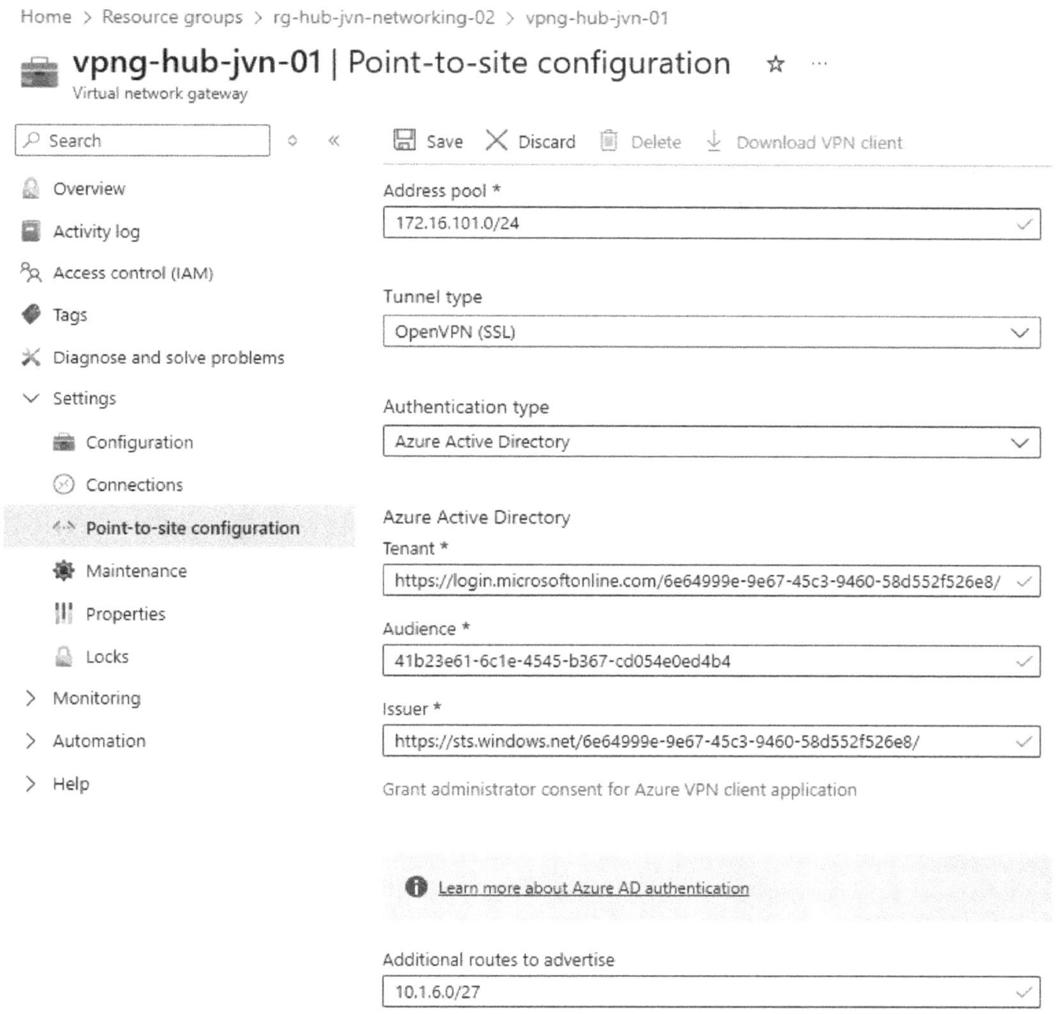

Home > Resource groups > rg-hub-jvn-networking-02 > vpng-hub-jvn-01

vpng-hub-jvn-01 | Point-to-site configuration ☆ ⋯
Virtual network gateway

⌕ Search	◌ «

🖫 Save   ✕ Discard   🗑 Delete   ↓ Download VPN client

- Overview
- Activity log
- Access control (IAM)
- Tags
- Diagnose and solve problems
- ∨ Settings
  - Configuration
  - Connections
  - **Point-to-site configuration**
  - Maintenance
  - Properties
  - Locks
- ⟩ Monitoring
- ⟩ Automation
- ⟩ Help

Address pool *
```
172.16.101.0/24
```

Tunnel type
```
OpenVPN (SSL)
```

Authentication type
```
Azure Active Directory
```

Azure Active Directory
Tenant *
```
https://login.microsoftonline.com/6e64999e-9e67-45c3-9460-58d552f526e8/
```

Audience *
```
41b23e61-6c1e-4545-b367-cd054e0ed4b4
```

Issuer *
```
https://sts.windows.net/6e64999e-9e67-45c3-9460-58d552f526e8/
```

Grant administrator consent for Azure VPN client application

ℹ Learn more about Azure AD authentication

Additional routes to advertise
```
10.1.6.0/27
```

Figure 11.44 – The P2S settings with Entra ID authentication

After saving the configuration, the IT admin can download it using the **Download VPN Client** button. This will include the HTML file that needs to be imported into the **Azure VPN client**. This client can be downloaded from the Microsoft store. More information about how to configure the Azure VPN client can be found here: `https://learn.microsoft.com/en-us/azure/vpn-gateway/openvpn-azure-ad-client`.

With the AVD environment configured for private access and the P2S connection configured, the user can connect over a private connection.

Summary

This concludes this chapter about securing Azure infrastructure. You have learned how to secure an FSLogix storage account and use NSGs and Azure Firewall to secure networks for AVD.

This chapter also concludes the technical chapters of the book. In the next two chapters, we will learn more about several use cases that an organization might have and how Windows 365 and AVD can help with them.

Part 5:
Use Cases

The last part of the book is dedicated to the question "When should we use Windows 365 or Azure Virtual Desktop to deploy desktops to our users?" We included various use cases for both Windows 365 and Azure Virtual Desktop to assist you in making the correct choice for your company and/or situation.

This part contains the following chapters:

- *Chapter 12, Windows 365 Use Cases*
- *Chapter 13, Azure Virtual Desktop Use Cases*

12

Windows 365 Use Cases

In the previous chapters, we covered how to secure Windows 365, Azure Virtual Desktop, and Azure infrastructure. From this chapter onward, we will move on from the technical areas as we explore use cases, starting with Windows 365. There are a lot of use cases that can be made for Windows 365, and in this chapter, we will cover the more common use cases to help you get started with Windows 365.

In this chapter, we're going to cover the following main topics:

- When to use Windows 365 as your personal desktop
- Windows 365 as a replacement for an on-premise VDI
- Windows 365 for contractors
- Using Windows 365 as a privileged access workstation
- How Windows 365 Boot helps to secure an endpoint
- Enhancing security by restricting access for Office 365 services to Cloud PCs
- Windows 365 Frontline versus Windows 365 Enterprise

When to use Windows 365 as your personal desktop

A really common question we get from companies and the community alike is, when can/should we use Windows 365? The conversation usually turns quickly to which sector a company is active in. But to us, it does not really matter what sector a company is active in. The way that users work and the applications that users use determine whether Cloud PCs are a good fit for a desktop or not.

Moving away from a local VDI environment or physical desktops to Cloud PCs brings additional features and settings that help companies and IT admins get the most out of a desktop.

Windows 365 as a replacement for on-premise VDI

An **on-premise VDI solution** enables companies to deploy virtual desktops to their users. These desktops can be reached via the internet to enable work remotely or locally from the network. If the on-premise VDI solution is reaching its replacement date or doesn't support the features that the company needs, IT admins will have to decide what's next. Do they either expand on the current solution or is there a better solution?

Why is Windows 365 a good alternative to an on-premise VDI?

Having an on-premise VDI solution can be very complex to manage in terms of licensing, support contracts, and finding IT admins with expert knowledge to make sure that the VDI solution works as designed. In addition, it can become quite tricky to expand on new(er) features, such as implementing Microsoft Teams to allow users to collaborate with each other via video calls.

If your company is in a situation where it is looking to replace the existing on-premise VDI solution, it makes a lot of sense to think about migrating to Windows 365.

Here are some key reasons why:

- Having an on-premise VDI solution brings a lot of complexity. Each component of the stack, such as storage, the server, the OS, the hypervisor, and the environment manager, needs to be managed, which requires specialist knowledge, especially since IT admins have to think about disaster recovery. Windows 365 as a **Software as a service** (**SaaS**) solution is a great way to simplify management, as all of the management is done via Microsoft Intune. This effectively reduces the technical knowledge that the IT admins need to have to manage the service.

  An on-premise VDI solution tends to span different individual solutions that require support and licensing. This can make an on-premise VDI solution a costly option. Windows 365 brings a recognizable desktop to the user without the need for a third-party solution. This approach can reduce costs as well as technical complexity.

- An on-premise VDI solution tends to be designed for a specific set of features. New features can sometimes be hard to implement in a safe and performing manner. Windows 365 integrates well with other Microsoft products, such as Defender for Endpoint or Microsoft Intune. It also supports gallery images and optimized images provided by Microsoft to improve performance at the operating system level, and it also improves Microsoft Teams performance.

- A VDI infrastructure tends to look at the number of concurrent sessions or the maximum number of users that will sign in at the same time. Using Windows 365 Frontline, companies can further reduce costs. Frontline can be used together with Windows 365 Enterprise. The license model used for Windows 365 makes it easy to calculate the license costs on a per-user/per-month basis.

- Choosing Windows 365 instead of competing products allows companies and users to use device actions, such as restarting their own Cloud PC. This helps to reduce the number of tickets on a service desk and improves the user experience.

Of course, there are more reasons why Windows 365 is a good alternative when compared to an on-premise VDI, but we hope these key reasons give you a good idea. Let's move on to the next use case, a specific use case on how to use Windows 365 for your remote workforce or contractors!

Windows 365 for contractors

Contractors are commonly hired for ongoing projects or temporarily assist a company with a specific task. Contractors can be hired from IT firms, or they can operate as freelancers. Contractors can be based in the same country, but they can also work remotely from other companies.

Most of the contractors are already equipped with a laptop and phone. But, often, contractors receive another laptop and phone when they are hired by a company. That laptop is enrolled into the Microsoft tenant and secured via Microsoft Intune. But does this way of working provide the best user experience and security?

Why is Windows 365 a good solution to provide a secure desktop for contractors?

While providing a laptop to a remote workforce or external users certainly has its benefits, it might be a good idea to implement Windows 365 and simply deploy a Cloud PC for these users. Here are some key reasons why:

1. Physical laptops have to be managed. They have to be deployed if they are already used, repaired if they become broken, and sent to the contractor. Using Windows 365, the only thing IT admins have to do is assign a Cloud PC license to the contractor. The Cloud PC will be ready in 30 minutes.

2. The contractor does not need the laptop once the project or task finishes, and the laptop will be sent back to the company. At this point, the laptop will be redeployed for later use. If there is no immediate request, then the laptop will sit on a shelf. Using Windows 365, IT admins can simply remove the Cloud PC license from the contractor and can be removed from the tenant if the license(s) are not needed anymore.

3. Contractors tend to have their own laptops to work with. Handing contractors a second laptop does not provide the best user experience, as they just become responsible for two laptops. Using Windows 365, contractors are able to use Windows 365 Switch to quickly connect to the Cloud PC of the company that hired them. This greatly improves the user experience.

4. Physical laptops can be forgotten about, lost, or even stolen. This scenario is a security risk to the company. Using Windows 365, Cloud PCs run in the data center at Microsoft. Forgetting about, losing, or having the Cloud PC stolen is not an option.

5. There are various solutions to protect data on an endpoint. Since Windows 365 Enterprise, and Frontline for that matter, are fully managed via Microsoft Intune, IT admins have all the tools at their disposal to make sure that data is securely stored in the data center at Microsoft. You can compare this to using RDP properties to disable the clipboard so that data cannot be copied to the local machine, using screen capture protection so that screenshots will result in black images, or implementing QR watermark codes to protect against someone taking a picture with a smartphone.

The flexibility of Windows 365 makes it a good candidate for a remote workforce such as contractors. Its easy management and many possibilities to secure the desktop make it a great choice! But there are more use cases when you're considering using Windows 365 in a secure manner. What about the next use case – using Windows 365 as a privileged access workstation?

Using Windows 365 as a privileged access workstation

An important way to protect a company against attackers is to implement privileged administration. Privileged accounts have the potential to do a lot of damage if they become compromised by attackers. Privileged administration contains a strategy, design, and implementation. Desktops are a part of privileged administration, which consists of three security levels:

- **Enterprise security**: This level is meant for regular users and roles, and it has the least amount of security configured.

- **Specialized security**: This level is meant for roles that have a higher business impact, such as developers, social media accounts, or executives.

- **Privileged access**: This level is meant for roles that have the potential to cause major damage to the company if they becomes compromised. Desktops at this level should have the highest security level.

A privileged access workstation is part of the privileged access security level. Here are a couple of roles that greatly benefit from using a Privileged Access Workstation (PAW):

- Microsoft Entra Global Administrators

- Identity management roles

- On-premise Active Directory roles, such as the following:

  - Enterprise admins

  - Domain admins

  - Schema admins

  - Local admin (built-in\administrators)

Creating a PAW is a technical exercise. Make sure to read up on all related articles (as there are many out there).

Why is Windows 365 a good solution as a PAW?

Windows 365 is managed via Microsoft Intune, and it integrates with a lot of other Microsoft solutions, which makes securing a Windows 11 desktop on a Cloud PC a valid option. Here are some key features of a PAW:

- **Restricted access**: Access to a PAW should be limited to authorized users who require elevated privileges. Cloud PCs are only accessible to the user to which it's assigned. Cloud PCs also have the local administrator disabled by default, increasing security.

- **PAWs should be isolated from other systems on a network**: Windows 365 supports this with its bring-your-own-network design. IT admins have the option to create a VNET and subnet for the PAWs to inhabit. Use an Azure network connection to connect a network to the Windows 365 service.

- **PAWs should be secured**: A PAW should be encrypted, protected against malware, and only accessible using MFA and other endpoint protection solutions to protect against cyber threats. Cloud PCs are encrypted by default on the session host. Data send to the storage layer is already encrypted. Additionally, data in transit (between various components and externally) is encrypted as well. Cloud PCs, just like physical desktops, can be enrolled into Microsoft Defender for Endpoint to protect against threats. IT admins can leverage conditional access to enforce MFA before the user can connect to their Cloud PC. This can be enhanced by using FIDO2 security keys as an authentication strength. Cloud PCs have their own security baseline, which can be used to further secure them.

- **Access to PAWs should be logged**: Microsoft Entra ID supports audit and sign-in logs, making sure that connections and changes to Cloud PCs are logged. Alternatively, you can use Microsoft Sentinel to log and access security information.

- **Perform regular maintenance**: Make sure that PAWs are up to date and compliant. IT admins can use Windows Update for Business or Windows Autopatch to keep the desktop up to date. Use **compliance policies** to make sure that PAWs meet the demands of a company.

Windows 365 can be used in many ways, even as a PAW. Remember that reading up on the latest documentation about PAW is very important, as new insights and recommendations become available over time.

Next, we will look at Windows 365 Boot, which is a great way to create a secure local desktop that connects to a Cloud PC.

How Windows 365 Boot helps to secure an endpoint

Windows 365 Boot was covered in *Chapter 1, Introducing Windows 365 and Azure Virtual Desktop*. It is a great solution to transform a Windows 11 device into a Windows 365 Boot device where users sign in directly into their own Cloud PC.

Why is using Windows 365 Boot a good way to secure a local desktop?

The **Windows 365 Boot feature** is free to use for companies that use Windows 365. Here are key reasons why using Windows 365 Boot helps to improve the security of a desktop:

- Windows 365 Boot allows users to sign in directly to their Cloud PC.

- No company data is stored on the local desktop.

- Device modes allow for a great user experience. The dedicated device mode looks like a regular Windows 11 sign-in screen, which includes a picture of the user. The shared device mode shows a company logo and the name of the company. This mode is intended when a group of users uses the same local device.

- If a Windows 365 Boot device breaks down, IT admins have the option to redeploy the device using Autopilot or simply replace the local device.

- Using Windows 365 Boot can extend the lifespan of a local device.

Enhancing security by restricting access to Office 365 services to Cloud PCs

While this might not be a true use case for using Windows 365, we feel that we should include this scenario in the book, as it adds a lot of additional security to keep company data safe.

The scenario of restricting Office 365 access to Cloud PCs

We mentioned previously that a desktop is at the heart of a user's workspace. This book covered a lot of features and methods to secure a Cloud PC to keep company data safe, but that only works if the Cloud PC is the go-to desktop that users work with. By default, users have the option to access their data using web apps, such as Word Online or OneDrive Online. The good news is that IT admins are able to make sure that other Office 365 services can only be made accessible from Cloud PCs.

How to restrict Office 365 access to Cloud PCs

Here are the key steps to take to restrict Office 365 access to Cloud PCs:

1. Create a Microsoft Entra group and add users to the group. These users will only be able to access Office 365 services from their Cloud PC once this process is complete.

2. Sign into **Microsoft Intune** and create a new Conditional Access policy.

3. Configure the following settings:

   I. Provide a good name for the policy.

   II. **Assignments**: Include the Microsoft Entra group that was created before.

   III. **Cloud apps or actions**: Make sure to include **Office 365**. Also, make sure to exclude **Azure Virtual Desktop** and **Windows 365**.

   IV. **Conditions**: Configure a filter for devices. Use the following expression – **device.model -startsWith "Cloud PC"**.

   V. **Grant**: Select **Block access**.

   VI. **Enable policy**: Select **On**.

Now, the specified users can only access Office 365 services on their Cloud PCs once the Conditional Access policy is created.

Windows 365 Frontline versus Windows 365 Enterprise

We introduced Windows 365 Frontline in *Chapter 1, Introducing Windows 365 and Azure Virtual Desktop*. Let's take a look at why companies might prefer Frontline Cloud PCs over Enterprise Cloud PCs.

Why should companies prefer Frontline Cloud PCs?

Frontline Cloud PCs have most of the features that Windows 365 Enterprise has. Both provide a PC in the cloud and are managed using Microsoft Intune. So, why would companies consider using Frontline Cloud PCs? The main reason is pretty simple – *Windows 365 Frontline should be used if licensing for concurrency makes more sense when compared to using a license for each individual user, to save costs.*

The best way to explain this is by looking at a couple of examples. I made the following assumptions for these examples:

- A Windows 365 Frontline license provides three Cloud PCs and one connection.

- We will use a 4vCPU/16 GB/128 GB SKU to compare Enterprise to Frontline.

- The costs can be seen on Microsoft's site as of April 2024. They are not partner prices.

- We used the following pricing (Enterprise – 66 EUR, and Frontline – 100.10 EUR):

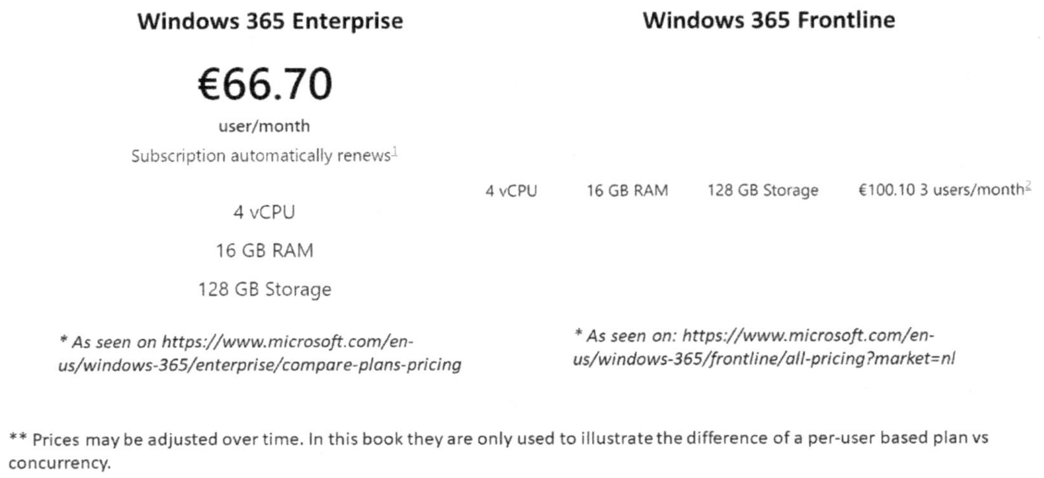

Windows 365 Enterprise	Windows 365 Frontline

€66.70

user/month

Subscription automatically renews[1]

4 vCPU	16 GB RAM	128 GB Storage	€100.10 3 users/month[2]

4 vCPU

16 GB RAM

128 GB Storage

* As seen on https://www.microsoft.com/en-us/windows-365/enterprise/compare-plans-pricing   ** As seen on: https://www.microsoft.com/en-us/windows-365/frontline/all-pricing?market=nl*

** Prices may be adjusted over time. In this book they are only used to illustrate the difference of a per-user based plan vs concurrency.

Figure 12.1 – Comparison information dating from April 2024

Example 1 – the easy example

A company has 30 users. Only 10 users need to sign in at the same time.

The Enterprise licenses needed are **30**. The Frontline licenses needed are **10** (as 10 licenses provide 30 Cloud PCs and 10 connections).

The total cost for Windows 365 Enterprise is €1,980 per month. The total cost for Windows 365 Frontline is €1,001 per month.

In this case, the company would save €979 per month by using Frontline Cloud PCs. which results in cost savings of 49.4 %.

Example 2 – concurrency wins

Let's discuss an example where we need to license for the number of connections, or concurrency. In this example, the company has 500 users but only 250 will sign in at the same time.

The Enterprise licenses needed are **500**. The Frontline licenses needed are **250** (250 licenses will provide 750 Frontline Cloud PCs and 250 connections).

The total cost for Windows 365 Enterprise is 33.000 EUR. The total cost for Windows 365 Frontline is 25.025 EUR.

In this case, the company would save 7.975 EUR per month by using Frontline Cloud PCs, which results in a cost savings of 24.1 %.

Example 3 – maximum user wins

In this example, we will explain the scenario where the company has a very low concurrency. Let's assume that the company has 500 users but only 150 users sign in at the same time.

The Enterprise licenses needed are **500**. The Frontline licenses needed are **167**. (167 licenses will provide 501 Frontline Cloud PCs and 167 connections. If you used 150 licenses, you would need 450 Frontline Cloud PCs, which means that 50 users would not receive a Frontline Cloud PC. These users would not be able to sign in, as there is no Cloud PC to boot from.)

The total cost for Windows 365 Enterprise is €33.000. The total cost for Windows 365 Frontline is €16.716,70.

In this case, the company would save €16.283,30 per month by using Frontline Cloud PCs, which results in cost savings of 50.6 %.

Does this mean that Frontline Cloud PCs are the way to go from now on? The answer is no. It really depends on the concurrency. The lower the concurrency, the higher the chance that Windows 365 Frontline is the right license model for you. Let's see what happens in the case of a very high concurrency, 100%.

Example 4 – high concurrency

Since this example is meant to illustrate what happens in case of high concurrency, we might as well go all out and find out what happens if there is 100% concurrency. The company has 500 users, and all of them need to be able to sign in at the same time.

The Enterprise licenses needed are **500**. The Frontline licenses needed are **500** (500 licenses provide 1,500 Frontline Cloud PCs and 500 connections).

The total cost for Windows 365 Enterprise is €33.000. The total cost for Windows 365 Frontline is €50.050.

The costs would increase by €17.050 per month. This is an increase of 51.6 %.

How to license for Windows 365 Frontline

Here are my key takeaways when licensing for Windows 365 Frontline.

- Make a list of all the users that will use Windows 365 Frontline
- Determine what SKUs are required (one or more?)
- Determine the maximum number of concurrent sessions per SKU
- Determine the number of Cloud PCs needed per SKU
- License for the highest number!

With this, we have come to the end of the chapter.

Summary

In this chapter, you learned about the more common use cases for Windows 365. You learned how Windows 365 can be used to simplify a VDI infrastructure and how it can replace an on-premise VDI. You learned how Windows 365 is able to deploy secure desktops to a remote workforce or contractors and how it can deploy highly secure Cloud PCs to privileged accounts, protecting against attackers by implementing a PAW strategy. You also learned how Windows 365 Boot transforms a Windows 11 device so that it can only be used to sign into a Cloud PC, without storing any data on the device itself. Lastly, you learned how to use a Conditional Access policy to easily restrict access to Office 365 services so that they can only be accessed from a Cloud PC.

This concludes the chapter about Windows 365 use cases. In the next chapter, we will continue our journey by exploring several Azure Virtual Desktop use cases.

13

Azure Virtual Desktop Use Cases

Welcome to the last chapter of this book. In the first 11 chapters, we learned about the importance of securing the cloud PCs and AVD environments. Similar to the previous chapter, this chapter is leaving the technical content behind and going to focus on some use cases where AVD can help companies.

This chapter will cover the following topics:

- AVD for external users using **Bring Your Own Device (BYOD)**
- Using remote apps instead of desktops
- AVD as a disaster recovery solution
- AVD for a break and fix scenario
- AVD running on Azure stack HCI

AVD for external users using Bring Your Own Device (BYOD)

Many companies these days not only have internal users but rely on external people to work for them. Since these external companies often don't work full-time for the company, it's not necessary to give these people a physical device. However, a lot of companies don't want external users accessing corporate data from their own physical devices using BYOD.

This is, of course, where AVD can help. Using AVD, external users can still use their own devices and connect to the AVD environment.

There are companies that want to prevent external users from having the same access as internal users. IT admins can therefore implement several security measures:

- **Separate host pools**: The security team might request that internal and external people don't work on the same devices. For this reason, it can be a good idea to create a separate host pool for external users.

- **Separate virtual networks**: Because external users often only need access to a specific system, the IT admin can choose whether to create a separate subnet or virtual network for external users. Often, this choice depends on the size of the organization.

- **Separate firewall rules**: The IT admin may also implement separate firewall rules for external users. This, together with the separate virtual networks, will make sure that external users don't have the same access as internal users.

- **Pooled or personal**: External users may need local admin access to the session hosts. For this reason, a personal host could be a good option. On a pooled device, it's recommended not to give local admin access.

- **Conditional access**: Particularly when users are working from their own devices, it's necessary to add an extra layer of security.

- **RDP properties**: As explained in *Chapter 4, Securing User Sessions*, the IT admin can configure specific RDP Properties for these kinds of host pools. This can help prevent external users from transferring data from the AVD session host to their own devices.

In *Chapter 1, Introducing Windows 365 and Azure Virtual Desktop*, we learned about the licensing for AVD. One of the options for enrolling in an Azure subscription is per-user pricing. When thinking about giving external users access to an AVD environment, per-user access pricing could be ideal for this.

Per-user access pricing has two tiers:

- **Apps**: This plan charges for each user that accesses at least one published remote app in the last month. This plan doesn't give access to a published desktop.

- **Desktops + Apps**: This plan charges for each user that accesses at least one published desktop or remote app in the last month.

Another advantage of per-user is that the end user doesn't need to be assigned an M365 license.

As you can see, this scenario is a good use case for AVD. Let's continue to explore the use cases and look at the remote app use case.

Using remote apps instead of desktops

These days, end-users are used to working on a physical device; in this case, the choice of a virtual desktop is easy. However, there are advantages to an IT admin not giving access to a virtual desktop but only to the remote apps that the end-user needs.

There are some key advantages when working with remote apps only:

- **More security**: When working with remote apps, the end-users don't have access to the OS. This makes it easier to control the OS but it also prevents the end-users from installing software on the session hosts.

- **Resource consumption**: An important benefit of working with remote apps is the fact that they consume fewer resources than a complete virtual desktop. This makes it possible to allow more users on a single host. Of course, this depends on the virtual machine's SKU.

- **Cost reduction**: A logical effect of resource consumption is that the IT admin doesn't need to provision the same amount of session hosts. This means that there is a cost saving when using remote apps.

When the IT admin has published a remote app, the end-user will be able to use it. The following image shows the Outlook app in the new Windows App that currently is in public preview:

Figure 13.1 – Remote app in Windows App

Next, we will have a look at why organizations might want to consider using AVD as a disaster recovery solution.

AVD as a disaster recovery solution

In *Chapter 3, Modern Security Risks*, we learned that virtual desktops can help organizations recover from a cyber-attack. A common target for a cyber-attack is the workstations of a company because it means that the end-users can't work anymore, and this has a big impact. Since companies want their employees to be productive again as soon as possible, they can consider AVD as a disaster recovery solution. Let's have a look at why AVD is a perfect solution for disaster recovery:

- **Scalability**: Depending on the size of the company, a lot of workstations can be impacted by a cyber-attack. AVD has the benefit that the IT admin can deploy a lot of session hosts at once and in multiple regions.

- **Location**: It may be that some end-users are impacted, but not physically at the office. Using AVD, the IT admin can make sure that the end-user has a workstation in the region where they are located. The user can then connect to an AVD session host using another device.

- **Costs**: Depending on the cyber-attack, it can take a while before the workstation of the end-user is fixed. Using AVD, the IT admin can make sure that they only pay for the machines when they are needed. The session hosts can be turned off and or deleted when they are not needed anymore.

There are a couple of components that the IT admin needs to have in place when AVD is needed for a large disaster, such as an entire Azure regional failure or cyberattack:

- **Networking**: The company needs to have enough IP addresses in Azure for the session hosts. It's a good idea to put this in the incident response plan if action needs to be taken for this during an attack. An advantage is that provisioning the virtual network will not increase costs, and it will also lower the recovery time.

- **Storage**: It's possible that the company already has a working AVD environment, but not all end-users are working on it. When all end-users suddenly have to work on it, the storage for the FSLogix profiles might need to be expanded. This is also a benefit of Azure Files because it can be expanded quickly without any downtime.

- **Identity**: When thinking about AVD in a disaster recovery solution, a key aspect is identities. The IT admin has to make sure that, especially when working with hybrid identities, the user has a line of sight to a domain controller. Another benefit of AVD is that it works perfectly without domain controllers with native Entra ID.

- **Images**: If the company is using a custom image, it's recommended to replicate it to every region that the company is using with Azure Compute Gallery.

Having these components in place will make it easier for IT admins if there is a disaster.

Let's have a look at the following use case and see why AVD would be a good idea for a break/fix scenario.

AVD for a break/fix scenario

Most companies give their employees a company device such as a laptop or desktop. How often does a hardware issue occur that needs to be fixed by the hardware vendor? Depending on the severity of the issue, the employee can't use the device for a couple of hours to a couple of days. In the worst case, the workstation is beyond repair and will have to be replaced by the IT admin.

It's in a situation like this that AVD can help. Let's see why:

- Users who need to wait for their device can request access to a pooled AVD environment. Since AVD is a very scalable solution, deploying an additional session host or adding the user to the host pool doesn't take much time.

- The IT admin can deploy an AVD host pool for this use case with the software installed like the Microsoft Office applications and Teams. This way, the users have basic functionality while they wait for their own devices.

- A break/fix host pool can help if the user is in a location that doesn't have local IT support.

- The benefit of this solution is that the IT admin can easily delete the session host when the user's workstation has been fixed. This way, the cost isn't very high.

Now that we know the advantages of using AVD as a break/fix solution, it's time to check out the last use case of this chapter.

Running AVD on Azure Stack HCI

Ever since AVD was introduced, IT admins have been able to run AVD in the cloud. This makes it possible for companies to provide a virtual desktop to end-users regardless of their location. However, a lot of companies have an on-premises VDI environment and can't move it to Azure for several reasons:

- Companies or organizations such as hospitals and governments are bound by geo boundaries and can't let their data leave their country or wider geopolitical area

- They have applications that are very sensitive to latency

Before we look at the benefits of the solution, let's have a look at what the solution is. Azure Stack HCI is a hyperconverged infrastructure, meaning that it combines the OS, storage, and networking. These devices can be bought from several manufacturers, such as Dell, HP, and Lenovo. A big advantage of these devices is that they can be managed in the Azure portal.

Let's have a look at the benefits of running AVD on Azure Stack HCI:

- Running AVD on Azure Stack HCI means that organizations such as hospitals and local government can also use AVD

- Using AVD on Azure stack HCI means that it's fully manageable from the Azure portal, creating a real hybrid environment

- IT admins can deploy AVD session hosts on the Azure Stack HCI machines directly from the Azure portal

As you can see, running AVD on Azure Stack HCI can solve a lot of issues that companies have relating to data and privacy.

It's recommended to create a separate host pool for the session hosts running on the Azure Stack HCI nodes. You can very easily deploy session hosts directly from the Azure portal, as shown in the following screenshot:

Add virtual machines to a host pool   ...

Basics   **Virtual Machines**   Tags   Review + create

A host pool is a collection of one or more identical virtual machines within an Azure Virtual Desktop environment. Here you can give details to create Azure virtual machines for your host pool now, or you can create and add them later, for example if you plan to add virtual machines from Azure Stack HCI. Learn more ⌕

Add virtual machines	◯ No
	⦿ Yes

Host pools are a collection of one or more identical virtual machines within Azure Virtual Desktop environments. Here you provide a common set of properties to update the Session hosts within your host pool.

Resource group	rg-prd-jvn-avd-shared-sessionhosts-01 ⌄
Name prefix *	vdh-prd-jvn ✓
	ⓘ Session host name must be unique within the Resource Group.
Virtual machine type	◯ Azure virtual machine
	⦿ Azure Stack HCI virtual machine

⚠ To create a session host virtual machine on Azure Stack HCI, you must be on Azure Stack HCI, version 23H2. Learn more

Figure 13.2 – Add session host to Azure Stack HCI

As you can see, running session hosts on Azure Stack HCI can be very beneficial for a lot of companies.

Summary

This concludes this chapter. We have learned that AVD can be used in several use cases. This can be for providing external users access to corporate resources in a secure way or running AVD on Azure Stack HCI. We have also covered why running remote apps using AVD can boost the security of an AVD environment.

This chapter was the last chapter of this book. We hope that you have enjoyed reading the book and that it will help you secure Windows 365 and Azure Virtual Desktop.

Index

packtpub.com

Subscribe to our online digital library for full access to over 7,000 books and videos, as well as industry leading tools to help you plan your personal development and advance your career. For more information, please visit our website.

Why subscribe?

- Spend less time learning and more time coding with practical eBooks and Videos from over 4,000 industry professionals

- Improve your learning with Skill Plans built especially for you

- Get a free eBook or video every month

- Fully searchable for easy access to vital information

- Copy and paste, print, and bookmark content

Did you know that Packt offers eBook versions of every book published, with PDF and ePub files available? You can upgrade to the eBook version at packtpub.com and as a print book customer, you are entitled to a discount on the eBook copy. Get in touch with us at customercare@packtpub.com for more details.

At www.packtpub.com, you can also read a collection of free technical articles, sign up for a range of free newsletters, and receive exclusive discounts and offers on Packt books and eBooks.

Other Books You May Enjoy

If you enjoyed this book, you may be interested in these other books by Packt:

Microsoft Intune Cookbook

Andrew Taylor

ISBN: 978180512-654-6

- Set up your Intune tenant and associated platform connections
- Create and deploy device policies to your organization's devices
- Find out how to package and deploy your applications
- Explore different ways to monitor and report on your environment
- Leverage PowerShell to automate your daily tasks
- Understand the underlying workings of the Microsoft Graph platform and how it interacts with Intune

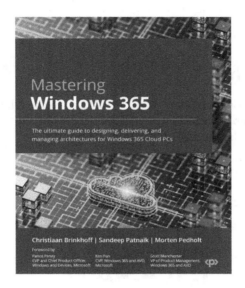

Mastering Windows 365

Christiaan Brinkhoff, Sandeep Patnaik, Morten Pedholt

ISBN: 978-1-83763-796-6

- Understand the features and uses of Windows 365 and Cloud PCs
- Extend your existing skillset with Windows 365 and Intune
- Secure your Windows 365 Cloud PC connection efficiently
- Optimize the Cloud PC user experience through effective analysis and monitoring
- Explore how partners extend the value of Windows 365
- Use the available tools and data within Windows 365
- Troubleshoot Windows 365 with effective tips and tricks

Packt is searching for authors like you

If you're interested in becoming an author for Packt, please visit `authors.packtpub.com` and apply today. We have worked with thousands of developers and tech professionals, just like you, to help them share their insight with the global tech community. You can make a general application, apply for a specific hot topic that we are recruiting an author for, or submit your own idea.

Share Your Thoughts

Now you've finished *Securing Cloud PCs and Azure Virtual Desktop*, we'd love to hear your thoughts! Scan the QR code below to go straight to the Amazon review page for this book and share your feedback or leave a review on the site that you purchased it from.

`https://packt.link/r/1-835-46025-9`

Your review is important to us and the tech community and will help us make sure we're delivering excellent quality content.

Download a free PDF copy of this book

Thanks for purchasing this book!

Do you like to read on the go but are unable to carry your print books everywhere?

Is your eBook purchase not compatible with the device of your choice?

Don't worry, now with every Packt book you get a DRM-free PDF version of that book at no cost.

Read anywhere, any place, on any device. Search, copy, and paste code from your favorite technical books directly into your application.

The perks don't stop there, you can get exclusive access to discounts, newsletters, and great free content in your inbox daily

Follow these simple steps to get the benefits:

1. Scan the QR code or visit the link below

https://packt.link/free-ebook/9781835460252

2. Submit your proof of purchase
3. That's it! We'll send your free PDF and other benefits to your email directly